BEN HALPERN & JEHUDA REINHARZ

ZIONISM

AND THE

CREATION

OF A

NEW

SOCIETY

BRANDEIS UNIVERSITY PRESS
Published by University Press of New England
Hanover and London

Published with the support of the

Jacob and Libby Goodman Institute for the

Study of Zionism and Israel

Published by University Press of New England, Hanover, NH 03755

© 2000 by Brandeis University Press

Printed in the United States of America

5 4 3 2 1

Originally published in hardcover by Oxford University Press,

Inc., 1998, reprinted by arrangement with Oxford University

Press, Inc., 198 Madison Avenue, New York, NY 10016.

Library of Congress Cataloging-in-Publication Data
Halpern, Ben.
 Zionism and the creation of a new society / Ben Halpern & Jehuda
Reinharz.
  p.   cm. — (The Tauber Institute for the Study of European Jewry series)
 Originally published: New York : Oxford University Press, 1998.
 Includes bibliographical references and index.
 ISBN 1–58465–023–0 (pbk. : alk. paper)
  1. Zionism—History.   2. Jews—Palestine—History—20th century.
 3. Palestine—History—1917–1948.
 DS149.H344   2000
 320.54'095694—dc21   99—88874

ZIONISM AND THE CREATION OF A NEW SOCIETY

The Tauber Institute for the Study of European Jewry Series

Jehuda Reinharz, General Editor
Michael Brenner, Associate Editor

The Tauber Institute for the Study of European Jewry, established by a gift to Brandeis University from Dr. Laszlo N. Tauber, is dedicated to the memory of the victims of Nazi persecutions between 1933 and 1945. The Institute seeks to study the history and culture of European Jewry in the modern period. The Institute has a special interest in studying the causes, nature, and consequences of the European Jewish catastrophe within the contexts of modern European diplomatic, intellectual, political, and social history.

The Jacob and Libby Goodman Institute for the Study of Zionism and Israel was founded through a gift to Brandeis University by Mrs. Libby Goodman and is organized under the auspices of the Tauber Institute. The Goodman Institute seeks to promote an understanding of the Zionist movement, and the history, society, and culture of the State of Israel.

Magdalena Opalski and Israel Bartal, 1992
Poles and Jews: A Failed Brotherhood

Richard Breitman, 1992
The Architect of Genocide: Himmler and the Final Solution

George L. Mosse, 1993
Confronting the Nation: Jewish and Western Nationalism

Daniel Carpi, 1994
Between Mussolini and Hitler: The Jews and the Italian Authorities in France and Tunisia

Walter Laqueur and Richard Breitman, 1994
Breaking the Silence: The German Who Exposed the Final Solution

Ismar Schorsch, 1994
From Text to Context: The Turn to History in Modern Judaism

Jacob Katz, 1995
With My Own Eyes: The Autobiography of an Historian

Gideon Shimoni, 1995
The Zionist Ideology

Moshe Prywes and Haim Chertok, 1996
Prisoner of Hope

János Nyiri, 1997
Battlefields and Playgrounds

Alan Mintz, editor, 1997
The Boom in Contemporary Israeli Fiction

Samuel Bak, paintings
Lawrence L. Langer, essay and commentary, 1997
Landscapes of Jewish Experience

Jeffrey Shandler and Beth S. Wenger, editors, 1997
Encounters with the "Holy Land": Place, Past and Future in American Jewish Culture

Simon Rawidowicz, 1998
State of Israel, Diaspora, and Jewish Continuity: Essays on the "Ever-Dying People"

Jacob Katz, 1998
A House Divided: Orthodoxy and Schism in Nineteenth-Century Central European Jewry

Elisheva Carlebach, John M. Efron, and David N. Myers, editors, 1998
Jewish History and Jewish Memory: Essays in Honor of Yosef Hayim Yerushalmi

Shmuel Almog, Jehuda Reinharz, and Anita Shapira, editors, 1998
Zionism and Religion

Ben Halpern and Jehuda Reinharz, 2000
Zionism and the Creation of a New Society

Contents

Preface

I came to Brandeis University in 1982 as a successor in the Richard Koret chair of modern Jewish history to my friend and mentor, Ben Halpern. Shortly after I arrived, he suggested that we collaborate on a book he had started some years earlier. It was intended as the second volume to his classic work *The Idea of the Jewish State*, first published in 1961 and revised in 1969. Ben and I collaborated on this second volume even as we each continued to work on other monographs. Thus, a project that we thought would last a year or two stretched to almost fifteen years. After Ben's unexpected death in 1990, I continued to work on our project as time allowed. Fortuitously and without prior design, this task was completed on the eve of the fiftieth anniversary of the State of Israel. My only regret is that Ben Halpern is not here to enjoy the bound volume.

I would like to thank Ben's wife, Gertrude, and their sons, Joe and Elkan, for their patience and cooperation throughout. Somehow they continued to have faith that this book would see the light of day, even when I had to postpone work on it as I took on more and more administrative tasks at Brandeis.

I am particularly grateful to my friend and former student Professor Mark A. Raider, who assisted me for the past few years on this and other projects. Mark checked facts, updated bibliographic notes, corrected mistakes, and generally served as an excellent and tough sounding board. Without his help, this volume might well have been delayed a few more years. I would also like to thank Professors Evyatar Friesel, Israel's state archivist, and Anita Shapira of Tel Aviv University for their comments and constructive criticisms. Finally, as so often in the past, Sylvia Fuks Fried, executive director of the Tauber Institute for the Study of European Jewry at Brandeis University, was helpful in myriad ways.

Waltham, Massachusetts   J. R.
November 1997

Note to the Paperback Edition

I would like to thank the staff of the University Press of New England, especially Phyllis D. Deutsch and Michael P. Burton, for making it possible for me to correct, in this paperback edition, numerous typographical as well as factual errors that found their way into the previous edition. I am very grateful to Mark Raider and Ada Paldor for their painstaking and careful reading of the manuscript, and to Sylvia Fuks Fried for overseeing the publication of the paperback.

Waltham, Massachusetts
January 2000   J.R.

ZIONISM AND THE CREATION OF A NEW SOCIETY

Introduction

This study is intended as a complement to *The Idea of the Jewish State*, published by Ben Halpern in 1961 (second edition 1969). In that volume, historical and sociological analyses are applied to the study of Jewish nationalism. Some of the methodology problems of such an attempt, with its combination of approaches, were dealt with briefly in the appendix to the first edition of *The Idea of the Jewish State* as well as in the prefatory note to the second edition. We will add here only comments necessary to clarify the differences in the problem and approach of this book in comparison with the earlier study.

The Idea of the Jewish State deals with the development of "the idea." It describes the emergence of a central conception—the notion of Jewish sovereignty—in the ideological complex that defines the historic purpose that present-day Israel seeks to realize. It is, then, a study in social and intellectual history, employing primarily standard historiographical methods, but with such additional minimum sociological assumptions as the problem seems to require. This volume, as indicated by its title, *Zionism and the Creation of a New Society*, deals with the emerging society that the Zionist movement sought to organize in accordance with its historically defined ideological purpose—in accordance, that is, with "the idea" and its varied institutional expressions.

A few other differences between the volumes are noteworthy. First, a history of the idea of the Jewish state clearly does not cover all the "ideas" involved in an attempt to convert the mass of immigrant Jews, widely different in background and outlook, into a cohesive social structure. A consensus that could establish a stable structure would have to include agreement not only on the ideas underlying the Jewish state but on the philosophies and attitudes at the heart of the disparate Jewish social, economic, political, and religious forces that constituted the Zionist organization and the Yishuv, the Jewish community in Palestine prior to the establishment of the State of Israel in 1948.

Second, the idea of Jewish sovereignty, whose history was traced in

The Idea of the Jewish State, is related chiefly (though not exclusively) to the specific problems with which the Jewish community—established in Israel (or seeking to establish itself there)—dealt historically. Thus, the earlier volume was concerned primarily with the history of relations between advocates of the Zionist idea and non-Zionist and anti-Zionist groups as well as relations between the Zionist movement and the gentile world writ large, particularly political entities in the international arena that concerned themselves with the Jewish problem and Palestine. This study, however, seeks to determine the outlines of the Zionist movement's emergent stable social structures, and it is concerned chiefly with domestic problems of the Yishuv and nascent Israeli society: with the relationships and strains that existed between different elements within the Palestine-based Jewish community itself, not those between the Yishuv and other groups—gentile or Jewish—outside of it.

Notwithstanding such gross differences between this work and *The Idea of the Jewish State*, there is one important respect in which the problems and methods of both studies are similar. In comparison to other countries not faced with such massive and rapidly shifting forces of change, a stabilized social structure in Israel is undoubtedly still not yet a fully established fact. To try to analyze the institutions that will define the social system of Israel when it no longer faces unpredictable forces of change is not feasible. One cannot assume, for example, as one generally does in the sociological analysis of stable situations, that certain fundamental ideas or values underlying the institutions of a society have been so decisively established by history that they may be viewed as permanent. Indeed, the ideas and values underlying contemporary Israel's institutions are obviously still being defined.

Nevertheless, it is true, as was pointed out in *The Idea of the Jewish State*, that the ideas underlying the several institutions of Israel are not unrelated to the core idea of the Jewish state: that of sovereignty as an instrument for the solution of the Jewish problem. National independence, as the specific means for solving the Jewish problem, is a concept reflected in all the institutions of Israeli society as well as in the political structure of the Jewish state. Thus the purposes of Israel, embodied in its cultural, economic, and social institutions, include the following: to develop Hebrew as the national language; to absorb mass immigration of Jews who cannot or do not wish to reside in other countries; to establish a community in Israel free from the social and cultural ills that historically attended the Jewish status as a minority people dispersed throughout the world; and to carry out necessary transformations in social and economic distribution, create appropriate socioeconomic institutions, and foster cultural changes necessary for the realization of such a revolutionary program. In all these efforts, the fundamental mythos of Jewish independence—the will to assert the right and acquire the capacity to control one's own national destiny and freely express one's own national individuality—is implied, though with varying clarity and in different forms.

By 1948, when the State of Israel was officially founded, this ideal crystallized not only through the clearest and most direct realization of the principle of Jewish independence: Jewish sovereignty. Other institutions of nascent Israeli society had also been established by that date in which the settled Jewish population realized less directly the same mythic idea: Hebrew was a spoken language and the recognized national tongue, social and economic institutions had been developed, occupational distribution was achieved, and cultural values were institutionalized that reflected the underlying idea of a self-sustaining, rounded community capable of controlling its destiny in the same way as other free peoples.

Following 1948, Israel, extending its welcome to all Jews who could not or would not remain in their old homes, received a massive immigration, which, for the most part, did not possess the national attributes already developed by the settled population. The tasks that faced the new state in consequence of this immigration policy included the following: to enable the newcomers to master the language and share in the other elements of social consensus existing in the settled community; to enable them to participate in the social institutions and cultural life of the settled community; and to transform the social and occupational distribution of the new immigrants so that they might become self-supporting and help the state become economically self-sustaining. The problem, therefore, was not primarily one of *defining* a national purpose, but of realizing it in actuality.

As in other countries that had—and have—to deal with mass immigration, the most general social problem to which national policy in Israel had to orient itself was to integrate the newcomers into the framework of the established institutions as they were historically determined, or to do so with the least possible departure from these institutions. This focus is precisely the one from which this volume considers the emergence of the Jewish state. It would seem to follow, then, that in order to deal with this chain of events, we must adopt an approach similar to that used in other studies that have considered similar issues: an essentially historical/sociological approach. We are concerned not solely with the historical determination of how the institutions of Israel's settled community came to be established, but also with the sociological deter-mination of how various Zionist groups adjusted to the new or estab-lished institutions and how strains upon the institutions arose and were dealt with.

Moreover, we are not concerned in this book with one central idea of Zionism and the specific institution of Jewish sovereignty. Nor are we concerned with the emerging Jewish state as a political entity and its relation to outside interests. Rather our examination comprehends the whole range of ideas and values attached to the Zionist enterprise in Palestine and the institutions built upon them. To this end, we trace the changing system of internal relationships of the Zionist organization from its early days to the eve of World War II. Our attention is focused especially on the impact of the ascendant Labor Zionist movement, whose relative strength was based on growing numbers and unity in Palestine and bolstered by the disunity of rightwing and traditional op-ponents. During the 1930s these factors brought Labor (and its socialist core constituency) to a position of political dominance in the World Zionist Organization, the Jewish Agency, and the Yishuv.

As the foregoing description indicates, even in describing the evolving definition of ideas—even, that is, in those sections of the book that are mainly historical—we cannot restrict our sociological observations to a few simple assumptions. By contrast, *The Idea of the Jewish State* re-quired only two basic sociological assumptions in order to establish the limiting social conditions for the autonomous development of the idea of Jewish sovereignty. In regard to the Jewish community, it was as-sumed that an effective social consensus established normative standards for the emotional quality and conceptual content of the Zionist vision of Jewish national independence. In regard to the international political context of Zionist doctrine, it was assumed that only legal and power-political considerations had a limiting effect. Within these constraints, it was possible to identify the autonomous history of the idea as though it were a rational matter continuously attuned and adjusting to the flow of changing events.

In this volume, however, although our problem is still one of the (anticipated) change and development of ideas, we are not concerned with a single idea and the relatively straightforward social contexts by which its autonomous development is limited. Instead, we are concerned with the whole range of related ideas underlying all the several institu-tions of the society—social, cultural, political, and economic—and con-sequently with the specific nature of the social contexts to which each is related, as well as with the relations between them all. The assumption of the two social contexts in the earlier volume—that of a social consensus in the Jewish community and that of contract-and-coalition in the realm of international law and politics—constituted minimum sociological criteria. These had to be included in the historical analysis in order to make possible a systematic account of the development of "the idea" as an isolated ideological concept and institutional value.

The historical analysis of ideological conceptions and institutionalized values addressed in this volume, which developed within the entire range of social contexts reviewed above, requires a set of comprehensive sociological assumptions. It appears, therefore, that while the analysis in this volume must be essentially historical, it must also to some degree be sociological. But it should be further noted that this undertaking implies an approach that is rather unusual from the point of view of the standard methods of both disciplines. Our problem is "historical" in a very unusual sense. The standard method of history is to rule out of consideration any but the already concluded effects of past actions, leaving the future to prophecy and unconcluded contemporary events to journalism and applied social science expertise. Our analysis, however, concerns itself precisely with the future historic effects of contemporary events. The problem is equally unusual in its "sociological" aspect, for the analysis of a social structure usually assumes stable conditions of two kinds—a stable, institutionalized value system and a more or less stable material environment—within which social interaction occurs and seeks its equilibrium. Analyses of the cumulative changes in the material environment (if this term embraces the economy, population density, ecology, etc.), on the one hand, and in the values of a culture are not unknown, but they are usually relegated to historical and special social sciences (other than sociology), which treat them in isolation from each other. Yet our analysis concerns itself precisely with the changes in institutional values and material conditions that may result from contemporary events; and, moreover, it considers these changing values and conditions not in isolation, but in relation to the whole range of institutions and activities of the Zionist social system.

It is our hope that this book, which relies heavily on the vast corpus of scholarly literature on the history and culture of Zionism and the Yishuv, will be accepted as a modest attempt to synthesize and summarize some of these works.

• 1 •

The Social Sources of Zionism

Israel is one of those modern societies whose early institutions were clearly shaped by an ideological movement. Israel's declaration of independence in 1948 was an immediate expression of the fundamental Zionist idea: it gave effect to a plan advocated by organized Zionists since the 1880s for solving the Jewish problem. Major Israeli political institutions, such as the party structure, embody principles and practices that were followed in the World Zionist Organization.

In this respect, Israel is similar to other new states whose political institutions directly derive from the nationalist movement that won their independence. But in addition, a wide variety of social, economic, and cultural institutions of the new Jewish state were initially developed by the Zionist organization and its associated bodies. In these respects, Zionism had an impact unusual among nationalist movements. It must rather be compared to social revolutionary and radical reform movements.

A national liberation movement typically arises among a people oppressed by foreign rulers in its own land. Resentment of the national enemy is so pervasive and intense that other national issues seem secondary, and nonnationalist or antinationalist popular movements are hard to sustain. Nationalist factions that are concerned primarily with aims other than the liberation struggle may have little effect. Both factional differences and opposition views are effectively submerged—if necessary, by force—for the sake of the all-absorbing fight against the national oppressor.

To these generalizations, the Zionist movement and the rise of Israel are outstanding exceptions. Jews did not face the common nationalist situation of being oppressed in their own land by a foreign ruler, the national enemy, who enraged all of them, whatever their class or kind, by the same painful contact to the point where they could focus their manifold hostilities in a single myth image. The Jewish people lived as a minority in numerous countries throughout the world, among many different ruling nations and under different regimes. The oppressions they suffered were different in kind, varying from intense to imperceptible, and no single foe could plausibly be held responsible for all Jewish frustrations.

Hence, when Jewish nationalism arose, rival ideologies did not succumb to it. They engaged instead in a sharp polemic through which their own positions became more fully elaborated and well defined. Nor did the whole nationalist movement concentrate upon the primary objective of national sovereignty. Numerous nationalist factions arose, each insisting that its own goal was most important and all others secondary.

But there is another side to this coin. Since no party enjoyed unquestioned, continuous, and universal dominance in the Jewish community, each was forced to compromise with others. The Zionists, for example, bore primary responsibility for building the Jewish national home in Palestine. But they were able to rely on substantial assistance from many non-Zionist factions in the community, and they were ready, within limits, to define their specific, immediate objectives in a way that made such cooperation possible. On the other hand, the chief rabbinate and Israel's plantation settlements were institutions primarily derived from non-Zionist sources, to which Zionists lent conditional support and cooperation.

Competing ideologies within the Zionist movement also had to cooperate with one another. The difficulties of achieving national sovereignty for Jews in a country where they were at first a tiny minority made even the most extreme "political" Zionists regard such sovereignty as an *ultimate* goal, to be approached by stages. This view opened the way for other Zionists, concentrating on nationalist cultural or social and economic aims, to enlist general *immediate* support for their objectives.

Cultural, social, and economic aims are normally the primary concern for humanitarians, social reformers, and social revolutionaries and are usually subordinate in national liberation movements. Because of the anomalies of the Jewish position, however, *all* Jewish ideologies since the eighteenth-century Enlightenment had to define cultural, social, and economic as well as purely political aims and adopt humanitarian, reform, or revolutionary rather than purely civil, political methods. This position caused not only Zionism but all modern Jewish ideologies to assume a distinctly different character from comparable movements among other peoples.

The Jewish protagonists of civic emancipation stood on the principle that Jews differed only in religion from their fellow countrymen. If this had been objectively true, the aims and methods of Jewish emancipation would have been the same as those of Catholic emancipation in England or Huguenot emancipation in France. Religious toleration and enfranchisement, which was the problem of all dissenting sects, should have sufficed for the Jews. But, in fact, all concerned, Jews and gentiles alike, considered the question to be one of "ameliorating" the Jews: that is, reforming their culture and improving their social and economic position, as well as abolishing their legal disabilities.[1]

In this respect, Jewish emancipation was more like the emancipation of serfs and slaves than of Huguenots, Quakers, or Catholics. Yet this parallel breaks down too. The Jew needed to be tolerated, like other dissenters, and not only elevated and advanced, like other depressed groups. Their problem consisted not only in having an unsatisfactory position but also in having an uncertain legitimacy, always questionable and frequently under attack.

Thus, the first aim of Jewish emancipation was to gain acceptance in gentile civil society. The proposed cultural, social, and economic "ameliorations" of the Jews were conceived as means, if not as prerequisite conditions, to that end. Zionists, on the other hand, abhorred the notion of suppressing characteristic Jewish qualities and aspirations for the sake of acceptance in gentile society. Yet they proposed to advance many of the very cultural, social, and economic reforms initiated by earlier modernists; but by relating them to a different purpose, the resettlement in Zion, they altered the nature and enlarged the scope of these reforms.

In addition to the goal of political sovereignty, Zionists proclaimed the following specific aims: to develop Hebrew as a spoken language and the foundation of a national consensus; to transfer to Palestine all Jews who could not or did not wish to live in diaspora countries; to establish a community in Palestine free from the peculiar social, economic, and cultural problems that beset the Jewish status as a dispersed minority people. When Israel arose, the Zionist idea of the autoemancipation of the Jews was realized in the clearest, most precise form, through the establishment of the Jewish state. This was a crowning achievement, the capstone of an institutional structure embodying many other, nonpolitical, Zionist aims. In 1948, Hebrew was a spoken language in Palestine, and the language of instruction in Jewish schools from the kindergarten to the university. Jews had demonstrated that they could be farmers and workers—and soldiers, if need be—as well as scholars and merchants. They had an economy firmly established on a base of Jewish labor in agriculture and industry as well as the service trades; the community had proved its capacity to absorb immigrants and expected rapid growth in the future.

Such results, whose influence extended to the greater part of the Palestine Jewish community (the *Yishuv*), were often achieved through the single-minded efforts of zealots devoted to a particular Zionist purpose. Hebraists worked and fought primarily for the revival of the ancient tongue; "religious"—that is, Orthodox—Zionists worked and fought for the dominance of traditional law and the rejuvenation of Jewish religious culture; and socialist Zionists worked and fought to build a nation of and through labor and in accordance with labor's interests and principles. Each enjoyed such success as they did because other Zionists shared these purposes in part, or, in any case, recognized them as defensible versions of their common idea of autoemancipation.

So, too, the institutions created by the whole body of Zionists often required support or acceptance on the part of many non-Zionist Jews in Palestine and abroad. Support and acceptance were granted only because the Zionist idea reasserted values that were part of a heritage common to all Jews.

I

The beginning of Zionism may be traced to the generation of European Jews who experienced the spread of political antisemitism on the continent since the 1870s, oppressive anti-Jewish nationalism in Rumania, *pogroms* (anti-Jewish riots), and, above all, the condoning of pogroms by Russian radicals, in the 1880s. The last struck home with traumatic effect among the Jewish intelligentsia: many who had hoped for a "rational" solution of the Jewish problem on liberal lines now turned in violent disillusionment against attitudes and assumptions they had previously shared. They not only denied the assumption that gentiles would generously grant emancipation to Eastern European Jews if Jews adapted themselves to Western humanism; they vehemently rejected so submissive a Jewish policy as worthy of contempt. Antisemitism, they contended, was not merely a symptom of historical backwardness among some gentile communities. It was rooted in permanent features of the Jewish situation: in their homelessness, their universal minority status, or their inexplicable, anxiety-provoking, millennial survival in exile. Consequently, antisemitism should be expected to persist wherever Jews lived in gentile society, whether or not liberalism was really the wave of the future. The Jews could only really be free—and, indeed, only deserved freedom—if they freed themselves by collective action: by an "autoemancipation."[2] So, too, they would regain a true culture not by slavishly imitating a general, Western Enlightenment but by cultivating their own historic heritage and national individuality.

Such stress on national individuality and self-reliance is, of course, not uniquely Zionist. Similar ideas and feelings were common in nationalist revivals everywhere. From the French Revolution to pan-Slavism, there were numerous models whose influence could have produced a Jewish nationalism, if Jews had been sufficiently susceptible to such influences.

But for most of the nineteenth century, Jewish responsiveness to a nationalist solution of their problem was effectively blocked. Pious traditionalists regarded the history of Jewish suffering as a penance to be lovingly borne until the messiah brought redemption, and they suspected any proposal for active efforts by Jews to end the exile as heretical. Modernists who favored action to end Jewish disabilities and improve their social and economic positions had other reasons to reject nationalist ideas: the contention that Jews were a separate nation was used as an argument against their emancipation by antisemites throughout Europe. Thus, the nationalist revivals that Jews observed around them did not give birth to a significant parallel movement of Jewish nationalism. Individual thinkers in the West developed a Jewish nationalist doctrine and some traditionalists saw messianic portents in the nationalist uprisings of the time, but no historically effective political movement arose until disillusionment with gentile liberalism set in among East European modernists. Under East European conditions in the last quarter of the century, secular-nationalist views not only were held by individual eccentrics but grew to be broadly characteristic of a definable group, the *maskilim*: traditionally trained young intellectuals living mainly in the Pale of Settlement, who had acquired some general European culture, usually solely through their own efforts, and who wrote or read modern Hebrew literature.

In the language of modern Jewish history, "Eastern Europe" is not so much a geographical as a political and social concept. It is, first of all, the area where the civic emancipation of the Jews was frustrated throughout the nineteenth century. The struggle for political emancipation was long and severe in Central and Western Europe too, but (disregarding the subsequent calamity) it was substantially complete by the 1870s. At that very time, the prospect for political emancipation in Eastern Europe began to seem hopeless, and it was in fact finally accomplished, in very ambiguous terms, only under the peculiar circumstances of World War I and the Russian Revolution.

Eastern Europe is also the area where legally enforced discrimination and exclusionary rules confined the Jews throughout the nineteenth century under conditions of mounting congestion, poverty, and economic rootlessness. By contrast, Western Europe, not to speak of the New World, was a domain of boundless opportunity for Jewish economic and social advancement.

As a result, confidence in emancipation as the anticipated, or even achieved, basis of Jewish life was shared by the entire consensus of Jews in Western Europe. In Eastern Europe there were very few periods during the nineteenth century when such confidence would have been truly possible.

There were, of course, advocates of modernist ideas like those of the Western Jewish Enlightenment among Russian Jews. They were found, first of all, among the wealthy merchants and investors, and the special categories of professionals, who were permitted to live in interior provinces, beyond the Jewish Pale of Settlement. They sought to introduce secular studies, preferably in Russian, and reforms in traditional folkways toward conformity with gentile conventions, as well as major changes in Jewish occupations in order to prepare Jews for emancipation. But in Russia, unlike the West, such a program held no hope for the community as a whole in the foreseeable future. Only an increasingly restricted few could expect the privilege of greater freedom and integration. That small group was consequently unable to exert a profound influence on the community of the Pale. Their superior status merely detached the privileged ones from their fellow Jews.

Within the Pale, efforts at enlightenment and reform which were made throughout the nineteenth century, often under pressure of the government, served only to crystallize rigid opposition among the community's traditional leadership. Even a liberal such as Dr. Max Lilienthal, who was appointed in 1841 to organize the tsar's new schools for Jews, became convinced that the government's real aim was conversion; he left for America. The traditionalist leaders rejected the whole project from the outset as an assault on Judaism. They often regarded those who supported any form of enlightenment as dangerous agitators who were subverting the foundations of the community.

The reformist attitudes of modernists who were active in the community within the Pale were not only more cautious but intrinsically different from attitudes common in Western Europe and among the privileged Jews in the interior provinces of Russia. The fundamental cause of the difference was a different position vis-à-vis both the gentile and the Jewish communities.

In Western Europe, modernists had no difficulty in recognizing the national complexion of the political community they desired Jews to enter. Nor did Jewish modernists who lived in Moscow or Saint Petersburg or even cosmopolitan Odessa have any difficulty in this respect. Western or modern civilization meant without question the French language and culture in France, the German language and culture in Germany, and the Russian language and culture in interior Russia. A single national community enjoyed undisputed dominance in government, the economy, and the status hierarchy of each country. It was obvious, in those cases, that to become modern or Western meant for a Jew to become French, German, or Russian in language and culture; this was also the key to the Jew's economic advancement and social and political acceptance.

In the Pale of Settlement and in adjoining territories to the west and south, there was a much more complex situation. These areas belonged to the multinational Russian, Austro-Hungarian, or, for much of the nineteenth century, the Ottoman Empire. The Jews lived mainly in regions populated by subject minorities rather than by the dominant, majority nationality. Therefore, the ideal of enlightenment could not be so easily identified with the language and culture of a single gentile nation: to choose any one, whether the subject or ruling nationality, meant to be regarded as a traitor or a rebel by the other. Some Jewish intellectuals and aspiring bourgeois did, in fact, choose each of these options, and occasionally suffered the consequences. Adepts of the Enlightenment in the heart of the Pale were spared this dilemma because, like the traditionalists, they were detached both from their Polish, Lithuanian, or Ukrainian neighbors and from the remote Russian rulers. Accordingly, their program for enlightenment and reform was directed toward the Jews' own cultural tradition and did not involve accepting gentile culture in its place. The main vehicle of their effort was the Hebrew (and, later, Yiddish) language, not Russian or Polish.

Criticism of the traditionalist community by the "enlightened" Hebraists was vigorous from the beginning and remained so well into the twentieth century, long after Zionist sentiments dominated Hebrew literature. Eastern European *maskilim* castigated traditionalist superstition and rabbinical tyranny as fiercely as any Western Jewish modernist had. In addition, they vehemently condemned oppression of the poor and weak by the rich and powerful in the community—a theme not stressed to the same degree in Western Jewish Enlightenment literature. On the other hand, since the 1870s, Eastern European writers had little occasion to paint in glowing Hebrew phrases the benevolence of enlightened monarchs and the amiable disposition of gentile society toward Jews who acquired enlightenment, themes that constantly recurred in the Hebrew Enlightenment in the West.

From the early 1870s, some Eastern European *maskilim* not only stressed different themes than did their Western counterparts, they accused them of undermining Jewish solidarity and threatening Jewish survival by submitting unreservedly to gentile standards. One may cite as an example Moshe Leib Lilienblum, who became a cultural hero for Eastern *maskilim* because of his battle with the traditionalists over issues of religious reform during the 1860s. He sharply rejected any comparison of his views with those of American and German Reform Judaism, and attacked them for discarding the concepts of a personal messiah and the restoration to Zion, for their innovations in the synagogue ritual, and for proposals to abandon the rite of circumcision and shift the Sabbath to Sunday. His contemporary Perez Smolenskin, in an early effort (a short story published in 1867, and in revised form in 1875, concerning enlightened young Jews who fought in the Polish rebellion of 1863), deplored the pointless sacrifice of Jewish lives in other peoples' quarrels. His critical and publicistic essays took on an increasingly sharp tone against Western Jewry for renouncing the hope of a national return to Zion and, above all, for abandoning the Hebrew language and culture.

Opposition to *both* the Western modernists and the Eastern traditionalists, their major antagonists in these debates, gave the *maskilim* of the Pale at least a negative sense of their special group identity; at the same time, their commitment to modern Hebrew literature gave it a certain positive content. Nevertheless, neither this group nor others who have been described as "proto-Zionists," such as the sponsors of a movement for Jewish settlement in Palestine in the 1860s, thought of themselves as a tight ideological formation, bound together in a broad opposition to rival viewpoints on the whole range of issues relating to the Jewish problem. But the shock of the pogroms of the 1880s produced just this sort of transformation among many of the *maskilim* of the Pale. Joining those traditionalist and modernist Westerners who remained committed to the project of Jewish settlement in Palestine, they formed a new ideological position in the culture of modern Jewry.

II

The idea of Jewish national sovereignty, and elaborate strategies for achieving it in Palestine, were anticipated by proto-Zionist enthusiasts long before the Zionist movement arose. The same may be said about the other, special Zionist objectives that were ultimately embodied in Israel's major domestic institutions.

The *Haskalah*, originally a movement to transform the Hebrew language from a sacred tongue to a medium of modern secular enlightenment, had existed for about a century before the 1880s. Its aims also included reforming the Jewish occupational distribution. Haskalah projects of occupational transfer were not directed toward resettlement in Zion, but were intended to prepare ghetto Jews, wherever they lived, for civic equality and social acceptance. However, since the 1840s, general education, vocational retraining, and a shift to "productive" occupations were also proposed as the way to build a sound social and economic base for the growing Jewish community in Palestine.

Jewish settlement in Zion was continually stimulated by organized groups of sponsors; since the 1860s at least, their aim was not merely to encourage prayer and study, but also to establish *self-supporting* settlers in the Holy Land. Yet their motivation remained religious rather than strictly nationalist. Such proto-Zionists did not hope to solve the problems of Jews in Europe by emigration, but aimed to build a community in Zion that would carry out biblical social, economic, and eventually political commandments that could not be observed in exile. By this means they believed the advent of the messiah might be prepared.

The proto-Zionists had little or no success in building self-supporting settlements in Palestine, and the number of migrants to Zion encouraged by them was minuscule. However, on several occasions when oppression became acute in some country during this period, there were also attempts to apply mass emigration, though not necessarily to the Holy Land, as a solution of the Jewish problem.

Thus, the major elements of a Zionist ideology—emigration to solve the Jewish problem, the return to Zion, occupational retraining and redistribution, and the revival of Hebrew as a medium of secular culture— were present long before the movement arose; but they were espoused in fragmentary, sometimes mutually opposed, forms by diverse Jewish groups. This diversity remained even in the 1870s, when a series of crises challenged all Jewish attitudes, traditionalist and modern, and strongly suggested a nationalist alternative. In Russia, a reactionary mood set in after the Polish insurrection of 1863 and was given sharp focus for the Jews by a pogrom in Odessa in 1871. At the same time, expulsions and persecution of Rumanian Jewry forced the Western Jewish communities to meet in international conferences at which radical proposals to solve the problem by mass emigration were seriously discussed. Then the Balkan wars and the Congress of Berlin in 1878 raised simultaneous questions concerning the future of Palestine, if the Ottoman Empire should collapse, and concerning the future of Balkan Jews under conditions of mounting oppression. But even after all this, inhibitions against a full-blown nationalist stand remained powerful. Nobody demonstrated this feeling better than some of the men who were soon to be counted among the forefathers of the Zionist movement.

The consideration of Palestine as a haven for Jewish refugees had become a familiar idea ever since the famine years of 1867–69, which severely affected the Pale of Settlement. Russian Jewish spokesmen of an enlightened Orthodoxy, such as David Gordon and Yehiel Michael Pines, argued that the refugees should be settled not only in America or in agricultural colonies in southern Russia but also, even primarily, in the Holy Land. The Alliance Israélite Universelle, under the influence of Charles Netter, at that time showed sympathy toward this view. An agricultural school, Mikveh Israel, was founded in the plain near Jaffa for any Jewish settlers, but especially for established residents, who could be induced to train for agricultural colonization in Palestine. However, active interest in fostering settlement in Zion was still largely confined to Orthodox elements, long dedicated to this purpose on religious grounds, and for that reason the *maskilim* maintained a lukewarm, if not cool, attitude.

In 1874, admirers of Sir Moses Montefiore planned to raise a testimonial fund in honor of the venerable philanthropist's ninetieth birthday, and in view of his long interest in Palestine Jewry, it seemed appropriate to apply the contributions toward improving the cultural and economic position of that community. The outstanding contemporary poet of the Russian Haskalah, Judah Leib Gordon, was asked if he, or alternatively Yehiel Michael Pines, would raise the funds in Russia, and was also asked how he thought the contributions should be used. He replied that if the goal were merely to build a school or hospital commemorating Montefiore, then, considering conditions in Russia, it would be better not to expose any Russian Jew to the risk of heading the committee. But if it had a more significant aim, such as purchasing land in Palestine for a settlement that might become the nucleus of a national revival, he himself would gladly serve, and he also highly recommended Pines for such a post. However, his agreement was conditional: he stipulated that the Jews already living in the Holy Land should first be removed, for their fanatical obscurantism could cripple the enterprise.

Even the pogroms, which produced an upheaval in the spirit of so many Russian Jews, failed to alter Gordon's cool and sober habit of mind. His nationalist views remained subject to the earlier reservations, and no sudden access of enthusiasm could make him overlook the obstacles to colonization in Palestine. Consequently, ardent new adherents regarded him as unsympathetic or insufficiently sympathetic to the cause. But right up to the traumatic pogrom experience that radicalized their whole view, some of those most prominently identified with the movement after 1881 had a similarly qualified sympathy for nationalism.

A striking example is the famous exchange between Eliezer Ben-Yehuda (formerly known as Yizhak Perlman) and Perez Smolenskin. Ben-Yehuda, a teacher, propagandist, and lexicographer of spoken Hebrew, to which cause he devoted his entire life from the day he set foot in Palestine in 1881, had the direct, single-minded approach of a Russian radical. He was a disciple of Smolenskin's cultural nationalism, heightened by the vogue of Slavophilism during the Russo-Turkish war of 1877–78. In 1878, while studying medicine in Paris, he wrote an outspoken, full-blown nationalist manifesto entitled "A Burning Issue"; Smolenskin renamed it more moderately "A Significant Issue" when he published it in 1879 in his journal *Hashahar*, a recognized organ for many varieties of proto-nationalist opinion. Ben-Yehuda argued that religion and Jew-hatred, which had preserved Jewish solidarity in the past, could no longer do so. In order to survive, the Jewish people would have to resettle en masse on the soil of Palestine and there create an autonomous national center and revive spoken Hebrew as the vehicle of a secular Jewish culture.

Although Smolenskin published this youthful effusion, he was far from agreeing at that time with such a radical, simplistic stand. An exchange of articles and open letters took place between the two in the period immediately before the pogroms; the last interchange, in fact, did not appear until after that turning point, although it was written before. Smolenskin's views then included the following: a return to farming, advocated by proponents of colonization in southern Russia, would solve no Jewish problem, for if Jews had civil rights they would enter all occupations, and without such rights they could not be aided materially; the Hebrew language would never revive as a spoken vernacular, but should be cultivated as the literary organ of a spiritual Jewish nationality; and while the resettlement of Jews in Zion was a messianic vision essentially bound up with Jewish history, and those who returned at any time deserved sympathy and support, the people were not prepared to undertake this as a practical, political plan for solving the Jewish problem.

The last interchange between Ben-Yehuda and Smolenskin was published, as noted, after the pogroms, although written earlier. In the very same issue of *Hashahar* Smolenskin published another article, written *after* the pogroms, which directly reversed his position on Palestine and was imbued with a totally different spirit. He began by attacking bitterly all those Russian Jewish leaders who had placed their faith in emancipation and enlightenment. The Jews were to blame for their own sorry plight, because they refused to see themselves as a nation and act accordingly. Their leaders had merely echoed antisemitic charges against their own people, and even though forewarned by himself (as Smolenskin acidly points out), they failed to anticipate the pogroms or do anything to forestall them. Even now they were resisting the necessary remedy, which a nationally minded leadership would readily understand: namely, mass migration of the Russian Jews to the only country where a better Jewish future was conceivable: the ancestral Zion.

The radical effect of the pogroms is equally evident in the changing views of Moshe Leib Lilienblum, an even more important pioneer of Zionism. He had become prominent in his early twenties through his battle for an essentially conservative doctrine of religious reform. He then turned increasingly agnostic and cosmopolitan under the influence of Russian positivist writers, but by the mid-1870s he had gradually reverted to the loyalties of his youth. At this point, he attacked the assimilationist inclinations of Russo-Jewish circles and showed a moderate sympathy toward projects for Jewish resettlement in Palestine which were being discussed in the press.

In 1874, an article in the *Odesskie Vestnik* ridiculing a reputed plan by Baron Edmond de Rothschild to buy Palestine for Jewish resettlement evoked a letter to the editor from Lilienblum defending the idea. In 1875, an actual project of this kind gained widespread attention. Haim Guedalla, who between 1876 and 1880 was chairman of the Turkish Bondholders of the General Debt of Turkey, proposed that the debentures be redeemed by the transfer of lands in Palestine and other Ottoman regions for Jewish settlement. At this time, too, a group of pious Jerusalem residents organized for colonization on the land; from this beginning came later the initial (abortive) settlement of the village of Petah Tikvah in 1878. A critical observer reported these events with measured approval in the Haskalah journal, *Hazfirah*, but he suggested that it would be a highly desirable preliminary step to convoke a Sanhedrin in order to reform traditions that, he said, precluded the successful founding of a modern Jewish state. Lilienblum, the erstwhile champion of religious reform, wrote, in a sharp rejoinder to the author, that this question should be shelved at a time when it might stand in the way of acquiring Palestine for Jewish settlement. Nevertheless, for Lilienblum too, Palestine was not yet a clear, ideologically defined goal, nor did he see mass resettlement and territorial concentration in a Jewish country as *the* solution of the Jewish problem. When it was reported, in 1878, that the Alliance Israélite Universelle proposed to purchase land in Russia for Jewish colonization, Lilienblum was a vigorous supporter of the project.

Lilienblum has given direct testimony, in his diary notations, of the emotional impact the pogroms had upon him. He was glad to have lived through the Odessa pogrom, he said; this intimation of what his forefathers had suffered served to reunite him with them. During this time, too, he came to a new intellectual conviction about the roots of the Jewish problem. He now believed that Jewish alienness was the fundamental cause of antisemitism, which, accordingly, was inevitable and ineradicable in the diaspora. The only remedy was resettlement in the historic Jewish homeland.

Sharing similar emotional and intellectual experiences, Lilienblum and men like him now felt identified with a distinct party and ideological movement. This group identity served the new Zionists as a common fixed point from which—each in accordance with his other predispositions—they severally took their bearing on current Jewish issues.

A group identity *may arise* out of a shared traumatic experience, but it is most effectively *defined* by opposition to the specific attitudes of rival groups. For the new Zionist movement, the role of ideological antagonist was performed by the Western European Jewish organizations and the Russo-Jewish leadership; further, the rise of a self-conscious Zionist opposition led these antinationalists to take a firmer, more ideological stand on current issues.

The questions debated in Russia in the 1880s were similar to those argued in relation to Rumania a decade earlier under similar circumstances. In both cases, a government indicated its deliberate intent to reduce the Jewish population by encouraging, if not compelling, emigration. In both cases, the Western and local Jewish leaders had to choose between opposing emigration—because it might imply abandoning a civil rights struggle—and aiding resettlement in order to solve the immediate problem. In both cases, the question arose whether America or Palestine should be the destination for assisted emigrants.

But the debate over the Rumanian problem in the 1870s did not line up nationalists and antinationalists in clear and consistent opposition. The idea of a mass evacuation from Rumania was favored not by a nationalist seeking to restore the Jewish state in Palestine, but by Benjamin Franklin Peixotto, an American Jew. He renounced hope only in the specific case of Rumania, not in the tolerance of gentiles in general, and what he proposed was not autoemancipation in Zion but emancipation in America. A proto-Zionist like Rabbi Zvi Hirsch Kalischer, who preferred Zion to America as a haven for Rumanian Jewish emigrants, was far less radical than Peixotto. Kalischer did not think in terms of an evacuation but of a minor movement; thus, one of his arguments in favor of resettlement in Zion was that, by proving Jews could become productive workers, the emigrants might induce the Rumanian government to grant civic rights to those who remained behind.

The Russian crisis consolidated opposed attitudes into rival ideologies. For all the reluctance of Western Jews to accept mass emigration from Rumania in the 1870s, the Alliance Israélite Universelle had not been disinclined to help immigrants to Palestine. Charles Netter, who founded the Mikveh Israel farm school at that time, was ready, as were other leaders, to cooperate with proto-Zionists. But in the 1880s, the resistance of Western and Russo-Jewish leaders to the whole notion of mass emigration was much stiffer and, what is more important, far more public. As emigration continued on a mass scale in spite of their efforts, they aided those who went to America or other places of refuge, but they resolutely refused (with minor exceptions) to help those who tried to reach Zion. The nationalists were thereby provoked to sharp protest, and they campaigned energetically, by circulating petitions and publishing open letters, to *compel* the Jewish organizations to change their attitude.

The Alliance reacted to such pressure in a letter to the London *Jewish Chronicle*, signed by none other than Charles Netter, and the reasons for *not* assisting Palestine immigration were given in detail. All the healthy and fertile areas, Netter argued, were already cultivated by Arabs. The Turkish administration was oppressive. In America, only lack of farm experience and capital had to be overcome, but in Palestine an additional handicap, the probable revival of biblical agricultural laws, doomed the project from the start. And, finally, he pointed out, if immigrants to America were unsuccessful as farmers, they would find a way to support themselves in the cities, while in Palestine they would simply be added to the existing pauperized community supported by pious donations. So sharp and decisive a tone encountered an equally partisan nationalist response. David Gordon, formerly a warm admirer of Netter, could find no other parallel than the following to describe Netter's betrayal: "In these words he defames the Holy Land more than did the spies in ancient time."[3]

Thus the lines were drawn, and henceforth positions were defined polemically—that is, increasingly in terms of principle rather than of the specific case. Before this time, proto-nationalists had been deviant individual voices in either the modernist or traditionalist camp. Their opinions were perceived as erratic departures from one of the ideological axes around which discussion revolved. With the pogroms, however, nationalism emerged as an independent axis of Jewish opinion. Particular views on the cultural, social, and economic reforms needed in the Jewish community were now related to the central nationalist end. Moreover, the opposing nonnationalist views had to be redefined ideologically in relation to the new Zionism.

For the nationalists themselves, what was now primarily important was their (essentially emotional) identification with the group, not the particular attitudes they adopted. Since nationalist opinion was no longer a matter of individual rebellion but rather an established ideological position, its definition was no longer an individual matter but a collective process, arising out of a group polemic against other groups. Accordingly, the new nationalists began immediately to adjust their personal opinions on particular issues to the needs of their group identity, leading in many cases to rapid shifting of lines.

The case of Lilienblum is characteristic. The immediate impact of the pogroms left him one certainty—his identification with his people's historic fate and destiny—but with no fixed opinion on how to achieve the national aim. He knew only that Jews could no longer rely on others, and that they must emigrate and set up their own autonomous state in their own ancestral land. When, shortly after the Odessa pogrom, university students asked his help in raising funds to purchase Palestine from the sultan, he had said that was a task for Western European Jews. But soon after, he was urging the Russian Jews to repair the omissions of their ancestors and raise funds to buy back Zion. He believed that Jews of all persuasions should settle there, without disputing religious issues, and that they must build not only individual settlements, but a state—for "if we do not get the right to set up a shadow government, we should do better to establish colonies in America, a country more settled and with better commercial prospects than the land of our fathers."[4] Not long after this statement, he reached his conclusion about the causal connection between Jewish alienness and Jew-hatred. He then decided that *only* in Zion—*no matter under what political conditions*—could the Jews ever be other than alien. His support for resettlement in the Holy Land had become absolute and unconditional.

Among the Russian-trained intellectuals converted to Jewish loyalty by the pogroms, it was not Zion but America that had the most immediate and widest appeal as the goal of a mass migration; but the rationale was distinctly nationalist even in this case. Such men founded the *Am Olam* ("Eternal People") movement, which sought national Jewish liberation through agricultural cooperative settlement, especially on the American frontier. Russian and Hebrew periodical articles on this subject stressed the possibility, under American laws, of qualifying for territorial home rule by settling 5,000 Jewish families in a frontier region, or even of constituting a state in the federal union if 60,000 families could be settled contiguously.

However, some young students preferred Palestine rather than America from the outset, because historical attachment gave *any* settlement there national significance, whatever its size, and the return to Zion made an immediate appeal to national sentiment. This was the most prevalent point of view among nationalist *maskilim*; and needless to say, it was the ruling opinion among the proto-Zionist traditionalists, who welcomed the new recruits to a cause they had maintained alone until then.

In the end, the course of events settled the issue of America versus Palestine for nationalists. The return to Zion became the only emigration policy with which a Jewish nationalist of that generation could identify. The migration to the United States continued and grew steadily more massive, but the dreams of Jewish autonomy, based on a dense Jewish cooperative farm settlement on the frontier, quickly proved chimerical. The Am Olam movement disappeared, and no national significance was thereafter attached by any ideological group to the mass exodus to America. The migration to Palestine, on the other hand, remained small and was repeatedly checked by Turkish opposition. Nevertheless, the idea of resettlement in Zion as the solution of the Jewish problem remained the central belief of a new, distinct ideological group.

In this group were united Russian-trained Jewish intellectuals, modernist *maskilim* who combined a self-taught European culture with traditional schooling, and some of the Orthodox laymen and rabbis who had long been involved with the project of resettlement in Zion. For the Russified intellectuals, as was already noted, their conversion to nationalism was an effect of the pogrom trauma, which shattered fully and finally their reliance on gentile liberalism and Russo-Jewish enlightenment. What they felt was, first and foremost, sheer revulsion against attitudes they had previously shared. To use a later parallel, the pogroms made them see themselves as "Uncle Toms."

The Hebrew *maskilim*, who had distrusted the assimilationist attitude even before, also experienced the pogroms as a severe emotional shock; but it produced not so much a conversion as a radicalization and politicization of their attitudes. Their views on all the cultural, social, economic, and political issues current among Eastern European Jews were no longer voiced as a form of marginal dissent on particular points, but now expressed a distinct group identity. Opinions on specific issues therefore had to flow organically from a common nationalist ideology, which yet remained to be positively articulated.

Traditionalists who became Zionists suffered no trauma from the pogroms. The direct and empathetic pain experienced was certainly no less for them than for other Jews, but they needed no intellectual or emotional reorientation to cope with it, for such trials and troubles were part of the familiar pattern of exile. That modernist Jews now became nationalists gave them new hope, for they saw this shift as a return of the prodigals to positions they themselves had long occupied.

A Zionist grouping thus emerged as a major ideological component of the Jewish community. Not all who joined it shared every position implied or expressed in the common program, as defined at a given moment, and many who would not join nevertheless sympathized with particular Zionist viewpoints. The varied initial composition and leanings of the group were favorable to divergent definitions of the nationalist aims from the outset. Such divergences, crystallized by the critical experiences of successive Zionist generations, resulted in a variety of ideological factions, each devoted to a particular nationalist purpose it held to be most essential.

III

Eastern Europe was the cradle of Zionism, but from its earliest days the movement developed significant relations with Jewish communities in the West. Oppressive conditions in its original Russian base hampered the movement in its work and compelled Zionism to seek support in countries of greater freedom. The waves of emigration from Russia, Rumania, and Austria-Hungary included a scattering of Zionist adherents who came to Western cities such as Berlin, Paris, London, and New York and built Zionist cells wherever they settled. Such societies were founded in the West from the beginning of the movement in Eastern Europe.

Western Zionism always had in its ranks—and often as its local leaders—native-born or fully integrated Western Jews. Such recruits shared, broadly speaking, their Eastern comrades' assumptions about the general nature of the "Jewish problem," but they came to Jewish nationalism by a different route, from a background of experience that they shared with some of their non-Zionist Western contemporaries.

One source of Western sympathy for Zionism was the tradition of supporting the Yishuv in the Holy Land. Western philanthropists who carried on the tradition in the nineteenth century did so in a new, modernizing spirit. Their benefactions were not simply acts of pious charity but also an extension overseas of the program of enlightenment and socioeconomic "amelioration" that they pursued on behalf of fellow Jews at home in the campaign for civic emancipation. The traditionalist community in Palestine, however, showed a stiff resistance to modernization, particularly in its opposition to secular studies, the mainstay of the Westerners' program. The Zionists, on the other hand, were no less committed than the philanthropists to projects of secular education, vocational retraining, and agricultural settlement. This position made cooperation with them an attractive option—but only if the Zionists would downplay their dangerous nationalist political intentions. When Zionists did so, under the pressure of Ottoman restrictions, cooperation with Western non-Zionists was indeed achieved. At the same time, there were from the beginning Western Jews who found ideological Zionism itself basically acceptable. Such men joined and frequently became leaders in early Zionism in such countries as Germany, England, and the United States.

One factor that predisposed such Western Jews to become Zionists was the tendency toward a more militant self-assertive style in the defense of Jewish rights and interests that was increasingly manifested in the nineteenth century. Early Jewish protagonists of Western enlightenment and civic emancipation had usually accepted that Jews must earn their equal rights by reforming their traditional ways, economic and social as well as religious. This attitude led many—notably in America—to eschew separatist Jewish political activity such as was clearly implicit in Zionism when it later arose. But by then a different, activist attitude was held by a generation of self-assured Jewish liberals. They considered civic equality to be an absolute right that must not be made conditional and withheld until Jews fulfilled demands for "amelioration." Moreover, it became clear by the 1870s that not only legal discrimination but also social prejudice against Jews, culminating in the rise of political antisemitism, required militant Jewish action, and therefore Jewish organization for self-defense.

The Alliance Israélite Universelle, formed in France in 1860 as an international Jewish body, and the Centralverein deutscher Staatsbürger jüdischen Glaubens, organized in Germany in 1893 to combat antisemitism, were founded by leaders of this activist inclination. Their avowed commitment to emancipation according to the principles of the French

Revolution was, of course, in direct conflict with the Zionist slogan of autoemancipation; their anti-Zionism became outspoken when this Zionist ideological position was proclaimed with special emphasis. But when they opposed certain other expressions of Zionist militancy, it was rather because of the challenge to their own dominance in the activist, militant, and implicitly political defense of Jewish interests. The conflict on these grounds frequently took the form of differences over tactics; but this kind of non-Zionist Jewish leadership shared with Zionists a fundamental strategy of activism rather than of passive, inner-directed accommodation in seeking to define the Jewish position in a gentile world.

Theodor Herzl belonged to a generation of young Jews in German lands whose sensitivity to the insults of antisemitism was strongly implanted in them in their student years. The 1880s saw German and Austrian political parties rise to heights of menacing strength. Even if the antisemites' electoral strength receded in Germany in the 1890s, students at the universities continued to be harassed and humiliated by antisemitic fraternities. In consequence of the rejection they encountered, Jews organized their own student societies: some were professedly nonsectarian though overwhelmingly Jewish in composition; others were proudly, if not defiantly, committed to positive programs of Jewish self-assertion. The founders of the Centralverein, as well as German Zionists such as Max Bodenheimer and the sociologist Franz Oppenheimer, not to mention Herzl himself, came out of this background. The wounded pride that those of that generation shared was expressed by the Centralverein's leaders in their militant defense of Jewish rights and by men like Bodenheimer, Oppenheimer, and Herzl in their Zionism.

With the rise of Herzl, Zionism emerged as no longer an essentially East European movement with marginal Western supporters and sympathizers. To be sure, even before Herzl, Western sympathizers played a vital role in the proto-Zionist movement (Hibbat Zion); the Parisian Baron Edmond de Rothschild had taken over the financial sponsorship of nearly all the Palestinian settlements founded by the movement, and Hibbat Zion had tried to overcome the handicaps the Russian government imposed on it by setting up headquarters in Paris. But what Herzl did in convening the Zionist Congress in 1897 was to project the Zionist movement boldly and effectively into the domain of international affairs—not as a pragmatic solution of the local problems of certain oppressed Jewish communities in Eastern Europe, but as the claim of Jews throughout their dispersion to be liberated as "a nation, one nation."[5] In this bold maneuver he was able both to revive the original impulse of autoemancipation among the Zionists in the East and—by a positive expression of Jewish pride—to attract a following among men like himself in the West. He posed Zionism once again as an ideological challenge to all Jews and as a solution for a problem that affected them all alike.

For Westerners, however, this move meant identifying with an ideology and a prescription for action that found its clearest application in the situation of East European Jews. Herzl did not boggle at this conclusion, arguing that the crisis that was clearly approaching in the case of Russian and Rumanian Jews was bound eventually to befall Jews everywhere in gentile lands. Others, like Bodenheimer (a proud German Jew who became a Zionist by identifying with the plight of Russian-Jewish refugees in 1891), might agree that in principle the basic Jewish situation was most clearly exemplified in Eastern Europe but would regard the case of Germany as a fortunate exception. The plea of exceptionalism was one that Western Jews in many countries, and Western Zionists among them, made in respect of their own case, but in their understanding of the situation of the Jews generally, as a single people, such Zionists accepted the East European situation, and the diagnosis and prescription appropriate to it, as the paradigmatic case.

One further element that made Zionism attractive to some Western Jews was their growing disquiet over the effects of the rationalist universalism of Jewish religious reform and of secularist liberalism in Western countries. Young Jews brought up in such a milieu too frequently dismayed their parents by abandoning their tribal loyalties; or, alternatively, the young might themselves find their parents' secularism or reformed religion to be distasteful expressions of a bourgeois lifestyle. Both situations could lead, among other deviations from the established Western Jewish consensus, to a heightened appreciation of the solid ethnic-rootedness believed to characterize the East European Jewish community. Zionism, as an expression of this quality, drew some German Jews of Orthodox religious background in the early years. Later, especially after closer contacts with Eastern Europe during World War I, an avant-gardist group of young Zionists in Berlin, Prague, and other centers of German modernist culture came to lead the German Zionist movement. Both there and in America and other Western Jewish communities, Zionism was taken up, like the vogue for neo-Hasidism inspired by Martin Buber and others, as part of a broader rebellion of the young against the older Western Jewish establishment.

◦ 2 ◦

The Setting

After an early period of conquest and expansion, the history of Ottoman rule in Palestine was one of protracted political disorganization and economic decline. Well into the nineteenth century, the territory was minimally populated by (in modern terms) a nonproductive, preindustrial society of some 200,000 to 300,000 inhabitants. However, there were sharp fluctuations in detail, some areas and some groups rising while others retreated in the scale of growth. The Jewish Yishuv and its major component sections experienced relatively large and rapid shifts in fortune.

The Ottoman conquerors took Palestine in 1516 in the course of campaigns against Muslim rivals that extended their dominion over Mesopotamia, the Arabian peninsula, and the North African Mediterranean coast. But the main thrust of their drive continued to be directed further into Europe, where the sultans carried forward the Islamic *jihad* against Christendom. After conquering Constantinople (Istanbul) in 1453, the Ottomans made it their capital; they chose a European base camp for attacking their main objectives, but it was not a suitable seat of central government for their expanding Asian-African, Muslim possessions. Their heavy commitment to military action made them disposed to leave local and regional administration to traditional or locally dominant leaders who paid homage to their authority and could provide necessary support for their campaigns. But by the late seventeenth century, a succession of military setbacks and the decline of internal institutions severely weakened the central government. Minor potentates, warlords, and clan and tribal leaders asserted increasing independence from the sultan, their nominal ruler.

In Palestine, unlike some other Ottoman territories, no major contender emerged to consolidate the area as a compact, semiautonomous power center. The country known in Jewish tradition as Erez Israel (the Land of Israel) was not a single administrative unit under Ottoman rule: it was divided between the province of Syria, formally governed from

Damascus, and a Lebanese-Palestinian region; a lesser administrative division was eventually created for the Jerusalem–Jaffa area. But effective authority flowed not so much from the central or provincial government as from a variety of local leaders who controlled daily life. The true political division of the country was that drawn by the bounds of their power.

Ottoman Palestine, as a result, had a chaotic history of feuding clans and tribal rulers. Given the available premodern techniques of warfare, the country was divided along lines of effective control that closely followed features of its physical geography. The lowlands—in the desert south, the coastal plain, and the valleys that cut across the north–south central mountain range—were open to Bedouin incursions and major invasions. The sedentary population sought safety by clustering in defensible hill villages, in towns, and behind city walls. Nearby lowlands were sporadically cultivated from these havens, and the extent of farming increased or shrank with the ebb and flow of external threats. Lands long untended deteriorated through nomadic overgrazing, seasonal erosion, encroaching sand dunes, and spreading malarial swamps at blocked watercourses. The coastal plain and valleys of Palestine, historic invasion routes of neighboring empires and nomad hordes, were also trade routes for Asian-African and Mediterranean commerce in times of peace. When relative security prevailed, cultivation of the lowlands increased together with the trade of the towns along the customary routes.

In the eighteenth and early nineteenth centuries, northern Palestine was controlled by powerful chiefs who installed themselves as Ottoman governors in Acre. A Bedouin chieftain, Zahir al-Umar, set an example of ruthless strength that was emulated with still greater ferocity by his successors. Other parts of the country did not enjoy such consolidated power. The southern wilderness was populated solely by nomads, and they overran the coastal plain and Jezreel Valley, which were repeatedly ravaged by warfare. In the central north–south mountain range, a settled population entrenched itself in defensive strongholds under the leadership of local clan chieftains. They joined together from time to time in feuds against similar combinations of local rivals, but no lasting political union emerged from these alliances.

Underpinning this precarious balance of divergent interests was a common commitment of the majority to the Sunni version of Islam shared with the Turkish rulers. When issues of property rights or personal status were brought before a court, they were submitted to judges who applied, whenever possible, the Islamic code, the *sharia*. Those who sat in judgment were generally chosen from families whose noble lineage and tradition of learning especially qualified them for this role. An upper class of scholars (*ulema*) also administered educational and charitable foundations (*waqf*) endowed with considerable tax-exempt funds. The protection from governmental exactions achieved by committment of lands and funds to a self-administered *waqf* was a base on which prominent clans built their financial power. Clerical office combined with control of *waqf* resources was particularly characteristic of the leading families in Al-Kuds, the walled city of Jerusalem. The holy city, unlike other parts of Ottoman Palestine, was decisively dominated by contending families among the *ulema*.

I

Napoleon's invasion of Egypt and Syria in 1798–99 drove home to Ottoman rulers the need to reform traditional institutions in order to defend themselves against the painfully obvious superiority of European power. The ruling sultans began to rely on European advisers and Western models and tried to scrap outworn Ottoman traditions, particularly their methods of military recruitment, training, and battle tactics. The innovations met with strong resistance from the imperial praetorian guard, the janissary corps, and others who enjoyed positions of privilege. After one sultan, Selim III, was deposed by the rebellious soldiery in 1807, his successor, Mahmud II, had to carry out a massacre of janissaries in 1826 in order to prosecute his reform program.

Mahmud was also able to bring under control the local strongmen who dominated major parts of Anatolia, the Turkish heartland, but his reign saw further erosion of Ottoman sovereignty in outlying European territories. Christian rebels in Serbia, Greece, and the Balkans were strongly supported by Russia as co-religionists or fellow Slavs, and there were militant Philhellenic sympathizers in England. In his long struggle to stave off inevitable losses, Mahmud relied on the support of his vassal, the Albanian-born pasha of Egypt, Mohammed Ali.

This powerful provincial ruler engaged in his own reforms in Egypt. He built a modern army and navy that sustained the Ottoman Empire against fanatical Wahhabi tribesmen in Arabia and temporarily held Greek nationalist revolutionaries in check. He also reorganized the Egyptian economy under tight control and opened his domain to European capital and civilian advisers. The ambitious pasha planned to establish his dynasty as provincial governor of broader areas, and he pursued this aim with military force as well as by diplomatic maneuvers involving

European powers. In 1831 he sent his son Ibrahim into Palestine, seeking to add the province of Syria to his domain; by 1833 Ibrahim was threatening to topple the Ottoman Empire in its heartland, Anatolia. The desperate Turks turned to Russia for help, thus setting off alarm bells in England and France. In order to avoid a general European conflict, the powers forced an agreement confirming Ibrahim's control of Syria, including Palestine, which he ruled for nearly a decade.

Mohammed Ali meanwhile extended his domination southward into the Arabian peninsula, and Ibrahim was thought to harbor dreams of replacing the Turkish Empire with a pan-Arab caliphate. The French, to whom the new Egyptian dynasts turned after some initial overtures to London, supported these moves, but the English foreign secretary, Lord Henry Palmerston, saw them as threats to the British lifeline to India. The sultan reopened the warfare with a new army trained by a Prussian general, Helmuth von Moltke, only to suffer another crushing defeat. The European powers again intervened in a confused tangle of moves and countermoves, ending in a British naval action in alliance with Austrian and Turkish forces which forced Ibrahim to withdraw from Syria in 1840. Palestine then reverted to Ottoman control, and an agreement was dictated by the European powers that conceded to Mohammed Ali's line a hereditary right to rule Egypt.

Ibrahim's ten-year occupation of Palestine began a new era of Western penetration and influence in the Holy Land. The Egyptian regime opened its doors to Western interests and ideas. When Ottoman rule was restored with European help, it too was accompanied by Turkish concessions to Western standards and expectations. Sultan Abdul Mejid, who succeeded upon the death of his predecessor at the height of the crisis, issued in 1839 the first of a series of Ottoman reform decrees, the Hatt-i Sherif of Gulhane. This was a gesture of propitiation to the Western powers who sustained him on his shaky throne. But it was also a measure of imperial self-interest, seeking to reconstruct Ottoman society and government on modern, functionally effective lines.

The Ottoman reform (*Tanzimat*) announced by the Hatt-i Sherif was only tardily given effect: resistance by local, traditional forces was powerful and persistent, while commitment at the center was neither determined nor consistent. Nevertheless—not without continual prodding by foreign interests—the structure of political and social relations was slowly reshaped by Ottoman policy. In 1856, after three years of the Crimean War (in which Turkey was embroiled because of conflicting French and Russian claims for precedence for their protégés in the rites at Christian holy places in Jerusalem), the European powers dictated a new reform measure, the Hatt-i Humayun, that substantially advanced the Westernization of the empire.

A team of Western-oriented civil servants, who controlled the central government until the 1870s, promoted a program of reforms to carry out the sweeping promises of the 1856 decree. Working on the assumption that the way to relieve the empire of unpleasant European pressures was to modernize its social and political institutions, they pressed ahead with a broad agenda. They pushed for an equal status of Ottoman citizenship, eliminating differences of civic rights and obligations between Muslims and the religious minorities (*millets*); for further extension of civil laws and courts and secular schools, based on equality for all citizens, to replace the distinctions of the traditional religious jurisprudence; and for the introduction of Western-style legal codes, suitable for commercial and industrial development on modern capitalist lines.

The reforms promulgated in Istanbul were not effectively administered locally. Efforts were made, accordingly, to discipline provincial and local governments by sending inspectors from the capital to review their operation. Seasoned bureaucrats, such as Midhat Pasha, introduced a more regular system of review, one purportedly applying Western methods of democratic control, advocated both for provincial governments and for the minority religious communities. In the latter case, the Ottoman authorities were interested in combating abuses of authority by churchmen, and they added lay leaders to the communities' autonomous governing bodies. A similar approach to provincial government—attaching an administrative council (including representatives of the millets) to the pasha's government—was demonstrated by Midhat Pasha amid general acclaim during his term of service as pasha in Baghdad. These experiments in democracy were limited to the appointment from above of local notables. They produced a stirring of interest in democracy and parliamentary government that, paradoxically, provided a new outlet for the discontent aroused by the heavy costs and unforeseen difficulties of the Tanzimat regime.

The reforms did not avail to overcome the fundamental difficulties of the Ottoman regime. They did not free the empire from the pressure of foreign powers. The Russians continued to extend their borders at Turkish expense and supported nationalist rebellions in the Balkans. Turkey and Egypt fell hopelessly into debt and were unable to satisfy their foreign creditors or cover the expenses of their domestic establishment. To meet the Ottoman debt, control of customs receipts and the budget had to be yielded to European bankers; Egypt, nominally still a part of the

Ottoman Empire and ruled by an autonomous native dynasty, was in effect taken over lock, stock, and barrel by England. Elsewhere in the Ottoman Empire, the reorganized government machinery did not confer clear benefits on the citizenry at large sufficient to give the reform movement the support of a solid consensus; it did, however, produce a generation of educated malcontents who could not inherit the traditional privileged status their parents once enjoyed and who were disaffected from the attitudes of the Tanzimat reformers.

Among such circles of young intellectuals, demands for a democratic, parliamentary constitution began to be heard, carrying further the ideas of men like Midhat. But by the 1870s, with the passing of the generation of the Tanzimat reforms, the sultan took over control of Ottoman policy from the bureaucrats and policed the country in the repressive style of authoritarian autocracy. In 1876, a rebellion by the chief minister Midhat and the discontented young intellectuals deposed Sultan Abdul Aziz (who died in prison) and proclaimed a new constitutional regime. A new sultan, Abdul Hamid II, eventually came to power amid domestic and external disorders. In short order, he dismissed and banished Midhat and let the parliament lapse after its first session. He quickly reverted to the autocratic methods and the pretensions to pan-Islamic leadership of his predecessor.

Abdul Hamid's long reign, begun amid internal and external crises, continued for 30 years in a posture of wary suspicion of dangerous foreign influences. The Zionist settlement in Palestine began and continued for a quarter of a century under this regime.

In Palestine, as elsewhere in the empire, the modernization initiated by Ottoman reformers met with strong local resistance, but it took hold slowly with accumulating effect. Another, perhaps more powerful, force for change arose indirectly from the rapid economic expansion and political upheavals of nineteenth-century Europe. Well into the century Palestine was still a country without paved roads; camels carried its export and transit trade to the Mediterranean beaches, where coast-hugging sailing ships anchored offshore. By mid-century, European steamships began to schedule stops at Haifa or Jaffa, opening up previously untapped markets and pouring into the country the mixed blessings of mass-produced Western industrial and agricultural goods. The first wheeled transport—two-wheeled wagons—were brought into Palestine by the Circassians, Muslim refugees driven from the Caucasus by the Russian invasion. Other Muslims, from Algeria and Bosnia, came in the wake of Christian dominance in those countries; Egyptian peasants and Bedouin also settled in waste areas of Palestine, seeking to avoid the exactions of their own Muslim rulers' Westernizing reforms. The Templars (a German pietist sect from Württemberg) built carriage roads and set up a stagecoach service. The model farms and urban colonies they founded demonstrated possibilities for developing Palestine on modern lines that set an example for the later Zionist settlers. By the end of the century, European investors and engineers, with some local Christian and Jewish participation, supplied Palestine with railroads and telegraph connections to Europe and the world beyond; European consuls provided regular postal service. And beyond the slow progress of indigenous reforms, these dynamic pressures from other continents swept Palestine into new, often unwelcome Western ways.

During the Egyptian occupation, Ibrahim tried to disarm the clans and introduced policies of military conscription and stringent tax collection that provoked a rebellion, repressed only with great difficulty in 1834. The restoration of Ottoman authority replaced Ibrahim's harsh rule with the more remote sway of the sultan; but it did not end the widely resented pressure of reform and foreign influence, nor did it persuade the local strongmen to accept a new rule of law peaceably. The old clans reasserted their claims and resumed their feuds in a struggle for local dominance. The 1840s and 1850s were a period of disorder in Palestine, as in Syria generally, and culminated in the bloody intercommunal war between Maronites and Druze in Mount Lebanon in 1860. The restoration of central control in the 1870s was a slow development until the accession of Abdul Hamid.

The Ottoman government, following the example of Ibrahim, tried to achieve effective central control by dividing and consolidating Syria and Palestine into appropriate administrative regional units. Jerusalem became the capital of an area stretching to the Mediterranean coast from Jaffa to Gaza, with a direct administrative tie to Istanbul; in Nablus, an administrative center for another consolidated region within the larger Syrian province was set up; and the capital of the area governed from Acre was in time moved to Sidon and then to Beirut. But these measures did not stabilize the unruly countryside or break the power of the traditional leadership in cities like Jerusalem.

The central government relied on three institutions in governing the reclaimed provinces: a civil governor, appointed by and responsible to the Porte (government); a military commander, also responsible directly to the Porte; and the administrative councils, selected from among qualified propertied men who ostensibly represented the local populace and assisted in civil government. The governor of Syria on the Jerusalem region labored under severe handicaps. He generally had no control over the regular army committed to his domain and only inadequate, unreliable forces to govern the immediate area of his official residence. Moreover, since he was usually appointed for a short term only, he had to depend on bargains that had been struck with long-established positions of traditional power. These men moved into control of the reformers' administrative councils and, because of the appointed governors' weak position, became dominant in the "reformed" power structure of their towns. In this way, the traditional leading families—especially those who won out over their rivals by superior strength or cunning—not only were able to delay and restrict the projected reforms, but they bolstered their position by preempting the power generated by the new political structures.

In the same period, an aggressive foreign presence, as stimulating as it was irritating, made itself felt in Palestine. The first foreign consulate in Jerusalem was welcomed during Ibrahim's occupation as a matter of Egyptian policy. Others rapidly followed after the Ottoman restoration—more, perhaps, under pressure from outside than by grace of the indigenous reform movement. Together with European consular protection came a sharp rise in the number of Christian pilgrims and missionary and monastic establishments in the Holy Land.

The European embassies and consulates in the Ottoman Empire were able to exercise extraordinary powers under their "treaties of capitulations." The early examples of such treaties—for instance, that between Suleiman the Magnificent and his ally Francis I of France in 1535—were based on mutual interest, particularly in fostering commerce. The French obtained exemption from local exactions and local courts for their trading colonies in Ottoman cities. The sultan obtained similar privileges for any Turks trading in France, a provision that remained largely academic. The French, usually on friendly terms with the Turks, extended their treaty privilege into a general right to protect Franciscan and other Catholic institutions in Ottoman lands. Other nations that entered into similar treaties of capitulations with Turkey demanded not only exterritorial rights for their own citizens but the right to protect one or another religious community in the Ottoman Empire with whom they could identify. The Russians aggressively championed the interests of Eastern Orthodox Christians and used the nationalist grievances of church-related Slavic groups as an instrument in their persistent drive to extend their direct rule or sphere of influence at the expense of Turkey.

After 1840, Palestine became an arena where all the major European powers competed for influence by bringing appropriate local clients under their protection. Consulates established in Jerusalem became the base upon which British, German, and American Protestant missionaries, French and Italian monks, and Russian and Austrian ecclesiastics were able to build with growing security their churches and monasteries, their hostels for pilgrims, and medical and educational missions for local co-religionists. The Russian patrons of Eastern Orthodox Christians supported Arab laymen in their quarrels with Greek priests. After the communal wars of 1860 in Lebanon, the French emerged as protectors of the Maronites, and the British defended the interests of the Druzes in the political reorganization of the country. In Palestine, Britain and Germany jointly (and later, in competition) initiated Protestant missionary activities, chiefly among Eastern Christians. The British also developed a strong interest in the Jews as potential converts, whether immediately or in the apocalyptic millennium; they were prepared to take under their wing those Russian Jews from whom the Russians withdrew their own protection. Not only the British, but other consuls as well liberally extended exterritorial rights to local residents who had questionable titles to such protection. The Turks, as well as the local Muslim community, became increasingly antagonistic to such foreign encroachments.

The spread of missionary influence was facilitated by the reforms in Ottoman land laws in the late 1850s. The Tanzimat reformers hoped to increase government revenues by developing a freer market in land. But the code of land tenure they issued in 1858 was not borrowed from European models, as were other codes they promulgated; it remained closely tied to the customary rules sanctified by Islamic law.

In the Islamic tradition of Ottoman society, land tenure was the special privilege, as military service was the special obligation, of Muslims. The tolerated religious minorities paid a poll tax for protection in lieu of service in the army, and their subordinate status seemed inconsistent with the dignity and power conferred by owning land rights. Thus, even though the Tanzimat reforms in principle conferred equal rights with the Muslims on Christians and Jews, the purchase and registration of titles to real estate, or the grant of building permits, were regulated by an administration dominated by local notables hostile to the implied empowerment of the subordinate millets.

Even stronger opposition, shared by Turkish officials as well as the Muslim Arab public, long hampered the efforts of foreign individuals and institutions to acquire land and build on it. The exemption from Ottoman jurisdiction that foreigners enjoyed under their treaties of capitulations would be particularly odious if it were extended to the privileged sphere of landed property. Not until the late 1860s did the Porte yield to pressure and provide a formal framework for land appropriation by foreigners. This was permitted on condition that a foreign state sign a treaty undertaking that its subjects and protégés would be subject to Ottoman jurisdiction and *sharia* (Islamic code) law for real estate rights they might acquire. The Württemberg Templars (in a way that prefigured the later experience of the Zionist settlers) were confronted with persisting obstruction in their efforts to establish self-sustaining villages: their building permits were held up for years after they secured land rights in the late 1860s.

While immigrant aliens such as the Ashkenazi Jews generally had to resort to indirect methods for acquiring real estate, Christian institutions and other foreigners with sufficient influence in government circles could purchase land rights and building permits under these treaty conditions. A burst of competitive ecclesiastical investment by Europeans injected fresh capital into the economy and provided educational and medical services that fostered a new phase of growth, particularly in the Christian Arab community. The Muslim Arab populace learned to appreciate the direct and indirect benefits derived from these imported foreign resources, but these advantages did not make them less antagonistic to projects, like the Templar colonies, that wished to maintain themselves by developing local resources, such as land, in competition with the native inhabitants.

The 1858 code and subsequent land regulations had a complex series of effects on the Muslim Arab population. In the traditional land tenure system (apart from a small amount of *mulk* property—privately owned real estate, mainly in the cities), the title of ownership was assumed to belong to the state by virtue of the early Islamic conquests. But this nominal title was frequently of little practical significance, since the *tenure* of land—that is, the vested, usually hereditary, right to its use—belonged to those who cultivated, grazed, built upon, or effectively held and defended it. Instead of formally documented appropriation, it was custom—an uncertain criterion in such unstable times—that determined who owned the right to use what lands and on what conditions. Boundaries were fixed not by precise measurement but by reference to landmarks and to traditions of occupancy. This was an insecure basis in the face of counterclaims by others, and force and influence were required to sustain property rights. In this environment, traditional clan chiefs and village headmen were the guarantors of the use rights of clients, who submitted to their authority.

In addition, the main tax payments for which the Muslim population was liable were the tithes taken from crops. Peasant cultivators were also subject to special levies from time to time and to forced labor or military service, if required. Provincial and subordinate officials who were appointed to deliver the tax assessed for their area would farm out their contract, usually at a profit, to local men of power and influence. The tax farmers would seek to extort greater returns from the tenants with vested rights, and they in turn would try to evade or reduce their tax obligation, in a periodic struggle of power and maneuvering. Here, too, village headmen and clan chiefs could protect the peasant client against extortion by others by becoming in effect the tax farmer themselves.

This system of land tenure and taxation presented serious obstacles to modernizing reformers bent on developing the country's resources and enhancing the government's revenues. Large estates held by the *waqf* foundations were exempt from most taxes and unavailable for acquisition by investors capable of a more productive use of their potential. Peasant villagers often held use rights in common (*musha'a*), sharing out plot allocations annually and paying collective taxes, subject to the bargaining power of their headmen and patrons. Neither effective taxation nor the most constructive use of land (which was not securely held from year to year by any single cultivator) could be expected under these conditions. The real estate that remained available for free disposal by the state was that not subject to local use rights—usually nonproducing land that was unoccupied for whatever reason. If peasants in peaceful intervals built homes unhindered, planted trees, or grazed their goats on such land, their use rights could be speedily established as customary.

The Ottoman rulers were for many years unable to dispense with the system of tax farming, but they tried persistently to reform the conditions of tenure. A decree was issued annulling claims of use rights on *miri* land (land held under customary, hereditary lease from the state) if left untended for three years, and checks were ordered on the actual state of properties declared to be *waqf*. A program of surveying and establishing clear boundaries and registering title deeds was initiated so that taxes could be levied directly on the registered owners—a prospect viewed with alarm by peasant-users. However, the program was carried out in painfully slow and halting advances and engendered measures of evasion that robbed it of much of its value as a fiscal measure. Yet the structure of society was radically changed by the reform measures and their unintended consequences.

Although the reform aimed to shake the traditional base of the dominant local families, it also offered opportunities to convert their customary, indefinite authority into new, formally defined power. Their wealth and status, reinforced with the positions they gained in the new regional governments and administrative councils where crucial decisions regarding land use were made, enabled them to emerge as large landowners and moneylenders in the growing real estate market. Peasant cultivators, fearing the menace of direct taxation, sought shelter in a new dependency as debtors, tenant farmers, sharecroppers, and landless farmhands under the patronage of those who were able to take advantage of the new system.

The cumulative effect of Western influence and Ottoman reform began to be felt in the growth of cities after the Crimean War. Improved conditions of health and security and the stimulus of Western investment brought about a rise in the population of Christian centers such as Jerusalem, now housed increasingly outside the cramped quarters of the walled-in Old City. Jaffa prospered as the port of entry for pilgrims and imports to Jerusalem, and Haifa began to rise at the expense of Acre, attracting new settlers from Algeria. The leading families of Jerusalem, as well as large landowners residing in Egypt and Lebanon, acquired control of land freed from the menace of Bedouin raids on the coast and in the lowlands. They drew rents from new plantations and peasant villages that were supplying the export and domestic urban markets. Only the old-established upland villages and towns remained relatively unaffected, as population growth moved slowly to the new centers of economic activity.

II

At the time of the Ottoman conquest of Palestine in 1516, the Jewish community numbered about 5,000. It was chiefly concentrated in the Galilee and was then made up mainly of indigenous, Arabic-speaking townsmen and villagers. Spanish-speaking (Sephardi) Jews fleeing the Inquisition sought a haven in the expanding Ottoman territories, and some moved into the Holy Land as soon as it came under Ottoman rule. The Ottomans, who saw themselves as still rolling back the Crusades, welcomed these victims of their enemies and hoped to find them useful allies. One of the refugees, Don Joseph Nasi, established an important banking and trade house in the sixteenth century and served as an influential adviser and political counselor to Sultan Selim II. In this capacity, Don Joseph Nasi successfully reestablished the old town of Tiberias, adding a new community to those in the other holy cities: Jerusalem, Safed, and Hebron. The Sephardi immigrants also brought new life to Jewish Jerusalem as well as to remote Hebron and other minor Jewish settlements in towns of the coastal plain, such as Gaza, Jaffa, Ramle, and Lydda.

Jewish immigrants built up the Galilean town of Safed to a Jewish community of 15,000—a major Jewish population center in terms of the urban concentrations of Jews common in the sixteenth and seventeenth centuries—and established a flourishing silk industry there and in surrounding villages. Safed became the most significant Jewish religious center of its time. It was the source of a code of Jewish law which, in different versions, is the basis of Orthodox practice to this day for both Sephardi and Ashkenazi communities. A mystical movement flourished there, around the shrines of ancient legendary rabbis, which powerfully influenced religious thought and feeling through the entire seventeenth-century Jewish world.

But by the eighteenth century, the glamorous era of Sephardi Jewry in Palestine was coming to a close. The Ottoman central government became feeble and corrupt, earning the name of the "Sick Man of Europe," and local authorities, janissaries, and guilds, not to mention Bedouins and bandits on the pilgrimage roads, showed Jews the same hostility and contempt they extended to all unbelievers. The Jewish communities of the Galilee depended on the changing fortunes of a banking family close to the ruling pashas in Acre. Jerusalem, Hebron, and other towns suffered from the wars, oppressive whims, and extortions of feuding local chieftains. Earthquakes and political turmoil continually afflicted Safed and finally reduced that community to insignificance in the nineteenth century.

The Yishuv was again in decline, dropping once more to a total of about 6,500 by 1800. By this time, the Ashkenazi Jews of Eastern and Central Europe had begun to immigrate in growing numbers. A count made for Sir Moses Montefiore in 1839 found Ashkenazim to be almost half of the depleted Safed community of 1,357 Jews, and about a sixth of the growing Jerusalem community of 2,943 Jews. There were also Ashkenazi groups in Tiberias and Hebron. Another survey, in 1856, showed Ashkenazim to be a majority in the Safed and Tiberias Jewish communities. The Yishuv in all Palestine had grown from about 6,000 in 1839 to 10,600. By the 1880s, when Zionist immigration began, the Yishuv had more than doubled in one generation, rising to an estimated 24,000; in Jerusalem, Jews had become the majority of the total population. Among Jerusalem Jews, 17,000 in 1880, thus constituting the major part of the whole Yishuv, Ashkenazim had risen to the substantial number of 9,000.

Soon after the seizure of Constantinople, Jews were tacitly, though not formally, recognized as one of the three privileged millets of unbelievers in the empire; their chief rabbi in the new capital was appointed Haham Bashi, the head and representative of all the Jews in the empire. When Palestine was later conquered, the Yishuv was absorbed into the general millet of Ottoman Jewry.

The refugees from Spain who came to Palestine relied for political protection on influential Sephardim close to the court in Istanbul, Damascus, or Acre. Religious enthusiasm was a major factor that led to their settlement in the holy cities of Erez Israel, and a significant number were committed to lives of scholarship and pious dedication. Many had close ties to supportive relatives in other Ottoman regions; others, the scholars and mystics as well as dependent widows and orphans, were maintained by the "distribution" (*halukah*) funds donated by the widespread Jewish diaspora. Controlling the flow of contributions gave those in charge a position of authority somewhat like that of the Muslim *ulema* in Jerusalem who performed similar functions; but the Sephardi leadership in Palestine was itself supervised—and usually selected—by a committee in Istanbul.

When small groups of Ashkenazim arrived, they were at first protected by the settled Sephardim and absorbed into their communal structure. However, those rabbis who led the immigrant movement, who were largely from various Hasidic sects and from the anti-Hasidic faction, the Perushim, soon established autonomous groupings, in accordance with the Jewish tradition of religious organization. As rival East European sects increased the number of their settlers in the holy cities, they created separate organizations for collecting and distributing donations from their supporters in Europe. Alongside the general *halukah*, numerous *kolelim* (sing. *kolel*, collectivity) sprang up, each claiming the sum contributed by its own sect, town, or province abroad. Specific institutions of learning and charity led by influential rabbis also competed in rancorous disputes over funds and authority.

Attempts to overcome the chronic disunity of the Yishuv led to the formation of new power centers in the diaspora and in Palestine. A group of pious supporters in Amsterdam, led by a prominent Ashkenazi banking family, the Lehren brothers, undertook in 1825 to rationalize the collection of *halukah* funds. They aimed to eliminate the expense (and, of course, spare diaspora contributors the trouble) of the emissaries sent by competing sections of the Yishuv. The Amsterdam committee built a network of regular contributors in Western and Central Europe and hoped to channel all funds through the Lehren bank. They were also able, with varying but appreciable success, to secure an allocations agreement between the Sephardim and Ashkenazim, and within the Ashkenazi sector, between Hasidim and Perushim. Their control over funding lent them the authoritative influence over communal affairs in the *halukah*-supported Yishuv that the Istanbul committee had exercised earlier.

The growth of the Ashkenazi component of the Yishuv brought some consolidation in the local administration of the *halukah* in the Holy Land as well. The most powerful organization was developed by the anti-Hasidic Perushim in Jerusalem. In 1866 they established a General Committee (Vaad Klali), claiming to represent the joint interests of all Ashkenazi *kolelim*. By the latter part of the nineteenth century, the Vaad Klali had become a major force in the affairs of the Yishuv; its constituents controlled a great part of the East European contributions, and the Vaad itself disposed of collections from countries such as the United States, England, South Africa, and Australia, which were represented by few if any of their countrymen in the Yishuv.

The growing influence of European countries in the Eastern Mediterranean decisively affected the Yishuv. One of the side effects was a wider divergence between the local situation of the Sephardim, who were integrally related to Ottoman society, and that of the Ashkenazi settlement, which was detached from Ottoman institutions and increasingly dependent on protection by European consulates.

Jews born and reared in a Muslim milieu adjusted to the slow modernization of Palestine in the same way as did other Ottoman subjects. They readily availed themselves of opportunities that opened up for Ottoman *dhimmis* (religious-ethnic minorities) by the advances toward equal citizenship and a freer market in land. Their familiarity with the languages and customs of Palestinian commerce allowed them to take part in the general economic expansion that was stimulated by Western investment and trade.

This group of Jews included both native-born residents and immigrants from other Muslim countries. When Sultan Abdul Mejid promised the Western powers in 1839 to grant equal security of life, liberty, and property for all his subjects, he offered similar pledges to French Jews. The Jewish millet was now formally recognized; the Sephardi chief rabbi of Jerusalem was invested with the office and dignity of Haham Bashi for the Yishuv; and Sephardi Jews long settled in the country shared in the subsequent economic development. The participation of Jews (almost entirely Sephardi) in the new Ottoman administrative structures, like popular participation in general, increased only minimally, but these Jews were alert to the new conditions these institutions imposed upon their private and communal affairs.

During the nineteenth century, the French and Russian expansion into Muslim lands set in motion a flow of migrants to Syria and Palestine. Not only Muslim refugees but Moroccan, Bokharan, and Daghestani Jews came. They were able to fit relatively smoothly into an environment that was reasonably similar to the one they had left, and in some cases to contribute to its new growth. Arabic-speaking North Africans established a new Jewish community in the town of Haifa. Emissaries sent to Persia, Afghanistan, and even far-off India on behalf of the Sephardi *halukah* reached isolated Jewish communities, strengthened their bond to Jewish tradition, and stimulated some individuals to make pilgrimage or settle in the Holy Land, adding to the color of the Jewish millet.

Like Jewish immigrants from all other areas, religiously motivated settlers from distant Muslim countries preserved their local variants of Jewish tradition in Palestine. Throughout this period, accordingly, traditional institutions continued to proliferate, particularly in Jerusalem. Immigrants to the holy city transplanted the time-honored customs and structures of their old homes—the synagogue and local style of worship, the kinship and charity affiliations, and the general communal organization, the *kehilah* (pl. *kehilot*)—adding to the mosaic of the Old Yishuv differently colored but essentially similar new pieces. Thus in 1844, a community of North Africans, mainly Moroccan, was established in Jerusalem, in addition to the already existing Sephardi and the two Ashkenazi (Hasidic and anti-Hasidic) communities. In 1849 the Georgian Jews, and in 1868 the Bokharans, founded *kehilot*. In 1877 Persian Jews, and in 1880 immigrants from Aleppo in Syria, set up their communities on traditional lines. In 1883, at the height of the first phase of Zionist immigration, Jews from remote Yemen—not only traditional but bearing the imprint of preindustrial society—came to Jerusalem, having been urged on by the chance visit of Shmuel Yavnieli, an emissary of the Ashkenazi *halukah*; they came under the mantle of the Sephardi community. Traditional *kehilot* were founded by Daghestani (Caucasian) Jews in 1887, Baghdadis in 1888, Afghans in 1900, townsmen of Urfa (on the Syrian-Anatolian border) in 1902, and Crimeans in 1909. However, the multiplicity of local religious traditions, languages, and self-enclosed communal entities that were preserved among the Jews from Muslim countries left the established Sephardi structure intact as the authorized representative, to the outside, of that part of the Yishuv that had an integral relation to Ottoman society. The Sephardi chief rabbi was the acknowledged ecclesiastical head of the Jewish millet for all such Ottoman Jews in Palestine.

The exception were the Jews of Ashkenazi stock and this "exception" became the numerically preponderant part of the Yishuv, as was earlier noted, by the time the Zionist settlers began to arrive. The Ashkenazim in Palestine were largely insulated from their Ottoman-Arab surroundings. Without influential connections in Ottoman society, they turned for support to the consuls and embassies of the European countries they came from and whose citizenship they retained—or to others, like the British consuls, who were willing to offer them their protection. Ashkenazim who enjoyed such legal and political protection were neither eligible for nor interested in participation in the new administrative and communal structures of the Ottoman reform.

The benefits of European political influence were not confined, of course, to Ashkenazi Jews. The native Christian Arabs, who suffered major attacks by enraged Muslims in the mid-nineteenth century, relied even more on foreign consular and ambassadorial protection. Both the Christian communities and the Sephardim enjoyed major charitable support for their religious institutions from co-religionists abroad. But only the Ashkenazim depended on donated funds not merely for the support of scholars and religious functionaries, or for needy widows and orphans, but to sustain an entire lay community as well.

The growing Ashkenazi population included some immigrants of independent means who came to end their days in prayer and study in the sanctity of the Holy Land, but there were also many who left Europe primarily because of oppressive conditions. Few of this latter group had scholarly attainments that merited sufficiently generous stipends to maintain them adequately. Nevertheless, since the Ashkenazi leaders viewed their entire community, and not simply individual votaries, as being endowed with a religious (or eschatological) mission, all immigrants belonging to one of the Ashkenazi *kolelim* were considered deserving of some support. The amounts available were both meager and unreliable, and poverty, malnutrition, disease, and high mortality rates were rife in the community. But the minimal support that was available maintained a far larger community than these Yiddish-speaking foreigners could sustain by their own efforts in the unfamiliar, backward Palestinian economy.

Like any other publicly supported institution, the Ashkenazi settlements had a domestic economy of their own, and those responsible for administering it had to maintain a more or less balanced, solvent relationship with the broader economic environment. The Yishuv's self-generated economy included the butchers, bakers, tailors, and other ritual specialists required by any tradition-bound Jewish community. A number of skilled artisans like watchmakers plied their trade in the broader local market. The high concentration of scholars and students yielded a rich crop of tracts and treatises as well as the first periodical journals published in Palestine; an energetic printing establishment provided the necessary production facilities. The *halukah* administration used its receipts from abroad as a base for credit operations: it borrowed extensively from Arab and other local sources and, when its cash box ran low, issued a kind of scrip that was widely accepted in payment in Palestine. *Halukah* funds, together with aid from diaspora benefactors and the investments of new immigrants, helped to build new Jewish quarters (alongside local Arab and foreign missionary construction) outside the walls of the Old City.

But more than keeping an existing situation in balance was required. The continual growth of the Ashkenazi population (by immigration, not by natural increase in this elderly and impoverished community) constantly drove up the rents paid to Arab landlords and worsened the congestion and unhealthy living conditions in the walled city of Jerusalem. The pressure of a growing population so far outran the economic capacity of the Ashkenazi Yishuv that many of the leaders strongly urged that only those should come from abroad who had the means to sustain themselves independently and would commit themselves entirely to study and prayer. Meanwhile, chronic hardships and occasional disasters compelled the community to send out repeated appeals for aid to the diaspora. Those who responded were a diverse, internally divided group, whose divergent views were, in turn, reflected or refracted in different ways by rival Yishuv interests.

A significant contributing cause for diaspora concern with the Yishuv was the rising Christian activity in Palestine, particularly when directed toward Jews. The seizure and torture of Jews in Damascus on ritual murder charges in 1840 was the occasion for the first major intervention of Western Jewry; such charges, brought by local Christians, became a recurrent feature of Ottoman Jewish life in the nineteenth century, paralleling similar antisemitic causes célèbres in Eastern and Central Europe in the same period. But it was a concern with Christian benevolence rather than such assaults, which were familiar to Jews from their premodern experience, that led to new diaspora efforts on behalf of the Yishuv—and to characteristically modern forms of such activity.

Christian missionaries pursued the conversion of impoverished Jews in ways that highlighted the severe social and economic faults in the Yishuv's structure. Alarmed Jewish leaders attributed the conversion of some Jews—slight as their number might be—to the medical and educational facilities and material support offered by the missions to the destitute and orphans in the Yishuv; even an attempt to settle Jewish converts on the land was initiated. This was a challenge that Jewish leaders felt must be met with similar methods undertaken from their side.

Modern, secular education, in the spirit of eighteenth century Enlightenment, as well as a restructuring of the vocational distribution of Jews, in order to further their emancipation and social-economic integration with their fellow citizens, were the very methods leaders of the Western and Central European diaspora tried to apply in their own community. These efforts, especially the proposed educational and religious reforms, alarmed traditionalist quarters and led to ideological conflicts that, in Germany and Hungary, produced denominational division and communal splits within Ashkenazi communities. A new separatist Orthodoxy arose in reaction to the growth of Reform Judaism.

Contributors to the support of Yishuv institutions before the rise of Zionism were drawn largely from the ranks of the religious conservatives. The Amsterdam bankers who mainly controlled Western and Central European *halukah* collections were staunch opponents of religious reform in Europe, and they were particularly hostile to modern innovations in the holy community in Palestine. However, others who began to concern themselves with the Yishuv's problems in the midcentury decades tempered their conservatism with certain reformist leanings, especially in regard to education. These differences were played out under the conditions imposed by differing responses of the various elements in the Yishuv itself.

Modern-minded Jewish philanthropists of the advanced Western countries (Britain, France, Austria, and Germany) concerned themselves with the welfare of the Palestine community, first through the efforts of influential notables such as Sir Moses Montefiore and Adolphe Crémieux, and after 1860 through the continuous activity of permanently organized, professionally staffed agencies such as the Alliance Israélite Universelle. They could not confine themselves to supporting the poor, pious, and scholarly; they aimed at practical, rational solutions for the Yishuv's problems through education and productive investment. Such objectives could not be pursued by the existing, traditional communal structure, but required new institutions: schools and hospitals, with appropriate staff and management; new residential quarters, suitably financed and administered; and even farms, factories, and workshops, with the necessary facilities to develop and maintain them. The teachers and physicians who settled in Palestine in their service, while generally themselves religious conservatives, constituted a new element of secular professionals in the community.

The schools built in Jerusalem by the Austrian Simon von Lämel or the British Montefiore and Rothschild were opposed with rigid hostility by the Yishuv's Ashkenazi leadership. Such efforts to introduce Western, secular subjects such as arithmetic, foreign languages, and history and geography into Jewish schools had been, in their experience, the entering wedge of religious infidelity, if not religious conversion, and they had fought it in Austria-Hungary and Russia. They issued anathemas and bans of excommunication and threats to withhold *halukah* support from any of their community who might wish to attend the new institutions. Their hard-line conservatism was supported, moreover, by the leading sponsors of the *halukah* in Amsterdam. Consequently, the new schools were used by Sephardi Jews rather than by Ashkenazim—and the schools managed to hold these circles, too, only by adhering to relatively conservative, traditional guidelines.

The *economic* reforms contemplated by Western philanthropists were more sympathetically received, though they too were subject to reservations voiced by the Ashkenazim. Proposals that could ease the burden of a growing dependent population were necessarily welcome to the hard-pressed Ashkenazi leaders (above all in Jerusalem, where the problem was greatest), since their community, unfamiliar with the languages of local trade and heavily burdened with old people, was the most dependent. They were, indeed, among the first to avail themselves of the opportunity to build new housing quarters. A more troublesome matter was that of vocational training for young people in the holy cities. Some were ready to concede that impoverished students who proved unable to master advanced religious studies might indeed benefit from learning a trade by which to support themselves; but the overriding consideration was that the Ashkenazi community was meant to devote itself to a life of pious devotion and study and should not be distracted from this paramount duty. Consequently, it was the Sephardi community whose young people, especially the poor and orphaned, made up the small group of students who were trained in vocational subjects.

A still more complicated issue was raised by proposals advanced by Montefiore and others to settle Jews on land in Palestine. The traditionalist Yishuv, both in Jerusalem and in Safed, showed a certain, continuing interest in the idea. Initial, abortive attempts conformed to the pattern of investment in land common in Palestine: Arab sharecroppers were to work the soil under Jewish management for the purchaser. The Yishuv establishment hoped to be the channel for investing the contributions made abroad and to gain added support for the *halukah* administration from the revenues of such projects. Jewish land settlement on such a plan would have left the local power structure intact, though (and, in a sense, because) it might do little to transform a significant part of the indigent Yishuv or a substantial number of immigrants into self-supporting farm settlers.

But it was precisely in this area that groups beyond the control of the *halukah* establishment, and committed in various ways to different goals became active. A widening split began to develop in this regard even before the appearance of Zionist settlers on the soil of Palestine.

Here again, Jewish activism arose against a background of rising Christian interest in Jews and the Holy Land, stemming in part from chiliastic cult-beliefs and in part from the periodic crises in the Ottoman Empire's political fortunes. As the year 1840 approached—a year of potentially eschatological significance in the calendar of Jewish mystics—Scottish and English missionaries followed the stirrings among certain Jews with keen interest. Somewhat later, American and German Christian pietists presented a telling challenge when they came to settle in Palestine in order to claim a special role for themselves in the imminently expected apocalyptic events. Similar perceptions, which however assigned a central importance to Jewish resettlement, were shared by men who combined their Christian evangelical enthusiasm with an acute awareness of imperial interests in the unstable Near East—notably, in 1838, by Lord Palmerston's nephew, Lord Anthony Ashley Cooper, later Earl of Shaftesbury. Finally, the nationalist awakening of the Greeks and Serbs aroused a sympathetic romanticism that, in the poetry of Lord Byron, led to sentimental appreciation of the legendary Hebrews as well. Thus, when the future of the Near East seemed open for reconstruction after Turkey was rescued by European intervention in the late 1830s and during the Crimean War, the visionary minds of such millenarianist-imperialist romantics gave birth to a series of daring proposals, projecting a major role for Jewish resettlement in Palestine's future.

As the nineteenth century wore on, the general perception that the Ottoman Empire was mortally weak played a prominent part in the maneuvers of rival European powers. England and France (and later Germany) feared that Turkey's collapse would lead to a dangerous aggrandizement of Russia. They acted as patrons and protectors of the Ottomans while competing in a struggle for influence over the sultan's government and economy and for positions that might enable them to take over large parts of his realm if the expected collapse should occur. Pending that terminal event, certain British and French enthusiasts, who favored the restoration of an autonomous Jewish settlement in Palestine, proposed this precisely as a solution for Turkey's ills.

They argued, in terms that Turkish reformers as well as others understood, that the Ottoman Empire needed greater, more reliable sources of revenue and that these depended on a healthier economy sustained by population growth and capital investment, which in turn required a legal system and judiciary attuned to modern commercial practices. The Turks had these broad aims in mind when they introduced piecemeal institutional reforms and when they granted Ottoman crown lands to Circassian refugees whom they settled in Syria. But Muslim refugees did not carry with them the capital needed for development. Christian immigrants, on the other hand, might mean the infusion of capital but would be regarded by the Ottomans as the entering wedge for dangerous Western penetration and disruption of their regime. The solution, such analysts concluded, lay in the Jews: they could not pose a threat to the Ottoman regime; they would draw in capital from wealthy coreligionists; and if they were given a legal status that protected them from the arbitrary and extortionate local administration, their intelligence and industry would prop up the Ottoman Empire—or, should the empire eventually collapse, would provide a strong, reliable, allied community for whatever European power sponsored their resettlement in Palestine.

The Jewish response to these developments was subject to serious inhibitions. In 1839 Sir Moses Montefiore proposed to the Egyptian pasha, Mohammed Ali, a plan to establish investment banks in his dominions in return for Jewish resettlement under an autonomous administration in Palestine. At that time, too, Rabbi Judah Bibas, according to a Scottish missionary's report, thought that since contemporary nationalist uprisings were a sign of the approaching messianic era, Jews should turn aside from their holy studies and learn the art of self-defense—a toxic medicine, perhaps, for the Jewish constitution, but one that was essential for curing their national illness, the exile. Neither Montefiore's nor Bibas's ideas were likely to be tolerated by those in power. Even more, they ran counter to the prevailing mood among Jews who viewed with suspicion anything reminiscent of the attempts in earlier centuries, by Shabbetai Zvi and Jacob Frank, to force God's hand and end the exile before its time.

Nevertheless, when defined in restricted, moderate terms, elements of both conceptions continued to be favored by Jewish advocates in the next generation. The idea of acquiring land for Jewish settlement, broached during Montefiore's 1839 visit to the area, was converted into a means for securing additional support for the existing communal institutions and their expanding clientele of scholars and impecunious dependents—but without significant changes in the established structure. Montefiore himself was careful in his subsequent activities to keep within the bounds that local leaders found acceptable. A similar basis of understanding was found for the advocacy of views expressing, in moderate terms, a messianist enthusiasm related to that of Bibas.

The Ashkenazi establishment, as was noted earlier, was based on the assumption that its very presence in the Holy Land was a religious service: to live in Erez Israel was a specific commandment of the Torah, which the Yishuv performed on behalf of the diaspora. The proto-Zionist rabbis, Yehuda Alkalai and Zvi Hirsch Kalischer, extended the argument and gave it enhanced eschatological significance: other commandments that could not be observed in the diaspora, such as rendering tithes from the crops of the Holy Land, could be carried out only by Jews engaged in farming and the other normal pursuits of an organic community in Palestine. Performance of these very commandments, Kalischer contended, was an essential prerequisite for the advent of the messiah.

Implicit in this approach, if it was put into effect, was the prospect that some who were totally dependent on the *halukah*, as well as new settlers who had been encouraged to immigrate, could become self-supporting. Their independence might detach them from the existing Ashkenazi power structure. But given the essentially eschatological project envisaged by Alkalai and Kalischer, and the limited practical possibilities for such development at the time, little more than symbolic expressions of messianic proto-Zionism was required or was likely to be accomplished. Hence, the matter could be regarded as a speculative issue of discussion within the community of rabbis rather than a threat of practical importance to the establishment.

Conditions that seemed favorable to bolder plans for Jewish settlement in Palestine recurred in the aftermath of the Crimean War. Once again the European concert of nations had restored the Turks to more stable power, and Western influence was in the ascendant. The reforms of the Hatt-i Humayun promised greater opportunities for European investment. The Porte, with not-always-welcome French and British aid, gradually enforced more effective central control, affording greater security to residents of Palestine, where the extortions and turbulence of local strongmen had earlier precluded ideas of Jewish settlement on the land. There now appeared new advocates who, in concert with old protagonists such as Kalischer, tried to give practical expression, in well-defined, limited ways, to the idea of Jewish resettlement in Palestine.

In 1860, the Alliance Israélite Universelle was founded and began its extensive program of education, legal and political intercession, and economic assistance for backward and oppressed Jewish communities. It was projected both as a brotherhood of Jews everywhere in aid of their co-religionists, and as a French Jewish agency working closely with the French foreign ministry. The Yishuv in Palestine, traditionally the focus of Jewish sentiment and concern, demanded their attention on both counts: it was a needy, oppressed community and existed in a country that France claimed for its sphere of influence. In the same year in Germany, the head of a boarding school in Frankfurt-on-the-Oder, Chaim Lorje, announced the organization of a Palestine Colonization Society, stirring up a lively discussion in the Jewish press. His active leadership lasted only four years, but his initiative consolidated a scattering of like-minded, religiously conservative, Central European supporters—including Kalischer and Rabbis Azriel Hildesheimer and Joseph Natonek—who continued to advocate and work for Jewish resettlement on the land in Palestine.

The Alliance Israélite Universelle, of course, approached its work in Palestine with the same methods that had been employed to seek greater Jewish integration into French society and were being applied in other regions where the Alliance worked: general education, including vocational retraining, general medical and social welfare services, and support for reforms in the Jewish economy and occupational distribution. The Central European pro-Palestine activists were drawn predominantly from among Orthodox Jews, but their Orthodoxy was of the kind that sprang up in the German culture sphere in the midcentury—committed, like French Jewry, to closer integration in the general society and economy of the host nation of the country whose citizenship they enjoyed or strove to acquire. Very soon, therefore, they beat a path to the doors of the Alliance and established a close working relationship with it for work in Palestine. The crowning achievement of this collaboration was the Alliance's founding in 1870 of an agricultural and vocational school, Mikveh Israel, on the Jaffa–Jerusalem road, an institution that was to remain significant in the history of the Yishuv.

The efforts of Kalischer, Hildesheimer, and Natonek, especially when coordinated with the French Alliance, presented the *halukah* leaders in Amsterdam and Jerusalem with the troublesome prospect of competition in soliciting funds for the Yishuv. Moreover, the new competitors—especially some of their peripheral supporters such as the historian Heinrich Graetz and certain leaders of British Jewry who examined the situation in Palestine—were occasionally free with their criticism of the *halukah* administration and of the pauperization of the Yishuv under its control. Polemics in the Jewish press and anathemas hurled by the Jerusalem hard-line traditionalists against their own critics and their works in Palestine, including the Mikveh Israel school, became the order of the day.

When Zionist immigrants arrived in the 1880s, they came into a scene already fluid and rife with polemics. Their appearance heightened old quarrels and crystallized still-incipient issues. The new institutions that accompanied their appearance provoked new disputes, which sharpened old lines of division in the Yishuv and created new ones.

o 3 o

The Yishuv, Old and New

Zionism determined the eventual shape of Israel's institutions through two separate, and sometimes opposed, channels: the diaspora movement and the immigrant settlers. The direct activity of the world movement in Palestine was controlled for a long time by a consensus based on values that arose and developed in the diaspora. Zionist immigrants originally shared similar values and often adhered to ideologies and factional organizations that were rooted in the diaspora, but they developed new ideas and grew to be an independent force as they faced the specific problems of life in Palestine. Among these were the continuous, frequently hostile pressures of the Ottoman authorities, the Christian, Muslim, and non-Muslim Arab residents, and the traditionalist institutions established by earlier generations of Jewish settlers.

The early development of the Zionist movement took place under peculiarly ambiguous conditions, both in Palestine and in the diaspora. In Rumania and Russia, acutely oppressive conditions continually gave point to the policy of emigrating in order to build a Jewish national home in Palestine. But the Zionist visionaries' capacity to carry out such a program was severely limited by local circumstances. Their recourse to the help of wealthy Jews in the free West meant relying on benefactors who did not always share the Zionists' rosy hopes and optimistic assumptions. Yet the combination of pressure and ambivalent support from outside forces was enough to keep a struggling movement alive in spite of disheartening setbacks.

Ottoman policy was generally opposed to the movement from the start. Repeated bans restricted Jewish immigration; land purchase, the establishment of new settlements, and the erection of homes and farm buildings were continually hampered by administrative obstruction. But in an empire governed by the arbitrary, capricious methods of inefficient autocracy, the restrictions were never clear and certain in practice, and attempts at evasion always had a reasonable chance of success.

There arose a standard body of irregular practices, so that properly instructed Jews knew what to do and how much it would cost to enter and settle in Palestine, and Turkish officials knew what pressures to apply and how much they could expect to gain from their dealings with Jews. The Porte was able to allow the situation to continue or to interrupt it when it chose, adjusting its policy to the anticipated rate of Jewish immigration and the risk of seriously offending interested European powers.

In adjusting to the rules of this game, Eastern European settlers relied on the support of influential Western European or Ottoman Jews. For example, the ban on land purchase for the settlement of Russian and Rumanian Jews could be circumvented by their registering deeds in the name of Ottoman Jews or Westerners, as well as by bribing officials with the customary gratuity (*bakshish*), which was useful at all stages, from land purchase and registration to the issuance of building permits and the settlement of civil suits.

Apart from administrative difficulties, the hardships of climate, infertile and unhealthy settlement sites, and rough, unfamiliar work threatened the new farmers with the loss of their investment and brought village after village to the brink of failure. In this crisis they turned to Paris and were rescued by the beneficence of one man, Baron Edmond de Rothschild.

This combination of circumstances produced an odd result, disheartening to the Zionist movement while at the same time containing enough promise to keep it alive. In spite of obstructions, waves of immigration to Palestine sporadically recurred, and for the first time, a part of the settlers established agricultural settlements. But most of them were able to maintain themselves only because Rothschild gave them regular subsidies, while funds contributed by the Hovevei Zion (Lovers of Zion Societies) helped to support others, albeit at a bare subsistence level. The institutions created by the settlers were thus strongly influenced by conditions in the diaspora. They shared a common background and common values with their Hovevei Zion supporters, and they had to conform to the demands that the Rothschild bureaucracy imposed as a condition for extending subsidies.

The whole enterprise also had to deal with the suspicions, and sometimes the hostility, of the local, overwhelmingly Arab population as well as the Turkish authorities. The early Zionists arrived in the 1880s, at a time when the pressures of accelerating change in the region were mounting. The encroachment of international, Western interests aroused resistance in both the governing circles and the native population. The incursion of Zionism was at once perceived as a form of Western invasion. The philanthropic sponsors of Jewish settlement could not deal with local authorities simply by relying on official inefficiency or corruption: they had to limit their activities, or disguise them, in order to allay Turkish and local Arab suspicions and fears. The settlers too, although sheltered by the influence and policy of their patrons, had to adjust their plans and practices to the pressures of the environment.

Such pressures came not only from gentile quarters, but also from the Old Yishuv, the traditionalist, pre-Zionist Jewish community. The secularism noted, or apprehended, among the Zionist settlers was offensive to the older settlers; the competition of Zionist demands on diaspora funds was also feared by the traditionalist leaders. Thus, the New Yishuv arose amid conflicts and confrontations as well as efforts at cooperation with the Old Yishuv, and its structure was influenced decisively at certain points by the encounter.

I

Zionism came upon the scene in Palestine in the 1880s at a time of hardening Turkish resistance to Western pressure. The French and British patrons of the weak, unstable Ottoman regime jockeyed for positions of dominant influence and strategic advantage in order to insure themselves against its ultimate collapse. Britain acquired controlling shares in the Suez Canal, built by French engineers. European investors secured payments on the swollen Ottoman and Egyptian debts by taking over major parts of Turkish and Egyptian financial administration. On the occasion of the 1878 Congress of Berlin (after the Russian advance at Istanbul and in Asia Minor had halted, following British threats to intervene), the sultan had to agree to the British occupation of Cyprus; France was compensated with a promise that England would not object when it added Tunis to its North African colonies, as it did in 1881. In the following year, England put down a nationalist, pan-Islamist rebellion in Egypt, restored the authority of the khedive, and appointed as its resident Lord Evelyn Baring Cromer, who effectively controlled the administration of that nominally Ottoman province.

Thus, the new Turkish ruler, Abdul Hamid, came to power at a time when his traditional European friends, Britain and France, began to seem no less a threat to his shrinking domain than the Russians. He accordingly adopted from the start a resourceful defensive policy of reducing his dependence on European powers by playing one off against the other. Since this was his dominant concern—and since he presented himself in Asia and Africa as a pan-Islamic leader—there was never a real chance that he would view Zionism as anything but another form of the European menace. Even earlier, in the 1870s, the rapid growth of the Yishuv relative to other communities in Palestine evidently did not go unmarked by the Porte. Jews, like the German Templars, encountered long bureaucratic delays and obstructions when they tried to acquire land. Nevertheless, the obscure methods of Ottoman policy and its limited freedom of action under external constraints left hopeful Zionists and their friends and patrons uncertain of the Porte's fixed intentions.

In the 1870s, early signs of the major migration of later decades began to be seen in the flight of oppressed Jews from Rumania. That nominally Turkish province, which arose from the union of the principalities of Moldavia and Wallachia amid the aftershocks of the Crimean War, was ruled by Christian princes even before the Congress of Berlin as a virtually independent entity. Their election was dictated by European sponsors, who were entitled to intervene under their treaty rights and were able to impose their will on the sultan. Under this regime, the Rumanian policy toward Jews, who had been coming in from Austrian lands, was one of such unrelenting hostility, including forcible expulsions, that mass evacuation to America was considered at an 1872 international Jewish conference on the problem. In 1878, the Congress of Berlin, which accorded full and formal independence to Rumania, also imposed on it the obligation to grant equal rights to all its citizens, without discrimination on grounds of religion. The Rumanians nullified this obligation by treating the Jews as resident aliens. Thus, even before the 1881–1882 pogroms in Russia made Jewish migration a cardinal concern for Western Jewish philanthropy, those who supported the Yishuv in Palestine, whether from humanitarian or pietistic-eschatological motives, began to take account of diaspora population pressures in formulating their policies and proposals.

Among the first and most explicit in doing so were Christian advocates of Jewish settlement in Palestine. Edward Cazalet, an English investor in Russian industry, and Laurence Oliphant, an influential journalist and traveler, took up this cause in the 1870s with the support of its early, high-placed evangelical enthusiasts, but they now placed their stress on secular rather than religious arguments. Cazalet argued that "Syria under our protectorate would offer still greater attractions" to Jews, who prayed for their restoration to Zion three times a day, than did America, where, according to him, 250,000 had already immigrated because of oppressive conditions in "Russia and the old Polish provinces which now belong to Austria, Germany, and Rumania." He also stressed the strategic advantage England would enjoy as the sponsor of Jewish resettlement: "No one . . . can . . . doubt that if the Jews were restored to their country under an English protectorate they would prove true to our nation and that Syria would become as firmly united to England as if it were peopled by our own countrymen."[1] Oliphant, a former foreign service officer and war correspondent in the Crimea, was even more emphatic in stressing the British national interest. After the Congress of Berlin, he obtained official assistance in a private mission to Istanbul, where he tried unsuccessfully to get a long-term agreement for Britain to administer the Syria-Palestine area and develop it by settling immigrants, mainly but not exclusively Jewish.

Jews at that time did not generally take so forthright and politically daring a position. A similar approach on the Jewish side, as was noted earlier, was put forward by Moses Montefiore in 1839 and by his nephew, Haim Guedalla, in the 1870s. But on the whole, such a sweeping strategy for the resettlement of Jews in Palestine did not seem relevant to Jewish communal leaders prior to the rise of Zionism. There was, to be sure, a movement to encourage Jewish land acquisition and settlement in Palestine in the 1860s, supported by rabbinical theorists such as Zvi Hirsch Kalischer and a diaspora organization led by Rabbi Azriel Hildesheimer, with aid from the Alliance Israélite Universelle. But the vision of this collection of enthusiasts (apart from the speculations of the philosophical essayist Moses Hess) was not based on a strategy of political action. It was inspired by religious imagination and was of limited (though, from a certain theological perspective, hypothetically critical) practical scope. Nevertheless, in their reaction to hostile pressures in Rumania in the 1870s, the advocates of Jewish settlement in Palestine were no longer simply acting out their religious enthusiasm: they were responding to the immediate crisis of a diaspora community.

When Western Jewish philanthropy in Palestine was represented mainly by individual notables, there were only sporadic and abortive efforts to acquire farmland, mostly prompted by Montefiore's early visits. With the rise of the Alliance Israélite Universelle, the propaganda among traditionalists for farm settlements in Zion became more constant and organized, with the hope of securing the Alliance's aid. Thus the Mikveh Israel farm school was founded in 1870 in response to the urging of rabbis and lay leaders in eastern Germany and Hungary, with support in France. But the policy followed at Mikveh Israel soon disappointed the enthusiasts.

The school was founded, and led personally for several years, by Charles Netter, an Alsatian merchant who was one of the original members of the Alliance Israélite Universelle. Under his guidance, roughly the same principles were adopted that were applied in France by reformers who sought the social integration of French Jews after their emancipation. Mikveh Israel aimed to prepare its students for farming or other occupations that could earn them a living, and it combined vocational with general education, stressing French and, to a degree, other useful languages. This policy aroused the usual harsh opposition from Ashkenazi traditionalists, and the school in its early years was able to draw students only from the Sephardi community, chiefly by providing stipends for needy orphans.

Criticism from another side was evoked by Netter's cautious, businesslike approach to settling Jews on farms in Palestine, which was the implicit function of a school that was conducted as a farm. Considering the failure of earlier efforts, Netter had concluded that new attempts at farm settlement should be deferred until Jews were trained in the necessary skills. But Mikveh Israel, in his time, did not succeed in training farmers, and its graduates found their livelihood in other occupations. Consequently, a man such as Yehiel Michael Pines (who came to Palestine in 1878 as the administrator of the British Jewish committee's funds for commemorating Montefiore's ninetieth birthday) attacked the school for neglecting its primary purpose. Netter's response drew a partial retraction from Pines, but subsequently, when Netter flatly opposed sending Russian pogrom victims to Palestine in 1882, he provoked an ideologically defined attack from a new quarter, the embryonic Zionist movement.

In the meantime, there were those in the Old Yishuv who attempted to create farm settlements themselves. After repeatedly failing to conclude purchases in Jericho, in the area now called Rehovot, and in the vicinity of Hebron, between 1872 and 1875, a Jerusalem group bought land northeast of Jaffa and created the settlement of Petah Tikvah in 1878. Earlier that year a group of Safed Jews of the Old Yishuv purchased land and settled on the site that later became the colony of Rosh Pina. Both the Jerusalem and Safed pioneers encountered severe difficulties, resulting in abandonment of the settlements. In both cases, the new Zionist immigration, from Rumania and Russia, infused money and labor and helped reestablish the colonies in 1882.

Thus, the essential ideas of "practical" Zionism (as well as the strategy and tactics of "political" Zionism) were anticipated by proto-Zionist enthusiasts. However, agricultural settlement in Zion was then an issue largely confined to the traditionalist community. The argument was conducted, in terms of traditional eschatology, mainly over such questions as the order of messianic events and the role of religious commandments relating to the Holy Land. Non-Orthodox Jews took little or no interest in such esoteric quarrels, and even among the Orthodox, the debate over these matters did not become an independent axis of ideological division. The traditionalist community, especially in Palestine, was driven by many conflicting attitudes and opposing interests that were built into its institutional structure: Sephardim and Ashkenazim, Hasidim and Perushim, and one *kolel* against another. The question of resettling Jews on farms in Zion was a secondary issue, cutting across these major factional cleavages: one could find supporters and opponents in almost every camp.

At most, one might say that in general the proto-Zionists, of all camps, represented voices of innovation and radicalism in the Old Yishuv, and the representatives of vested interests were generally sensitive to this menace. But the innovators did not become a cohesive, militant group possessed of esprit de corps. They usually sought prior authorization from the establishment for their projects; if they adopted a more rebellious tone and were attacked by the dominant clique with the customary polemical zeal, the conflict often reflected older, long-standing rivalries not arising primarily out of their proto-Zionist position.

Thus, sponsors of cooperative urban housing projects in Jerusalem were at first unable to persuade the *halukah* administrators to invest in this venture; but in the end the *kolel* heads boasted of the new Jerusalem residential quarters as their own achievement. Proto-Zionist promoters in Jerusalem not only obtained authorization but enlisted the leading Ashkenazi rabbi, Meir Auerbach, as a charter member of their cooperative association to form an agricultural colony. In Safed, the leading proto-Zionist figure, Eleazar Rokeah, was a young *maskil* and scion of a Jerusalem Hasidic family—on both counts antagonistic to the *halukah* administrators. His advocacy of a self-supporting Yishuv was accompanied by direct attacks on the *halukah* administration, attacks that often became bitterly personal; his opponents in turn were unrestrained in their methods of fighting him and his project. However, it is to be noted that one of the expedients they adopted themselves was to sponsor the group that initiated the settlement of Rosh Pina—a project that later enlisted the aid of Rokeah, against strenuous objections from the establishment.

Thus, the controversies over proto-Zionist farm projects divided the Old Yishuv along lines of tactical advantage rather than strategic principle. There were, nonetheless, certain contentions, traditionally formulated but objectively related to the nature of the problem, which recurred in the arguments made on either side. Some issues were highly practical.

Supporters of agricultural settlement argued that it would serve to refute charges that the Yishuv was made up of demoralized paupers. Opponents argued that Jews could not succeed as farmers under Palestinian conditions and that the promoters were leading their followers into financial and personal disaster. Other issues were more far-reaching. Supporters held that the restoration of a self-sustaining community in Palestine was a direct religious duty and believed it would rehabilitate the Jewish people, purge the corruption, and avert the dangers afflicting them in exile under modern conditions. Opponents held that only the specific commandments tied to the Holy Land—the temple service, agricultural tithes, offerings, sabbatical years, and so on—were religious duties, that it was positively risky to live in Zion, because of the inherent difficulties, and that modern Jews were religiously disqualified from performing these observances. The only safe way to live in Palestine was the traditional one of complete dedication to study and prayer, whose purifying effect was undeniable. Agricultural colonization not only multiplied the risks of transgression, voluntary or involuntary, but it diverted men and support from the purely devotional life, as already practiced in the Old Yishuv.

From the 1880s on, the movement for farm settlement in Zion was no longer confined to traditionalist circles, though they continued to play a major role. The participation of modernists, even secular nationalists, raised new issues and presented the old ones in a new light. The result was the crystallization of firm ideological positions dividing the Yishuv in new ways.

One problem implicit in this development was the question of pious Jews' associating with unbelievers or religious liberals in the same community. This was an issue on which some of the traditionalist circles most prominent in the Old Yishuv had already declared themselves decisively in Europe. The *kolelim* of Hungary and of Holland and Germany were recruited in good part from partisans of so-called Trennungsorthodoxie (Orthodox Separatists). Only recently they had fought successfully at home for the right to secede from the liberally inclined general Jewish community and set up a separate, officially recognized Orthodox community. The rise of a New Yishuv, led by avowed secular nationalists, evoked the characteristic response of separatism and avoidance, and it gave a new, more ideological edge to the old arguments against innovators. Under this pressure, traditionalist Zionist settlers had to define their positions on two fronts: in the Old Yishuv they had to defend their collaboration with unbelievers, and in the New Yishuv they had to fight for the interests of Orthodoxy.

Yehiel Michael Pines's career can serve as a paradigm of this development. He was intimately tied by birth and marriage to leading anti-Hasidic families of the Old Yishuv. As a youth in Russia, he became known as the chief representative of traditionalism among *maskilim*, and he was the trusted literary spokesman of the foremost Lithuanian rabbis. When he arrived in Palestine in 1878 as administrator of the Montefiore memorial fund, the Jerusalem leaders of the *kolelim*, who were encouraged by Montefiore's personal sympathy and support for their efforts, expected Pines to be guided by them and to channel his investments through them. But Pines's instructions from the London committee were opposed to such a connection and dictated, in general, a very skeptical attitude regarding the constructive capacities of the Old Yishuv. Thus, Pines appeared as a rival of the establishment. The ultraconservatives eventually placed him under the ban on charges of favoring secular schools ("shkoles") and other dangerous innovations.

Pines not only came into conflict with the traditionalists but became allied with the New Yishuv, a connection initiated by the first wave of immigration, which began soon after his arrival in Zion. He pledged his word to Eliezer Ben-Yehuda to speak to him only in Hebrew, thus sharing the honors for creating the movement to revive the national tongue. He not only became the sponsor, together with Rabbi Samuel Mohilever, of pious settlers in Petah Tikvah, but also purchased land in Gedera for the secularist Bilu settlers. On the other hand, he soon came into conflict with the secular nationalists too, and in a polemic over religious issues he developed the elements of a partisan religious Zionism.

The issues of avoidance or cooperation with unbelievers in the national movement and of the religious evaluation of their work in the Holy Land—whether one should condemn it as a profanation and menace or praise it as a consecration, a meritorious act of messianic import—these questions continued to be debated among traditionalists. But they matured as fully developed, mutually opposed ideological positions only after the British occupation.

II

The literature on the rise of Israel used to present Zionist immigration since the 1880s as a clean break with the past. The "New Yishuv" founded by the Zionists was described as sharply distinct from the traditionalist, dependent "Old Yishuv." Later scholarship, not without its own polemical intent, attempted to revise this account, claiming that presumably Zionist sources of Israel's institutions were anticipated by "forerunners" in earlier generations.

It is the accepted convention to divide the flow of Jewish immigrants into a series of *aliyot* (sing., *aliyah*), or waves of newcomers, each of which made a characteristic contribution to the New Yishuv's developing institutional structure. The final product, the base upon which Israel was founded, is pictured as a stratified deposit of the historic achievements of the successive *aliyot* from 1881 to 1948.

Like most historical generalizations, these too are useful mainly as points of departure. The actual course of events does not follow closely the lines they lay down, but the profile of history *is* illuminated when one plots the curve of deviations from these initial assumptions.

The First Aliyah, from 1881 to 1903, is said to have brought those pioneers who first established Jewish plantation colonies, the *moshavot* (sing., *moshavah*), the mainstay of Israel's private agricultural sector. This observation merely provides a skeletal (and incomplete) framework rather than a full description of Israel's institutional development during that period. From 1881 to 1903, Palestine Jewry is estimated to have increased from about 22,000 or 24,000 to about 47,000 or 50,000, mainly because of immigration in 1881–84 and 1890–91. Of the 20,000 to 30,000 newcomers, only 3,000 settled in the new *moshavot*, the characteristic achievement of the First Aliyah. On the other hand, Jerusalem, the stronghold of the established institutions of the Old Yishuv, increased from 14,000 to 28,000, by far the greater part of whom were undoubtedly absorbed into the traditionalist community. Thus, considered in the light of demographic statistics, Jewish immigration to Palestine from 1881 to 1914 was largely a continuation of its pre-Zionist past. The specific historic importance of Zionism in the population transfer is nevertheless said to have been that a number of Jewish plantation villages and the beginnings of a farmer-worker class were established.

This conclusion, too, has been contested. The polemical bias of the criticism is sometimes transparent, but it has underscored significant qualifications nevertheless. Characteristically Zionist innovations such as the revival of spoken Hebrew were "foreshadowed" by "precursors" in earlier generations. Opposition to the revival of spoken Hebrew became a hallmark of the Ashkenazi traditionalist establishment only after Zionism arose. In earlier decades, many had defended the holy tongue in Europe as one of the main points in their resistance to religious modernism; in Palestine, there were traditionalists who practiced Hebrew speaking as a religious exercise, and even dreamed of its revival as the national vernacular. Moreover, the rigid ideological separation of the two camps *after* Zionism arose was neither immediate nor complete; some settlers belonged to both the old and the new social structures.

A notable example is the checkered career of Eleazar Rokeah. In

1880, after a fruitless appeal to Yehiel Michael Pines in Jerusalem for support for the hard-pressed Safed farm settlers, he left for Europe on their behalf. He came to Rumania, where he conducted an energetic campaign for his clients, from synagogue platforms, in personal solicitation, and in the press. However, he combined this activity with attacks on the *halukah* administration and, after gaining initial assistance from the local representatives of the Alliance Israélite Universelle, fell into a quarrel with them; the result was that the Safed group got no funds and in the end had to abandon its project. But in the meantime Rokeah found a new constituency among oppressed and uprooted Rumanian Jews. He organized "a hundred families" in Bucharest who were interested in settling on the land in Palestine.

Under his guidance, they wrote (after Rokeah's breach with the Alliance) to the Anglo-Jewish Association, the Montefiore fund, and the London *Jewish Chronicle*, describing their situation and their hopes. The letter was published in the *Chronicle* on November 1, 1880, and evoked an unexpected, greatly heartening response: a letter from Laurence Oliphant (whose Istanbul negotiations had been made public in the *Chronicle* in January) was published in the journal on September 24. Oliphant offered both help and advice, promising to raise funds among non-Jews to supplement Jewish contributions. He called attention to the possibility of securing land grants from the Turkish government—not in the Jerusalem district, to be sure, but in adjacent areas—if the settlers would submit to Ottoman jurisdiction.

A rapid rise of enthusiasm among Rumanian Jews for settlement in Palestine aroused by this exchange was given further impetus by the pogrom wave that broke out in Russia in April 1881. The ensuing refugee crisis posed an immediate problem—and an ideological issue—for Jews everywhere and forced itself on the attention of governments. It stimulated the growth and tighter, broader organization of the Rumanian movement, which now saw itself not simply as a limited, local charitable project but as part of a major, international, Jewish effort, connected particularly with the parallel Russian movement.

A general conference of Rumanian pro-Palestine societies in January 1882 addressed itself not so much to the problem of reforming the economic base of the Palestine Yishuv as to that of Rumanian Jewry's need to emigrate. This focus sharply heightened the saliency of political implications, both in proposing to alleviate the hardships of Jews in Rumania by reducing their number and in choosing to resettle the emigrants in Palestine—options that posed a nationalist challenge to the established alternatives of liberal modernism and traditional quietism.

Nevertheless, under Rumanian conditions these implications were largely covered over by a broader consensus than was possible, for example, in Russia. The pro-Palestinian organization that arose was built by extending the ranks of earlier, traditional supporters of the Yishuv and came under the aegis of recognized lay and rabbinical leaders; even the traditionalist Hasidic cult leaders, who stood aside, did not actively oppose it. The argument that emigration in general would reduce Jewish population pressure and, consequently, antisemitism in Rumania, and the arguments for choosing Palestine rather than other destinations— that it was close and less costly to reach, that Muslims were not antisemitic, and that Jews would preserve their traditional piety there and not fall away as in America—were points that the established leadership could understand. Moreover, the leaders of the Rumanian government not only granted the movement legality but expressed willingness to support Zionist desiderata in Istanbul that went much further than those the new Zionists themselves were ready to advance. Hence, some of the Rumanian settlers who began to leave in August 1881 were sponsored by a diaspora organization and enjoyed communal support, but, as we shall see, they soon discovered in Palestine the problems inherent in working under imposed supervision.

The Russian movement faced a significantly different situation. Like the Rumanian Jews, they were under pressure from a hostile government, but it developed in a sharply different way after the pogroms. Initially, Count Nikolai Pavlovich Ignatiev, the minister of the interior, permitted a statement to be published in his name that if Jews wished to leave, the western borders of Russia were open. At that time he was also drafting regulations restricting Jewish residence in villages *within* the old-established Pale of Settlement. These were issued as "temporary rules" in May 1882 and were maintained in force with little change until tsarist Russia collapsed. Thus, there was continuous pressure to emigrate after the initial shock of the pogroms.

Unlike the Rumanian authorities, however, the Russian government offered no encouragement or support to the Zionist project. Russian officialdom was suspicious on principle not only of emigrants but of any kind of popular organization among the national minorities. Having allowed one interviewer to publish his statement inviting the Jews to leave, Ignatiev shortly afterward conveyed a contradictory message through another intermediary. At an 1882 Saint Petersburg conference of Jewish notables called to consider the pogrom crisis, the financier Samuel Polakov reported the minister as saying that any Jewish effort to conduct emigration in an organized manner would be considered "an incitement to sedition."[2] Not until 1890, after years of cautious lobbying, were the Zionists able to secure a severely restricted legalization of their work.

The new Zionists were thus unable to function under normal conditions, directly pursuing their aims in the most effective manner. But they could operate on much the same terms as a good deal else in Russian Jewish life, by evasive methods of modestly disguising and indirectly advancing their purposes. When a conference to unite the numerous European Hovevei Zion societies was held in 1884, it had to take place in the Prussian border town of Kattowitz (Katowice), even though most of the new Zionists were Russians. Within Russia, Zionist propaganda and polemics had to be conducted under police surveillance and censorship.

In Russia, as in Rumania, Jews felt the pressure of popular as well as official hostility; but in this respect, too, the Jewish response developed under significantly different conditions. The pogrom wave of 1881–82 was not only a more violent and sudden expression of Jew hatred than was the case in Rumania; it struck with particular force at that element among young Jews who had been committed, at least in principle, to the cause of revolutionary, populist action on behalf of the Russian peasants. In their disillusionment with the equivocal response of Russian radicals to the pillage and murder of Jews, some turned to a more radical, ideologically trenchant kind of Zionism than developed spontaneously and independently in Rumania. In 1882, it found its symbolic expression in Leon Pinsker's brochure, *Auto-Emancipation*, which formulated in clear terms their repudiation of emancipation by others in the lands of exile, and their espousal of the Jews' self-emancipation in a land of their own, as the solution of the "Jewish problem."

The young Zionist radicals, to be sure, were few in number and formed a minor part of even those active in the new movement. Many who were traditionally committed to the maintenance of the Old Yishuv now extended their support to the migrants who wished to flee to Erez Israel. Also a major part of the emigrants came from the same pious circles that had been the base of the Old Yishuv, and they were moved by the same sentiments. Others (as in Rumania) simply found in Palestine an accessible haven of refuge from the mounting pressures at home: among them, some were impecunious drifters and some, individually or by clubbing together, hoped to invest their savings in Palestine and seek their livelihood there.

These were motives not unknown to the Yishuv and its supporters in earlier days. The disputes they gave rise to, however sharp their occasional expression, had been contained within the familiar limits of a pragmatic consensus: quarrels grounded in different versions of common religious principles were not allowed to undermine traditions of mutual aid that enabled one part of the community to expect and another to extend material support in times of hardship. But the implicit assumptions of the new, secular Zionists, given explicit form in the ideological writings of Moshe Leib Lilienblum, Leon Pinsker, and others, posed a new challenge for both the traditionalist and modernist establishments— a challenge that was accommodated within a pragmatic consensus only after protracted encounters.

The ideological challenge of Zionism was less clear and immediate for traditionalists than for the modernist liberal establishment. The ideas that the new radical Zionists themselves considered most revolutionary— that antisemitism was a permanent, structural feature of life in the diaspora, and only the restoration of the Jews to national autonomy in their own land could eradicate it—sounded to traditionalists like echoes of the ancient Jewish mythos of exile and redemption. What made them wary was the intrusion of secularists, even by way of partial rapprochement with tradition, into an area held especially sacred: the Jewish settlement in the Holy Land. Some of those long associated with support of the Yishuv, through both the *halukah* and the other Orthodox-organized organizations, fell away from the new movement because of the active involvement of unbelievers and transgressors. Others, who continued in the new framework, had to keep close watch against the threat of importing infidelity into Zion, the sanctuary of religious commitment.

For the reform-minded Western philanthropists who concerned themselves with the Yishuv and the Jewish refugee problem, ideological Zionism was an immediately perceived, acute problem. The main issues of the debate in the Jewish community after the pogroms were practical, to be sure, rather than ideological: they were centered primarily on the relative advantages and drawbacks of supporting the immigration of Jewish refugees to Palestine versus the Americas. The "practical" arguments in favor of Palestine (for example, that Jewish loyalty to tradition would be better preserved in the Holy Land than in America) obviously rested on deeper assumptions (that emancipation in the exile threatened the survival of Judaism through assimilation) widely held among the traditionalists in opposition to the ruling consensus among Western Jewish philanthropists. But since the only program of action that these assumptions entailed among traditionalists was a defensive retreat to seclusion, and reliance on the divinely appointed messianic redemption, this position presented no real challenge to modernism. Ideologically explicit secular Zionism, however, in spite of its own modernism, was seen as a direct attack on the established program of integration into the nation-state, which renounced Jewish nationality and retained only the (rather loose) tie of religion. Thus the debate over the practical issues had a sharper polemical edge when conducted between Zionists and the establishment modernists.

But practical considerations quickly forced the secular Zionists to moderate their positions, at least as to immediately relevant action. The Rumanian pro-Palestine movement found within a few years that the obligations it incurred to support settlers were far beyond its means. Only the intervention of Baron Rothschild saved the settlements that Rumanians had begun to build in the valley east of Safed and the upland plain south of Haifa. Relieved of this responsibility, the Rumanian organization relapsed into virtual dissolution. When the 1884 Kattowitz conference created a new, international center for the Hovevei Zion, the Rumanian movement was incapable of participating. The prime movers in that conference were the Russian Hovevei Zion. Their main concern was to build a more effective organization for carrying out the responsibilities they had assumed, to support those remaining new settlements in Palestine that Rothschild had not, at that time, undertaken to maintain. They too were fully aware of their dependence on support from Western Jews. This consideration led their chosen leader, Leon Pinsker, to suppress the ideological contentions of his earlier position, stated in the brochure *Auto-Emancipation*, and set forth a program confined to practical, humanitarian aid for resettlement in Palestine, on lines calculated to propitiate the leaders of emancipated Western Jewish communities.

But while their working program was adapted to non-Zionist specifications, the Russian Hovevei Zion and the *maskilim* and intellectuals associated with their movement carried on a lively ideological debate in the Hebrew and Russian press. Divisions within the movement were sharply defined and developed in more complex articulation. The practical work in Palestine sufficed to keep the organization alive, in spite of the handicaps under which it labored in the diaspora and in Palestine. But the compromises it was compelled to accept were a source of constant frustration to those young *maskilim* and radical intellectuals who shared in a cultural revival inspired by the mythos of autoemancipation.

° 4 °

Settlers and Patrons

In three years, 1882–84, eight permanent Jewish settlements were founded in Palestine, including the rebuilt villages of Rosh Pina and Petah Tikvah. Then the movement came to a temporary halt under the pressure of Turkish opposition to the influx of Jews.

It was not immediately clear how decisive was the policy adopted by the Turkish government; nor was it evident from the start that Jewish immigrants would face a focused hostility from the Arabs. Anti-Western hostility in the nineteenth century had led primarily to attacks against Christians; Jews suffered in such upheavals mostly as an effect of violence directed against others. As for the government, some officials showed an appreciation of the argument that Jews, as well as Muslim immigrants, could prove to be a safe and useful resource for economic development that would expand the imperial tax base.

Thus, Laurence Oliphant was encouraged in his 1879 project by Midhat Pasha, then governor of Syria, and by the incumbent grand vizier in Istanbul. Under their guidance, he argued that his plan for settling Jews in Gilead, east of the Jordan River, would provide employment for Muslim immigrants and would help the Porte free itself from foreign influence, as the Jews would become loyal Ottoman citizens and not claim exemption from Turkish jurisdiction under one or another treaty of capitulations. He attributed the rejection of his scheme to, among other fortuitous circumstances, the sultan's dismissal of his liberal ministers and the turn to centralized, autocratic rule.

Abdul Hamid's hard line was certainly evident in the persistent opposition the Porte thereafter adopted against Jewish settlement in Palestine. Yet the sultan occasionally showed himself well disposed to Jews, both as a people oppressed by those who also menaced Turkey and as potentially loyal and useful subjects—but only if they settled elsewhere than in Palestine. What tipped the scales after the Congress of Berlin was the clear evidence from the press and from reports of Turkish agents abroad that the impending surge of Jewish immigrants was probably driven by nationalist aspirations that could further disrupt the integrity of the empire.

Thus, the Cazalet proposals presented to the Porte in the fall of 1881 evoked a statement, published in November, excluding Jewish "immigrants" from Palestine; "scattered groups" would be allowed to settle elsewhere in the empire if they accepted Ottoman jurisdiction in all matters and were prepared to apply for citizenship. Notwithstanding the publication of this decision, groups of Russian, Rumanian, and Bulgarian Jews began to arrive in the spring of 1882; a specific order was then sent to the governor of Jerusalem not to permit them to land in Jaffa or Haifa or to settle in the four holy cities. But since capitulations treaties—including that with Russia—guaranteed the rights of foreigners to travel, trade, and acquisition of land in Ottoman areas, the rule was revised to permit Jews to enter Palestine for purposes of pilgrimage and business only, on 30-day visas, subject to a deposit returnable upon departure. Later, in 1884, pilgrims alone were to be admitted, on the grounds that Palestine was not a place suitable for business.

This restrictive order was at first applied to all Jews. But the Haham Bashi was soon able to secure the exemption of Ottoman Jews; in practice, the policy was directed mainly against selected countries from which most new settlers came, particularly Russia. Bureaucratic delays and obstructions also hampered the registration of land purchases and construction of buildings. These obstacles were far from being insuperable, especially when foreign consulates and embassies granted protection to those who evaded or resisted the Ottoman decrees and administrative decisions. However, they were sufficiently effective to discourage immigrants, and together with other problems—the settlers' unpreparedness, and opposition from those whose toleration or support was required—brought immigration to a halt after a few years until it was renewed in the 1890s.

I

The immigrants were a mixed company, reflecting the diverse composition of the diaspora movement from which many were drawn. What they had in common, in distinction from their predecessors in the Old Yishuv, was a new perception of the meaning of *aliyah* to Erez Israel—one in which escape from acute oppression in Russia and Rumania and vague, as yet undefined hopes to rebuild their lives free of the chronic anomalies of diaspora conditions played a prominent part.

Within this broad area of consensus, a wide variety of ideological leanings characterized the immigrants. These differences, relatively muted among the early Rumanian settlers, began to arise more ominously among those from Russia. Some were simply impecunious refugees who fled from hardships in their old homes; they exerted no ideological pressure on communal institutions beyond posing the problem of providing for their support and integration. Others were relatively well-to-do settlers who, either individually or by clubbing together, wished to invest their savings in Palestine and build homes and seek their livelihood there. Many of these were religiously traditional, particularly close to the modernizing elements in the Old Yishuv. Others were of a more secular bent. The student-organized Bilu group (very few of whom actually came to Palestine) formed a third element of young radicals who played a significant part in the ideological battles of the First Aliyah.

The pogrom refugees who gathered in the Austrian town of Brody in the summer of 1881 compelled the Jewish public to face the problem of directing, as well as assisting, the flow of migrants. In the following year, continuing pogroms, arson, and anti-Jewish government policies increased the refugee stream. Some, responding to lively agitation in the Jewish press by pro-Palestine advocates, now turned to Odessa, or further on to Istanbul and Jaffa. There the penniless among them produced a relief problem similar to that of the refugee throng in Brody, which some pro-Palestinians hoped would in fact force Western Jewish philanthropists to aid resettlement in Erez Israel. Those settlers who expected to invest in land or trade and commerce usually made an effort to explore the possibilities before moving from Europe. Others joined the thousands of uprooted Jews wandering aimlessly around the streets of Jaffa.

When a similar mixed multitude had accompanied the sectaries who formed the Old Yishuv in earlier years, the communal leaders could only urge that immigrants lacking a specific religious commitment should be discouraged. The early Zionists were no less embarrassed by the uncommitted mass who flocked to Palestine with no clear prospects or objectives, but they could not simply take the position adopted by the traditionalist leadership. They were carrying on a heated debate in the press with opponents who advocated America rather than Erez Israel as the preferred haven. Thus, the spectacle of a dependent refugee population in Jaffa undercut the philo-Zionists' argument. They had to prove that Jews could be successfully established on the land or in urban trades and industry in Erez Israel: success or failure in doing this was a critical test of an ideological position, and not only a humanitarian issue for them.

One energetic activist, Zalman David Levontin, publicized, in the Hebrew press and in extensive correspondence from June to December 1881, proposals to settle a hundred young families and to found a model colony in Palestine. He arrived in Jaffa on March 8, 1882, armed with commissions to buy land in Erez Israel for two Russian philo-Zionist societies. After little more than a week of travel and consultation, especially with Yehiel Michael Pines in Jerusalem, he addressed himself to the immediate problem of the prospective investors and hapless refugees in Jaffa. On March 18, Levontin, Pines, and a few associates formed a committee to organize an association that would purchase land, build houses, and manage their farms and finances for its members until they could take over independently. But the committee not only failed to unite its intended constituency, it swiftly developed an internal split—a characteristic disagreement between leaders of a small, inchoate project with no clear prospects for success. The majority rejected Pines's plan to direct activities from Jerusalem, where he resided. They contended that traditionalists in the holy city, already at odds with Pines, would hamper their work and that Jaffa, where the immigrants were concentrated, should be chosen instead. Thereafter, Pines turned against Levontin and his projects and Levontin became equally hostile to Pines and those connected with him.

Hoping to place a number of indigent families on the land that his group would acquire, Levontin felt entitled to solicit aid from diaspora sympathizers, on both humanitarian and philo-Zionist grounds. After a series of false starts, which compelled him to return funds to investors and cut back the scope of his plan, a reduced group of associates established the first philo-Zionist agricultural settlement, Rishon Lezion, late in July 1882. In token recognition of the broader aims of the plan, Levontin's uncle, the major investor, sold part of his land at reduced prices to six refugee families, and the other ten settlers agreed to initially bear in common the expenses and labor of farming. Levontin set out for Russia to seek aid, and Joseph Feinberg, another settler who had come as the agent of a diaspora society, left in August on a similar quest. In Paris, in October 1882, Feinberg was able to obtain a substantial grant and the promise of further aid from Baron Edmond de Rothschild.

With the founding of Rishon Lezion, two new elements in the Yishuv's institutional history made their appearance: the new settlers were led by nationalist *maskilim*, and their project was based in Jaffa rather than Jerusalem or Safed. They thus detached themselves from the influence of the traditional establishment. Petah Tikvah and Rosh Pina, resettled by an infusion of new immigrants in the same year, remained umbilically tied to the Old Yishuv in spite of the difficulties of their relationship.

From its beginning in 1878, Petah Tikvah struggled with severe problems. There were quarrels among the founding group and other Jerusalemites who settled on an additional, malaria-infested tract; and when land for housing was later purchased, at over an hour's remove from the malarial stream, there were official delays and obstructions in granting building permits. By the summer of 1881—and with the approach of the sabbatical year, when Jewish land should not be worked—the project was on the verge of dissolution. Nevertheless, the founding settlers persisted and tried to replenish their funds by selling parcels of their land to new recruits. They turned to Pines for help and published an appeal to sympathizers in the diaspora to become investors or to join as settlers. Pines tried to interest Levontin and his associates in buying into Petah Tikvah, by then an abandoned village. Failing in this, he helped the Jerusalemites send an emissary to Russia, where he succeeded in selling parcels of land and gaining new settlers from Bialystok and other north Russian towns.

The resettlement of Petah Tikvah was, thus, in large part the work of an original group in the Old Yishuv who turned to the diaspora immigrants to sustain their settlement. The founders not only kept their project alive, but retained dominant control after it was resuscitated by the newcomers. A somewhat different development in Rosh Pina also produced a village of a strongly conservative cast.

The Safed group who bought land in an Arab village in 1878 staked their own meager savings on the chance that others would come to their aid and fund the expenses required to achieve their goal. When their first sponsors, the local *halukah* leaders, failed them, they turned to Eleazar Rokeah, but he too failed them. Little more than a year after they settled, they had to abandon their land. In 1882, shortly before the establishment of Rishon Lezion, an agent sent by the pro-Palestine committee of the Rumanian town of Moinesti bought out the property and cabled the glad news to his principals. Within a few weeks, in mid-August, a group of young settlers, some 30 families equipped with tools, building materials, and a rifle for each man, left for Palestine. They formed part of a larger contingent, 228 immigrants in all, who had responded to the agitation of the Rumanian central pro-Palestine committee as well as of the local Moinesti society. On shipboard, differences over religious commitment led to a split in the group enrolled for the Moinesti project, and only the conservative traditionalists debarked at Beirut and established Rosh Pina on December 12, 1882.

The others joined the group sponsored by the Rumanian central committee and landed at Haifa. The committee bought the land of Samaria south of the city that was first settled on December 6, 1882, and it became, after many tribulations, the village of Zikhron Yaakov, a Rumanian counterpart of the Russian Rishon Lezion.

A third type, more sharply distinguished from both the others than were the secular nationalists from the religious conservatives, was represented by the Bilu society, which arose in an immediate response to the pogroms in southern Russia. It was formed by a band of young people, many of them students in Kharkov, on January 30, 1882, the day of the communal fast following the outbreaks. The society at first dedicated itself to propaganda in favor of emigration to Erez Israel. The organization expanded to other towns, eventually seeking allies in Rumania and as far away as the United States. After a time, some of the members undertook not simply to preach but to organize the emigration movement, and to symbolize this aim, they adopted the acronym Bilu (*Bet Yaakov lekhu venelkha*: House of Jacob come, let us go [Isaiah 2: 5]) as their name. They intended to rally young people to follow the example of the Russian *Narodniki*, populist agitators who "went to the people" to rouse them in revolt against tsarist oppression while sharing their lives. Bilu members were to join the Palestine-bound immigrants in the same spirit of self-sacrifice as exemplars and leaders of the masses. While their populist, physiocratic themes—returning to the soil and retraining displaced Jews for "productive" occupations—were common among all sectors of the migration to Palestine and its diaspora supporters, the personal commitment that the *Biluim* (pl. of *Bilu*) brought to their project gave their movement a challenging militancy and ideological edge.

As it turned out, there was more symbol than substance in the perceived challenge of Bilu. The organization, unable to consolidate a coherent central authority and an agreed-upon policy, flared off its energies in several directions. While some continued to seek funds and gain recruits in Russia, a three-man delegation left in May 1882 for Istanbul, where Oliphant was negotiating with the Porte. Shortly before they arrived, Oliphant had already warned publicly that the mounting tensions in Egypt had created an unfavorable political climate for his activities. In meetings with the Bilu delegates, he left no hope that he could obtain land for them in Palestine but led them to believe that they might be able to settle on state land in northwestern Syria on terms acceptable to Istanbul and the local pasha. Both the Bilu leaders in Russia and the delegation in Istanbul were at first ready to accept this compromise, seeing it (as some Zionists later viewed similar proposals) as a way station to Zion.

Meanwhile, the delegation, together with others gathered in Istanbul for whom they assumed responsibility, grew desperately short of funds. Under pressure of their deteriorating situation, they came to feel that waiting for the Syrian option to materialize would destroy the movement's morale. On June 28, they decided, with the unanimous approval of a meeting of all Bilu members in Istanbul, to send a group to Palestine immediately in spite of the Turkish ban; there they would attach themselves to others who possessed the means to purchase private land and would somehow settle as pioneers, hoping to lay a foundation for a substantial Bilu settlement in the future. This rash decision, coming on the heels of long-mounting frictions between the Istanbul and Odessa leaders, led to a split that signaled the rapid decline of the movement in Russia, a decline that was already well advanced by a history of continual setbacks. Those still active in Istanbul and those who began to arrive in Jaffa soon developed their own differences: the former continued to cherish hopes for mass organization in the diaspora while the latter—especially one of the founders of Bilu, Israel Belkind—were intent on consolidating the foothold they wished to secure in Erez Israel.

The fourteen Bilu members who left Istanbul on June 29 (some of them students, others young people recruited by them; two additional settlers had preceded them on their own initiative) expected at first to join the projected settlement of Levontin's Jaffa committee; those remaining in Istanbul would continue to seek a land grant from the Turkish authorities. Levontin, who had still not completed the formal acquisition of land for Rishon Lezion, met them at the dock and arranged for their admission to the country but could do no more for them; he hoped, in fact, that they had brought funds to contribute to his project. They found work for most of the men in the Mikveh Israel farm school, while the leading members busied themselves with movement negotiations and the young women in the group kept house in the two-room apartment they rented near Jaffa.

The Biluim continued in their unaccustomed, backbreaking toil as unskilled labor in Mikveh Israel through the hot summer and parched fall months of 1882, under the unsympathetic eyes of a cost-conscious administration and Arab workers. The strain of poverty and fading hopes caused some to leave the country, while others continued to arrive. Growing embitterment among some of the working members against the appointed leader-representatives whose unproductive negotiations their work supported began a series of continuing splits in the remaining group.

Support for mass emigration of Jews from their homes was a decision forced on the philanthropic leaders of Western Jewries, not one they willingly adopted. Their ideological difficulties were compounded, because of the nationalistic implications of the proposal, when Palestine rather than America was advocated as the place for resettlement. But the hardships of the displaced masses in Istanbul and Jaffa were compelling reasons to extend charitable assistance in the tradition of Jewish mutual aid.

Moreover, qualms about nationalism were not so potent, in some cases, that they could suppress sentiments of attachment to Erez Israel. This was certainly true of Charles Netter and, as became clear in time, of Baron Edmond de Rothschild. And in Palestine itself there were Yehiel Michael Pines and Laurence Oliphant (who came to live near Haifa), both ready to help the new settlers and possessed of ties to potential supporters in Europe, though their actual resources were limited.

Netter, whose warning against sending settlers to Palestine was widely published in March 1882, nevertheless was responsible earlier, in December, for sending a group of refugee children from Brody, Austria, to be trained in Mikveh Israel. With them, he sent two young Russian teachers, Isaac Oshri and Joshua Ossovietzki, who later played a significant role in the Rothschild settlements. In Brody, too, Netter met Rabbi Samuel Mohilever, an active organizer of pogrom- and refugee-relief, and helped pave the way for the rabbi to present his plea to Rothschild for aid in settling his protégés in Palestine. That summer Netter discussed Palestine resettlement with Rothschild in Paris. He opposed a large, unselected influx, which, in his view, would only produce a pauperized mass dangerously susceptible to missionary blandishments (a prospect that both Netter and Rothschild suspected was the very design of some Christian philo-Zionists); but he favored trial projects, both for training qualified young people to be farmers and for applying improved agricultural techniques that might enable Jews to support a modest European standard of living in Palestine. In the fall, Netter went to Palestine to pursue these plans, but within a few weeks he fell ill and died. In the meantime, however, he had met the Biluim and the Rishon Lezion settlers and sent back favorable reports. Joseph Feinberg's meeting with Rothschild, like Mohilever's, owed something to Netter's encouragement. Those meetings initiated Rothschild's long career as patron of the Jewish settlements in Palestine, in the spirit of a tribute to Charles Netter.

Rothschild's first commitments were cautious and limited. He promised training in Mikveh Israel for a few young immigrants chosen by Mohilever, with the prospect of financing their settlement later if they proved satisfactory. He contributed funds anonymously for housing and well-digging in Rishon Lezion, supplementing the investments already made by the founding group and subsidizing support for the needy settlers who were added to their number. But the conditions Baron Edmond attached to his gifts implied a disposition to assert greater responsibility—as it turned out, more than some who solicited his aid would welcome.

The ten family heads to be chosen by Mohilever (eleven were in fact sent, together with a group leader representing the rabbi) were from the start expected to depend entirely on Rothschild. For nearly a year they were put up as farm workers in Mikveh Israel (they had been farmers from childhood in Russia) before land could be bought for their settlement; then another year passed in legal formalities before their families could be moved onto the village site of Ekron. During the stay at Mikveh Israel they were the baron's stipendiaries, and they continued in that state while their homes were set up and their farms were equipped and cultivated in anticipation of the first harvest. The baron owned the land, and supervisors he appointed provided the livestock, tools, seed, and personal needs of the initial group, plus many others sponsored by Mohilever. It was on this model that Rothschild prepared to conduct the other settlements he began to assist, or himself create, with prudent care.

Such tight control seemed vital in view of the gross miscalculations (together with the huge, unforeseen expense of dealing with Ottoman obstructionism and other misfortunes) that forced settlers to apply for the baron's help. The discipline he imposed was meant to ensure that his generosity would speed rather than retard the settlers' transition to self-supporting independence. But closer study of the materials he had to work with gave a turn to his plans that greatly extended the anticipated period of dependency, inflated the investment costs, and entailed more rigid bureaucratic control of the baron's settlements.

Much of the heavy investment cost of the Rothschild enterprise was unavoidable, given the local conditions. Land available for the first Jewish rural settlements was located in marginal areas, where Arab cultivators could not raise enough to sustain themselves and also pay their taxes, rent, or the landlord's share in the crop. Rishon Lezion was built on light, sandy, unwatered soil from which native farming methods could not extract an adequate grain harvest. In Petah Tikvah and elsewhere there were swamps to be drained, and in all cases there were heavy, unpredictable outlays involved in dealing with administrative delays and other causes of litigation. These were burdens that exhausted the capacities of the original settlers. But Rothschild bore them without question, once he had committed himself to a particular undertaking. His caution was confined to making sure that the commitments were those he himself chose, in line with a broad strategy, and that his funds were dispensed under his appointed administrators' strict control and not in response to what he might consider unfounded demands of the ultimate beneficiaries.

A major factor that further prolonged the period of settler dependency was the baron's developing strategy for Jewish rural colonization. His determination to introduce European methods and standards of cultivation was strongly biased toward the model of southern France, where his family owned world-renowned vineyards. He judged that highly skilled horticulture yielding premium crops, together with agriculture-based light industries producing wine, preserves, and perfumery essences, was better suited for future Jewish cultivators than the rough, heavy labor of peasant farming. He spared no expense in perfecting his favored branches of farming, using entire villages for experimentation and pilot projects. But since his plan for a viable farmstead relied in good part on plantations that could not produce cash returns in the first season of cultivation, as cereal crops could, the settlers were consigned to a long period of enforced dependency while their future vineyards and orchards matured. During that time they were subjected to the dictates of the baron's administrative staff.

In one settlement after another, the system of administrative supervision and control led to fierce disputes between the directors and the settlers. The hard-pressed settlers of Samarin rebelled against the administrators appointed by the Rumanian central committee even before Rothschild took them over. The baron's demand that they turn over their land and property and subscribe to a compact of near-servitude under the supervisor he would impose on them was rejected by some at first, but in the end, all submitted in order to receive his support in their desperate need. This village, renamed Zikhron Yaakov (i.e., James's Memorial) in honor of the baron's father, was a Rothschild favorite thereafter, but frictions between the director and settlers persisted, ending in an open clash in 1888 which was put down by the expulsion of some rebellious settlers and the formal submission of others.

The same scenario, more or less, was played out at the other settlements that Rothschild initially chose to take under his wing. The settlers in Rosh Pina readily accepted the transfer of their land and property to Rothschild's proxy (since the baron wished to disguise his connection) in return for the settlement of their debts and support for the foreseeable future, but they soon quarreled with Isaac Oshri, the young Russian administrator set over them. He was transferred elsewhere only after the offending settlers apologized formally for their insulting insubordination, and the system was maintained with a new administrator.

A more complicated situation existed in Rishon Lezion. The baron's initial commitment to the village was more limited than to Rosh Pina. The land, registered in the name of a Sephardi sponsor, was transferred to Rothschild's proxy, but the assets of the founding group were not effectively taken over. Baron Rothschild supplemented the founders' investments by paying for public utilities and services out of a general subsidy and supplying an expert farm manager. Thus, the lines of authority were not as clearly drawn as elsewhere, since the settlers retained, together with their property, a certain authority in their village. The stage was set for the creation of factions around rival leaders in the event of differences that might arise.

The pressure to call on Rothschild's aid at Rishon Lezion arose from costly failures to find water after digging to considerable depths and from the heavy expense of maintaining a group in which a relatively large number were unable to pay their own way. The subventions were understood to apply to both problems. Early frictions arose when Rothschild proposed to transfer the Biluim from Mikveh Israel to Rishon Lezion. The six needy families, who feared that bringing in penniless newcomers would deplete the funds contributed for their support, resisted the acceptance of the Biluim. Others complained of the damaging effect that the presence of godless young people would have on the settlement. In November 1882, the Biluim moved to Rishon Lezion on the following stringent terms: they could have no share for two years in the internal governance of the settlement; they could not form a separate entity in the village but would have to abide by existing and future regulations adopted by the other settlers; and they would observe a traditional, Jewish-religious lifestyle on pain of expulsion for breaches of ritual commandments or conventional decorum. Moreover, although the elder Levontin had promised them the use of his land, he was not to register the deed in their name for two years. In addition to working the land allotted to them as tenant farmers, the Biluim supported themselves as laborers on Rothschild-financed public works. In spite of these restrictions, the young enthusiasts, given to disputes among themselves and not easily disciplined by others, added an additional element of dissension in the village.

At the point when financial embarrassment forced the leaders of Rishon Lezion to appeal for Rothschild's aid, their authority was already undermined by an opposing faction of more conservative settlers. The village council was disbanded, and Rothschild's local representatives asserted a growing control. This situation bred resentment, particularly against Justin Dugourd, the farm director whose work brought him to the village frequently. As the fall rains drew near and the purchase of plows, wagons, and horses for the planting continued to be delayed by the administration, the settlers chose a new committee of five of their number—now including one from the six needy families and the Bilu spokesman, Israel Belkind—to press their claims. Quarrels ensued, causing the offended Dugourd to leave the colony and the Rishon Lezion committee to send cables and letters of grievance (drafted in French by Belkind) to Paris. In response, there were sent, first, instructions to Samuel Hirsch (the director of Mikveh Israel and a reluctant supervisor of Rothschild aid to Rishon Lezion, which he found burdensome and probably doomed to failure) to take stern measures; then an irate, insulting letter to the settlers from the baron, replete with epithets; and finally the specific demand that they ban Belkind from the village. For months, the regular Rothschild stipends were withheld until finally Belkind had to agree to leave.

Subsequently, Rishon Lezion was provided with a communal administrator, Joshua Ossovietzski, chosen from the teaching staff of Mikveh Israel, who eventually became the target of a second, more serious "revolution," which shook Rishon Lezion in 1887. He was welcomed at first as one who could understand the settlers, sharing with them a common background.

Leading settlers formed the Rodef Shalom ("peace seeker") society, a kind of broad encounter group, open to all Rishon Lezion settlers and others as well, that attempted to overcome internal frictions by public discussion and social pressure. At first Ossovietzki joined in. But the group sessions increasingly aired complaints against his administration; moreover, its leaders encouraged an organization of landless workers employed in the expanding village economy. Ossovietzki then parted company with the "peace seekers" and founded a rival society.

The tension between the factions broke into open war over a temporary worker, Yehiel Michael Halperin, whose militant enthusiasm had won him considerable notoriety earlier in Russia. The scion of a wealthy family of distinguished rabbinical antecedents, he distributed much of his inheritance in various quixotic, quasi-revolutionary projects. In Palestine he attached himself to the Rishon Lezion dissidents, particularly to the embryonic workers' organization, and became their most flamboyant spokesman. When Ossovietzki then ordered him evicted, and his belongings were removed from his rented room, Halpern and a crowd of his supporters broke into Ossovietzki's house to confront him. The panicky administrator fled, after firing some random shots to hold off possible attack and to summon Turkish militia. The scandal provoked by this incident, which aroused not only the Yishuv but the philo-Zionist press worldwide, ended in the standard way: those who were held responsible for the rebellion were expelled—including Joseph Feinberg, who was forced to sell his property to the baron—and Ossovietzki was transferred to another Rothschild settlement. The settlers remaining in Rishon Lezion committed themselves to new stringent restrictions on their rights to form associations, hire workers, and shelter unauthorized guests like Halperin.

II

While Rothschild's patronage effectively closed down the Rumanian philo-Zionist movement for a number of years, the Russian societies continued to be active. Petah Tikvah was not given Rothschild support until 1887, and even then the baron purchased only part of the settlement. The colony continued to engage the efforts and attention of the Russian societies and was a particular concern of Mohilever and the traditionalist wing of the movement. Another major concern, to which the secular philo-Zionists were especially sensitive, was to provide for the village of Gedera, where Pines helped a Bilu group settle after the Rothschild administration washed its hands of them.

Some of the very first Biluim to arrive in Palestine settled in Jerusalem and were joined there by others in 1883. They undertook to learn industrial crafts in a project sponsored by Pines and Eliezer Ben-Yehuda, and they formed a close group associated with their mentors. Another division in Bilu ranks occurred when later immigrants who had first joined the group in Rishon Lezion withdrew from there, for ideological as well as personal reasons, and found work in Mikveh Israel. Meanwhile, the continuing dispute between the Bilu contingents in Palestine and the movement delegation in Istanbul ended with the abandonment of the negotiations in the capital and the departure of the delegates for Erez Israel. They joined the workers in Mikveh Israel and together with them continued to press for the movement's larger objective: a model Bilu settlement as a training farm for pioneer settlers and as the center of a worldwide movement. They viewed the tendency of Belkind's group to settle down in Rishon Lezion as a lapse into narrow egoism. During the spring and summer of 1883 (in collaboration with Pines, whom they now viewed as their presiding sponsor), they planned to restructure their organization, leaving the Rishon Lezion contingent in order to settle down as individual immigrants, finally detaching themselves from the larger purpose of the movement.

All this ideological ferment detracted from the initial sympathy of Western philanthropists for the young idealists; the administration in Mikveh Israel saw it as distracting the workers from their routine duties. After various proposals by Hirsch for a permanent solution for the Biluim were rejected, he advised them to present a proposal of their own to Rothschild. They framed it in the form of a "constitution," providing for an independent, model Bilu colony as the movement's center, and laying out a structure of discipline and personal dedication and an avantgardist strategy for leading the whole Zionist undertaking.

This proposal was presented to Rothschild in the fall of 1883, just when the first "revolt" in Rishon Lezion aroused his ire. From Mikveh Israel he received reports of the unruly behavior of the Biluim and their contentious relations with their instructors and the Arab workers, and complaints about their general slackness and inefficiency at work. The baron refused to treat them as an autonomous entity or finance a new settlement for them. His administration would deal with them only as individuals. Moreover, the baron indicated that he would now consolidate the villages already taken over and consider no new projects until he saw how the first ones turned out.

The Biluim remained in Mikveh Israel in continually worsening relations with their milieu. In the spring of 1884, a number of them, including the leaders who had come from Istanbul less than a year earlier, were granted funds to leave the country. After Passover, Hirsch dismissed all but one of the remaining workers, and the problem of their immediate future became acute. A partial solution was found through the efforts of Pines and some of the Russian philo-Zionist societies. Pines, who had been negotiating land purchases and selling parcels to diaspora clients and supporters, acquired a sizable block in the Arab village of Katra. He persuaded some of the purchasers to allot their land for the Biluim among other prospective settlers. Meanwhile, the Warsaw philo-Zionist society raised a thousand rubles for the Bilu settlers, who founded Gedera at the end of the year.

In the absence of Rothschild's support, this settlement relied on the uncertain resources of the Hovevei Zion. In addition, the philo-Zionist societies were committed to support Petah Tikvah and Yesud Hamaala, an independent settlement founded in 1883, as well as individual landowners in Rishon Lezion who had expected to be self-financed and at first dispensed with Rothschild aid.

From the beginning there were attempts to unite the local Hovevei Zion societies in a comprehensive organization. Doing so became urgent when settlements they initiated or supported required continuous, increasingly onerous financing. In November 1884, a conference held in the Silesian border town of Kattowitz created a body that persisted in a precarious but unbroken effort to promote the Jewish resettlement of Palestine as a common project of the movement at large.

The initiative was taken a year earlier by the Kattowitz philo-Zionist organization, Bnai Brith, at a preliminary conference intended to unite the German, Austrian, Russian, and Rumanian societies. This effort remained without effect, but it stimulated more active discussion and correspondence in which the Hovevei Zion of Warsaw, Bialystok, Moscow, and Odessa assumed the leading roles. What emerged from the 1884 conference was a framework for coordinating primarily the Russian societies.

Leon Pinsker, who was induced to accept a role of active leadership, opened the conference with an address that sought to gain the support of Western Jews by allaying their apprehension of overassertive nationalism. He stressed that the movement was not political in purpose but rather aimed to relieve Jewish distress—and also to dissolve a purported source of gentile hostility—by resettling Jews as farmers in Palestine. Prior to the conference, the Warsaw society had energized the floundering Hovevei Zion by a new fund-raising campaign: poster photographs of the aged philanthropist Moses Montefiore, honoring his hundredth birthday, were widely distributed. In the same spirit, the conference decided to adopt the name of "Moses Montefiore Holy Land Foundation" in the obvious hope that the London trustees of the similar fund created ten years earlier, in 1874, would cooperate with the new, consolidated philo-Zionist organization. It was also decided to create a provisional executive committee as a short-term stopgap until a permanent center could be established in a Western metropolis such as Berlin. But these hopes were not to be realized. The Londoners decided to honor Montefiore with charitable work in England and terminated their contributions previously funneled to Palestine through Pines. The philo-Zionists could not build a movement center in Berlin; the Russian-based provisional executive elected in Kattowitz became the permanent leadership.

Twenty-five participants at Kattowitz chose a "central committee" of eighteen (including some not present and some who declined the appointment) to lead the movement for one year and take decisions on proposals not brought to a conclusion by the conference. The central committee, broadly representing the local societies, delegated authority to two subcommittees. One in Odessa, headed by Pinsker with Lilienblum as his part-time paid secretary, was to determine policy and exercise general supervision. The second, subordinate body in Warsaw (where the Montefiore fund-raising project had been initiated by an activist who now became a salaried officer) was to administer the movement finances and conduct its correspondence with the constituent societies.

The program of action adopted at Kattowitz and assigned to the new executive reflected a certain duality of purpose, even among the secular nationalists. Pinsker's attempt to conciliate Western Jews in his opening address was dictated by perceived necessity, not intrinsic preference. The draft of his remarks met with considerable criticism in preliminary discussions held by the Odessa group because it watered down the nationalist theses of his 1882 brochure, *Auto-Emancipation*. There was a persistent undercurrent of distrust for Western Jewries in the Russian movement, leading some to warn against relying on philanthropists. For them, the consolidation of an independent East European organization was the desirable alternative. What was endorsed at Kattowitz purported to be at least a coordinate body, not one subordinate to Western supporters of the Yishuv. Thus, the elected executives were committed to the following tasks: to secure legalization in Russia; to channel locally collected contributions through the central executive and set up the receipts of the Montefiore fund as an endowment under its control; to send a mission to Palestine in order to examine the settlements that required support, to study the prospects for future work, and to propose candidates residing in Palestine to direct the movement's local activity.

Given the conditions under which the Hovevei Zion had to operate, the efforts to carry out these assignments fell far short of their aims. Legalization was not won in Russia for five years, until the situation changed in 1890. After a partial remittal of locally collected funds to the Warsaw center, the flow dwindled and the constituent societies often chose to support preferred projects directly rather than allow Warsaw or Odessa to set priorities. The movement relied on a Parisian, Michael Erlanger (Rothschild's erstwhile proxy for land purchase in Palestine and a leader of the Alliance Israélite Universelle), to transmit its contributions to the Yishuv.

The mission to Palestine (with a fruitless stopover in Istanbul) was undertaken by the Moscow-based tea magnate, Kalonymus Wissotzky, who took along Eleazar Rokeah as his aide. They failed to establish a solid, representative Hovevei Zion agency there. Local liaison and supervision were provided by volunteer leaders, with Rokeah as a salaried secretary: at first, by a Moroccan-born Sephardi merchant, Abraham Moyal, and after his untimely death, by Samuel Hirsch. Hirsch, whose primary responsibility was the Mikveh Israel farm school, set up a committee to assist him composed of representatives of the villages that required Hovevei Zion support. He co-opted those Rothschild-management personnel who could conveniently supervise the work. His ties with Rothschild enabled him to facilitate needed cooperation from that quarter and to obtain essential supplementary aid from the baron when the Hovevei Zion was unable to meet emergencies that arose.

Growing dissatisfaction with the movement's condition in Russia and Palestine generated pressures for change that came to a head in 1887. A second conference—long demanded by the discontented Moscow society and Rabbi Mohilever's Bialystok group but delayed for fear of upsetting the delicate negotiations to secure legalization—was finally held. Mohilever made clear his unhappiness at the domination of the movement leadership by secular Zionists and his desire to take personal control. This objective was not won, but the reorganization that emerged significantly changed the structure. An executive committee of seven was chosen, with Pinsker as its chief and a consultative, advisory panel of six—three secular and three rabbinical members. Pinsker and Lilienblum remained in control of general policy and the work in Palestine, though not without submitting to a stream of advice and complaints from the rabbinical board members. Warsaw's special role in the movement's leadership was eliminated.

The conference led to a reorganization of the work in Palestine as well. The rebellion in Rishon Lezion a few months before the conference had created an unbridgeable breach between Rothschild associates such as Hirsch and reputed associates of the rebels such as Rokeah. Following the conference, a meeting was arranged between Pinsker and Rothschild in Paris in order to restore cooperation. The baron stated plainly that he needed no socialists or freethinkers in the settlements he supported, and he expressed his willingness to lend assistance to the conservative pious settlers of Petah Tikvah, until then solely dependent on the Hovevei Zion. He pledged his aid in the final settlement of litigation over construction on land that Pines had acquired in Petah Tikvah and resold to Russian Jews. In turn, Pinsker undertook to persuade the investors who had not settled on their plots to sell them to Rothschild. In the aftermath of these discussions, the Hovevei Zion Palestinian representation was eventually reorganized. Hirsch resumed his responsibilities, with a new executive secretary, Yehiel Michael Pines, who moved from

Jerusalem—not, to be sure, to Jaffa, where a Hovevei Zion office was opened, but nearby in the vicinity of Petah Tikvah. In addition, Pines was appointed as the director of Gedera with the enthusiastic approval of its settlers, and as the religious inspector (*mashgiah*) of the villagers' observance of ritual piety.

At that time, too, the difficulties imposed on Jewish resettlement by Ottoman officials had reached a new peak, and Rothschild's ability to intercede, bargain, and exert pressure was vitally necessary. Although official impediments were encountered everywhere, they were especially severe in the Jerusalem district. The central government's policy was stricter in this religiously sensitive region, and the Jerusalem governor, Rauf Pasha, became notorious among Jews for his rigid, incorruptible application of all bans.

In 1886 and 1887, the pasha ordered Jews who overstayed their 30-day pilgrimage passes to be arrested on the streets and in their homes, and he also tightened the controls at the port of Jaffa. The Russian and Austrian consuls, who had guaranteed the departure of their Jewish citizens, aided in carrying out the detentions and expulsions, creating a near panic in the whole Yishuv. But thereafter, the new American ambassador in Istanbul, Oscar Straus (scion of a prominent New York Jewish family), protested vigorously, having been instructed that the United States could not accept religious discrimination against any of its citizens. He was joined in protests by the French, British, and other diplomats. In February 1888, the Turks relaxed the rules, permitting Jews a three-month stay on pilgrimage, but continued diplomatic pressure was maintained on the principle of nondiscrimination. Finally, in October 1888, the Porte responded to the protests, explaining that the Jerusalem pasha's orders were not to prevent individual visitors from staying in the country, since the ban was meant to affect only the immigration of Jews en masse. Though this statement suggested a change in policy, Rauf Pasha continued to require Russian and Rumanian Jews to depart after three months. Effective easing of the restrictions became evident with his departure for a post in Beirut in 1889. He was replaced by a new Jerusalem governor, Reshad Pasha, who signaled his commitment to a liberal policy of development by dropping the ban against Russian and Rumanian Jewish settlers.

These developments eventually brought about a sharp change of course in the diaspora Hovevei Zion organization. During the 1887–89 period, Pinsker reluctantly carried the burden of leadership under mounting difficulties of ill health and persistent, nagging criticism by the rabbinical opposition. At last, in 1889, he resigned, his stamina exhausted, and the movement was confronted with the need to reorganize at a conference planned for that summer in Vilna. Mohilever's demand that leadership be entrusted entirely to rabbis fell short of a complete victory. A three-man executive was chosen, with an advisory council of five, in which Mohilever was granted a clearly dominant position.

During that time of trouble for the Hovevei Zion, Alexander Zederbaum, a publisher of Jewish journals, had been lobbying in Saint Petersburg for legalization of the movement. The Russian government held it inadvisable to sanction a philo-Zionist organization so long as the Turks banned Jewish immigration to Palestine. A change came with the turn in Turkish policy in 1889. After several months of further negotiation, Zederbaum was able to announce that the movement had been officially recognized for charitable work in Palestine, within narrowly defined limits.

A legally sanctioned philo-Zionist organization clearly had unassailable advantages over the insecure and uncertain existing structure, but the terms of its charter posed severe problems for the shaky balance of opposed interests. The "Odessa Society," as it came to be known, was to be constituted on a basis of direct individual membership, not of constituent local societies, and to be run by a committee of persons resident in Odessa, elected by those personally attending a meeting of the members in Odessa. This system placed in question the rights of the local societies who had previously been represented by delegates at the conferences and in the elected governing bodies. A compromise was effected by appointing the heads of the local societies as "correspondents" (although a proposed provision for such a function had been eliminated by the government and later was explicitly forbidden in the Polish provinces). A five-man executive resident in Odessa was headed by Pinsker and dominated by secular nationalists, but it also included a representative of Mohilever. In addition a broad basis for advisory consultation in executive decision-making was agreed upon, providing a channel of influence for displaced older leaders and their supporters.

Shortly after the first assembly of the new Odessa society in April 1890, a pilgrimage group of Hovevei Zion leaders went to Palestine to study the movement's commitments there, to plan for renewed work, and to propose a new set of local officers. The leading member of the group was Mohilever, and the visit was conducted in his spirit. But in the end, the three-man control board that he proposed—Pines; Yizhak-Eisik Ben-Tovim, who was Mohilever's personal *homme de confiance*; and Vladimir Tiomkin, a young engineer—was reshaped by giving Tiomkin authority superior to that of his two traditionally inclined colleagues. In this posture, the Hovevei Zion office in Jaffa encountered the heightened responsibilities brought on when Russian policy expelled a new stream of refugees in the following year.

III

With the easing of Ottoman restrictions, land became available for purchase in Palestine, and philo-Zionist activity in the diaspora increased. Oppressive Russian policy, especially the mass expulsion from Moscow in 1891, made the resettlement of Jewish refugees an acute issue once again. The legalization of the Odessa Society led many to believe that they could expect aid if they left Russia to resettle in the promised land. Societies sprang up in many Russian towns—and soon also in Jewish immigrant colonies in England and America—hoping to purchase plots of land in Palestine on regular, deferred payments. They included both relatively well-to-do members, who expected to have their tracts planted and tended for them for years before emigrating, and others of very modest means who would rely on immediate employment, loans on easy terms, or outright support to achieve their resettlement.

Earlier settlers of the 1880s emerged as active agents in the renewed movement. Yehoshua Hankin, a Bilu member who married Israel Belkind's sister, became a major land agent after he sold his land in Gedera and moved to Jaffa in 1888. In the following year, he borrowed money for a deposit on 2,500 acres of land south of Rishon Lezion, which he sold to a group of Warsaw settlers, who founded the village of Rehovot on the Purim holiday in 1890. Hankin then went on to further extensive land deals, including the purchase and resale of some 7,500 acres on which the village of Hadera was founded in 1891.

The sharp increase of immigration created a land boom that attracted many such dealers, both Jewish and non-Jewish, in a frenzy of speculation. The Hovevei Zion committee in Jaffa—as well as the local agents of Baron Rothschild, who were long active in this market—appreciated the urgent need to impose controls that would protect the settlers from exploitation and prevent the undermining of their own project. Under Tiomkin's vigorous leadership, Hovevei Zion induced many potential purchasers, particularly representatives of newly organized diaspora groups, to accept the Jaffa office as their central agency. Tiomkin collected their deposits and, using Hankin as his chief land agent, made commitments for purchases which the client societies were to pay off in installments. Hankin undertook to carry out the delicate and tedious work of registering deeds, securing the demarcation of land purchased from other lands held by Arab peasants in the same village or area, and, when the settlers insisted, obtaining building permits.

But the boom was sharply checked when the Ottoman authorities reacted with renewed restrictions. The sudden spurt of Jewish immigration was given alarming political significance in Turkish eyes by Western support for it, particularly in England. The 1890–91 refugee movement occurred at a time when immigration restrictions, in response to to the pressure of the recent Jewish influx, were being pressed in both England and the United States, and Jewish philanthropists were casting about for other havens, particularly in undeveloped and underpopulated territories. The Protestant-evangelical tradition of support for the restoration of the Jews, and the secular-diplomatic turn given to it by men like Oliphant, was revived in America by William Blackstone's "memorial," presented to President Benjamin Harrison with an impressive list of signatures. It called for an international conference "to consider the condition of the Israelites and their claims to Palestine as their ancient home."[1] In England, leading figures of the Anglo-Jewish establishment— particularly the staff officer Colonel Albert Michael Goldsmid, and the banker and Liberal MP for Whitechapel Sir Samuel Montagu—joined forces with a rejuvenated Hovevei Zion movement among East European immigrants and took over its leadership in July 1891. Under their direction, both William Gladstone, the British Liberal leader, and Lord Salisbury, the Tory prime minister, were induced to indicate support for the Zionist aspirations.

Salisbury, in response to Montagu's appeal, ordered an inquiry through the British embassy in Istanbul as to whether the Porte would welcome British sponsorship for an ambitious Zionist plan calling for the grant of crown lands to Jewish settlers. This drew an immediate rejection in July and later a detailed reply in October 1891 that made clear the intention of the regime to prevent a disproportionate rise in the Jewish population. Meanwhile, rumors were being spread about a British-supported Jewish plot to raise an armed force of 5,000 men and seize control of Jerusalem. Leading Jerusalem Arabs, who dominated the local administrative council, wired a protest against any lowering of bars to Jewish settlement. In August 1891, the Porte tried to ban Russian Jews, and in October all Jews, from entering the empire; a year later, the Jerusalem governor was instructed to bar all sales of *miri* land (land held under hereditary lease from the state) to Jews. The protests of foreign diplomats made these measures ineffective in the long run, but the shock of their announcement and initial application was enough to collapse the immediate pressure of immigration and the land boom and to precipitate a new crisis in the affairs of the Hovevei Zion.

Societies that had planned to purchase land through the Jaffa office withdrew after the Ottoman crackdown and demanded refunds of their deposits. But Tiomkin and his associates had committed such funds to already initiated projects, often without express approval from the committee in Odessa. The ensuing financial collapse of the Jaffa office left the Rothschild administration alone in the field. The baron's agents had been active in extending their holdings in and around the established villages, as well as in remoter areas such as the Transjordan plateau. He now rescued a number of projects begun in the boom years by the Hovevei Zion, and began to buy land reserves for future settlement, which were made available to the Hovevei Zion societies who survived the crisis or were renewed in the years that followed.

By the 1890s, Rothschild's support had significantly advanced the philo-Zionist resettlement even though his enterprise still remained essentially experimental. The villages he sustained developed in a way that had substantial economic effects beyond simply maintaining the plantations and planters' families that he sponsored. Having installed vineyards, he also built wineries in Rishon Lezion and Zikhron Yaakov, purchasing the grape yield at prices that were fixed at a level that would support the producers, with no assurance that the market could absorb the final product at somewhere near the cost. Such agro-industrial enterprises—including a failed glass and bottling plant, silk worm, perfumery, and other horticultural production—introduced a layer of craftsmen and technicians into the settlements, together with teachers, doctors and nurses, and religious functionaries employed in Rothschild-supported public services. The impact of this investment and activity was felt in neighboring Arab villages, where the new market and the availability of seasonal farm work attracted a growing population. In the towns that served the new villages, particularly in Jaffa, a supporting structure of both Jewish and gentile land agents, importers, and suppliers, together with services for an urban population, grew up alongside the burgeoning officialdom of the Rothschild regime. The baron's beneficence, along with that of other Western philanthropists, was also felt in Jerusalem and Safed, not only sustaining the established Sephardi and Ashkenazi settlement but expanding the group of modern-minded professionals in the holy cities.

These were unintended consequences of the baron's policy, though certainly for the most part they contributed to his broader aims. But when the Rothschild administration began to serve as a central land agency for the Hovevei Zion societies, it moved onto a new level and adopted a new strategy of resettlement planning. By harnessing the spontaneous efforts of philo-Zionists throughout the diaspora to his management team, Rothschild committed himself to their particular needs while confining them to his administrative methods.

The Rothschild bureaucracy agreed with the Hovevei Zion Jaffa office in seeking to impose central control over Jewish land acquisition, but viewed with apprehension control by others than themselves. They contended that the crisis that followed the land boom was the inevitable consequence of the openly political aspirations and loud publicity that were characteristic of a popular movement. They now pursued in their own discreet way, based on years of close connections with Ottoman landowners and officials, a broad program of land acquisition, increasingly directed to more remote markets as well as to available tracts that could support the growth of already established settlements. The new, more remote acquisitions, such as land purchased east of the Jordan River, were now offered to philo-Zionist land-purchasing societies that were considered able, with reasonable credit facilities, to carry the expense of a new settlement.

The Russian Hovevei Zion had to face continual demands for readjustment beginning with the legalization of the Odessa Society and the 1890–91 boom–bust cycle. The Odessa Society enjoyed unchallengeable superiority in managing (to the extent it proved possible) the Palestine projects directly sponsored by the Hovevei Zion. But its officially sanctioned bylaws restricted its permissible activities both in Erez Israel and in the diaspora. The society was chartered for support to artisans and farmers resident in Palestine, but not for bringing in immigrants and new settlers. It was authorized neither to maintain the old network of Hovevei Zion associations throughout the Jewish-populated parts of Russia nor to participate in contemplated international Hovevei Zion connections. It managed to sustain a continuing program of work in Palestine, within the limits of the resources at its disposal. However, the Odessa Society deferred to other, officially tolerated but not legally authorized, organizations that the movement improvised in order to sustain and develop Hovevei Zionism in the diaspora.

One such body, the secret society Bnei Moshe—organized in 1889 and led by the young merchant Asher Ginzberg, who rose to fame under his nom de plume Ahad Haam ("One of the People")—became the seedbed for certain ideological alternatives in Zionism, to which we shall recur. Others in the movement aimed rather to recover the lost ground and previously cherished possibilities that were restricted under the Odessa Society's charter. Initial hopes to name regional representatives to the Odessa Society's governing board, and so retain an integrating center and extend the cover of legality over the entire Hovevei Zion network, were soon extinguished. In 1893, therefore, Mohilever set up a "spiritual center" (*merkaz ruhani*, hence "Mizrahi") in Bialystok in order to communicate with the scattered remnants of the Russian movement and, under his traditionalist guidance, stimulate their revival. Attempts to reach out beyond the borders of Russia and consolidate the movement internationally began even earlier.

In 1891, at the time of the expulsion from Moscow, the Russian government responded favorably to an ambitious proposal from the railroad financier Baron Maurice de Hirsch to organize the mass emigration of Jews. Having concluded that Jewish immigration to advanced industrial countries could spread the virus of political antisemitism, Hirsch favored concentrated resettlement in new, underpopulated territories— in particular, Argentina. Palestine, to which he had given some attention in the 1880s, did not seem to him a promising haven for Jewish resettlement, and he was content to let Rothschild bear responsibility for the work there. But in 1890 the Hovevei Zion still hoped that Hirsch might be induced to aid their work as well. At a preliminary meeting to organize the legalized Odessa Society in 1890, a proposal was adopted that the executive of the new society should send a delegation to seek his assistance.

The Odessa executive soon concluded that its statute did not permit it to undertake such a mission, but others took it up in the spring of 1891. The activities of influential Jews in London and Paris at that time encouraged diverse Hovevei Zion leaders to hope that an old dream of theirs, to set up an agrarian banking institution in Palestine to finance fixed and current investment by the settlers, might gain support from major Western capitalists. Those who waxed enthusiastic over the plan ranged from the Bnei Moshe to Rabbi Mohilever and included substantial industrialists among the Moscow, Minsk, and Warsaw Hovevei Zion. They began with a campaign in Russia for subscriptions to shares in the proposed bank and then sent a three-man delegation to line up support and sponsorship in Berlin, Paris, and London.

The initial responses of Western leaders were guarded but favorable enough to encourage high-flying hopes. Baron Hirsch, even while developing his preferred plan for colonization in Argentina, expressed willingness to aid Jewish resettlement in Turkey-in-Asia on certain conditions: in addition to the intercession in Istanbul against the threatened bans, desired by the Hovevei Zion, he demanded an initial feasibility study by an impartial, expert committee, including persons chosen by the Alliance Israélite Universelle and his own representative. Also, if co-operation with the Hovevei Zion were to become effective, they must set up a joint center in the West for their internationally scattered component parts. The Alliance, for its part, added its own condition: before it could sponsor the survey committee that Hirsch proposed, the Hovevei Zion would have to mobilize the necessary funds from various sources. Then, in London the Hovevei Zionists not only found a ready ear in the British movement, actively pursuing its own, parallel project, but learned that Lord Nathaniel Mayer Rothschild might be willing to support his Paris kinsman, Baron Edmond, in his Palestinian work.

Upon returning to Russia, the delegates set to work to capitalize on the seemingly enhanced opportunity. The leading Warsaw activist, Saul Pinhas Rabinowitz, envisioned an immediate future in which not simply the Hovevei Zion but "all of Israel," and particularly the leading Western Jewish organizations and their funds for aiding Russian emigrants, would assume the responsibility for the resettlement in Erez Israel—a proposal recurrently advocated in Zionist history until it was realized by Chaim Weizmann in the form of the Jewish Agency in 1929. At a meeting in Warsaw in the fall of 1891, nominees were chosen to represent the Russian Hovevei Zion on the "central committee" of the projected all-Jewish body in Paris or London (other organizations that were expected to join were the French, German, British, and American Hovevei Zion, the Anglo-Jewish Association, the French Alliance and its Austrian counterpart, the Israelitische Allianz, and other various German funds to aid Russian refugees); a delegation was to go to Istanbul to seek the relaxation of immigration restrictions and for other political tasks; and Tiomkin was to tour Russia and raise the Russian contribution to the funds needed for a major expansion of the resettlement, the creation of the agrarian bank, and all the anticipated new tasks, such as aiding the establishment of Jewish workers in the villages and the promotion of trade and industry.

All these bright vistas were soon darkened. At a conference in Berlin in October (where Russian Zionists were not represented but submitted briefs arguing on nationalistic or traditionalist lines for Erez Israel rather than other havens for the refugees), the German philanthropic agencies decisively rejected any involvement with the Palestine project, on ideological as well as on practical grounds. Meanwhile, the Turks made their opposition to the Zionist aspirations unmistakably and officially clear. The fund-raising campaign in Russia expired in feeble fits and starts.

Baron Hirsch, whose Argentina project took concrete shape in the foundation of his Jewish Colonization Association (ICA) in September, withdrew from cooperation with the Hovevei Zion.

The movement dwindled in all countries of the diaspora. For its continued work in Palestine, it fell back on the exclusive land-acquisition facilities now enjoyed by Baron Rothschild, with whom relations were consolidated. This affiliation enabled the "practical" labors of its Odessa Society and other Hovevei Zion groups to continue, with a much reduced agenda, but it left other adherents dissatisfied, especially those not directly engaged in resettlement projects.

The proposal to reorganize the movement internationally around a center in the West continued to be raised. It was vigorously advocated by Nathan Birnbaum, a young Viennese activist, in his journal *Selbst-Emanzipation*, which had a devoted following among East European Jewish students in Austria, Germany, France, and Switzerland. The British, American, and French leaders who had been involved in the earlier approaches to Hirsch were able, in January 1894, to convene a meeting in Paris that did indeed set up an international Hovevei Zion center. But Baron Rothschild ordered his officers not to cooperate in the new body's broadly conceived agenda; the committee he had set up in Paris for work with the Hovevei Zion would confine itself to the role of land agent. This decision left the international Hovevei Zion center in a state of impotence, especially after the British leadership then withdrew.

IV

The growth of the Jewish settlement in Palestine continued through the 1890s under conditions of balanced uncertainty. The Zionists were not granted the concessions that were essential for them to undertake their more ambitious aspirations. On the other hand, the restrictions announced by the Ottomans were checked by the opposition of foreign diplomats relying on their treaty rights. This was, moreover, a period of economic expansion, driven by European investment in railroad construction, which opened up opportunities both for the population at large and for official corruption. In Palestine, the infiltration of Jewish settlers under the aegis of philanthropic patrons and foreign diplomats was a significant element in the growth of neighboring Arab villages and the wider economy.

It was also a period when disquiet and dissatisfaction rose among those concerned with the resettlement, producing a drumfire of criticism and the beginning of alternative approaches. The vicissitudes of the movement were reported in detail and actively discussed in the flourishing Jewish press. Journalists and publicists such as Ahad Haam, Lilienblum, and Zederbaum in Russia, Birnbaum in Austria, and the editors of Jewish newspapers and journals in London and New York were philo-Zionist activists; they vented their frustration over the halting, inadequate achievements in the field, critically analyzing the movement's current methods and results and the diverse proposals for change.

It became clear in the 1880s that the existing political economy made Palestine unfit to absorb a large, immediate influx of immigrants; a few years of experience led to the same conclusion about Argentina in the 1890s. The mass migration was drawn spontaneously to advanced, Western, industrial countries such as England and America. Two problems, however, were generally perceived in this outcome: both nationalist and antinationalist Jewish circles sensed that large-scale Jewish immigration was provoking antisemitic reactions in the West; nationalists also feared that both the cultural traditions and the ties of a common Jewish peoplehood would be dissolved in the process of assimilation to Western conventions. Both arguments were used in the Zionist defense of Erez Israel rather than America as the destination of a nationally oriented Jewish migration policy. But there arose a division in Zionist ideological perspectives that led to emphasis on another line of argumentation.

For Lilienblum, the issue was decided by his perception of antisemitism as structurally inherent in the situation of a total diaspora, a dispersed minority everywhere. Hence, Zionist policy had to direct Jewish migrants to Palestine in sufficient numbers to make the ancestral land effectively their national home, a place where they could not be treated as strangers; this was an achievement that could never be accomplished in America, for example, as all Zionists agreed. This fact of life shaped his analysis of the unsatisfactory results and flawed methods of the philo-Zionist project. Like most of his contemporaries, he decried the mass influx of penniless refugees—but only as an error in timing. The national home under construction was meant precisely to accommodate refugees who fled antisemitic oppression, but first the ground had to be prepared in Palestine. This meant that the first stage in resettlement must be the immigration of men of means, able to finance development on the land as well as in industry and commerce. Only after they had laid the foundations, with reasonable support from philanthropic or publicly donated credit facilities, could the general mass be absorbed. The failure of men of means to play their essential role—a dereliction of duty that he sharply condemned—was the reason the Hovevei Zion movement had been loaded with an insupportable burden.

A different approach was represented preeminently by Ahad Haam. He shared the common perception that an indefinite commitment to the unlimited demands of whoever fled to Palestine was fatal for the movement. But this thinking led him to the radical conclusion that Zionism could not, and should not, seek to solve "the problem of the Jews"— that is, to provide a haven for the undifferentiated mass driven by oppression and poverty from Eastern Europe. Let this stream follow its natural course to the advanced economies of the West, he reasoned, where the forces of individual self-interest sent them in overwhelming proportions. It was true that the problem of national autoemancipation could not be solved in America. But this problem—or as Ahad Haam preferred to call it, the "problem of Judaism"—was specifically different from the immediate refugee question, the "problem of the Jews." To solve the former, one must rely not on the spontaneous impulsions of self-interest but on the disciplined idealism of an elite corps of pioneers who would address themselves to the primary Zionist task: to regenerate the national will, or consensus, without which autoemancipation could not be achieved. The "problem of Judaism" required a "qualitative," not a "quantitative" solution.[2]

This was the rudimentary programmatic position from which Ahad Haam began when in 1889 he became the head of the new Zionist secret society, Bnei Moshe, to which a good part of the more active and disgruntled philo-Zionists were attracted. He came to inspect the work in Palestine in 1891 as a recognized leader, with a strong influence in the Hovevei Zion office in Jaffa and the new settlement of Rehovot. After a three-month tour, he returned to Odessa and published in the press scathing reports of his findings and impressions. He diagnosed the root of the movement's difficulties far differently than did Lilienblum, who bemoaned the failure of venture capitalists to do their duty. There was too much investment, too recklessly applied, to the accompaniment of too much publicity, he contended. He condemned the blind reliance on planting vineyards according to the changing recommendations of French advisers, without their checking experimentally to see whether what grew well in France would succeed in Palestine and whether there would be a market for the eventual product. What the movement needed were prudent, informed, and well-trained settlers, not driven by fantasies of speculative wealth, but willing to live modestly on the annual yield of ordinary farming and build more lucrative specialties gradually, as their means permitted.

The distrust in Rothschild's French-oriented administration and the resentment of the dependency to which settlers were reduced, common in the movement, was keenly felt by Ahad Haam. He was equally offended by the loud propaganda, sometimes reaching a level of arrogant bluster, that prevailed in the Hovevei Zion movement and characterized some of the settlers. He denounced the land speculation and land-agent chicanery that he found in Palestine and pointed to the likelihood of adverse Turkish reactions. He urged that new settlements should not be attempted until they could be established openly with full Ottoman, legal approval. He noted in passing, as symptoms of the arrogance instilled by inflated movement propaganda, the excessive demands of immigrant laborers for support and the sometimes offensive attitudes of Jewish planters to their native Arab workers. He concluded with a bitter reflection inspired by a visit to the Western Wall, implying that the New Yishuv was perhaps cut from the same pattern as the Old: "If a land is destroyed, and the people is still full of life and strength . . . they will return and rebuild it; but if a people is destroyed, . . . whence will come its aid?"[3] The immediate task of philo-Zionism, accordingly, was not to rebuild Zion, but to build up "love of Zion." What was done in Palestine, no less than the work in the diaspora, must primarily serve this purpose.

Ahad Haam's critique was sharply rejected by Lilienblum and others. They attacked it as defeatist gloom mongering that could undermine the movement's morale. His reports did not prevent Hovevei Zion associations in Russia, Rumania, and the United States to continue their efforts to buy land for their members, using the facilities now being extended by Rothschild. Nevertheless, the main counts in Ahad Haam's indictment voiced doubts that were widely shared. The attempts to reorganize the movement from a Western center in the early 1890s, in which Ahad Haam took an active part, reflected precisely such doubts and fears, and the inadequate results left many with a sense of frustration. This was particularly true of the largely East European student Zionists in Germany, Austria, Switzerland, and France.

In 1896, Theodor Herzl burst upon the Zionist scene with his pamphlet *Judenstaat* ("The Jews' State") and his bold, well-publicized visit to the sultan in Istanbul. Failing to win over Hirsch, Rothschild, or the wealthy British philo-Zionists (whose sobering experience with their own direct, political initiatives a few years earlier made them wary of Herzl's parallel approach), he turned to the already existing Hovevei Zion movement. His proposal to convene a Zionist congress coincided with an objective that was being actively pursued in their ranks at the time. The impatient young student Zionists in Austria and Germany immediately responded enthusiastically to his call. Other Hovevei Zionists found his approach both rash and unreliable, especially in its failure to focus exclusively on Erez Israel as the projected Jewish homeland. Careful adjustments had to be made in Herzl's program to bring it to the First Zionist Congress in 1897 and keep it in the organization established in Basle.

Herzl, like Ahad Haam, favored suspending new Jewish settlement projects in Palestine until the political rights and guarantees needed for effective work were secured—although his alternative, in sharp contrast to Ahad Haam's, was to mount an immediate, direct, publicly proclaimed campaign to secure the political objective. This was a position that threatened the slow, cautious methods of work to which many of the Hovevei Zion had reconciled themselves, however reluctantly. To get such veteran philo-Zionists to come to the projected congress, Herzl offered certain assurances and concessions, which were embodied in the Basle program that was adopted at the First Zionist Congress. He tried to allay fears of an adverse Turkish reaction (which in any case occurred, though in a relatively moderate form) by stating the aim of political Zionism to be not explicitly a "Jewish state," but a Jewish "home in Palestine secured by public law": that is, a certain autonomy in the Ottoman Empire, not independence from it, was implied. Instead of a flat rejection of continued settlement until the needed political conditions were secured, the Basle program vaguely allowed for "appropriate" (*zweckdienliche*) activity of this kind. In addition, the program extended a rhetorical olive branch to the cultural nationalism of Ahad Haam's followers by committing the movement to foster "national consciousness" (*Volksbewusstsein*).[4]

During Herzl's brief remaining life span, the "cultural" and "practical" work done by his Zionist organization was minimal. It was closely restricted by an overriding commitment to political activity that fully absorbed his energy. Nevertheless, the groundwork was laid for new institutions that later became critically important in the social and economic development of the New Yishuv. In the last year of Herzl's life, under the combined force of a failed diplomacy, criticism from the Zionist ranks, and the renewed crisis of Russian Jewry, Herzl himself took greater interest in practical measures to relieve the pressure of immediate needs for resettling refugees.

At the First Zionist Congress in 1897, proposals for a Jewish land-purchasing fund and a Zionist bank were advanced. The Jewish National Fund (JNF), which was to buy land in Palestine as the inalienable possession of the Jewish people for Jewish settlers to cultivate under long-term leases, was formally approved by the Fourth Zionist Congress, held in London in 1900. It was 1907 before its legal status was finally acquired; a requirement that it raise a capital of £200,000 from public contributions before beginning its operation also delayed its practical application.

The proposed Zionist financial institution, approved at the Second Zionist Congress in 1899 under the name of the Jewish Colonial Trust, was meant to raise £2,000,000 by selling shares at £1 a share to the Jewish public—that is, to those whom the Zionist organization could reach. This was Herzl's fallback expedient after he failed to enlist the leading Jewish bankers in this cause before turning to the Zionist "masses." His chief concern in setting up the trust was to command large funds which could be offered as a loan to the sultan in return for a "charter" that would permit large-scale resettlement of Jews in Palestine. Thereafter, of course, the funds of the trust would finance the resettlement project. But not only was no charter obtained: the capital subscribed by the Zionist public fell far short of the goals envisioned, and the pressure to employ the modest accumulated sum in practical work grew irresistible. This situation led Herzl to turn to East Africa as an immediate outlet for the pressure of the refugees' needs, since Palestine was blocked. But at the same time he took greater interest in the immediate use of existing Zionist facilities in Palestine.

In 1902, the Jewish Colonial Trust set up a subsidiary, the Anglo-Palestine Company (later the Anglo-Palestine Bank) to engage in credit transactions, especially in Palestine and the adjacent territories. Zalman David Levontin, after a long period away from Erez Israel, returned in 1903 to handle the bank's operations in its new Jaffa branch. At this time, too, the "Colonization Commission," which had been regularly appointed by the Zionist Congress and had remained inactive, was replaced by an impressive and active Commission of Experts: an agronomist, Selig Soskin; the eminent botanist Otto Warburg; and the well-known sociologist and proponent of cooperative rural settlement Franz Oppenheimer. These were to become significant factors in renewed Zionist "practical work" in the period that followed.

The creation of the World Zionist Organization (WZO) in 1897, which provided the Hovevei Zion with the effective international center it had long sought, brought to an end its effort to apply its united forces immediately to the expansion and strengthening of the Palestine settlement. Most of the existing societies, together with new ones drawn largely from sources that shared the same sentiments as the old Hovevei Zion, were absorbed by the new body and were constrained by the limits imposed by Herzl's policy. However, some—in particular, the Odessa Society—continued their previous work outside the new Zionist organization, even though many of their supporters became individual members of the WZO.

The mainstay of the continued resettlement in this period was the Rothschild administration. The Odessa Society eventually gave up giving minor support grants directly to settlers in favor of support for their communal institutions. The Hovevei Zion clubs that were organized for land purchase applied to the Rothschild land agency. Rehovot, the major settlement independently organized by the Hovevei Zion—a village dominated by members of Bnei Moshe—followed the Rothschild pattern in planting vineyards; consequently it depended on the Rishon Lezion winery to purchase its grapes at subsidized prices. Hadera, also founded by Hovevei Zion investors, not only followed the same pattern but was rescued from collapse by a heavy infusion of Rothschild funds, and especially by the swamp drainage and sanitation he financed in order to stem the ravages of malaria that decimated the village.

As the Rothschild project extended beyond limited experiments to a general patronage of resettlement, it increasingly stimulated development beyond the bounds of its effective control. The baron's agents sought new lands to accommodate the needs of the children of their older settlers, as well as the demands of diaspora groups and local candidates for settlement. As their vineyards matured and new plantings in the independent Hovevei Zion settlements brought in new supplies to the Rothschild wineries, a network of marketing depots in foreign ports in Asia and Europe had to be developed. Apart from the agents being directly hired by Rothschild, a marketing organization, the Carmel Company, was set up with the baron's assistance by a Rehovot settler, Eliahu Lewin-Epstein, with exclusive rights for sales in Russia and Poland. It was floated by investments raised by Lewin-Epstein among Hovevei Zion supporters, and it depended on a market appeal that drew largely on the traditional, as well as Zionist, attachment of diaspora Jews to Erez Israel. In addition, the growth of the farm settlements, more than doubled during the 1890s, was an economic stimulus that—together with the general growth of the Palestine economy—expanded and variegated the structure of the New Yishuv. The older rural settlements became embryonic townships, with administrators, farm workers, lay and religious service professionals, and artisan and winery workers residing among the planters' families. Arab workers, both in the Jewish villages and in neighboring Arab villages, were a major appendage of the structure, as was a growing Jewish urban society, in Jaffa and Jerusalem, that had close ties to the rural settlements.

Not only did the collateral extensions of Rothschild's influence develop along their own lines; the settlements he sponsored themselves showed patterns of growth that were not what he desired. He wanted to create a core group of Jewish farmers, who would free themselves from the disreputable middleman occupations forced on their community by diaspora conditions even while preserving the Hebrew language and religious traditions of their fathers. His ideal was a self-supporting, self-respecting, modestly living Jewish farmer who would, if necessary, employ Jewish workers. What he got departed from these designs, in good part as a consequence of administrative policies he himself imposed: the plantation system forced years of dependency on the farmers; Arabs, not Jewish workers, became a major element in the plantation economy; instead of a commitment to Hebrew culture and traditionalist frugality, the French-reoriented administration set a tone that made Paris the model to which the settlers' children were taught to aspire; and the recurrent losing battles with the administration undermined the self-respecting independence of the settlers.

When these flaws in his work were pointed out by critics such as Ahad Haam, or provoked outbursts of rebellion in the settlements, it was not in the baron's nature to listen patiently. Moreover, the hard line he took on such occasions in the 1880s brought the settlers to their knees, while the independent Hovevei Zion had to resort to his aid in their own repeated failures. But these victories were won at a cost that grew more onerous and more evident each year. Toward the end of the 1890s, at a time when the baron feared that his days were numbered because of ill health, he received reports from two of his own agents in Palestine about serious deficiencies in the state of Zikhron Yaakov and other favorite settlements. Much of the accounting he received echoed criticisms that were familiar in Hovevei Zion circles. What may have been more telling was the demonstration that his policies in regard to wine production, which guaranteed a viable income to the planters and a reasonable margin of profit to the independent marketing organization, were producing a huge, accumulating deficit for the wineries, which were carried at his own expense. Soon after, the baron drastically altered the organization of his cherished enterprise.

Some years before, in 1896, a new agency had become active in promoting Jewish rural resettlement in Palestine. Baron Hirsch's ICA organization, which continued his work after his death, began to support educational projects and purchase land for settlement in Palestine. The relative ease and lower price of land acquisition in Galilee, outside the Jerusalem district, led the agency to concentrate its work in that region. Soil conditions there, less suited for vineyards and orchards than the light, coastal lands, suggested a policy of general farming and cereal crops. ICA's technical staff favored a modest peasant style of farming on social-economic grounds as well, and they set aside suitable areas for training prospective settlers before committing themselves to their permanent colonization.

In 1900, Baron Edmond transferred his holdings to a new Palestine commission established by ICA of which he himself became the active leader. While doing this did not mean relinquishing personal involvement, it did signal his adoption of the methods favored by ICA—and the abrupt abandonment of his previous lavish largesse. The transition from the philanthropic patronage of the baron to the ruthless laissez-faire economy imposed by ICA, however salutary in its eventual effects, was a rude shock that produced widespread consternation. For the planters, it meant an immediate drastic cut in the price paid for their grapes to a level intended to balance the books at the wineries. Vineyards producing unmarketable crops were uprooted. In the course of time, unprofitable ventures such as a silk factory in Safed and a perfumery in Yesud Hamaala in Galilee, were eliminated. An immediate effect of the ruthless retrenchment was the dismissal of most Jewish hired workers.

In their first reaction to such blows, the settlers, urged on by the Odessa Society, sent a joint delegation to Paris in February 1891 to petition the baron to reconsider the ICA policy. He received them with bitter reproaches of his own. The rebuff was so humiliating to one of the delegates, Ahad Haam, that he said he would withdraw from public activity—but not without publishing in the press acid comments on the disastrous encounter. In the longer term, however, the more solidly established planters in the older villages were able to consolidate their position, after amortizing ICA loans; they also gained control of the wineries and of the marketing of thriving citrus crops, conducting both ventures as cooperative enterprises.

A more intractable problem was that of the Jewish farm laborers. It was one of Baron Edmond's clear aims, firmly conveyed to his administration, to ensure that Jewish workers would be employed in the villages. This task was relatively easy in initial stages of plantations; but as vineyards (or later, citrus orchards) matured and as mainly unskilled, seasonal labor was required, chiefly at harvest times, it became more complicated. The older Jewish villages could draw upon an increasing, low-paid supply of farm labor from neighboring Arab villages. Jewish workers not only were mainly new to the work, but required facilities—housing, medical care—and a wage beyond what Arab labor cost the planter. These were supplied, at the baron's behest, on the same plan as the subsidies to the planters: that is, as a form of welfare payment, not as a return for marginal productivity. Even then, the wage level for Jewish workers in the Rothschild villages provided a bare living for young bachelors but was inadequate to support a married worker and his family.

The problem of Jewish labor in the villages arose, accordingly, from the beginning. It was acute by the late 1880s in the oldest settlements and was eased for a time by the establishment of Rehovot and Hadera, only to reappear when those settlements reached greater maturity toward the end of the century. The baron's policy shift in 1900 and the retrenchment enforced by ICA soon after brought the problem to a critical point, as had happened after the collapse of the 1890–91 boom. The sponsoring agencies, including the Odessa Society, were compelled to consider once more the painful expedient of raising funds to aid in the *emigration* of unemployed workers from Palestine to lands of greater opportunity.

Various solutions were discussed by the Zionists faced with an odious situation. They were unable to contribute enough to make the workers' position in the villages tenable, and they could not be happy with the degrading consequences of this policy when the baron applied it. An alternative policy, to assist the workers in becoming landed settlers themselves, ran into the limits of Jewish ability to buy land and finance settlement. Hovevei Zion opinion was divided between those who wished to follow this line on a large scale, together with subsidies for the workers in existing villages, and Ahad Haam's preference for select, demonstration-model settlements of veteran workers intended to test and prove the efficacy of such an approach. Still others pinned their hope on Yemenite Jews and others from Muslim countries who might compete successfully with Arab laborers. All, however, were compelled to reckon with the situation after 1900, when not simply Rothschild's new approach, but a revision of Turkish law was announced.

Complications in Ottoman relations with foreign diplomats since 1880 over Jewish resettlement led the sultan to reorganize the control system that had been developed in order to restrict new immigration more effectively. At the same time, he ordered a cessation of the harassment of illegal settlers long resident in the country; they were henceforth to be free to move and acquire property without hindrance. This redefinition of the Jewish status had its own loopholes, which were thoroughly exploited. But it made clearer than ever certain conclusions about what Jews, Zionists, and their philanthropic associates alike could and could not expect to accomplish in the near future. The prospects for large-scale new immigration seemed decisively reduced, but expanded resettlement could continue more easily than before by drawing on local resources: the growing second generation in existing villages, young people in the Old Yishuv who desired vocational retraining, and also veteran farm workers whose experience (and, as some hoped, small savings) qualified them as potential settlers on the modest lines contemplated by ICA.

Both Herzl and the Odessa leaders could accommodate themselves to the limited possibilities this plan offered. Herzl's control group in the WZO, the Viennese-based executive (the "Smaller Action Committee"), defined the Basle program's provision for "appropriate" practical work in Palestine as permitting resettlement of already resident Jews under officially sanctioned conditions; the Odessa activists accepted such limits perforce. Their differences persisted in subsidiary matters.

Both Herzl and the social critic Max Nordau were asked to be participants in the Odessa Society's appeal to Rothschild in 1891, but they both preferred to abstain from acting on an issue that implied submission to a policy of surreptitious "infiltration." At the same time, Herzl found scattered enthusiasts among Jews in Palestine, particularly in the New Yishuv, and maintained a correspondence with them, taking a helpful interest in their practical concerns. The crisis of 1900 and its aftermath led some of these supporters to build a Palestine Zionist "federation" that sought recognition from the Vienna executive, but Herzl preferred to avoid irritating the Turks at that time by so public a nationalist manifestation.

In 1903, Menahem Mendel Ussishkin came to Palestine to reorganize the work of the Odessa society there. Among his projects was an attempt to buy land to resettle veteran workers. He pursued this assignment with deliberate publicity in order, as he said, to make clear the limited scale and objectives of his purchase and thus lay to rest any suspicions of far-reaching, conspiratorial aims that local Arabs and Turkish officials might otherwise entertain. Herzl, however, viewed such an approach as unduly provocative so long as the sultan had not yet responded positively to his own diplomatic campaign for a Zionist "charter." In Palestine, Ussishkin enlarged his mission by convening a meeting, not simply of Zionists, but of a broadly representative group of leaders of the Yishuv at large to set up an authoritative communal organization. Thus, Herzl was challenged not only by his own ardent supporters, who demanded recognition of a Palestinian Zionist "federation," but by what could be a rival organization outside the WZO framework, one probably no less provocative to the Turks.

In 1903, too, Ussishkin published his "program" calling on young Zionists to volunteer for a three-year stint of labor in Palestine at minimal wages. This plan for a rotating corps of workers would supply Jewish labor in the villages without requiring funds for their establishment as landed settlers. It was thus an implicit acknowledgment of the limited possibilities for Zionist resettlement at the time. But it also was, even at the time, a break with the self-imposed limits of Herzl's policy, subordinating practical work to the needs of his political action. In the tradition of Zionist historiography and the popular Zionist mythos, it is recognized as one of the signal lights of a post-Herzlian era that was soon to follow.

o 5 o

The Conflict of Tradition and Idea

Early Zionism had a history of continual frustration. Yet oppressive conditions in Russia and Rumania, together with the corrupt inefficiency of the Ottoman administration, kept the philo-Zionist movement alive, and traditional sentiments, together with the responsibility for a common project of social and economic reform, bolstered the uneasy union of its disparate elements.

Theodor Herzl's World Zionist Organization, committed as it was to a strategy of open politics, was hampered by the same legal difficulties as the Hovevei Zion in Russia. Special circumstances induced the government to sanction a national convention of Russian Zionists in Minsk in 1902. The new minister of the interior, Vyacheslav Konstantinovich von Plehve, was visited by Herzl in the following year and gave him the impression that public Zionist activity would be permitted, on condition that it be confined to removing Jews from Russia (which the government considered desirable) and refrain from nationalist activity within the country (which the government considered dangerous). In spite of Herzl's hopes, however, legal sanction was then ordered withdrawn from the Zionists. They were unable to function freely until the 1905 uprisings, which for a time brought broader political liberties to all Russian parties.

After Rothschild's providential beneficence was granted in 1883, the philo-Zionist movement found itself in a rather stifling alliance with its ideological opponents. The Alliance Israélite Universelle continued to be firmly opposed to any nationalistic implications in the Palestine venture but worked closely with Rothschild. By 1894, the creation of the international Hovevei Zion headquarters in Paris was a formal acknowledgment of the dominant influence of Western European notables.

The spread of Russian, Rumanian, and Austrian Jews to other countries produced a scattering of Hovevei Zion societies all over the expanding Jewish world. In Paris and London, native Jews, especially some who had shown proto-Zionist sympathies through the Alliance Israélite

Universelle or other Jewish bodies, joined immigrant *maskilim* and Orthodox Zionists in the movement. In New York, Chicago, Boston, and Philadelphia, immigrants found native Jews or older settlers who supported their efforts. In German and Swiss universities, students forced to go abroad by the restricted Jewish quota (*numerus clausus*) in Russian schools formed Zionist or Jewish student organizations. In the course of time, they attracted Western students who sought a different form of Jewish identification than was offered in their native community.

The heart of the movement remained in Russia, Rumania, and Galicia, the Polish province of Austria-Hungary. Even under the restrictions at home and the obstructions in Palestine, there was enough to do and room enough for hope to sustain the movement. The resettlement of Palestine after 1880 produced results that were certainly very disappointing to the new Zionists who had arisen in that generation, but these goals had been sought in vain by the generation of the 1860s. The Rothschild-supported, bureaucratically administered village made a mockery of the slogan of autoemancipation, but it realized dreams that traditionalist proto-Zionists had been working for in vain for 20 years. The daily small-scale activities of the Hovevei Zion—fund collections for Palestine settlers, celebrations of Sir Moses Montefiore's centenary anniversary, agitational addresses to synagogue gatherings (one of the few legal locales for work), savings societies for land purchase and future immigration, and so on—were far from the ambitious aspirations of the Zionist intelligentsia, but they had at least the attraction, especially at first, of bringing them back into the heart of their people. Beyond this, Zionists buoyed themselves with the seemingly reasonable hope that Turkish policy might change, or that the Ottoman Empire might collapse, or that settlement might be possible in the Ottoman areas adjacent to Palestine.

And if the inadequate scope of Hovevei Zion activities or the enforced alliance with its ideological opponents crippled the movement, early Zionists could conduct a lively ideological debate, free and fierce beyond the Russian borders and quite active even in Russia, in spite of the censorship. For such disputes, not only sharp outer opposition but the heterogeneous composition of the Zionist movement itself provided more than sufficient grounds.

I

The much debated distinction between "proto-Zionism" and historic Zionism rests essentially on the latter's commitment to seek a secular solution to the Jewish problem through the return to Zion. The emotional source of the Zionist commitment was revulsion against the passive submission with which traditional and modern Jews alike adjusted to exile. Positively stated, the emotional core of historic Zionism was expressed in the slogan of autoemancipation.

This emotion was most effective, even to the point of trauma, among the Russian-oriented intelligentsia and young *maskilim* who joined the movement. Little more than this emotion was definite at the outset. The only thing clearly perceived were those aspects of Jewish life against which Zionists rebelled. They knew what they passionately rejected: the economic dependency of a people of middlemen; the enslavement of traditional Jewish culture to petrified codes, and of Jewish modernists to gentile fads and fashions; and, above all, the political incapacity of the Jews to defend themselves, or act militantly in their own behalf, because of the collapse of their social cohesion and discipline. These abhorred conditions made the new secular Zionists favorably disposed toward *anything* that seemed inherently opposed to or likely to counteract them.

In the first shock, all logically possible theories regarding the ultimate and proximate aims, the strategy and tactics of the movement, could be held at one and the same time—or even by the same person. Indeed a wide variety of such theories were formulated that at first had a provisional, academic character, and frequently varied in accordance with polemical needs. In the later development of the movement, critical issues forced a choice between alternative Zionist theories and programs. Partisans, especially those whose Zionist identification matured at such moments, constituted factional groups based on their stands on the current controversies. The persistence of such factions gave Zionism its pluralistic ideological pattern.

For the religious proto-Zionists who had been active since the 1860s, much of what the new Zionist converts deemed most radical in their views was, as was noted earlier, common ground, reminiscent of traditional attitudes towards exile and redemption. Nevertheless, by moving the focus of the pro-Palestine moment from religious-eschatological to secular Jewish concerns, Zionism posed latent ideological issues for the traditionalists in the movement—issues that became open and acute in time.

Men such as Mohilever, Pines, and Rokeah came into Hovevei Zionism out of the same background as the antecedent proto-Zionist movement. They were as much involved with that religiously based, traditionalist milieu as with the new pro-Palestinian coalition with secular Zionists, and their strategies and tactics reflected both connections. The prickly relations between Pines and Rokeah, for example, had much to do with Pines's kinship and cultural ties with leading Perushim and with Rokeah's similar connection to leading Hasidim in the Old Yishuv. Mohilever's initial problems with the Old Yishuv, and his way of dealing with them, were the same as those of the earlier proto-Zionist leaders in relation to the *halukah* establishment. Competition for funds collected in the same traditionalist circles, by essentially the same methods, produced frictions, which were resolved from time to time by agreements on the coordination of their separate efforts and by statements of support for the *halukah* by the Zionist traditionalists. And when the Turks reacted to what they perceived as a wave of nationalist immigrants by pursuing Jews in the streets and in their homes for overstaying their permitted pilgrimage time, the Old Yishuv establishment joined in the Zionists' efforts, with Western help, to have the harsh Ottoman policy rescinded, blocked, or otherwise evaded.

The major difficulty inherent in a coalition with secularists could be met by the religious conformity that the traditionalist Zionists were able at first to impose on their secularist Zionist associates, particularly on those who settled in Palestine. Secular Zionists such as Ben-Yehuda and the Biluim in Gedera (in both cases, closely associated with Pines) were willing, at least initially, to abide by the norms of traditional orthopraxy. Pines, as their friend and sponsor, supervised their outer religious conformity while being himself constrained by the suspicious surveillance of the established Old Yishuv leadership. On this basis a traditionalist Zionist could straddle both camps without being obliged by a decisive break between them to side with one against the other.

Decisions were forced in 1888–89 by an issue that set the Old Yishuv leaders against the Rothschild administration more immediately than against the Zionists. That year was another sabbatical year in the Jewish calendar, like 1880–81, which had precipitated the abandonment of the initial settlement of Petah Tikvah. The commandment to abstain from cultivating Jewish land in Erez Israel was one of the restrictive traditional rules that had turned modernists like Judah Leib Gordon away from Palestine as a place for the resettlement of immigrants. Mohilever and other Zionist rabbinical leaders in Europe were approached in 1887 by settlers in Rishon Lezion and by Rothschild's Paris representative to find a way out of the impending difficulty. After considerable debate, the rabbinical philo-Zionist leaders, backed by the dean of the Lithuanian rabbinate, Rabbi Yizhak Elhanan Spektor, agreed to authorize the cultivation of Jewish land by applying the legal fiction of a sale at a nominal price to a non-Jew for the duration of the sabbatical year, with an exclusive option to reclaim possession at its close. The sales, however, were to be executed by the rabbinical court in Jerusalem. Rothschild promptly conducted such a sale of all his holdings in Paris and expected his settlers to continue cultivation.

However, two paradoxically related complications swiftly upset this arrangement. Pines, on behalf of the Hovevei Zion, and the Rothschild administration also approached the Jerusalem rabbis for their approval. The Sephardi rabbis speedily agreed—all the more readily in view of an inquiry from the Jerusalem district governor whether a way could not be found to obviate the loss of tax revenue that failure to farm Jewish owned lands would entail. But the leading Ashkenazi rabbis in Jerusalem issued a strong, violent objection. This had a chilling effect on the baron and especially on the rabbis in Russia: they had to respect the traditional primacy of the local rabbinate in matters regarding its own territory.

A second complication that gave an even harder edge to the first was the attitude of many settlers. The sabbatical year approached on the heels of a series of particularly bitter disputes between the settlers and the Rothschild administrators. The revolt in Rishon Lezion was followed by further altercations, some involving what settlers regarded as administrative offenses against their religious sensibilities. In Ekron, settled by pious farmers, the attempt by a new Rothschild director to reduce them to hired hands was strenuously opposed. Moreover, the rabbi who had guided the settlers in their old Russian home declared himself firmly against working Jewish land in Erez Israel on the sabbatical year. Thus, the order to work the land not only ran counter to their religious loyalty but was viewed as part of the bureaucratic tyranny against which they were in revolt.

Another dispute that pitted religious traditionalism against the Rothschild administration occurred in Zikhron Yaakov. After his dismissal from the Hovevei Zion Jaffa executive, the ubiquitous Eleazar Rokeah came to live in Zikhron Yaakov, where he launched a new feud with the director of the settlement. He sent scathing reports of the religious laxity tolerated by the Zikhron administration to the journal *Havazelet*, published by his kinsman, Israel Dov Frumkin. There also came to Zikhron Yaakov a physician trained in traditional rabbinical studies who considered himself designated by Rothschild to minister to the spiritual needs as well as the physical health of the settlers. He too challenged the local administrators, particularly on matters of religious practice. The rivalry led, as in Rishon Lezion, to an explosion that ended in the usual way. The leading rebels left Zikhron Yaakov, as did after a while the director, and the settlers were reduced to submission, or were replaced by others. In the following year, Zikhron did not observe the sabbatical abstention from working its land.

Another settlement, however, did so, presenting a special problem for the Hovevei Zion. In the late 1880s, Gedera found itself in such straits that there were those in the Hovevei Zion, particularly the more rigid traditionalists, who proposed that the hapless—and godless—Biluim be encouraged to leave Erez Israel with the aid of the movement. Their patron and guide, Pines, feared that if they continued farming in the sabbatical year, even under the conditional license of the philo-Zionist rabbis, the Biluim would attract a further storm of criticism and he himself, the inspector and mentor of their religious conformity, would come under attack. Thus, together with Ekron and the traditionalist settlers of Petah Tikvah, Gedera complied with the decrees of the Ashkenazi rabbis in Jerusalem and left the land untilled in 1888–89.

This situation led to troublesome problems for all concerned: the settlers, Baron Rothschild and his agents, the Hovevei Zion of all religious colorations, and the Old Yishuv's Ashkenazi establishment. Existing relationships came under strain, and rifts that signaled the inevitable—and for Zionist traditionalists, unwelcome—development of new alignments began to appear. The secular Hovevei Zionists as well as the Rothschild administration were shocked and outraged by the settlers who complied with the Jerusalem decree of sabbatical rest and who expected to be supported in idleness. Leaders of the Zionist-rabbinical coterie, very reluctantly, were driven into a position of antagonism toward the rabbis in Jerusalem by the overriding need to mend their relations with the baron. The Ashkenazi Old Yishuv establishment, for its part, had assured the settlers that their needs would be supplied by others if their current patrons failed them—a pledge that they were unable to make good.

The uproar over these issues eventually was stilled as all the involved parties tried to restore a measure of essential tolerance. The sabbatical year was handled on subsequent occasions in the manner proposed by the Zionist rabbis. But, despite the attempts of men like Mohilever to restore their former position, bridging the gap between the Old and New Yishuv and firmly anchored in both, the role of traditionalist Zionist had become distinctly more problematic. The dispute over the sabbatical year was a crux that forced such men to align themselves openly with Western modernists and the New Yishuv. This action placed them under pressure from those who criticized their association with sinful unbelievers. But now a new crisis arose over the aggressive secularism that traditionalists perceived in the educational and cultural activities of

Ahad Haam and the Bnei Moshe. Men like Pines then joined ranks with the Old Yishuv establishment in attacking the secularist radicals.

With the appearance of Herzl's political Zionism, which tended to suppress the issue of secular versus sacral Jewish culture, Pines and like-minded traditionalist Zionists returned to the nationalist movement. Religious Zionism continued to reflect the tension of its bipolar anchorage, and its protagonists had constantly to justify themselves before two courts of public opinion, which were ruled by often opposing norms.

Asher Ginzberg, before he became famous under the nom de plume Ahad Haam, was a member of the committee that Pinsker and Lilienblum consulted in Odessa before the 1884 Kattowitz conference and one of the severe critics of the restricted aims Pinsker was forced to adopt. In 1889, he assumed responsibility as official leader of Bnei Moshe and president of the society's Odessa lodge and began to write a series of trenchant publicistic essays that marked an epoch in Hebrew letters. Through these channels he exerted a widespread and lasting influence.

Ahad Haam and his associates directed their unsparing attack against the policies of the Hovevei Zion over the whole range of pertinent issues. The leader himself was the most radical and outspoken in his criticism of the main activity of the Hovevei Zion, the colonization of the Holy Land. He demanded that no more immigrants be settled or colonies be built unless a secure legal basis were obtained first. He condemned the Rothschild-supported villages because, under the paternalistic administration, the settlers became dependent and lost their initiative along with their personal liberty. He argued that the whole project had been run without consideration of economic return, and he demanded that no more vineyards be planted until it became clear that their produce could compete in the world market. He also attacked sharply the pettiness, personal as well as organizational, to which the pointless activities of diaspora Hovevei Zionism reduced its leaders and members. He called for a new approach, sober rather than adventurous, realistic rather than fantastic, concentrating on quality rather than quantity. Above all, he demanded concentration on the preparation of the people for national tasks rather than on premature undertakings in the homeland, on "spirit" rather than "matter." He insisted in particular on education and a Hebrew cultural revival, both in Palestine and in the diaspora, in order to achieve the first prerequisite of Jewish nationalism: the reconstitution of national discipline, cohesion, and commitment to a historic goal.

The Bnei Moshe, either directly or through its influence in the general Hovevei Zion movement, carried out many specific endeavors that gave a more radically nationalist color to the activities of the 1890s. It founded the colony of Rehovot, which remained independent of direct Rothschild support and supervision. In this settlement Hebrew was spoken, and young Jewish laborers found employment when other, more traditionalist, villages rejected them as freethinkers and radical troublemakers. In the diaspora, members of the Hovevei Zion founded publication houses and produced books, journals, and pamphlets through which the Hebrew literature of the period enjoyed a nationalist, modernist revival. *Maskilim*, trained in a holy tongue and a sacred literature, rediscovered in the ancient Jewish heritage elements of a national and popular mythos: holy days not only of penitence but of national freedom and victory; legends not only of martyrdom and piety but of rebellion and heroism. They revealed to the Western and Russified intelligentsia the vision of a new Judaism, not dry, legal, ceremonial or rationalistic, but vital, epic, spontaneous, and romantic.

Such a cultural revival had much in it to reconcile the mutually estranged elements of Eastern Jewry—the traditionalists, *maskilim*, and Russified or Westernized intelligentsia. But it also had in it the elements of conflict and factional division: Bnei Moshe, the vital center of the rebellious Hovevei Zion, became, in fact, the center of the sharpest early Zionist disputes.

In spite of the great esteem in which Ahad Haam was held and the position of leadership bestowed upon him by the Bnei Moshe, his views were not shared in detail by all of the order's varied membership. The *maskilim* and Russian intelligentsia among the Hovevei Zion shared a mood of rebellion against the frustrations of the movement, and leading Hovevei Zionists everywhere were glad to join an elite secret order that sought radical new paths. For Ahad Haam himself the priorities were clear: the first thing was the revival and activation of the Jewish national consensus, through patient cultivation of a free, creative Hebrew culture. This implied severely restricting, if not abandoning, other activities, especially the ill-starred Palestine colonization, which he regarded as premature and positively demoralizing. Lilienblum, who for a brief period joined Bnei Moshe even though he fought Ahad Haam on these very issues, agreed that under existing circumstances the primary aim was to make the movement strong; but he contended that only organized activity, and especially the continuous colonization of Palestine, would build the movement. The members of Bnei Moshe were impatient with the established Hovevei Zion leadership, with which Lilienblum was identified, but on the underlying issue many were inclined to share his view rather than that of Ahad Haam, their leader and mentor. The essential

Zionist mood of this elite was militant: they wanted action, not patient preparation.

Bnei Moshe gained a powerful position in the Odessa Society, and the Jaffa office set up to organize the spurt of immigration and land purchase in Palestine in 1891. One of those identified with them was Vladimir Tiomkin, who risked large sums on behalf of the movement in the very kind of ill-advised real estate transactions that Ahad Haam abhorred. When the Turkish government's enforcement of old bans on immigration and land purchase collapsed the wave of speculation, the resulting loss of funds involved both the Jaffa committee and Bnei Moshe in a major scandal.

Even more notoriety and conflict developed over the order's attitude toward traditional Judaism. This was from the beginning a potentially divisive question among the heterogeneous membership. In an attempt to bridge differences, the initiation oath of Bnei Moshe invoked the "name of the God of Israel," a formula which Lilienblum, for one, found acceptable because of its nationalist reference (much as David Ben-Gurion in 1948 approved of the phrase "the Rock of Israel" in the new state's Declaration of Independence), while he held that such a term as the traditional "Lord of the Universe" would have offended the scruples of skeptics. In the same spirit, the order committed itself to the following, among its proposed functions:

> Without intervening in any way in the party strife of those who dispute matters of religious faith and practice, and with absolute tolerance toward their private beliefs and opinions on matters between man and God, it [the order] will raise the common national standard over all of them, endeavor to implant in all of them a common belief and opinion on matters between man and nation, and strive to make all of them cherish the common national heritage that forms our national spirit in all its various aspects; the land of our forefathers and its settlement, the Torah, language, and science of Israel, the memory and history of our forefathers, and the basic customs and national way of life of our forefathers from generation to generation.[1]

This was less than some in the traditionally minded Bnei Moshe wanted. They had tried to make such "basic customs" as Sabbath rest and the dietary laws, as well as the rituals of family purity, mandatory for all members.

On the other hand, there were those who saw at least a hint of religious coercion in the provisions adopted. Ahad Haam himself felt that "the form of the undertaking, which begins, 'In the name of the God of Israel' etc. will make it harder for many of our best people to join us—on both sides, of course—while the truth is we could well believe in men like our brethren without their invoking such guarantees. . . ." Accordingly, he had the oath changed to read "by my heart's faith and in the name of all that is precious and holy to me."[2]

In addition to such inner differences, a persistent, violent attack by traditionalist elements in Erez Israel involved the order in religious scandal and notoriety. The bone of contention was the secular-nationalist educational reform initiated in Jaffa by immigrants who formed a communal structure independent of the Jerusalem establishment and were seen as increasingly opposed to it.

The economic expansion driven by general Western investment and Rothschild and Zionist support of the new settlements built up a rapidly growing, heterogeneous urban society in Jaffa, the main Palestinian port. Alongside the large influx of Arab workers, landowners, and merchants, there was a significant accretion of Jewish residents. Some came from Sephardi communities elsewhere in the Ottoman Empire or from North Africa and were at first the predominant Jewish element (as was true in Haifa as well). With the wave of Ashkenazi immigrants in the 1880s, Russian, Rumanian, and other European Jews, together with internal migrants who moved from Jerusalem to seek new livelihoods, soon became an element of equal, and growing, weight in the community. From a small settlement of about 400 in 1812—200 Sephardim, 120 Maghrebim (North Africans), and 15 Ashkenazi families—the Jews in Jaffa increased to some 2,700 by 1891. Of these, there were now 1,600 Ashkenazim and 1,100 Sephardim and Maghrebim.

Jews in Jaffa were not generally supported by the *halukah*. They not only provided for their own needs, individually and communally, but organized institutions designed to deal with broader responsibilities arising from Jaffa's strategic location as the center and headquarters of the new Jewish resettlement project. An activist group formed in the town, made up of new immigrants with leading roles in the Hovevei Zion and Bnei Moshe together with influential Sephardim and officers of the Alliance Israélite Universelle–Rothschild combine. They built a library for the Jewish town dwellers, organized aid for newcomers arriving in Jaffa, and took a leading part in the local activities of the major Western agencies as well of the Zionists who built the New Yishuv.

In 1888, on leaving Gedera, Israel Belkind set up a private school in Jaffa, planned along the lines of the modern Hebrew schools promoted by secular nationalists in the diaspora. After two years, he was no longer able to carry the financial burden of his school and turned to the Jaffa leadership of Bnei Moshe. It was able to take over the school and expand it by forming a partnership with the Alliance, with some aid from the Hovevei Zion in Odessa. This project became a major force in the revival of Hebrew in Erez Israel—but also a central issue in disputes that arose between its sponsors and the traditionalist establishment.

The teachers, who were identified with Bnei Moshe and shared its aims, hoped to make the Jaffa school a full-scale training institute that would develop a modern curriculum, with Hebrew as the language of instruction in all subjects, and prepare teachers who would propagate the Hebrew revival throughout the Yishuv, particularly in the new settlements. The Alliance, however, imposed a much more modest program: only a few years of elementary education were provided; the use of Hebrew as the language of instruction was resisted; and a curriculum was adopted that aimed not at the education of a future cultural elite, but at vocational training for skilled or semiskilled workers. The mutually opposed objectives were pursued in a competition of Zionist teachers with Alliance-oriented trustees and administrators, which ended in compromise: the school was divided between an Alliance-directed boys' division and a girls' school conducted by the Zionists. Meanwhile, young men who wished to go on to more advanced studies went either to Mikveh Israel or, with Rothschild aid, to French schools and universities.

The Jaffa school, in spite of its limited ability to carry out the full nationalist cultural program, served as a catalyst for the consolidation of an activist group committed to that goal. Associated with the group were Zionist-minded teachers who pressed vigorously for a Hebrew-based secular program of education in the rural settlements. Here they encountered not only the resistance of some Rothschild administrators but in places like Petah Tikvah or Rishon Lezion the much more direct and open competition of traditionalists allied with the Old Yishuv establishment.

When the Jaffa school and its secular-nationalist teachers became the focus of the wider controversy, old alliances were broken and latent ideological issues that were formerly downplayed among the Hovevei Zion emerged in an embittered polemic. In particular, the bonds between Pines and such nationalists as Ben-Yehuda and the Bnei Moshe were severed. Pines, who had been assailed by the ultratraditionalists for his support of worldly education, now joined them in an assault on a school whose staff included freethinking pedagogues who publicly profaned the

Sabbath. Ben-Yehuda, who previously had accommodated his public behavior to the norms of traditionalist decorum, made his new journal *Hazvi* an organ of militant opposition to the traditionalist establishment.

In 1894, a vicious imbroglio was touched off by a Hanukkah homily published in *Hazvi* by Ben-Yehuda's father-in-law. This preachment praised the Maccabees and urged contemporary Jews to emulate their spirit. It was seized upon by the Jerusalem ultratraditionalists and laid before the Turkish governor of the city in a distorted Arabic translation as evidence that the Hovevei Zion were rebels not only against God, but also against the state. Ben-Yehuda was arrested. The *maskilim* and intelligentsia, many of whom held Jerusalemite intriguers and informers already responsible for such setbacks as the 1882 immigration ban, broke into furious outcries in the Jewish press against their foes. The traditionalists answered with a concerted campaign of vilification through the mails, addressing themselves to pious supporters of the Hovevei Zion movement. The attack was directed primarily against the pernicious secret influence of the Bnei Moshe. It succeeded, during more than a year of violent conflict, in sowing dissension and suspicion among Hovevei Zionists on whose friendly support Ahad Haam relied.

On this occasion, Yehiel Michael Pines developed themes that had been previously sketched by traditionalists at early Bnei Moshe assemblies into a full ideological attack upon secular Jewish nationalism. He thus defined the rudiments of an opposing, religious (Orthodox) Zionism.

Pines was one of the three Bnei Moshe members who constituted the Jaffa executive committee of the Hovevei Zion at the time of Tiomkin's ill-fated real estate operations. The relations within this executive committee had been strained and quarrelsome, and the subsequent investigation by Ahad Haam led to Pines's expulsion from Bnei Moshe. Now, soon after the inception of the ultratraditionalists' attack, Ahad Haam published an open letter on the role of Hovevei Zionism in reviving the "petrified" Jewish tradition. Pines, in response, formulated a critique of secularism within the Hovevei Zion camp, basing his case on broad ideological grounds.

Hitherto, he said, he had seen some value in secular Zionism, if it served to bring estranged Jews back from assimilation into the fold. But Ahad Haam and his band wanted to sow secularism among the faithful. Not only did they use their secret control of Hovevei Zionism to discourage practical settlement in Palestine, in the name of preliminary cultural preparation, they also conducted Jewish education on lines that could only encourage apostasy. Their program proposed to "eliminate everything sacred to Israel and make mere history of the Torah, poetry of the prophets, and a national language of the Holy Tongue."[3] Their whole approach, he argued, was full of logical contradictions, since the Jews were not an ordinary nation. The only national characteristics they had were a holy tongue and a common bond of history and solidarity. These could not be used, as the secularists proposed, to *create* a national consensus, since they were themselves products of an existing "national" consensus based on faith; and, within the realm of nature, an effect could not be its own cause. Apart from logic, this new secularism had to be sternly opposed because of its vicious effects. Jewish nationalism could not be separated from Jewish religion, which was its source. Jewish education had to be religious in spirit, no matter how modern in content. Accordingly, teachers without faith should be rejected because they were incapable of rearing properly educated, loyal Jews.

Following the Palestinian "boom and bust" cycle of 1891, in which the Bnei Moshe was so equivocally involved, Ahad Haam had retired from active leadership of the society, a role for which he felt ill suited and believed he had ill performed. However, he remained responsible for the secret society as its spiritual guide. During the 1894–95 conflict with the ultratraditionalists, Ahad Haam and another Bnei Moshe member of the Odessa committee offered their resignations in protest against the attacks. An investigation not only cleared the Bnei Moshe but evoked an apology from one of its most influential opponents. Yet Ahad Haam felt that the secrecy of the order, always distasteful to him, now had to be abandoned, because it had lent credence to suggestions that a powerful conspiracy was at work in the Hovevei Zion movement. In the following two or three years, the society made fruitless efforts to reorganize as an open Zionist faction, while Ahad Haam retired to the new editorial duties he assumed at that time.

In this capacity, he was the focus of controversies that served to differentiate Zionist ideologies still further. His role was no longer that of the young critic of the establishment, leader of a rebellious cultural nationalism against the practical, philanthropic Zionism of the Odessa committee and against the tyrannical Orthodoxy of the ultratraditionalists. Now *he* was the conservative editor against whom creative younger men rebelled. Ahad Haam's editorial policy favored informative and analytical material over belles lettres. He had a didactic bent reminiscent of the positivists who had dominated Russian criticism in the 1860s and whose disciples held sway in Hebrew letters in the 1870s. In addition, he demanded concentration on *Jewish* rather than general topics, since, he believed, the main object of Hebrew literature was to cultivate the national spirit, the characteristic ethos of Judaism, and to develop the national consensus, not to adulterate it with importations foreign to its essential character. This attitude provoked younger writers to vigorous dissent, as they were committed to a universal (that is, contemporary Western) culture in which aesthetic sensibility was more highly valued than moral rigor. The antihistorical influence of Nietzsche was strongly felt among them.

The same generation of younger Zionists also turned impatiently against Ahad Haam's Zionist policies. Cultural Zionism was all very well—though it became sterile and parochial under the control of Ahad Haam's neo-Judaism—but the immediate material interests of the suffering Jews were far more pressing. It was a time of political oppression and economic misery, and those who matured in that rebellious generation could not be told to work patiently toward a remote future when decisive action would become possible. They responded eagerly to challenges for immediate action, and these were offered freely in the revolutionary and workers' movement and in the lively ethnic politics of the turn of the century in Central and Eastern Europe.

Like a moving storm center that spins opposing winds out of a quiet atmosphere, Ahad Haam provoked sharply defined opposition by the controversial positions he took as political critic and editor. But not even when he was chief of Bnei Moshe did his ideology confront opponents with the choice of submission or rebellion because of policies he imposed on an organization to which they belonged. The opposition, no less than his own stand, represented an essentially academic rather than organized, factional partisanship, no matter how sharply defined and polemical the tone of the debate.

In the Zionist organization reconstructed by the genius of Theodor Herzl, all the old Zionist views, together with the new political Zionist ideology, were brought within the framework of a disciplined body, committed to action. Ideological differences in this setting eventually had to be organized in the form of factions, if they were to survive. In the course of time, such factions did emerge. The ideological positions by which they were defined often paralleled the alternative positions abstractly outlined during the long, many-sided debate with Ahad Haam.

II

Ahad Haam has given the following succinct account of the last period in the history of the Bnei Moshe: "So it continued to 'exist' in a state of neither life nor death for about another year. And in the summer of

1897, when the political Zionist movement arose, the society spontaneously dissolved under the impact of the tumult in Basle."[4]

The description applies, to some extent, to the effect of political Zionism on the whole Hovevei Zion organization. Already a weak and declining movement at the time of the advent of Herzl, Hovevei Zionism was largely absorbed into the new world organization. But the process was neither so rapid nor so simple and complete as in Ahad Haam's sketch of the demise of the Bnei Moshe.

Hovevei Zionism in 1897 consisted of three elements: first, a dwindling popular base, increasingly traditionalist and conservative in character, still organized in residual groups in Eastern Europe and the immigrant colonies in major cities abroad; second, disgruntled intellectuals, once consolidated to a degree by Ahad Haam, but now organized mainly in the form of Eastern European student societies in Western universities; and third, leadership groups in places such as Odessa, Saint Petersburg, Berlin, London, Paris, and New York, who gave modest support to Palestinian colonization in cooperation with influential, non-Zionist, Western Jewish philanthropic agencies. Herzl's new organization absorbed all three elements, but not completely, nor all at once, nor at the same rate, nor without incurring the growth of an internal opposition. The reports of the First Zionist Congress aroused a lively response among the popularly based local organizations. Herzl enjoyed the immediate and lasting support, not to say adulation, of rank-and-file Hovevei Zionists. The rise of political Zionism not only restored the enthusiasm of the existing groups and brought old members back to activity, but extended the movement's ranks far beyond the old limits. At the same time, the old societies represented vested interests: even those who did not question the new views and loyally supported the new activities did not so easily submit to the discipline of the new organization in local matters.

Student Zionists were among the most enthusiastic participants in the First Congress. They had been urging the convocation of a new Zionist assembly to revive the movement in the years before Herzl appeared, and some of them took an active part from the beginning in Herzl's preparations for the congress. But they were also fully conscious of their status as veteran Zionists, with a longer, more intimate knowledge of the movement's aims than Herzl possessed. Committed as they were to Herzl's leadership, they were also responsive when Ahad Haam launched a caustic attack upon Herzl's methods. They, too, felt uneasy about Herzl's autocratic and adventurous tactics and his shallow disregard of cultural Zionist concerns. They were increasingly disturbed by the implied total suspension of colonization in Palestine while Turkish authorization and international support by European powers were fruitlessly pursued. They were prominent among the first of Herzl's factional opponents, and before the end of his brief, galvanic leadership they established a formally organized party of dissent.

The most resistant to the enticement of Herzlian political Zionism were the leadership groups of Hovevei Zion who conducted the movement's Palestine activities and maintained contact with non-Zionist philanthropic agencies. They had a vested interest in the existing resettlement efforts, which Herzl made the butt of his most vigorous attacks; they also had a vital stake in good relations with the Western philanthropists, who, by rejecting Herzl's overtures, had made themselves his most immediate foes. Nevertheless, political Zionism was a direct expression of the mystique of autoemancipation, which had made most of them, especially the Russians, into Zionists in the first instance. Eventually, many such persons became active in the World Zionist Organization and, through their leadership in the local, countrywide organizations, exercised a powerful influence in the congress. At the end of Herzl's career, such men too were prominent in the organized opposition to his policies.

Herzl's own attitude toward Zionist parliamentary politics was every bit as odd and equivocal as one might expect in the founding father of so improbable a liberation movement. His strategy for securing a Jewish state did not call for a parliament as an instrument of policy. His analysis indicated that the keys to success were financial power and imaginative diplomacy: by offering, on behalf of a society of Jews, to solve Turkey's fiscal difficulties, he might obtain a charter for a Jewish company to colonize Palestine; and by offering to remove excess Jews from areas of severe antisemitism, he might obtain the support of European powers. Both objectives, he at first assumed, could be most effectively attacked if he could persuade the powerful Jewish philanthropists to adopt his plan and establish the necessary instrumentalities. Only when the Rothschilds and Hirsches rebuffed him did he resort to a popular movement. He now regarded the World Zionist Organization as his "Society of Jews," the platform for his diplomacy; and he expected the WZO to establish the "Jewish Company" in the form of a bank (funded by popular subscription, if wealthy financiers failed him) to serve as his financial instrument.

Herzl was well aware, of course, that constructing the Zionist Congress in the likeness of a Jewish parliament was his own decisive historic achievement. But this form of organization presented certain immediate tactical difficulties. He could build his diplomacy on the base of the congress only if it appeared firm, united, powerful, and reasonable in its social as well as political aims. Herzl could achieve this public effect at the congress only by applying all his skills in order to control the inherent tendencies of a popular movement toward impulsiveness, factionalism, indecisiveness, and irrationality. His task, as he saw it during the First Congress, was to perform in public "an egg dance" upon the following array of eggs, visible only to himself, the performer:

1. Egg of the *N. Fr. Pr.* [*Neue Freie Presse*, the Viennese newspaper where he was employed] which I must not compromise or furnish a pretext for easing me out.
2. Egg of the Orthodox.
3. Egg of the Modernists.
4. Egg of Austrian patriotism.
5. Egg of Turkey, of the Sultan.
6. Egg of the Russian government, against which nothing unpleasant may be said, although the deplorable situation of the Russian Jews *will* have to be mentioned.
7. Egg of the Christian denominations, on account of the Holy Places . . .
   Egg Edmond Rothschild.
   Egg Hovevei Zion in Russia.
   Egg of the colonists, whose help from Rothschild must not be queered, *tout en considerant leurs miseres.*[5]

With such a view, even though Herzl proclaimed the Zionist congress a Jewish forum where at last the Jewish problem would be raised for free, frank, and public discussion, he could not welcome unrestricted debate, let alone the organization of factions. He counted it one of the benefits inherent in the Zionist movement that it made room, for the first time, for the whole range of current ideologies within a Jewish consensus; but he was firmly convinced that Zionists should wait until the state was founded before organizing in rival political parties.

Among the ideologies that could be expected to produce factional organizations, Herzl had a well-defined, rather subtle attitude toward two: socialism and Orthodoxy. Herzl's political models were such modern conservative virtuosos as Disraeli and Bismarck, who understood how to steal the thunder of popular and labor radicalism. He regarded the appeal of leftism to the oppressed Jewish déclassés as a major danger, and he believed Zionism could provide an outlet for their frustrated energies. This was not only his personal view, but a good argument with which to win the sympathy of European powers. Thus Zionism, incorporating everything valuable in socialist programs, would make rebellious socialism unnecessary, even after the Jewish state arose; and certainly there was no need for socialist parties in the Zionist Congress at a time when the immediate objective was to obtain the support of the powers and the sultan's consent for a charter to resettle Palestine.

Herzl's attitude toward Orthodoxy—in his eyes, the Jewish analogue of clericalism in a Christian state—manifested the same conservatism and aristocratic sophistication. It goes without saying that traditionalist Judaism could make no claim on one's private belief, but it deserved to be publicly respected and cultivated as a bulwark of popular loyalty to the national cause. The power and magnificence of the "courts" of Hasidic *zadikim* fascinated Herzl. His diaries refer repeatedly to the "Wonder Rabbi of Sadagora" as he speculates about the possible uses of the rabbis in creating and sustaining the Jewish state. He is equally interested when he believes he has penetrated behind the pious facade to the shrewdly cynical tactics by which these clerics maintain their power, and even when he has to deal with clerical politicians at the Zionist Congress. His comments then show none of the contempt and anger with which he assails the motives of other Zionists who, at one time or another, obstructed his aims. They reveal instead tolerant, if amused, appreciation.

Thus, if Herzl wanted to prevent the emergence of a religious Zionist faction, it was not, as with socialism, because he thought that one of the functions of Jewish nationalism was to serve as a substitute for religion. He simply wished to eliminate from the congress debates any issues that could divide the Zionist camp and divert attention from the political objectives he considered primary. This did not mean, of course, that Herzl ignored political crosscurrents that affected the course of his policy, whether in the Jewish community at large or in the narrower confines of the Zionist movement. He was, in fact, sensitive to the smallest maneuvers of friend and foe alike; and, in his efforts to impose his own view, he frequently found useful allies among the Orthodox Zionists.

Such leaders did come to the Second Zionist Congress in 1898, and in some force. However, they showed little interest in signing a counterprotest against the "Protest Rabbis," who issued an anti-Zionist manifesto before the First Congress. Instead, they formulated demands, to which Herzl responds in his diary:

During the Congress I also had a secret contest with the rabbis of the blackest stripe who had come to join the movement. They wanted concessions, which I denied them. I felt that they were yielding and wanted to salvage whatever they could from their defeat. When I made no concessions to them, they went along even without them.[6]

Herzl's diaries generally show little interest in the congress sessions, and this was not one of the exceptional meetings that captured his imagination. Consequently, his record reflects only obscurely what actually happened.

Orthodox leaders from Russia and Poland had no reason to share the anti-Zionism of Western "Protest Rabbis," who feared that a Jewish congress might produce an impression of "dual loyalties" or suggest a "state within a state," thus imperiling civic emancipation. The rabbis from Eastern Europe were no less interested than the secularist Zionists in strengthening the internal discipline and autonomy of the Jewish community—of course, under their own control; they had even less faith in, or desire for, social integration among the gentiles; and they had been lending practical support to Jewish settlement in Zion since long before secular Zionism arose.

Fifteen years of cooperation with secularists in the Hovevei Zion movement had led them to develop new ideological distinctions. They now accepted, and adopted as their own, a "pure Zionism" that went beyond the religious proto-Zionism of the 1860s by seeking both an economic solution for Eastern European Jewish emigrants and the political conditions for such a solution in Palestine. They rejected, on the other hand, the new "cultural Zionism" represented by Ahad Haam and his followers. These distinctions were sharply focused in the preliminary conference held in Warsaw by the large Russian delegation on its way to the Second Zionist Congress in Basle.

The majority of Russian delegates wanted to draft resolutions for the congress session committing the world organization to the "practical" and "cultural" Zionism pursued in Russia. They hoped to realize the following objectives, vaguely outlined in subparagraphs of the First Congress's Basle Program as means for attaining the main aim, a national home for the Jews in Palestine:

1. The promotion on appropriate lines of the colonization of Palestine by Jewish agricultural and industrial workers;. . . .
2. The strengthening and fostering of Jewish national sentiment and consciousness.[7]

The latter point touched off all the differences over the issue of Jewish culture developed in the Hovevei Zion movement over the past years. Among Orthodox Zionists it triggered well-established responses.

During the period of Rabbi Samuel Mohilever's dominance, a council of eminent rabbis was appointed to oversee Hovevei Zionist activities, though it had no well-defined authority. Now at Warsaw it was proposed that a rabbinical conference be held, at Zionist expense, to create a rabbinical committee authorized to supervise all Zionist educational endeavors, as well as all WZO propaganda and agitation. The already existing Zionist executive would be left free to administer "pure Zionist" activities, such as diplomacy and resettlement, as it saw fit. Another, more moderate rabbi favored a second expedient also reminiscent of Mohilever: since cultural programs could not be pursued in unity by Zionists, the WZO should undertake no cultural projects of its own but should support the existing projects of secularists and traditionalists alike, under proper safeguards that respected Jewish tradition.

These Orthodox views were rejected in Warsaw, and the Russian delegation came to the congress with a resolution that strongly supported cultural Zionist programs. The Orthodox delegates, however, tried to press their own proposals. Rabbi Elijah Akiba Rabinovitz of Poltava, who had fought in Warsaw for a rabbinical committee to supervise all Zionist educational, propaganda, and agitational work, now lobbied for the same demand at Basle. He thought he had achieved a compromise with the chairman of the cultural commission, the Haham (rabbi) of the Sephardi congregation in London, Dr. Moses Gaster. The commission was to propose the appointment to the Zionist Action Committee of a group of rabbis who should be consulted on "every spiritual question relating to our holy religion." In addition, the cultural commission was to report to the congress the original Orthodox proposal for an independent rabbinical council with clear-cut and broad authority over all Zionist education, propaganda, and agitation. On these conditions, Rabinovitz agreed not to present his resolution from the floor. But Gaster neither submitted a proposal for a rabbinical group in the Action Committee nor reported the Orthodox proposal. The cultural commission's resolution included no more than Herzl had already promised the Orthodox faction when he failed to appease them at an earlier meeting— a promise that the Zionist movement would never do anything offensive to religion:

Zionism seeks not only the economic and political, but also the spiritual (*geistige*) renaissance of the Jewish people, while it stands on the ground of modern culture, holding fast to all its achievements. Zionism will undertake nothing contrary to the religious laws of Judaism.[8]

This formula was reluctantly accepted by most of the Orthodox leaders at the congress, but not by the Rabbi of Poltava. While declaring himself still a "pure Zionist," he published a strong attack on the perfidy displayed at the Second Zionist Congress. He canvassed other opponents, with a view to creating an organized body of Orthodox opinion that could negotiate on equal terms with the Zionists for an agreement to unite through allocating the functions of "pure" and "spiritual" Zionism according to the Orthodox proposal he favored.

The rabbis who stayed with the WZO did not conceal their displeasure either. Under such pressure, Herzl came to regard the cultural debate as an unnecessary nuisance at the congress. He made his attitude clear to the Third Congress in his reply to critics during the "general debate":

> Dr. Tschlenow also finds our report lacking in respect to the cultural question. Ladies and gentlemen! Yesterday I had a private conversation with Dr. Gaster. I shall abuse no confidence in what I tell you here. I merely want to mention what I asked him. What I asked was this: It is possible that the cultural question may come up while I chair the Congress. Now, I should not like it to seem as though I don't understand the matter. Tell me please, what is it? What is this cultural question, which, as I hear, is being so vehemently discussed in the corridors and committee rooms? (Stormy applause and handclapping.) As this was a private conversation, and anyway of a friendly and humorous kind, I shall not tell you the answer.[9]

Despite Herzl's reluctance, the "cultural question" continued to be discussed regularly at the Zionist congresses, and regularly produced disputes between the Orthodox and cultural Zionists. Since nothing significant was done by the world Zionist movement in spite of the resolutions adopted, the Orthodox Zionists remained reasonably satisfied with the situation. But proponents of Zionist cultural programs were seriously discontented; and this was an important factor in the growing opposition to Herzl.

As the Fourth Zionist Congress was held in London, Herzl was even more anxious than usual to cut off ideological squabbles on side issues that could spoil its effect as a political demonstration. The Orthodox came in force and were well represented on the cultural commission. Cultural Zionists on the commission, concerned that previous congress resolutions had been without effect, tried to frame one making it obligatory on all Zionists to work actively toward the moral and national elevation of the spiritual condition of the Jews. Since no agreement could be reached, a compromise proposal was offered by one member, in the commission and in the plenary session, amending the draft to read "religious, moral, and national." This proposal merely provoked violent debate. Herzl, in any case, was anxious to suppress the whole issue, and it had been scheduled for consideration late in the session. The result was that, by a slim margin of five votes, all action on the cultural question was tabled.

The protagonists of cultural Zionism were angered by this outcome but also encouraged by their demonstration of strength. They began to organize with an eye to the next congress in the following year. The initiative was taken by Zionist student societies in Western universities, with Chaim Weizmann, then a young chemistry instructor in Geneva, playing the most active role. In Russia, they were supported by Zionist youth societies, study circles, and incipient labor groups—that is, by all those who wanted to formulate a "progressive" or "democratic" Zionism in order to attract youth, labor, and the intellectual avant-garde. They felt that Herzl's personal style and his combine of bourgeois and traditionalist Zionists were, in good part, to blame for the alienation of such elements from the nationalist movement, and they wished to make good the loss. At the Fifth Zionist Congress, in December 1901, the "Democratic Faction" appeared as an organized force, expressed opposition on a number of issues, and produced a particularly stormy incident over the cultural question.

Although the Democratic Faction represented the first attempt at organized opposition to Herzl, he was not completely antagonized by its appearance. At the first reports of a projected conference of Zionist youth, Herzl was indeed concerned at the possibility of reckless talk that might disturb his current negotiations. But these fears were alleviated by Weizmann's assurance that the conference would avoid public sessions and take up no specifically political issues. Herzl considered the main source of his troubles within the Zionist organization to be the vested interests and veteran Hovevei Zion leadership of local affiliates. Any new leadership that arose might be preferable and perhaps also more responsive to his own influence. Thus, at the Fifth Zionist Congress, he secured changes in the structural principles of the movement that made it easier for new groups (including, therefore, ideological factions—something that was not his intention) to organize outside the framework of the existing Zionist territorial organizations and come in direct contact with the central governing bodies of the world organization. He also demonstrated his confidence and the hopes he placed in the young rebels by entrusting successively to two of them, the German students Berthold Feiwel and Martin Buber, the editorship of his own paper, the organization journal *Die Welt*.

Nevertheless, the cultural question provoked a severe clash between Herzl and the Democratic Faction at the Fifth Congress. The young rebels, led by the Berlin Russian student chief Leo Motzkin, had shown their militancy in a number of preliminary demonstrations before this delicate issue arose. The faction was determined not to repeat the history of the fourth and previous congresses, when resolutions on cultural activities were delayed until the end of the congress, a procedure that crippled discussion and blocked the adoption of effective decisions. Because of their pressure, Martin Buber was able to present cultural resolutions relatively early in the session. But when the discussion grew lengthy and Herzl proposed to put off action until other—in his view, more immediately necessary—actions had been adopted, the Democratic Faction marched out in protest. Herzl stood firm on the procedure he favored, and in the end the faction returned to the session. They then saw resolutions more or less satisfactory to them adopted under Herzl's aegis.

The Democratic Faction was now well launched and had reason to intensify its efforts in order to achieve more decisive success. The group did initiate a number of significant activities: journalism and publishing (the *Jüdischer Verlag*), a statistical bureau, and a fairly detailed project for a Jewish university. But all these projects were conducted independent of the factional organization and of each other. The faction itself failed to build an effective structure. After the next congress, it disappeared altogether because of a new issue that divided Zionists: Herzl's proposal to investigate Uganda as an alternative, at least temporarily, to the exclusive concentration on resettlement in Zion.

On this question, most of the Democratic Faction members found themselves in agreement with some veteran Zionists, such as Menahem Mendel Ussishkin, who had previously opposed the progressives as a divisive force. The new partners developed an ideological synthesis, counterposing "practical Zionism" to Herzl's "political Zionism." After Herzl's death in 1904, a long struggle ensued during which this school of thought grew increasingly influential and gradually took over full power in the World Zionist Organization, as well as in the Eastern European territorial organizations. They thus had no need to organize in the new forms created by the Fifth Congress, which enabled ideological minorities and other independent Zionist groups to enjoy a direct relationship to the central Zionist leadership structure. This possibility was utilized by other groups, stimulated more or less immediately by the developments at the Fifth Congress. First to do so (apart from nonideo-logical Zionist societies and fraternal orders) were the Orthodox Zion-ists, who organized Mizrahi. Somewhat later, labor Zionist groups, some of whom had begun to develop within the milieu created by the Dem-ocratic Faction, emerged as independent socialist Zionist parties.

The demonstrations and relative success of the Democratic Faction at the Fifth Zionist Congress in 1901 had an ominous look not only to the Orthodox but to many of Herzl's partisans in Russian Zionism. At the suggestion of the latter, an Orthodox leader, Rabbi Isaac Jacob Reines of Lida, convoked a meeting in February 1902 in Vilna. Most of the participants were opposed to cultural activity by the WZO and com-mitted to "pure" or political Zionism. Others, notably the Orthodox scholar and intellectual Rabbi Zev Jawitz, could not conceive of Zionism without a positive cultural program. Their view, fully developed by Ja-witz in later years along the lines of his close associate Pines's doctrines, specified an inherent functional relationship between Zionism and Ju-daism: the two were mutually dependent in the fullest sense. There could be no true Zionism except one that was thoroughly traditional, and no vital Orthodoxy except one revived by applying itself to all the social, legal, and cultural problems of a free Jewish society in Zion. In 1902, however, this was a minority viewpoint which was not elaborated, even in documents written by Jawitz such as the first manifesto of the new organization. The majority view was also expressed in the form of the organization adopted at Vilna. It was decided to organize not an inde-pendent religious Zionist body, but a "spiritual center" for Zionism, like that of Rabbi Samuel Mohilever (and under the same name, Mizrahi), which would be integrally related to the territorial organization of Rus-sian Zionists.

The new ideological factions clashed at the conference of Russian Zionists held in Minsk in September 1902. By this time Mizrahi was sufficiently strong to bring to the conference double the delegate strength of the Democratic Faction, but the nonfactional delegates outnumbered the combined strength of both factions by the same proportion.

The cultural question was, as usual, hotly debated. The main pres-entation on this topic was made by Ahad Haam, as it had been in 1898 in Warsaw. He proposed, first, that a worldwide nationalist cultural organization be organized, which would be independent of the World Zionist Organization but would cooperate with it. Weizmann, on behalf of the Democratic Faction, opposed this suggestion, just as he had re-jected a similar proposal by Ahad Haam to the young progressives when they were planning the Democratic Faction itself. On the other hand,

Ahad Haam's second suggestion, that the Zionist federation set up separate commissions for secular-nationalist and religious educational and cultural activity, was endorsed by Weizmann. In plenary session, the Orthodox passionately repeated their usual plea to avoid the divisive cultural issue, which could only alienate the community from Zionism, but they were won to a different position in private conferences. They accepted the proposal for two distinct trends of Zionist educational and cultural work. In a sign of agreement, Reines shook hands with Weizmann amid tumultuous applause, and one of the rabbis pronounced the blessing for peace from the platform.

The issues that were opened up in Mizrahi's first year were not finally decided by the measures adopted then, but continued to be discussed in the movement. The beginning that was made in Russia attracted attention elsewhere, and in 1904 it was thought necessary to consolidate the Orthodox Zionists on a global scale. A convention was called in Pressburg (Bratislava), the center of Hungarian Orthodoxy, which was renowned for its hard-bitten conservatism and for maintaining a separate community from the liberal and moderate Hungarian Jews. To organize a religious Zionist world organization in this environment was a triumph for Jewish nationalism. But the move also marked a drift toward greater independence within the Zionist organization. An Orthodox ideological movement on a world scale required a more elaborate structure than a "spiritual center" within the Russian Zionist organization. The convention also added to the existing "spiritual center," commanded by Rabbi Reines in Lida, a second headquarters for work in Central and Western Europe. This was located in Frankfurt, which, like Hungary, was a center of Orthodox communal separatism. As Russia entered into a new time of troubles in 1904–5, control of the whole movement was assigned to the Frankfurt headquarters. Under its aegis, Mizrahi completed the transition to a full-fledged independent Zionist federation (or "world union," as these formations were later named).

At this time, the World Zionist Organization entered into a period of frustration, reorganization, and bitter personal and factional strife. Herzl's proposal to consider resettling in East Africa in 1903 threatened the unity of the movements, and indeed after his death the conflict over Uganda caused splinter groups to break away. Herzl's action implied recognition that the chances of obtaining a charter to resettle Palestine en masse were remote. The Young Turk revolution of 1908 produced an explicit Zionist acknowledgment of this fact. Alternative Zionist activities—small-scale, gradual colonization in Palestine, Hebraist cultural activity, and intensified concern with Jewish social politics in the diaspora communities—were pressed by practical and progressive Zionists, particularly by the Eastern European territorial organizations, and were rather reluctantly adopted by the World Zionist Organization.

Nevertheless, the Zionist Congress continued to elect to the presidency of the movement a devotee of Herzl's policies, David Wolffsohn, who insisted on the same highly centralized, even personal, control of the movement that Herzl had exercised. This stand produced a condition of endemic rebellion in the Eastern territorial organizations against the central leadership. Yielding to this pressure, and also to a growing cardiac weakness that caused his death a few years later, Wolffsohn agreed to a reorganization plan, formulated at a Zionist conference in Berlin in 1910 and adopted by the Tenth Zionist Congress in 1911, which enabled the practical Zionists to gain effective control of the organization.

The Orthodox Zionists knew what to expect at the Tenth Congress, for the Zionist "peace" conference of the previous year clearly foreshadowed significant changes. With the practical Zionists about to take command of the movement, one could certainly anticipate an attempt to make the world organization actively responsible for a cultural program.

In anticipation of the approaching debate, the Orthodox Zionists met in Berlin shortly before the congress and agreed on a resolution of their own:

> It is the duty of every Zionist, all Zionist organizations, groups, and federations to contribute to their full capacity to the advancement of the Hebrew language and literature. Each federation, in its own spirit and according to its own conscience, shall render account to the Congress of its cultural activity.[10]

The discussion of the cultural question at the congress was, for the first time, introduced by a presentation in Hebrew and conducted by the chairman in Hebrew. After further consideration in committee, the following report and resolutions, presented by the cultural commission, were approved:

> The commission constituted by the Congress, consisting of representatives of all groups and federations, declares: The several trends and factions in the Congress agree in the conviction that our cultural and educational activity is intimately bound up with the Hebrew language and with the whole cultural legacy accumulated through millennia by our people.
>
> The commission, on the grounds of this conviction, has the honor to submit to the Congress for adoption the following resolutions:

I. The Tenth Zionist Congress instructs the Smaller Action Committee to organize and control cultural activities in Palestine and the Orient.

II. The Tenth Zionist Congress declares its intention that nothing which is contrary to the Jewish religion should be undertaken by any institutions for cultural activity created by the Zionist organizations.

III. The Congress declares cultural activity in diaspora countries to be an autonomous concern of the several territorial organizations and federations; but it obligates every Zionist and all territorial organizations and federations to work for the advancement and dissemination of Jewish national culture in all fields of Jewish creativity and folk life.[11]

This formula was accepted, however reluctantly, by rabbis representing the Orthodox in the cultural commission. But even as the congress debated it, some Mizrahi members made clear their intransigent opposition. A party conference was held in Berlin immediately after the congress to consider the situation. The Frankfurt leadership proposed that Mizrahi should now leave the Zionist organization. Upon the defeat of this proposal, some of these leaders themselves withdrew and, in the following year, joined German Orthodox separatist leaders and Eastern European traditionalist opponents of Zionism in forming a general Orthodox world organization, Agudat Israel.

In the course of time a clear, hard ideological distinction developed between this body and Mizrahi. Agudat Israel eventually set itself up in direct opposition to the Zionists both in Erez Israel and in the diaspora: while the Zionists claimed to be authoritative spokesmen of the political will of the Jewish people, Agudat Israel's rival claim to be the Jewish people's legitimate spokesman rested on the authority of a council of rabbis, considered to be the authentic interpreter of the divine law to which all Jews were bound. The religious Zionists defined maximum and minimum objectives that enabled them to work within the consensus of the world Zionist body. They aimed ultimately to persuade or maneuver the whole Jewish people, through Zionism, into complete submission to traditional Jewish law, adapted to the new demands of a restored Zion; and in the meantime they cooperated directly with the political and economic Zionist activities and conducted parallel cultural activities, so long as the Zionist organization respected Jewish tradition in its public appearances and facilities. Agudat Israel, on the other hand, began with separation from the secularist Zionists and later opposed them vigorously on their own chosen ground, the political affairs of Palestine.

It was not until the end of World War I, however, that this opposition was fully crystallized. The founding conference of Agudat Israel declared its intention to avoid political matters; members of Mizrahi not only participated on this occasion but continued a relationship with both organizations for some time. Moreover, some Mizrahi activities remained under the influence and authority of men who were now more closely associated with Agudat Israel.

Thus, the development of the characteristic partisan Zionist character of Mizrahi, both in ideology and in practical activities, was masked and retarded by the continuing obscurity of its relations with Agudat Israel. After the war, however, the break between the two became clear and irrevocable. At that time, Mizrahi intensified and expanded its specific Zionist functions, stamping its own ideological image on many emerging institutions.

III

As the diaspora conducted an ideological struggle over the issue of culture and religion, significant developments of immediate practical effect took place in Erez Israel. Local needs and local initiatives rather than the policy of nationalist leaders abroad brought about a critical advance in the revival of spoken Hebrew and a major development of secular education conducted in Hebrew under the direction of nationalist pedagogues.

Despite the restricted Jewish influx from Europe in the latter 1890s, internal growth and new settlers from other Ottoman regions and Muslim areas, together with travelers who overstayed the legal term, continued to expand the Yishuv's institutional structure. The old-style schools of the Ashkenazi and Sephardi establishments expanded, and immigrants from North Africa, Syria, Yemen, and remoter Asian territories set up their own communities and schools on traditional lines. Access to the modernizing influence of Western Jewish philanthropists was available in schools maintained by the Alliance Israélite Universelle, the Austrian Israelitische Allianz, and the Anglo-Jewish Association. After the Hilfsverein der deutschen Juden was founded in 1901, it embarked on a vigorous campaign to rival the French Alliance Israélite Universelle as a sponsor of Jewish education in Palestine. In the Western-supported schools, foreign languages and other secular studies were provided as a supplement for a core curriculum of traditional Jewish religious studies; in most cases, the schooling provided was limited to the elementary requirements for self-support as an artisan or trader at the existing stage of economic development in Palestine. These schools provided an opening for some nationally minded, Hebraist teachers—especially so the Hilfsverein schools.

Zionism implied a commitment to broader, more ambitious objectives. In the absence of responsibility for institutions comparable in scale to those of the Old Yishuv or the Western philanthropists, proponents of cultural Zionism were free to develop far-reaching plans for education in the spirit of secular nationalism. They pressed for schooling that was not restricted to four elementary grades but advanced to the *gymnasium* level and, beyond that, to a Hebrew university in Palestine. Their militant activists insisted on Hebrew as the language of instruction not simply in Jewish studies, but in all subjects, including the most technical—a proposal that implied an extraordinary, deliberately accelerated development of a language that had been confined to very narrow uses for centuries. They envisaged a program of retraining aimed not only to make self-supporting artisans or tradesmen out of indigent, dependent Jews, but to transform every aspect of their character and lives, which were held to be degraded by centuries of oppression in exile. The new Hebrew-speaking Yishuv was to be based on productive working farmer families, rooted in their own soil. They were to be free and proud soldiers, if need be, and to possess a broad liberal culture as well as an intimate understanding and creative mastery of the Hebrew heritage. Erez Israel was to be transformed socially as well as economically by their dedicated labors.

Thus, when in 1906, under a resolution of the Seventh Zionist Congress of the presiding year, Bezalel, a Zionist-inspired arts and crafts school, was established in Jerusalem, it aimed not simply to provide vocational training for the local Yishuv, on the lines of already existing philanthropic institutions; its founders, the artists Boris Schatz and Ephraim Moses Lilien, hoped to create a new Jewish-Palestinian art style, embodying Eastern and Mediterranean influences with the traditions of craftsmanship that Jews brought with them from their varied backgrounds. At the Eleventh Zionist Congress in 1913, a proposal to establish a Jewish university in Palestine, originally advanced at the First Congress in 1897, was at last launched—at least in the form of an exploratory commission headed by Chaim Weizmann. In the circumstances of that time, the projected university could be imagined as the capstone of the Hebrew educational network that already existed in a rudimentary form in Erez Israel. Creating the elementary and secondary schools that such a university could draw on was not the achievement of the WZO, however, but of local activists neither guided nor supported by it. The WZO carefully avoided the prickly cultural question in Herzl's time; it adopted vague resolutions favorable to cultural nationalism at the Fifth (1903) and Tenth (1911) Congresses but did not commit itself to any specific direct responsibility as a central body.

A more active, though still secondary role was played by the Russian Hovevei Zion. Bnei Moshe, and its offshoots that continued to be active after its demise, had a major impact on the nationalist Hebrew revival in the diaspora; it had a more diffuse effect in Erez Israel, achieved mainly through the initiative of individuals who were once associated with the order. The Odessa committee extended some aid for secular Hebrew education in Palestine, especially after the prospects for major resettlement projects dwindled. Given the limits of its fiscal resources, the Odessa committee could not attempt major administrative tasks on the lines of the Rothschild–ICA project. It did become a source of grants for communal services in the villages and for other applicants who proposed suitable undertakings—a procedure that imposed a much lighter burden of supervision on the beneficiaries and reduced the Odessa committee's power of direct control.

The most significant contribution of the Odessa committee to the Hebrew revival in Palestine was its role in the organization of a teachers' union, an association that became an active local force behind nationalist reforms in the schools of Erez Israel. This came about as an incidental effect of a broader aim repeatedly pursued by Hovevei Zion leaders: to unite all elements in the Yishuv in a common, representative communal organization. During Mohilever's pilgrimage in 1890, he sought not only to smooth relations between the *halukah* and the Hovevei Zionist fund collections but to bridge differences between Sephardim and Ashkenazim in the Old Yishuv. Ahad Haam, coming shortly after, urged the agents of various land-purchasing societies to work through the Hovevei Zionist central agency in Jaffa. Success in both cases was significant but temporary. The most ambitious attempt was that of Menahem Mendel Ussishkin in his 1903 mission to Erez Israel. He was able to assemble a broad selection of leaders from both the New and Old Yishuv, including activists in the Zionist and philanthropic services; at the same time, he sponsored a meeting of Jewish teachers at which they united in a general, professional union. The major objective, to unite the Yishuv in a generally shared communal structure, quickly collapsed under the pressure of internal strains and the coolness or opposition to it of the Yishuv's diaspora sponsors, both Zionist and philanthropic. The teachers' union, however, survived and flourished—if not as a functional apparatus, then as a coherent, persistent influence for nationalist, progressive pedagogy in Erez Israel.

The teachers' union did not directly control a nationalist school system, but it set standards and provided models for a growing corps of dedicated adherents. Teachers among its leaders prepared textbooks, aiming at a graded Hebrew-language curriculum in all subjects taught by its devotees in elementary and secondary schools. Its professional publication and periodic conferences transcribed into Hebrew, for the public as well as for its members, relevant materials from current progressive pedagogical literature, especially in Central Europe. It provided a certification service for teachers and school committees who wanted standards of qualification to provide instruction, and provided educational guidance for schools committed to the secular nationalist aims; in the same vein, it offered standard examinations for various stages of the projected school system. In every case, it could only offer these services but not impose itself as a professional authority. Those willing and eager to accept the guidance provided formed a force within the community that moved it in the direction of secular nationalism. Thereby they aggravated existing tensions and provoked the protagonists of traditional Judaism, especially among educators and rabbis, to sharper opposition— but also to rivalry by emulation.

A hard line of total avoidance and excommunication was the primary and most salient but not the exclusive response of the traditionalist Ashkenazi establishment to the challenge of modernist education. In one sector of the growing Yishuv, the new rural settlements, they undertook to compete with the modernists on the same ground. As a consequence of this rivalry, there were recurrent clashes between protagonists of secular nationalist schooling and the conservative adherents of the old ways of Ashkenazi religious education in the villages. Younger settlers often welcomed the free spirit introduced by Zionist schoolteachers, forming social bonds with them and looking to them for what they felt was needed for their children as they began to form families. Among the older settlers, who considered the lifestyle that attracted the young to be libertine and impious, the radical-Zionist teachers and young workers were seen both as dangerous to religious tradition and as provocative to the Ottoman authorities and the Arab milieu. They looked to the Old Yishuv for the kind of elementary instruction that would implant traditional culture and loyalty in the settlements. Jerusalem supplied rabbinical support—including *halukah* grants to a small number of settlers—and provided the teachers for such settlements as Petah Tikvah and Ekron, as well as for the conservative faction in other settlements. Old-style classes were maintained in such villages in competition with the secular-nationalist schooling that was being slowly and persistently developed by Zionist pedagogues.

The area of competitive struggle spread to those sectors in the cities where some elements in the growing middle class desired the advantages of modern schooling in a developing market economy but feared the seduction of religious license. The issue was forced by the rise of secondary schools in Jaffa, Jerusalem, and Haifa in the early twentieth century, particularly by the foundation in 1906 of the Hebrew *gymnasium* (or as it was later called, the Herzliya Gymnasia) in Jaffa.

Postelementary education, primarily oriented toward vocational training, was provided by Western-sponsored schools in Jerusalem earlier. These institutions were avoided by the Jerusalem Ashkenazim and served primarily the needy among Sephardi boys and girls in the city. Modern-minded, Zionist-inclined teachers on the staff of Western-supported schools successfully urged the German Hilfsverein to build a teachers' seminary in Jerusalem when it began its work in Palestine in 1903. By that time, tolerance for such schools within recognized limits had become conventional in the variegated Jerusalem community.

The Jaffa *gymnasium* was born and developed in a more challenging manner. Its founder, the teacher Yehuda Leib Metman-Kohen, embarked upon his career inspired by a report, delivered by Ahad Haam in 1899 upon returning from Palestine, on the need for a Hebrew professional intelligentsia in the Yishuv. Metman-Kohen organized a student group in Odessa whose members undertook to train as physicians and teachers and immigrate to Erez Israel. The young enthusiasts constituted themselves as a communal group and adopted as their first priority the aim of establishing a Hebrew *gymnasium* in Palestine. Metman-Kohen himself went to the Swiss university of Bern in 1900 to study pedagogy, joining a noted group of Russian student-Zionist émigrés there. Here too he formed a group dedicated to the cause of Hebrew and committed to the creation of an institution for secondary education in Palestine as the foundation for a future Hebrew university.

Upon hearing that Rishon Lezion was seeking a principal for its school, the group decided that Metman-Kohen should apply for the position. In 1905, he and his young wife moved to Rishon Lezion as teachers, hoping to build the *gymnasium* there with the help of the Russian Hovevei Zion. His conduct of the school alarmed conservative village elders in Rishon Lezion by celebrating the Maccabean victories with eight nights of torchlight parades and Zionist flag-raising; his policy of promoting Hebrew instruction at the expense of a reduced French course also contributed to the village leadership's decision to discard the plan for a *gymnasium*, to which it had initially committed a building plot. Metman-Kohen and his wife left for Jaffa, where he soon carried out the design for a *gymnasium* on his own.

The announcement of a projected postelementary private school in

Jaffa in the 1905–6 academic year clearly met the need of a number of local parents. After the first year, Metman-Kohen was able to invite one of his old Bern comrades to join him, and in the following year the remaining member of the Bern triad joined the *gymnasium* faculty. In the second year, a local support group was formed to help finance the school, supplementing the tuition fees paid by prospering parents. The school not only drew on local children, but (implementing part of the design of the initial Odessa group) attracted young people who were sent to Jaffa by Zionist families in the diaspora to be brought up in a Hebrew environment.

The curriculum announced at the opening of the school covered, in addition to "the studies dear to the heart of every Hebrew," classes in French, German, English, and Latin; arithmetic, geometry, and algebra; bookkeeping and commercial subjects; physics, chemistry, zoology, botany, and elements of geology and mineralogy; history and geography, and drawing and painting. In the early years, however, the self-proclaimed "gymnasium" actually conducted only preliminary classes at the elementary level. Additional terms were added each year, until the school was confronted with the problem of accreditation so that its graduates could enter universities. After considering different options, the school settled on conforming its curriculum to the requirements for admission to Ottoman universities.

The Jaffa *gymnasium*, which was widely discussed in the Jewish press, as well as the development of secular-nationalist education in the new settlements and the cities, broadened the horizons of parents and young people in the Yishuv. They presented a particular challenge to religiously conservative middle-class urban settlers, who grew in number with the economic expansion of the towns. These families could not rely on the instruction provided by the Old Yishuv as readily as could villagers of similar religious leanings. The skills their children would need in order to compete in the growing urban economy seemed to require secular schooling not available in the traditional Ashkenazi curriculum. In 1904 a group of parents in Jaffa organized a private school to provide religious education for their children—based on the traditional texts, with instruction in oral Yiddish translation, but also offering courses in history and arithmetic taught in Hebrew. They set up a board headed by the recently arrived Rabbi Abraham Hacohen Kook (who assumed responsibility for the religious guidance of Jaffa and the agricultural settlements) and appointed as director a rabbi who changed the name of the school (now called Tahkemoni) and who brought his own ideas for reforming the traditional curriculum.

After its first years, the new school began to prove too costly for its local board alone to finance. It sought help from Mizrahi, which until then had not been active in promoting education in Erez Israel. But the lively discussion provoked by the opening of Metman-Kohen's project in Jaffa, together with internal development in the religious Zionist organization, led to a decision of the diaspora leadership in 1908 to take over the school as a countermeasure against the perceived threat of the secular-nationalist Jaffa *gymnasium* and similar institutions.

From its earliest days, Mizrahi was divided between two tendencies in regard to its proper role in Zionism. The dominant opinion favored confining both the Zionist movement as a whole and Mizrahi's involvement in its work to what was called "pure Zionism"—that is, political Zionism and such "practical" activities as were of common interest, but not controversial such as the issues between Orthodox and secularist Jews. A strong minority view, however, held that religious Zionists should be especially interested in cultural activity—on strict Orthodox lines, to be sure—and should favor it particularly as a Zionist function. The compromise adopted at the 1902 Russian Zionist conference in Minsk—the agreement that the Zionist movement should support *separate* secular and Orthodox cultural activity—was a program that this group wished to see Mizrahi pursue actively within its own sphere, both in the diaspora and in Erez Israel. But for years Mizrahi refrained from any cultural work in Palestine, confining itself to diaspora activities: pro-Zionist agitation among Orthodox Jews and study groups among its own members. This was also the program it tried in vain to impose on the Zionist Congress in 1911.

Thus, the decision to assume responsibility for the Tahkemoni school in 1908 as the first step toward active engagement in cultural work in Erez Israel was a significant break with past policy. But the practical effect of the decision in terms of concrete educational reform, was limited. The divided opinions among Mizrahi leaders on the subject remained in evidence, and what central control the diaspora movement could exercise remained in the hands of the Western Orthodox conservatives. Still the Russian advocates of an activist cultural program gained influence gradually. They found in Rabbi Kook an ideologue who took up the themes of messianic Zionism sketched out in an earlier generation of Rabbis Alkalai and Kalischer and who developed them with greater depth and radical definition—though with a clarity beyond what like-minded Mizrahi leaders were themselves prepared to subscribe to at that time.

Kook asserted not only that Zionist work in Palestine represented a preliminary stage of messianic redemption, a prerequisite condition of its final consummation, he drew the further, radical conclusion that all those who built the New Yishuv in Erez Israel were instruments of God's purpose and will, however profane their deeds and heretical their ideas. He also concluded that the true role of religious Zionists must be not simply to recruit support among the pious but to bring the Torah into the camp of the profane unbelievers who, despite themselves, were laboring in the holy cause. Not simply tolerance of the secularists and openness toward them, but a militant, benevolent campaign to bring them back under the yoke of the Law must be the immediate agenda of religious Zionism.

Both of Kook's doctrines—the justification of working together with secularists and the goal of restoring the rule of the Torah over them—were in principle acknowledged by all religious Zionists. However, those actively involved in the movement who were closest to his position were bound by the demands and responsibilities of which he was free. Their openness to working more closely with secularist nationalists—which they continually had to defend against the inclination of others to withdraw further—was gradually constrained as a result of external pressures and the rapid development of embryonic parallel cultural projects they had just begun to create. An aggressive campaign to win over the secularists to traditional piety was more than they were prepared to undertake.

The drive to build a Mizrahi counterpart to the Hebrew cultural revival promoted by secularists in Palestine did not yield substantial achievements until the British mandate produced a radically different environment for Zionist work. The militancy implicit in Kook's teachings really came to fruition only after the foundation of the State of Israel.

• 6 •

Zionism and the Left

Socialist and labor Zionist groupings appeared in Russia and Austria during the turbulent years that bridged the nineteenth and twentieth centuries. At the Seventh Zionist Congress, in 1905, they were no longer represented merely by individual delegates, but appeared as organized factions in the WZO.

Jewish labor parties arose out of the same anomalous situation that produced Zionism itself, as well as all other modern Jewish ideologies. Because Jews were both a dissident religion and a depressed group, the liberal leaders of Western Jewries found they could not rely solely on civic emancipation and religious toleration to solve the Jewish problem. They had to develop programs of cultural, social, and economic amelioration. The late-nineteenth-century leftist ideologues, who were concerned primarily with social and economic issues, similarly found that they could not deal with the problems of Eastern and East-Central European Jewries without confronting the issues of emancipation and antisemitism. Because liberals and leftists focused on different aspects of the same anomalous general-Jewish situation, and they arose in different regions at different periods, they developed their views in response to characteristically different gentile counterparts or adversaries.

The debate between Zionists and the liberal leaders of Western Jewry was over what Zionists called "assimilationism." It centered on the assumption of the Western liberals that, once emancipated, Jews should not differ from their countrymen in anything other than their "religion," and that too was to be redefined in the narrowly ecclesiastical sense of Western churches and reshaped in the style of the locally dominant Christian denomination.

In practice, the non-Zionist West did not, or could not, fully abide by the logic of this assumption. Emancipation was followed by a remarkably successful acculturation, economic advance, and, to an extent, social assimilation of the Jews. But this very success became the grounds for the recurrent rise of new, increasingly virulent forms of Jew-hatred.

Until the emergence of Zionism, Jewish modernists adjusted to the anomaly in practice, while evading it intellectually, within a general ideology of liberalism. Excluded from German Masonic orders and student *Burschenschaften* or *Korps*, Jews formed their own parallel societies, but in theory they conducted these as "nonsectarian" bodies. The local Jewish community, nominally organized for purely cultic functions, actually performed a considerable variety of intracommunal welfare services. Special agencies such as the Alliance Israélite Universelle were active on an international scale, conducting a range of cultural, economic, and political projects no less comprehensive than those later envisioned by the Zionists; but they presented these activities in the guise of "philanthropic" assistance to "co-religionists." Under the publicly acceptable titles of general philanthropy and of a special responsibility for the need of one's own church, these quite evidently ethnic functions veiled their national character.

Western Jewish philanthropy that extended to the Jewish community in Palestine made possible Zionist cooperation with non-Zionists and at the same time gave cause for disputes over strategic and tactical theories. The roots of difference were ideological, but cooperation in practice became possible when underlying ideological issues were covered over by either reciprocal or one-sided concessions.

Leftist Zionism arose in a confrontation with socialist or social-revolutionary Jewish ideologies, primarily in the Russian and Austro-Hungarian Empires. It had to contend with a Jewish opposition, usually dominant among the local left-oriented elements, that did not propose to reshape the Jewish community as a Western-style religion purged of ethnic attributes, but rather regarded Jewishness, whether religious or ethnic, as a historical irrelevancy and a present-day encumbrance. That Jews were at once a religiously and ethnically defined community, a faith group and a nationality, was not a matter of debate in Eastern and East-Central Europe. The question at issue was how this undisputed fact was to be dealt with in practice.

In the multinational Austro-Hungarian Empire, the ethnic quality of the Jewish situation was magnified by the factor of an ethnically divided electorate. The curial system permitted a number of Jewish representatives to be chosen even under a highly restricted as well as easily manipulated franchise.

The liberal Jewish deputies, spokesmen for the established community leadership, adopted a singular policy. In a parliament where all other deputies grouped themselves according to ethnic interests and openly defended these, Jews alone took the mandate of their Jewish electors as instructions to submerge their ethnic identity. They were like the editor of the *Neue Freie Presse* about whom Herzl ironically remarked, "He belongs to a species which I have never seen: he is an Austrian." They needed a neutral identification with the state in order to deny "the existence of a Jewish people."[1]

But there was no "Austrian" national formation with which to identify directly. The political establishment of the Dual Monarchy was based on a compact through which the Germans, dominant over the empire as a whole, generally recognized Magyar dominance in Hungary and the dominance of Polish conservative aristocrats in Galicia. The Jews demonstrated that they were Austrian primarily by identifying with the German liberals but also by joining the "club," or bloc, of Polish deputies if elected in Galicia. Similarly, German-speaking Jewish notables stood politically with the dominant Magyars in Hungary. But under this multicolored camouflage of "Austrian" neutrality, the Jewish deputies nonetheless defended special Jewish interests.

Thus, the theory that Jews were simply a religious sect, indistinguishable in all other respects from their fellow countrymen, was combined with patently ethnic practices by Jewish liberals. When Jewish nationalists arose, they sought to widen the functions and democratize the structure of the ethnic community, but they found it already constituted on a fairly wide, factually ethnic base. Consequently, "nationalism," the issue on which they differed radically from the Jewish establishment, expressed itself not so much in their practice as in their theory of Jewish social policy.

Viewing the activities of Jewish organizations in an openly ethnic perspective rather than as humanitarian aid to co-religionists, the nationalist program radicalized and politicized the whole range of already existing functions evoked by the anomalous Jewish situation. Not only ought emigration to be properly directed to produce an autonomous, concentrated settlement in a Jewish homeland; local welfare and political activities too, in the view of the nationalists, should be critically reviewed in terms of the principle of autoemancipation. The aim of cultural reform should no longer be to introduce European culture into the Jewish ghetto in whatever language was convenient. Instead, the national language, Hebrew, or the folk language, Yiddish, should be cultivated as the organ of a distinct cultural individuality. The aim of vocational reform should no longer be to remove complaints against Jewish usury and make Jews acceptable in gentile society. Instead, vocational retraining, producers', consumers', and credit cooperatives, and political and trade union struggles were proposed to gain the rights and protect the interests of oppressed Jewish workers. The social integration sought should be one that solidified and activated an inner Jewish, autonomous consensus, not one that established Jews as a fully absorbed part of gentile society. And Jewish political activity should serve openly Jewish ends, whether it were directed toward the international problem of Jewish migration or the local problems inherent in each country's domestic politics.

Views like these were held not only by Zionists, who were most clearly and comprehensively committed to them. Eastern European Jewry produced a variety of nationalist movements that differed with the Zionists over questions of strategy: for example, whether Palestine was the proper place for concentrated Jewish resettlement, or whether working for minority rights in the diaspora should not be the nationalist aim instead of seeking the solution of the Jewish problem in emigration. Moreover, a Jewish socialist movement which was strongly and explicitly concerned with the Jewish problem as an ethnic problem developed in Eastern Europe. Its approach to issues of Jewish social policy was based on presumptions more like those of the Zionists than of Western Jewish liberals. In 1897, the very year when Herzl founded the World Zionist Organization, the Bund (*Algemeyner yidisher arbeter bund in Rusland un Polin*), a Jewish social democratic, general labor organization, was also founded.

Socialist Zionist parties arose within a political experience whose polar antipodes were the Bund, on one side, and the World Zionist Organization on the other. Jewish workers' groups and radical intellectuals, attracted toward both organizations and unable to accept either fully, formed new parties which were suspended in dynamic tension between organized Zionism and organized socialism and seeking to unite both ideas in an original synthesis.

I

In Russia the sudden economic and political shifts of the middle decades of the nineteenth century severely shook established Jewish settlement and occupational patterns. The emancipation of serfs and the expulsion of Jews from rural areas destroyed traditional Jewish livelihoods and produced a stream of migrants. Many of the displaced Jews, resettling in metropolitan centers of industry, commerce, and administration such as Lodz and Bialystok, Vilna and Minsk, Odessa, Budapest, and Vienna, as well as London and New York, emerged as a new Jewish working class. But the existence of such a class began to be noted by ideologists only toward the end of the nineteenth century.

Socialist tradition did not include the Jews in its roster of class and ethnic groups who were potential bearers of the revolution. The record of early socialist attitudes toward the Jews is a virtually solid history of hostility and contempt. Agrarian populists, witnessing the legendary eminence of the House of Rothschild, assimilated this figure of menace into traditional anti-Jewish folk images. Socialist theoreticians agreed in defining the Jews as the classic embodiment of the capitalist spirit. Nor did it help the Jews' cause among radicals that they were undoubtedly one of Europe's oppressed minorities. What defined them as a minority was primarily the reactionary criterion of religion—and, at that, a religion long left behind in the march of history. One might also classify them as an oppressed *nationality*, but if so, they clearly belonged to the class of small, retrograde, economically insignificant ethnic fragments who only cluttered the machinery of progress and who ought to be absorbed into large, economically progressive and politically viable national states.

This attitude was not altered but, if anything, reinforced by the fact that Jews (or persons of Jewish descent who were still identified as such in spite of themselves) played a significant role in radical movements. A roster that includes Heinrich Heine, Ludwig Boerne, Karl Marx, Ferdinand Lassalle, Rosa Luxemburg, and Leon Trotsky obviously stands comparison with any other ethnic contribution to the history of the Left. Second-rank Jewish leaders were equally numerous in the socialist parties of every European country. However, until the rise of Jewish nationalism, such intellectuals found no real place for themselves within a Jewish community that remained staunchly conservative in Eastern Europe and became solidly identified with bourgeois liberalism in the West. In any case, the Jewish radicals usually shared in full the leftist stereotypes concerning their ancestral stock.

The rise of political antisemitism presented an increasingly irritating problem to Jewish socialist leaders. They were politically embarrassed, at the very least, by the lively response of the gentile masses to antisemitic motifs. In order to protect not only themselves but the party, which could be damaged by antisemitic attacks on Jewish socialist leaders, men like the German Paul Singer and the Austrian Viktor Adler avoided any involvement with Jewish issues. This pattern was manifested as late as 1891, at a meeting of the Second International, when the American Jewish delegate Abraham Cahan presented a resolution denouncing antisemitism. Such a stand appeared dangerous to other Jewish socialist leaders, and they rejected it. Instead, they substituted a resolution denouncing both antisemitism and philosemitism in a feeble attempt to dissociate socialism, and some of its Jewish leaders, from the Jewish question.

Jews became active in the Russian radical movement only in the late 1860s. Like their gentile comrades, these Jewish activists concerned themselves primarily with the Russian peasant. Early attempts to conduct socialist propaganda arose among a group of students at the Jewish teachers' seminary in Vilna, led by the young *maskil* Aaron Samuel Lieberman. Lieberman's determined efforts to organize Jewish unions and socialist circles in Vilna, Berlin, London, and Vienna, using the Hebrew and Yiddish media, led his gentile contemporaries to accuse him of nationalistic separatism. Lieberman defended himself by saying that his particular skills could best be applied in this field and by these methods for the benefit of the general socialist cause.

> The fact that I have tried to assemble a certain number of persons in order to publish a paper in a language spoken by about four million people in Russia—this is far from being nationalism. It would be different if I dreamed about a victory for the synagogue over the Roman church or about taking possession of Palestine with leaden or golden bullets. . . . You well know that I hate Judaism exactly as I hate all other nation "hoods" and national "isms". . . . I am an internationalist, as you equally well know, but I am not ashamed of my Jewish descent, and, among all the other oppressed, I love that part of humanity whom the ruling national and religious principles single out as Jews. And again, indeed, I do not love them all, but only the suffering masses and those capable of joining us. Otherwise I should not deserve the name of socialist.[2]

The pogroms of 1881–82, which sharply altered the climate of general Jewish opinion, also directly affected Jewish radicals. Even before this they were no doubt accustomed to occasional expressions of hostility and repudiation that were let slip by gentile comrades in unguarded moments. Lieberman's apologia, quoted above, came in reply to reproaches for having dared, though a Jew, to present himself as a *Russian* spokesman at an international socialist conference. But until the 1880s, these could be regarded as exceptional cases, mere pinpricks, which need not seriously disturb the cosmopolitan amity and comradely intimacy between Jewish radicals and other revolutionaries—especially when intermarried. The pogroms were another matter. A deep-seated revulsion swept Jewish leftists when some radical circles condoned the outbreaks or, seeing in them the beginning of general revolution, actively promoted further attacks on the Jews.

Most of the Hebraist *maskilim* among the leftists immediately became committed nationalists and thereafter devoted themselves primarily to Jewish concerns. For example, Lieberman had counted, or hoped to count, among his socialist cadre the writers Yehalel (Yehuda Leib Levin), and Moshe Leib Lilienblum, who now became ardent Hovevei Zionists. He also maintained contact with Sholem Jacob Abramovitz (Mendele Mokher Seforim), who became a classic Yiddish and Hebrew novelist, the famous "grandfather" of all modern Jewish literary nationalists. Another of Lieberman's supporters had been the *maskil* Isaac Kaminer. Kaminer's daughters, who married radical activists (including a non-Jew), were prominent among early Jewish socialist leaders, and his home in Kiev served as the center for a socialist group led by his son-in-law Pavel Akselrod in the 1870s. After the pogroms, Kaminer's poems constantly sounded themes of penitence and Jewish loyalty. He voiced bitter remorse for his early cosmopolitan backsliding and for his failure to implant traditional national values in his children.

Reactions were more diverse among those Jewish leftists whose background or identification was mainly Russian rather than Hebrew or Yiddish. Some, especially among those who became Hovevei Zion, turned away from radicalism. Others, in particular among those who joined the Am Olam societies, confronted the world with the novel phenomenon of utopian socialists who identified with the Jewish people. Still others came through the traumatic experience relatively unmoved, but not without an interval of severe confusion and self-questioning.

Men like Pavel Akselrod and Lev Deitch, political émigrés at the time of the pogroms, were undoubtedly shaken by their inability to react effectively against antisemitic tendencies in the radical ranks. They did not believe Jews like themselves could persuade Russian workers that pogroms were counterrevolutionary, and they were unsuccessful in their attempts to induce gentile comrades such as Georgii Valentinovich Plekhanov, Peter Lavrovich Lavrov, or Sergei Mikhailovich Kravchinsky to take up the Jewish cause.

The reaction was particularly intense in the case of Akselrod. In his youth, as he tells us in his memoirs, his first "political" activity was an effort "to 'cultivate' Jewish youth, to liberate them from religious and national superstitions by spreading among them those ideas, concepts and tendencies which developed in my mind under the influence of . . . Russian authors." But, having read Lassalle, he found that "the 'Jewish question' seemed trivial in comparison with that of one 'idea of the fourth estate,' which included the radical solution of all particular problems from which arise various injustices and misfortunes of the masses."[3] However, the pogroms revived in him old sentiments, and he was drawn to the Hovevei Zion ideal preached by his father-in-law, Isaac Kaminer, and by others of his old circle. His comrade Lev Deitch, who remained skeptical of this as well as the Am Olam idea, nevertheless agreed to solicit the opinion of Elisee Reclus, the eminent geographer. The combined arguments of these two sufficed to bring Akselrod back to standard leftist cosmopolitanism, for we hear of no more nationalist deviations in his life.

Men like these, who held fast to their cosmopolitan attitudes, nevertheless found themselves with two new fronts to defend after the pogroms. Within the Jewish community, there was the new secular nationalist ideology to be combated. And in the Russian radical movement, it was necessary to convince the gentile comrades that the pogroms were not harbingers of revolution, but a tool in the hands of reaction. However, the circumstances were such that it was unnecessary to tax dialectical ingenuity and develop ideological innovations in order to find satisfactory solutions for these problems.

After the first pogroms, tsarist support for the anti-Jewish outbreaks grew increasingly blatant. Official propaganda began to identify Jews and radicals as one and the same subversive threat to Holy Russia. Thus, what Akselrod and Deitch felt unable to do and could not induce Plekhanov or Lavrov to do, the tsar now did for them: circumstances, rather than persuasive arguments, caused gentile radicals to adopt a more or less acceptable position on antisemitism.

The other ideological issue raised by the emergence of a nationalist movement in the Jewish community also developed in a way that permitted the cosmopolitan leftists to rely on standard clichés in meeting the challenge. No group of leftist nationalists firmly established itself in the generation of the first pogroms, beyond the initial reaction period. Am Olam, the nationalist organization with the most strongly marked utopian socialist, populist character, speedily dissolved under the test of American conditions. The Hovevei Zion movement absorbed some of the radicals, without offering any opportunity for the development of their characteristic views. Its internal conflicts arose over issues of secularism versus Orthodox traditionalism or of practical colonization versus cultural activity. When men were absorbed in such quarrels, their social radicalism and utopian ideas, being irrelevant to current concerns, receded into the background. They developed no nationalist ideology couched in standard radical terms. Hence, the cosmopolitans needed no dialectical ingenuity in order to refute them. It was sufficient to damn the whole nationalist movement as bourgeois and obscurantist.

For political émigrés at the center of international socialism and for Russian Jewish radicals intimately involved with the main revolutionary groups, intra-Jewish ideological disputes were in any case too trivial to be concerned with. But other radicals moved together with the mass of Jewish emigrants to cities such as London and New York, where Jewish workers were virtually the only Eastern Europeans among whom a Russian radical could conduct propaganda and agitation. The intelligentsia in these cities did not have to seek out the people idealistically, as did the populists in Russia, but were thrown in with them by necessity, since many of them had to become proletarians in order to support themselves.

Radical immigrants were thus part of the Jewish immigrant community and, almost in spite of themselves sometimes, they organized and propagandized on a distinctly ethnic basis. Russian was the recognized language of social enlightenment in their circles, and they tried to maintain it even in America; but necessity drove them to rely increasingly on Yiddish. They sought the company of Russian and German socialists, and when they organized Jewish workers, they preferred to call their unions "international." But the principle of ethnic organization was accepted in the established trade unionism of America; and where there was a clearly identified federation of German unions, it was impossible for long to avoid calling the Jewish unions by their own name. Yiddish journalism was advanced in significant measure by the publications of Jewish anarchists in London in the early 1880s and thereafter by Jewish socialists in New York. Jewish trade unionism was first firmly established by social democrats in New York in the late 1880s; and in the first two congresses of the Second International, their delegates appeared as Jewish representatives.

Yet none of this activity led to the development of a specifically Jewish socialist doctrine, nor did Jewish problems arouse any serious ideological discussion among these radicals. The major disputes among them were between social democrats and anarchists over the strategy of the social revolution. The Jewish milieu in which they performed their routine labors on behalf of radicalism in no way affected this debate. Their attitude toward the Jewish community was a simple dualism: Jews were divided into the workers, among whom they were active, and all the rest—nationalist, traditionalist, and plutocrat reactionaries. Ideological communication with the latter groups was confined largely to a fierce antireligious campaign, conducted mainly by the anarchists but also sustained by the social democrats.

Jewish workers in Russian cities also provided a field of activity for Jewish radicals, beginning in the late 1880s, but conditions were different from those in London and New York. Necessity did not unite the intelligentsia with the Jewish workers, for in Russia radicals did not have to support themselves by working in factories. But the growing influence of Marxism turned the attention of radicals to urban workers, among whom Jews were a significant part. Nor had Russia anything like the established patterns of trade unionism, which, in America, favored organization on ethnic lines and the pragmatic use of languages spoken by the workers. Nevertheless, the current *theories* of socialist strategy and tactics that radicals applied to the Jewish field led them to commit themselves increasingly to the support of Jewish linguistic traditions and ethnic interests.

In Russia, Jewish ethnicism could not be adopted merely as a pragmatic tactical requirement for successful organization, as in America. A double challenge compelled the radicals to work out their policy in explicit ideological form. After the pogroms and the rise of Hovevei Zionism, anyone who hoped to lead Jewish masses had to speak rather openly in favor of ethnic interests. Moreover, the Polish and, later, the Russian socialist movement opposed Jewish separatism so outspokenly that a specific defense of the policy could not be avoided.

In the 1880s, the leftist Jewish intelligentsia worked among Jewish laborers in traditional forms of "propaganda": that is, they taught small circles the elements of general education and science, from which they progressed to radical social theory. The medium of this propaganda was the Russian language. By the 1890s, the increasing trade unionist militancy of Jewish workers, together with the growing vogue of Marxism and the examples of German and Polish social democracy, suggested the possibility of going beyond small propaganda circles to mass agitation. This approach opened up the prospect of a renewed political activism, built on the concrete economic interests of Jewish workers; but it also meant abandoning Russian lessons and using Yiddish as the primary medium of agitation and organization.

The latter point led to sharp polemics between advocates and opponents of the new course. The intelligentsia who favored mass agitation argued that the old study circles merely turned out a select group of workers, many of whom took advantage of their training to become bourgeois. Elite workers countered by arguing that mass agitation in Yiddish, by abandoning Russian education, closed the door of general culture to workers, leaving it a monopoly of the intelligentsia. A nationalist variant of this position held that the Jewish economic structure was such that the workers needed vocational training and enlightenment, not the class struggle. After two years, opposition to the new course was finally overcome toward the end of 1894, on condition that study circles would be maintained in order to prepare worker activists for mass agitation.

The issue between "agitation" and "propaganda" was a general one among Russian radicals; and the pamphlet "On Agitation," written by Arkady (Aaron Kremer) in order to influence Jewish workers in Vilna, became a major instrument for converting the entire Russian radical movement to the method of mass organization. But among Jewish workers, the argument involved special ethnic issues beyond the choice between Russian and Yiddish. There was a definite pressure for a more nationalist line in Jewish labor agitation.

By May Day 1895, such a line was formulated in a programatic statement by Julius Martov (Yuli Zederbaum), the leading social democratic ideologue then active among Jews:

> In placing the mass movement at the center of our program, we were compelled to see to it that our agitation and propaganda should be adapted to the masses, that is, we had to make them more Yiddish. . . . Our slogan, "Everything by the people," does not permit us to await the emancipation of the Jewish proletariat—its emancipation from economic, political and civil enslavement—either by the Russian or the Polish movement. . . . Any class which cannot fight for its freedom does not deserve freedom.[4]

When the General Jewish Workers' Bund was organized in 1897, these views were firmly established among its basic principles.

Even such a vaguely defined nationalist position needed a specific defense in view of the attitudes toward the Jews prevalent among socialists. The notion of autonomous organization on national lines, within an empire or within the radical movement, was not unfamiliar. But when influential socialist leaders took up the ideas of federative organization and national autonomy, they were not ready to apply them to the Jews.

The Austrian socialist movement had to face the nationality issue at its Bruenn convention of 1899, when the South Slavs presented a proposal to reorganize Austria as a federation of *nations*, not of territories. That is, the principle of "exterritorial" (or, as it was later called, "personal") national autonomy would be adopted, granting members of all ethnic groups throughout Austria the right to belong to national entities, autonomously administering their linguistic and cultural affairs. The party gave qualified recognition to this view in a novel compromise, later explained and elaborated on as a new socialist nationality theory by Otto Bauer and Karl Renner. The party proposed to reorganize Austria as a democratic federation of *territories* that were constituted, as far as possible, on nationally homogeneous lines. Autonomous *regions* for each major nationality comprised within larger territorial units dominated by another nationality were to be designated and serve as the base for *unions* organized over the whole area of the federation to administer the national affairs of each ethnic group. As for the Social Democratic party itself, an earlier convention at Vienna in 1897 had already organized it as a federation of the socialist parties of the constituent nationalities of all Austria, without reference to territories.

It was quite obvious, and explicitly stated by the authors of the new policy, that all of this had no application whatever to Jews. The countrywide national unions of the Bruenn program were based on autonomous national *regions*, not on the personal national identification of scattered *individuals*. Essentially, the scheme was a method to bring some dispersed national minorities, such as the Germans in Bohemia or Bukowina, under the protection of a national entity based on a territory where they were dominant. It was not intended to extend to a minority like the Jews, who were dominant in no major territory.

Whatever the intentions of its authors, the Bauer-Renner theory admirably served the purposes of the Bund in Russia and Poland, especially if construed as justifying the principle of exterritorial autonomy in the form originally propounded by the South Slavs. The Bundists most committed to a Jewish "national" line (which they always carefully distinguished from a "nationalistic" line) could not rest content with their first formulas, taking up the struggle for Jewish civil and political rights. A generation of Zionist critics of Jewish liberalism had stamped this kind of thing as a species of bourgeois assimilationism. Not only Zionists but socialists now talked, however vaguely, of national political self determination and of national cultural rights as being essential elements in any nationalities' program.

Nevertheless, a long and tedious internal discussion was required before the Bund could define its position on these matters. In 1899, the third Bund convention confined its Jewish demands to civil equality; it ignored national rights. The fifth convention, in 1902, split so evenly over the right of the Jews to foster their own nationality and claim cultural autonomy that no resolution was adopted and the entire debate was dropped from the published account of the proceedings. Not until the sixth convention, in 1905, was a program of Jewish cultural autonomy finally adopted.

The Bund was interested primarily in another feature of the Austrian model: the federal structure of the Social Democratic Party, based on countrywide constituent parties of the several nationalities. Attempts to adopt this principle on behalf of Jewish autonomous labor organization met with sharp opposition in Congress Poland, the semiautonomous Russian province annexed at the Congress of Vienna. The Polish Socialist Party (PPS) strongly opposed separate Jewish labor organizations in its area and insisted that if any such body arose, it should at least support the PPS's demand for full territorial autonomy for Russian Poland. In regard to the All-Russian Social Democratic Party, founded a year after the Bund, a different situation at first prevailed. The Bund played a decisive role in founding the Russian party, supplied some of its foremost leaders, and was one of its most successful exponents of mass action—largely confined, to be sure, to the centers of dense Jewish settlement in northern Russia. Under the circumstances, the Bund was conceded autonomy in the beginning, without much argument, for the purpose of organizing the Jewish workers.

But by 1903, at the second congress of the Russian Social Democrats, opposition to Jewish separatism was widespread. The Bund proposed to reorganize Russian social democracy as a federation, with its constituents being the socialist parties of the various Russian nationalities *without reference to the territories where they lived*. The latter point was of immediate concern, for the Bund was beginning to extend its activities to south Russian Jewish communities, and there it encountered the same kind of opposition from the Russian Social Democrats as from the PPS in Congress Poland. The Bundists were fully aware of the general hostility likely to be provoked by such demands. Accordingly, they declared their "federative statute" for the All-Russian party to be a "basis for negotiation," not an "ultimative" demand.[5] But their efforts were of no avail. They were so sharply rebuffed that the Bund was forced to leave the All-Russian party it had so signally helped to create.

Other conflicts at that time completely broke up the unity of the Russian Social Democrats, and the party was not reestablished until 1906. The Bund was among the parties then invited to rejoin and help reconstitute the All-Russian party. Its demands were now slightly altered. It no longer spoke of a federal organization of Russian social democracy, since in any case socialist parties of various nationalities were recognized by their invitation to the reunion convention. It no longer asked to be recognized as the *only* socialist party entitled to organize Jews, but for the right to organize in *all* Russian territories. The Bund had by then adopted a program of Jewish national cultural autonomy. Not daring to insist on the adoption of these principles by the All-Russian party, the Bund asked only that its own right to advance them be recognized. In the outcome, the Bund rejoined the All-Russian party with only partial satisfaction of its demands. Its right to organize Jewish workers was conceded, but the assembly avoided giving any sanction whatever to the Bund's national cultural program by a simple declaration that it had not considered this question.

The vacillations and hesitations of the Bund on Jewish national issues are easily understood if one considers the hostile attitude of other Russian radicals to the notion of a Jewish nationality. The opposition the Bundists encountered sometimes gave them a sense of a special hostility toward them as *Jews*; the uneven record of Russian progressives toward the Jews' civil rights struggle, let alone their demand for national autonomy, was capable of strengthening that impression. Pogroms and open antisemitism were no longer condoned or encouraged for tactical reasons as they had been by Russian radicals in the 1880s. In the meantime, it had become accepted in European socialist circles that antisemitism was an instrument deliberately employed by the reactionaries precisely in order to win popular and labor support away from the Left. At the same time, for this very reason, leftists and liberal progressives were reluctant to expose themselves to antisemitic attacks by fighting for Jewish causes too vigorously. Compared to the social revolutionaries and liberals, the Russian Social Democrats showed themselves particularly reserved in this respect.

It was a distinct handicap for the Bund among nationally inclined Jewish workers that it felt compelled, at great cost, to find its place in the ranks of social democracy. Under this pressure, it was unable to hold out uncompromisingly for a more satisfactory attitude toward Jewish interests even on elementary issues like civil rights and antisemitism. On the other side, progressives and labor elements in the Zionist camp found much to criticize in the WZO, in many cases sharing the attitude of the Bund. Within a few years after the WZO and the Bund were founded in 1897, such circles began to group themselves in a variety of socialist Zionist formations.

II

We have noted the ideological embarrassment of Jewish liberals and leftists forced by diaspora conditions to conduct an ethnic policy. This problem posed inherent ideological difficulties for Zionists as well. The most clearly distinctive feature of Zionism in Eastern Europe was not the slogan of "autoemancipation," for this expressed an emotional attitude shared by other nationalists and, in some sense, by Bundists as well. What singled out Zionists was their doctrine that an exodus from diaspora countries to Zion was the way to carry out this autoemancipation. Such a doctrine, if construed with rigid and simplistic consistency, would preclude Zionists from any concern with the domestic politics of the countries they planned to leave. Leftist anti-Zionists took just such a simplistic view of Zionism, attacking it as a defeatist, reactionary movement that diverted the Jewish masses from the barricades of the social revolution.

But Zionism was no more committed to a single principle than was any other ideological movement. The rather complex compromises with cultural Zionism that were involved in the formulation of the Basle Program are a case in point. The fact that Herzl's early adherents included men with a strong commitment to both socialism and ethnic politics also had significant effects.

Noteworthy among them was Nathan Birnbaum, the most prominent pre-Herzlian Austrian Zionist. In his varied career, he ultimately went from liberal Zionism to traditionalist anti-Zionism. By the late 1890s, his increasingly intimate identification with the folklore, language, and vital interests of the Eastern European masses had made him a socialist and Yiddishist.

While Birnbaum naturally was suspicious and resentful of so meteoric a newcomer as Herzl, he saw in him a man with a dynamic political style who might be used to break the hold of the bourgeois establishment that dominated Hovevei Zionism as well as all other Jewish communal institutions. Together with followers such as Saul Raphael Landau, a young Galician student activist and Zionist journalist, he hoped to remold Zionism according to his own strategy through the revived Zionist organization initiated by Herzl. In the group of Zionist leftists were also the French Dreyfusards Bernard Lazare (Lazare Marius Bernard) and Jacques Bahar. As newcomers to Jewish nationalism, like Herzl himself, they had no preconceived designs, but when they came into the movement, their sympathies aligned them with the Austrian radicals.

Herzl, for his part, was interested in the support of Lazare and Bahar and in the technical cooperation of Landau—though not of Birnbaum—because he felt he could use such men in molding Zionist policy and organization according to his own design. Given the narrow compass of early inner-Zionist politics, confined as it was to a small group of men, this was a situation bound to end in bitter personal clashes. Apart from personalities, there were also strategic and tactical disagreements, centering on the issue of involvement in diaspora politics.

At the time of Herzl's appearance, Austrian Zionists were engaged in controversy with a variety of antagonists in their immediate environment. They were opposed to the Jewish Reichstag deputies who conducted a pro-German "Austrian" instead of an ethnic Jewish policy. They were critical of the Jewish magnates who maintained control of Jewish institutions by means of a restricted community franchise. They were sharply opposed to official anti-Jewish discrimination. They were up in arms against Polish and German antisemitic politicians, who pretended that there were no Jewish proletarians and that all Jews were bourgeois oppressors of the autochthonous workers and peasants. They were hardly less critical of Social Democratic leaders, some of them Jewish, who also ignored the existence of the Jewish poor and Jewish workers and who refused to commit their party to a firm and open stand against antisemitism. Landau, who became editor of Herzl's new Zionist journal, *Die Welt*, wanted to devote this organ to a militant attack on all these fronts, as well as to the main aim, propaganda for a charter to resettle Zion. Birnbaum had more understanding for Herzl's view that Zionists must maintain neutrality on local issues. Consequently, he favored the idea of a Jewish People's Party, like other Austro-Hungarian nationality parties, in which Zionist and non-Zionist ethnic militants would join in action on diaspora issues.

Herzl's approach to these matters may well be called simplistic, but it was certainly far from rigid. The compelling tactical reasons that made him try to suppress cultural questions (even though the Basle Program specified them as Zionist concerns) applied equally well to domestic politics in the diaspora (to which Zionists did not commit themselves in Basle). The issues involved here could divide Zionists no less dangerously than their differences over culture. It is easy to see why Herzl wholeheartedly adopted at least one strategy of the diaspora ethnic politicians, the attack on the undemocratic plutocracy that controlled the Jewish community: he could not act for Jews in the diplomatic sphere if the community repudiated him. But he did not restrict himself entirely to those diaspora issues where Zionism as such was under attack. He also was ready to use *Die Welt* to support the linguistic concession offered by the Austrian government to the Czechs, in pointed contrast to the liberal Jewish leaders who supported the German parties in their determined opposition. His main reasons, other than the joy of defying the Jewish establishment, were tactical: he hoped to gain sympathy for Zionism from the government by demonstrating his usefulness.

But this was one of the very cases where Landau, who tried to conduct Jewish ethnic politics through *Die Welt*, broke with Herzl's editorial policy. The line Landau favored was one of complete neutrality on this and other disputes among Austro-Hungarian gentile nationalities. He wanted the Jews to be recognized as an independent political interest and not subordinated to any other national bloc.

Another source of irritation was Herzl's rather equivocal attitude toward the publication in *Die Welt* of attacks on antisemitism. He welcomed such attacks when leveled against Social Democrats who failed to disavow Jew-hatred, but he was sometimes less than enthusiastic about complaints regarding anti-Jewish discrimination by public officials. In his view, antisemitism would be ended not by Jewish agitation against it, but rather by the exodus Zionism would ultimately organize; and for this end, Zionism needed an understanding with the authorities, who were antisemites themselves.

Two opposed interests heightened the friction. Herzl's efforts to set up Zionist financial instruments and gain the support and confidence of substantial investors aroused acute suspicions among the radicals. And he for his part was cool to their efforts at labor organization and strongly rebuffed their attempts to obtain labor representation in the WZO.

The personal sympathy of Herzl for oppressed workers, certainly for the Jewish poor, was frequently expressed. His antipathy toward the wealthy Jewish employers and community leaders, who were the main objects of radical attack, was equally open. But, considering the legal complications that already hindered the effective functioning of the Zionist executive, even in relatively liberal Vienna, Herzl thought it essential, as a rule, to avoid Zionist involvement in European domestic politics. Above all, he rejected any Zionist association with socialism, for it was precisely the suspicion of such a connection that he knew would shut certain doors to him in high quarters. He did not hide his displeasure when Max Nordau—one of his closest collaborators—made a speech in Vienna leaning too far toward the socialists. He was at pains on several occasions to explain away incidents that betrayed radical sentiments among Zionist congress delegates, directed especially against the Russian and Turkish autocrats.

Given these circumstances, it is not surprising that the most active radicals, Birnbaum, Landau, Lazare, and Bahar, soon left the WZO. Birnbaum remained active for a while, and Landau for a longer period, in radical nationalist formations outside the Herzlian Zionist movement. No opponents earned angrier and more contemptuous epithets from

Herzl's pen than these men and their associates. They, for their part, joined in a chorus of criticism leveled against the Zionists by their opponents. Not only traditionalists and liberals, but ethnically oriented critics conducted this polemic since the beginning of Zionism. The latter foes not only shared the Zionist mythos of autoemancipation, but claimed to be its most authentic protagonists. It was the very point of their attack on the Zionists to charge that the Hovevei Zion and the WZO had betrayed the spirit of autoemancipation.

Such a tone was frequently taken in the circles from which the Bund arose. We have already noted Martov's dictum that "a class which cannot fight for its freedom does not deserve freedom." This obviously echoes the Marxist slogan that the workers' liberation must be won by the workers themselves. It even more clearly evokes overtones of the Zionist cry of "autoemancipation," for the "class" in question is pointedly identified with the Jewish ethnic group. Moreover, while making the proud claim that they themselves were the fighters who would achieve Jewish autoemancipation, the socialists coupled this boast with reproaches to other Jews who shamefully failed the task:

> Upon us, the Jewish proletariat, fell the unpleasant fate of being exploited by the lowest, most shameless bourgeoisie in the world. Robbed not only of political rights, like all the Russian bourgeoisie, but also of civil rights, our bourgeoisie does not seek ways to better its lot but simply waits for the gracious kindness of the Russian government. It does not even occur to our bourgeois intelligentsia that only through energetic independent action can Jews expect any improvement of their position.[6]

The "bourgeoisie" referred to here implicitly includes the Hovevei Zionist movement. After Herzlian Zionism arose, Bundist propaganda, now issued in the name of a countrywide movement, took occasion to make this point explicit:

> The Zionists kowtow and lick the hand of the slaughterer of the whole Jewish people, the tsarist autocracy, the atrocious, thieving tsarist autocracy that made paupers, beggars, sick, weak, and feeble wretches out of the Jews. . . . You tell us to hide in a corner so that, God forbid, no one should notice and trample on us; keep our heads bowed as lowly as possible, so we should not catch anyone's eye; speak quietly, like a beggar at the door; beg for mercy and kindness. . . . That's how the Zionists talk, the same Zionists who always yell about national and personal self-respect, national pride and self-consciousness and other such jabber and

keep attacking "slavery within freedom"! . . . If the West European Jewish bourgeoisie is sunk in "slavery within freedom,"[7] then you, the Zionist Russian bourgeoisie, are sunk in a still bigger pile of muck—in "slavery within slavery."[8]

A similar critique of Zionism developed among populist, progressive intellectuals. In the course of his variegated, mercurial career, Chaim Zhitlowsky was a brilliant founder and paradoxically, leader of both Zionist and anti-Zionist nationalist labor factions. In an open letter from "A Jew to the Jews," published as a Russian pamphlet in 1892 by the populist Fund of the Free Russian Press in London, Zhitlowsky scolded the Jewish intelligentsia for neglecting their own people. He elaborated his program through a critical appreciation and analysis of the Hovevei Zionist alternative.

Zionism, he noted, was "a sheer utopia" in its positive program, but in other respects it was "a national movement . . . not incapable of certain progressive elements," and its "critique of the present situation [was] . . . in accord with the simple truth" at many points:

> The Hovevei Zion criticize the Jewish position on two main points, which are indeed the most serious. The first point is the ethical degeneration of the Jewish people, a degeneration which is the necessary consequence of an urban commercial life; the second point is the severe decline in autonomous national activism among the Jews, who place all their hopes for reform and improvements on influential intercessors in high quarters.

But, because of its utopian character, Zionism could not be the instrument for either of the remedies correctly indicated by this analysis. Instead, it degenerated into a reactionary force striving "to preserve among the people the mystique of religious nationalism and, with its own hands, pulling chestnuts out of the fire for the future Jewish landlords and kulaks in Palestine." The solution of the Jewish problem must, therefore, be undertaken by the radical intelligentsia through a revised populist tactical approach. They must first organize the Jewish masses, together with all Russian workers and peasants, in order to accomplish the revolutionary seizure of political rights, and after the revolution they must organize the mass of Jews for rural resettlement in Russia. The return to the soil would mean the end of antisemitism. Finally, as producers and no longer parasites, the Jews would be under no pressure to assimilate but would be recognized as one of the family of equal nationalities in Russia.[9]

The rise of Herzl caused another critic, the liberal constitutionalist Simon Dubnow, to write a series of articles that constitutes the most extensive critique and elaborate alternative to Zionism by a non-Zionist nationalist. He began to publish his "Letters on Old and New Judaism" in *Voskhod* in 1897 and continued them as a running argument with various schools of Zionist thought; he laid bare the "utopian" character of Zionism and expounded his own "autonomist" proposals, elaborated on the basis of the nationalities theory of the Austrian Social Democrats.

In the sixth letter, originally published in 1898, he offered the following analysis of Herzl's recently concluded congress:

> Political Zionism is thus a web of fantasies: the dream of the creation of a Jewish state guaranteed by international law, the dream of colonizing a great part of the Jewish people, and the dream of finding the solution of the Jewish problem in this manner. What remains of the Basle Program in practice? I believe only the second and third [sub] paragraphs of the Program: the "organization of the Jews" and the "strengthening of the national consciousness." These principles, which are also included in [Dubnow's] theory of autonomism, together with the gradual extension of the settlement of Palestine, will be the outstanding results of the Zionist effort. To this end, however, the Zionists must become sober, and understand that the "return to Judaism" [proclaimed in Herzl's congress address] is the chief goal and not a means for the (illusionary) establishment of a Jewish state. Otherwise the failure of political Zionism may cause even greater spiritual disillusionment than the despair brought about by the failure of assimilation.[10]

Thus, at the turn of the century, radical but ethnically oriented critics outside the WZO had established a canon for the progressive nationalist attack on official Zionist policy. It condemned Herzlian neglect of the political struggle in the diaspora, demanded immediate action to improve the social and economic position of the Jewish masses, and tended to defend the right of the Jews to preserve their national, cultural individuality in perpetuity in the diaspora. All these themes also occur in the polemics against the official line conducted by the Democratic Faction within the WZO.

Within the Zionist orbit, programs of diaspora activity were referred to as *Gegenwartsarbeit*—that is, activity concerned with "immediate" rather than "ultimate" Jewish problems. Such a program was obviously timely, in view of the halting progress of Herzlian diplomacy toward the ultimate goal. Consequently, Herzl's followers, as well as the internal opposition, formulated pertinent proposals. Herzlians stressed the generally accepted Zionist assumption that Jews could pursue a true *"national* policy" only in relation to Zion. In the diaspora, there could be only Jewish *"social* policy."

> For us Zionists, who strive towards a radical solution of the Jewish problem and regard all immediate policy (*Gegenwartspolitik*) as only a means to an end, a "way station," *Jewish social policy remains as before only a provisional program (Gegenwartsprogramm)*, which we break down into the *special problems of the spiritual, economic, and corporal advancement* of the Jewish people.

On this basis, it was argued that Zionist diaspora activities must be restricted to the "forum internum"—that is, such diaspora politics as Zionists conducted should be confined to the "conquest of the communities."[11] But within these limits a fairly elaborate program of Zionist social reform and welfare activities in the diaspora was outlined.

The internal Zionist opposition viewed the matter in a rather different light. They, like Dubnow and other nationalist critics outside the WZO, held Herzl responsible for neglecting diaspora affairs, and they proposed a *Gegenwartsprogramm* as a major reform in Zionism. Where he had antagonized men such as Birnbaum and Lazare, they hoped to attract not only such veteran progressive Zionists, but also the progressive Jewish youth. Through activity in local diaspora affairs, they hoped to decentralize and democratize the Herzlian Zionist organization. In the presentation of the theme of *Gegenwartsarbeit* by Martin Buber, all these positions were derived from a theory that, like Dubnow's or Ahad Haam's, placed primary emphasis on the reestablishment of Jewish solidarity and consensus.

The Zionist interest in *Gegenwartsarbeit*, he said, was not produced because of the fading prospects of achieving the Herzlian ultimate goal. In fact, faith in the future goal made work on the tasks of the present possible. The rational, objective necessities of Zionism had the primary effect of arousing enthusiasm among disoriented Jews. The actual tasks of Zionism, however, had not fully satisfied the subjective needs of young progressives until the movement reached its present, new stage. A new, reflective Zionism, understanding the objective and subjective significance of the movement as one, had now attained the level of historical self-determination.

Inward and outward awareness complemented each other: we became more autonomous vis-à-vis the movement. We went our separate ways; but *one* idea united us: we share in a movement where political action represents only the indispensable ultimate consequence, requiring the strictest and tightest centralization, and where organization and agitation are only widely ramified and indispensable instruments, which must be relatively decentralized and be entrusted to those specifically qualified. The essence and soul of the movement, however, we see in the transformation of national life (*Volksleben*), in the education of a truly *new* generation, in the development of the Jewish people (*Stamm*) into a strong, united, autonomous, healthy, and mature community (*Gemeinschaft*). That is, in those processes which, at the moment, are inadequately expressed by the slogan of "advancement" (*Hebung*) conveyed to us by the London [Fourth Zionist] congress.[12]

Following the London congress, Austrian Zionists held a convention at Olmuetz (Olomouc) on March 24–25, 1901, at which the Herzlian and opposition elements established a unified territorial organization for the whole Austrian monarchy. A proposal for diaspora activities was introduced by Berthold Feiwel, of the emerging Democratic Faction, and adopted by the convention. It developed in greater detail the lines of action familiar to Austrian Zionists since before Herzl, and more recently revived in a Zionist party platform prepared on the occasion of communal elections. Under the heading of economic advancement, it was proposed to establish Zionist employment exchanges, vocational training in the crafts, planning and control of communal social welfare work, trade unions, and producers', consumers', and credit cooperatives. Under the heading of cultural advancement, it was proposed to establish adult education centers (Toynbee Halls), reading rooms and libraries, mobile libraries and newspaper exchanges, courses, lecture series, educational publications and services, Hebrew language and Jewish art societies, and clubhouses. Under the heading of corporal advancement, it was proposed to establish athletic and gymnastic societies, medical services, and medical and recuperative centers.

Another line of nationalist diaspora activity discussed at that time was Zionist participation, through a Jewish ethnic party, in general elections and political affairs. The pre-Herzlian Austrian Zionists had committed themselves to this line; indeed, diaspora nationalists had contended with strict Hovevei Zionists within the movement over primacy for local ethnic politics or for Palestine resettlement in the Zionist program. In September 1900, Adolf Stand, a veteran leader of Galician Zionists, proposed to Herzl that the movement put up candidates in the elections to the Austrian parliament, about to be held. However, it was decided to maintain the policy of not presenting Zionist candidates. Instead, other candidates were to be asked to indicate their sympathy for Zionist aims in order to earn Jewish support. Only after the call for elections to the first Russian Duma in 1905, and the broadening of the franchise in Austria in 1907, did Zionists participate as an ethnic party in general elections and politics.

On the issues that arose within the WZO at the turn of the century, Zionist radicals joined in opposition to the Herzlian policies that had estranged such men as Birnbaum and Lazare. Among those closely associated with the group that founded the Democratic Faction was the stormy petrel of the movement, Nahman Syrkin, whose socialist views, fully developed in his 1898 essay "The Jewish Problem and the Socialist-Jewish State," were often and vigorously proclaimed at the early Zionist congresses. In Russia, the potential popular strength of the Zionist opposition was concentrated largely in newly organized study circles and workers' organizations, similar to those of the socialists. These societies maintained contact with the WZO through a center for correspondence conducted by a Russian member of the Zionist Action Committee, Jacob Bernstein-Kohan, a man whose brother was famous as a revolutionary and political prisoner and who was himself kept under surveillance by the authorities because of his reputed radical connections.

In spite of these bonds and affinities, outright socialism found little more room in the Democratic Faction than it had earlier in the WZO. From the earliest discussions about founding a progressive Zionist students' and workers' faction, Nahman Syrkin tried in vain to gain support in the Democratic Faction for his socialist Zionist theory and strategy. He proposed two separate plans of activity, both to be conducted on socialist Zionist principles. In Palestine or in another suitable territory, a Jewish socialist commonwealth would be created by cooperative settlements of immigrant workers. In the diaspora, Zionists would cooperate with the social democratic revolutionary parties, on condition that the latter abandon their hostility to Jewish nationalism. When these proposals were rejected, Syrkin embarked on a series of attempts to create a socialist Zionist movement of his own, in direct rivalry with the emerging Democratic Faction. The faction itself considered proposals to pursue the economic advancement of the Jewish masses through training, cooperative institutions, and similar nonpolitical methods in the diaspora. But in the end, it lost its specific progressive coloration completely, merging into the common front of practical Zionists produced by the Uganda issue.

III

The attempts to create a socialist Zionism discussed so far were made by leaders, largely drawn from student circles, who had already defined themselves as Zionists before Herzl, during the Hovevei Zion period. The socialist organizations of their time were markedly indifferent to Jewish questions. The result of their efforts was insignificant, for they were unable to establish permanent organizations. But at that same time, a younger generation of Eastern Europeans was engaged in parallel efforts. These men, mostly in their teens at the turn of the century, reached political awareness and attained a mature identity under different circumstances than did Birnbaum and Syrkin. The Zionism that they personally encountered was represented by Herzl's WZO. On the other side, they confronted new socialist organizations, especially in Russia, for whom the Jewish question, far from being ignored, was a subject of bitter ideological disputes.

The primary ideological conflict was against the Bund in the major centers of the Pale of Settlement in Poland and Lithuania. In the Ukraine, Bessarabia, and Crimea, and in Austrian Galicia and Bukovina, the Bund, or its local surrogate, was slow to appear on the scene, and the chief opponents were Jewish ideologues of the German, Polish, or Russian socialist parties. The main issues concerned the relation of Jews to the revolution: were they qualified by their history and class structure to participate in it, and need the doctrine of social revolution include any specific provisions for Jewish problems? These questions produced a triple division, setting the cosmopolitans, Bundists, and socialist Zionists against each other.

The Jewish cosmopolitans in the German, Polish, and Russian socialist parties generally held that radicals need have no special doctrine for Jews. The "Jewish people" was an anachronism destined to disappear by assimilation, and Jews would thus be freed as human beings in the general liberation produced by the social revolution. They held any Bundist or Zionist attempt to defend specific Jewish interests to be irrelevant, if not diversionary. Also, they considered that the Jewish social structure—an undifferentiated, unstable mixture of petty bourgeoisie, pre-industrial craftsmen, obscurantist clerics, rootless migrants, and miscellaneous déclassés—made Jews almost as unsuitable as gypsies for any kind of progressive political organization. The rebelliousness produced by their hopeless position could be usefully employed only in a general movement of (Russian, Austrian, or Polish) workers, peasants, and intellectuals.

The Bund, as we have seen, dissented from these views. After some ideological hesitation, it came out in defense of a political struggle for Jewish rights, including cultural autonomy. Above all, it insisted on organizing Jewish workers separately, undeterred by the peculiar Jewish social and occupational distribution. There was in all this a restricted, ambiguous, not fully avowed but nonetheless quite distinct, quasi-nationalist commitment. Indeed, the Bund claimed to represent the Jewish people's interests more truly than either the Zionists or diaspora nationalists like Dubnow.

The socialist Zionists were certainly committed to activity on behalf of Jewish workers, but they took very seriously the argument that Jewish interests and the interests of the revolution were to a great extent unrelated. They were able to face this possibility openly because of a nationalist commitment far more uninhibited than the Bundists could consciously sustain. Marxists who were cool to Jewish labor organization could cite the fact that the true Russian proletarians, the factory hands in the most advanced and basic industries, were not Jews but urbanized Russian peasants. Bundists had to justify their extensive organization of Jewish workers on the narrow grounds (hardly relevant from a strict Marxist standpoint) that the general social revolution alone, without revolutionary Jewish political organization, would not truly or effectively emancipate the Jews as Jews. Labor Zionists, however, openly advanced the proposition that general social and economic advances could not solve the special problems of the Jews as workers.

They noted that precisely when machines were introduced, Jewish workers (e.g., the original laborers in the Borislaw oil fields) were dispensed with. Even Jewish manufacturers preferred to hire casual peasant labor for work in their factories while subcontracting certain operations to Jewish supervisors who sweated their Jewish fellow workers at home. From facts like these, labor Zionists derived a law of history, generalizing an earlier observation of the German economic historian Wilhelm Roscher. According to Roscher, mobile Jewish capitalists, not having the security of territorially rooted ethnic groups, contributed prominently to all such progressive but risky economic innovations as early capitalism. Once established, the new economic pursuits were taken up by the ruling ethnic groups, and Jewish capitalists were expelled or otherwise displaced. This rule held for Jewish labor as well, said the labor Zionists; consequently, economic upheavals brought about by capitalism would not cause Jews to be absorbed, like Russian peasants, in the industrial proletariat—certainly not in basic industries. They could point to the Jew-hatred evinced by gentile laborers of their own time as a convincing illustration of the point.

The problem of the Jewish worker was not merely one of his or her "surplus labor" that was being expropriated, but of finding employment in the face of ethnic discrimination, not to speak of inappropriate training. The ordinary methods of economic class struggle were, indeed, necessary to raise the sweatshop workers' wages, limit their hours, and improve their working conditions. But both worker and boss—particularly when the employer was himself a worker on subcontract to a larger industrialist—faced the same problem of finding work.

The solution must therefore be a constructive one, of common concern to all Jews—except, of course, the thin stratum of plutocrats, who were mostly assimilationists estranged from their people. As an immediate palliative, vocational training and producers' cooperatives were needed. A fundamental solution, however, was possible only by settling the Jews in compact masses in a territory of their own.

This, moreover, was the prerequisite which alone would make it possible for the normal revolutionary patterns to apply and the normal revolutionary methods to be effective in the Jewish situation. In their own land, according to some socialist Zionists—those influenced by the Russian populists and social revolutionaries—the Jews would create directly a socialist society, eliminating the whole travail of capitalism. Others, notably Ber Borochov, the foremost Marxist ideologist, projected a neo-Marxist dialectical pattern of development: the Jewish petit bourgeois, displaced by gentile competitors who enjoyed preferential ethnic treatment, would ultimately be driven to invest capital in Palestine, the ancestral homeland, a resource-poor country which no other capitalists would care to develop. Jewish capitalists would draw after them Jewish labor and thus produce the necessary conditions for a normal class struggle between different classes of a single people occupying its own land resources (or "strategic base") and then produce socialism according to the Marxian prescription.

Such propositions, in sharply conflicting versions, were developed under the acute pressures of the renewed pogrom wave and the revolutionary Russian situations that provoked it, as well as the inner-Zionist disputes arising from the so-called Uganda proposal. The impulse to form volunteer cadres to work in Palestine in response to the crisis that afflicted the New Yishuv in 1900 had already affected young people, many of whom had vague socialist, populist, and cooperativist views—

but these were few in number. It was the pogrom wave and the organization of Jewish self-defense units, in which young radical Zionists
played a prominent part, that brought about a large influx of student
and worker recruits to the Zionist ranks, organized separately from the
previously existing bodies. They arose in the midst of acute divisions
that the Uganda affair produced among Zionists. This, together with
their ideological affinities with socialism as well as Jewish nationalism,
thrust them at once into contention with rivals on both flanks as well
as with opposing positions within their own ranks.

When Herzl presented to the Zionist Congress in 1903, the tentative
British offer to open East Africa for Jewish settlement, a group of outraged opponents stormed out of the hall in protest. He was able to pacify
them sufficiently to conclude the immediate debate with a resolution to
set up a commission (not to be funded by the WZO treasury) that would
explore the proposal before the next congress. Before that congress convened two years later, Herzl had died, leaving the issue of diverting
Zionist efforts to various areas remote from Zion (the British East African offer having virtually been withdrawn in the meantime) to be
fought out by his passionately divided followers.

While Herzl retained the loyalty of a majority of the congress in 1903,
including some veteran Russian Zionists and the leaders of Mizrahi and
the Zionist federation in Palestine, the bulk of the Russian Zionist movement joined the opposition, the so-called "Nay-Sayers." There were no
Herzl loyalists among the scattered groups of Poalei Zion, the young
socialist Zionists, whose numbers were rapidly expanding, but concern
for the immediate problems of the Russian Jews, which had greatly contributed to Herzl's Uganda proposal, was also their dominating concern.
Abandoning hope to reestablish the Jews in Palestine, leading young
intellectuals met in Odessa in December 1904 and organized the Zionist
Socialist Workers' Party (SS), committed to a "territorialist" ideology
that sought to build a new "Zion" in some other available country. At
the Seventh Zionist Congress in 1905, this group, under the leadership
of Nahman Syrkin, left the WZO and formed a broader Socialist-
Territorialist party that joined in the Jewish Territorialist Organization
(ITO) created by Israel Zangwill.

Opponents of Ugandism in the WZO were concerned by the rise of
territorialism among the Poalei Zion and were anxious to support efforts
to counteract such defections in a growing sector of Jewish nationalist
organization. But both in the older Zionist ranks and among the young
socialist Zionists there were parallel differences regarding what approach
to adopt in this common struggle. The division in both cases was defined

by two issues: the question of the proper tactics to take in opposing the territorialists at the coming Seventh Zionist Congress, and the related question of the proper attitude to adopt toward a new antiterritorialist movement among Jewish nationalists, the Vozhrozdenie (Revival) group of intellectuals. The older anti-Ugandists were led by two veterans of the former Moscow Bilu group, Menahem Mendel Ussishkin and Yehiel Tschlenow. Ussishkin, who was intent on ousting the territorialists from the WZO, also took a distinctly cool approach to the Vozhrozdenie. Tschlenow favored a moderate line toward the territorialists in order to preserve the unity of the WZO; he and those who shared his approach also responded warmly to many aspects of the Vozhrozdenie program, which appeared well suited to the conditions that a new parliamentary regime in Russia seemed to promise.

The Vozhrozdenie activists, who emerged as a dominant force among the Poalei Zion groups opposed to the territorialist SS, took a line similar to that of the Ahad Haam–Dubnow critique of Herzlian Zionism. They questioned whether Jewish mass emigration could be readily absorbed and form a concentrated national polity, either in Palestine or in another territory, under existing circumstances. Their immediate hope, buoyed up by the current revolutionary enthusiasm in Russia, was to build Jewish national solidarity and strength in the diaspora by creating a "Sejm"—a representative governing body—for Jews as a recognized nationality endowed with cultural and linguistic rights on a basis of personal, exterritorial autonomy.

This course, they claimed in the early days of 1904–5, would eventually make it possible to achieve the territorial concentration and independence to which the Zionists aspired. But from the beginning it was apparent that their approach, seeking to build a political base that would encompass the whole Jewish community, was likely to downgrade their attachment to the Zionist organization, reducing it to a partisan body. In their subsequent development, they organized outside the WZO in 1906 as the Jewish Socialist Workers' party. Though Chaim Zhitlowsky emerged as one of their leaders, the organization did not ultimately identify with the Russian Social Revolutionary party, of which he was one of the early associates. Nor did they end as Social Democrats, in spite of the strong Marxist influence among them. In their final metamorphosis, the Sejmists were Dubnowian nationalists, identified primarily with Yiddishism and the principle of personal national autonomy.

In 1905, however, the Vozhrozdenie seemed likely to become the dominant influence among the antiterritorialist Poalei Zion. At first, they alone, had a clear ideological position and an impressive leadership cadre. But their equivocal stand on the immediate relevancy of work in Palestine was disturbing to those who insisted on exclusive, and urgent, concentration on this task. Among the agitators whom Ussishkin enlisted in his campaign to oust the territorialists from the WZO was the young radical philosopher Ber Borochov, who devoted his efforts mainly to the Poalei Zion. He succeeded in stemming the Vozhrozdenie campaign by meeting its challenge in the lists of Marxian dialectical argument. When Ussishkin forced the withdrawal of the territorialists at the Zionist Congress, the developing doctrine of Borochovism, which purported to prove that Jewish concentration precisely in Palestine and in no other territory was a historical necessity, became the prevailing orthodoxy of the Poalei Zion, who, in 1907, organized as a separate "world federation" within the WZO.

Nevertheless, the Palestine-oriented Poalei Zion federation that emerged could not remain immune to contemporary pressures for *Gegenwartsarbeit*. The Austrian Socialist-Zionists who joined had in any case a considerable tradition of local cooperative and trade union activity. In Russia, the local activism began with self-defense during the pogroms and involved Zionists of all kinds in the electoral politics generated by the convocation of the Duma. At a 1906 convention in Helsingfors, Russian Zionists, under the leadership of Tschlenow, Vladimir Jabotinsky, and allied Jewish journalists, adopted a program of immediate practical work in Palestine but also sketched an extensive, highly politicized program of *Gegenwartsarbeit*. They proposed a full parliamentary regime for Russia, among other general demands, and called for national autonomy for Jews, administered by democratically elected representative institutions. Ussishkin did not attend the Helsingfors convention, and those aligned with him remained cool to its radical diaspora nationalism; but the Poalei Zion organizations adopted the Helsingfors principles in various forms according to the possibilities in the several countries where they were organized. The world federation sought admission to the socialist Second International as the social democratic party of the stateless Jewish people.

Other issues further complicated the diverse activities of Poalei Zion parties and made for differences and divisions among them. The Russian and other parties inclined to turn Borochovism into a neo-Marxian orthodoxy. They tended to question participation in the Zionist Congress on the grounds that it was a policy of discredited "class collaborationism," and they accepted in practice, if not in principle, the elevation of Yiddish as the Jewish national language by the 1908 Czernovitz (Cernauti) conference—it was certainly the language of the Jewish proletariat among whom they worked. Also, cleaving to the "prognostic" pro-Palestinism of Borochov, which anticipated a "stychic" process of the "inevitable" flight of Jewish capital followed by Jewish labor to Palestine, they lacked a theoretical base for stimulating idealistic pioneering migration to Zion.

But these trends were accompanied by countervailing tendencies among the Poalei Zion and other young Zionists attracted to socialist ideals. Borochov himself, before developing his "prognostic" Palestinism, had strongly argued for an idealistic, "therapeutic" movement of a pioneering elite to lay the foundations for a gradual transition to mass immigration. His old vision could not be totally suppressed by his later theories, and it reemerged in various forms in his last years during and immediately after World War I. Other Poalei Zionists held to Palestinism "in principle"; the commitment to Hebrew rather than Yiddish also had its devotees among them. Outside the Poalei Zionist ranks, other young Zionists whose attraction was to voluntaristic, even utopian, rather than Marxist, socialism or to populism were organizing within the framework of the regular Zionist federations under the name of Zeirei Zion. In both cases, the principles of these young enthusiasts were logically consistent with, and conducive in principle to, immediate *aliyah* to Zion as pioneers (*haluzim*) without the sanction of the Borochovist stychic process. They contributed the leadership that gave the Second Aliyah its distinctive historic significance in Palestine.

◦ 7 ◦

The Young Workers

The State of Israel was founded in 1948 under the dominant leadership of men and women who came to Palestine in the Second Aliyah, between 1904 and 1914. For nearly 30 years, they governed the new state through shifting coalitions, always controlled by their own (variously named) labor party. Their hegemony rested on the base of a network of cooperatives, communes, and a comprehensive labor union organization of extraordinary scope, considered to be the authentic fruit of seeds they planted in the time of the Second Aliyah.

As with the First Aliyah, however, those responsible for these historic achievements were a minor fraction of the immigrants. The Yishuv grew from 55,000 to 85,000—at a faster rate than the generally expanding Palestine population, which, at a rough estimate, rose to about 700,000 by 1915. Two-thirds of the Jewish increase is attributed to net immigration: over 40,000 arrived, but nearly half that number of Jews left the country. Most of the net growth was in the traditional holy cities, particularly Jerusalem, whose Jewish population rose from 28,000 to 45,000. Jewish farm settlers also increased from 3,000 to 12,000, largely through the growth of the plantation villages that were the characteristic achievement of the First, not the Second Aliyah. The immigrants were divided mainly between traditionally oriented groups, both Sephardi and Ashkenazi, who were drawn to the Old Yishuv, and petty bourgeois settlers who joined the emerging New Yishuv in the towns and *moshavot*. About a fourth of the immigrants were young people seeking work, but the vast majority left, disheartened by the difficulties they encountered. There were in addition some 2,500 Yemenites, who were no longer fully absorbed into the Old Yishuv as their predecessors had been in the 1880s; many settled as workers in the plantation villages. The total number of Jewish farm workers, for example, rose from perhaps 5,500 to about 12,000 before the period was closed because of the war in 1914. Approximately 7,500 were actively engaged in agricultural labor but only a few hundred of these were the *haluzim*, the pioneering volunteers who are celebrated as the founders of Israel's labor movement. The collective settlements for which they became famous were built on marginal resources initiated near the end of the Second Aliyah.

But what this handful of pioneers began represented a radical change in the direction of the developing New Yishuv. The crisis of the First Aliyah, following the abrupt transfer of the Rothschild villages to ICA in 1900, was given a new turn and a sharply heightened impact by the upheavals in Russia and in the affairs of the WZO after the Kishinev pogrom of 1903. The *haluzim* who came to Erez Israel in the Second Aliyah were formed in the crucible of those events. One significant effect of the pressures upon their generation was the militant mood that emerged among radical nationalists in the New Yishuv. They asserted themselves as an independent force in ways that sometimes demanded unwelcome decisions from their diaspora supporters.

The conditions for advancing the Zionist project in Palestine were significantly affected by the sharp changes that the successive shocks of the period produced in the politically oriented institutions and partisan groupings of the diaspora. After Herzl's death and the tumultuous divisions his Uganda proposal provoked at the subsequent congress, his successors reluctantly suspended the pursuit of evanescent diplomatic victories and gave renewed attention to the immediate possibilities of resettlement and development in Palestine. The Young Turk revolution of 1908, which established a parliamentary republic on the ruins of the Ottoman sultanate, led Max Nordau, Herzl's close ally, to declare that, given equal treatment under the new regime, Zionism did not require a colonial-style charter. The WZO's "practical" efforts were now implemented by a Jaffa office headed by Arthur Ruppin, and within a few years, control of the organization passed entirely into the hands of old opponents of Herzl's policies.

Both ICA and the WZO now followed policies that offered new opportunities for young idealistic volunteers. The colonizing agencies purchased *miri* land in remote areas that had to be occupied and prepared for permanent settlement. Failure to cultivate these acquisitions could lead to their seizure by the government in three years, or to their immediate invasion by neighboring Arab villagers or Bedouins who moved plant crops or graze flocks on them and so established their own claims. The Jewish land-settlement agencies found it useful to protect their rights by bringing in unskilled immigrants to prepare them as farmers in training centers on not yet allocated land purchases, under the guidance of professionally competent managers and instructors. Moreover, because the agencies were interested in avoiding overdependence on their support, and because many of the professional staff were recruited from the same regions and communities as their clientele, they were prepared to entrust greater responsibility, and sooner, to the settlers and to the worker-trainees. A tradition of cooperation between such patrons and their clients began to be formed—though not, of course, without recurrent friction and sharp clashes.

There was at the same time an awakening of nationalist activism in the towns. Hebraist educators and young Zionist entrepreneurs developed campaigns for modern, Hebrew-language schools, built new Jewish housing quarters in Jaffa (Tel Aviv) and Haifa (the Carmel), and promoted modest new industrial and commercial undertakings. Projects of this sort that exceeded the capacity of individual investors were supported by the Zionist Anglo-Palestine Bank and the Palestine Land Development Company (PLDC), created by the WZO Jaffa office. In many ways—particularly in the campaign to make Hebrew the common spoken language of the Yishuv as a whole—the New Yishuv's urban activists worked in close harmony with the young, Second Aliyah worker-immigrants.

In all of this activity there was the beginning of a self-conscious, self-assertive pretension of the New Yishuv to determine the policies essential to its own healthy growth. This meant not simply a claim to some local autonomy but, increasingly, a claim to a privileged voice in the councils of the WZO.

At the same time, the most active element among the radical Palestinian Zionists, the newly arrived young worker-volunteers, frequently had ties to diaspora parties or organizations involving ideological commitments unrelated to the local scene. They were preshaped by traumatic experiences that set them apart from their predecessors and, in different expressions, produced internal strains among them, despite all they had in common.

I

Among Russian Jews in the first decade of the twentieth century, the fin de siècle mood of disorientation, pervasive among educated young Europeans of the period, was raised to a high pitch of political awareness and irritability. The shock of renewed pogroms, amid the general demoralization of Russian society, struck a generation of young Jews already trained by Zionism and socialism in an ethic of active resistance. Reaching a scale of violence exceeding earlier attacks—though merely foreshadowing the greater disasters of later years—the Kishinev pogrom gave Zionist radicals a base in immediate, personal experience for their militant ethos of autoemancipation.

In terms of ideology, the labor Zionists were sharply divided since the earliest days. What they shared, and what united them with other Zionists, was the myth of autoemancipation. The emotional core of Zionism was nowhere more clearly stated or elaborated with more refinement, than among these radicals—except perhaps in the writings of Hebrew poets and essayists, teachers and intellectuals, who were contemporaries of the Second Aliyah.

Adverse circumstances, as was previously noted, allowed the Zionist movement to give little or no expression to its basic drive. But in Hebrew literature, emotion and imagination ran free. The mythos of autoemancipation, in sharply opposed interpretations, was elaborated in the sociological or aesthetic categories of currently fashionable thought.

Ahad Haam was a major source and storm center of this debate. In his rethinking of Zionist doctrine, the original, merely political, connotation of autoemancipation was broadened into a general nationalist principle of social and cultural revival. The first task of autoemancipation—a task requiring personal commitment—was to rebuild the social consensus and revive the secular culture that Jews had lost in the long exile. Doing so required not ancient priests nor modern administrators or diplomats, but enthusiasts like the ancient bands of prophets.

Underlying Ahad Haam's call for self-dedication to the national revival were general assumptions drawn from the vitalistic, organismic sociological theorists of his time. In the spirit of that school, he decried alienation from the self and the bondage of the living present to past or future. He attacked the Eastern traditionalists for crushing the national will under the burden of an ossified past; but they at least were not false to the national self. The more contemptible role, and perhaps the greater threat, he felt, was that of the Western modernists, who made themselves slaves in the name of an illusionary future. Some sought in vain to deny that national self, concealing it from themselves and others under the transparent veil of a Jewish mission to the gentiles. Ahad Haam poured out his bitterest scorn on this attempt to subordinate Jewish life to the universal good and its present existence to a transhistorical goal.

In Ahad Haam these underlying themes, occasionally stated in bare, brief dicta, were never directly attacked on a speculative level but crop up as leitmotifs in his polemics on current public issues. Yet they had a greater, more widely effective impact than his various political positions. Haim Nahman Bialik, an enthusiastic admirer of Ahad Haam, stated the

essentials directly with a poet's bold intuition. His essay praising the
legal rather than the homiletical aspects of Jewish tradition stands as a
defense of the living present of action against the past of traditional
passivity and the future of millennial dreams. In one of his poems evoked
by the Kishinev pogroms, Bialik, the disciple, drew from the depths of
Ahad Haam's gospel the following manifesto of vitalistic radicalism—
expressed with a stark intensity that may have startled, if not repelled,
the master:

> If there be justice—now let it be shown!
> But if I must be blotted out under the skies
> Before justice arise,
> Then forever be blasted his throne![1]

The younger literati of the Hebrew nationalist revival—the "Young
Ones," as they called themselves—took up such themes with ardor. Led
by Mikha Yosef Berdichevsky, they cultivated a Hebraic Nietzscheanism
whose primary demand was to free the living present from the dead hand
of the past.

Their immediate ancestor in Hebrew letters, as they were vividly
aware, was Ahad Haam; and yet he was also the target of their attack.
Berdichevsky says of Ahad Haam's first volume of collected essays:

> Not since I began to read books have I read anything so cogent which yet
> aroused—together with feelings of heartfelt respect—a resistance to many
> of his thoughts, his expressions and ideas, so powerful that they forced
> me to come to an opposite conclusion on these matters.[2]

Ahad Haam, he felt, had betrayed the vital message of his own doctrine
by his inconsistency and halfheartedness. In spite of all that Ahad Haam
had said against the hidebound traditionalists and in favor of openness
to the demands of new times, he was unable to sustain an unlimited
tolerance toward innovation. He regarded a particular tradition—the
austere, rational, universalistic ethic of impartial justice—as being organically identified with historical Judaism. He therefore rejected incompatible ideas: not only the Christian doctrine of altruism (an inversion
of egoism, Ahad Haam thought, wherein the self is sacrificed to the
selfish interests of others) but also the neo-Hellenic hedonism that was
preached, albeit in a severely pessimistic, melancholic, and quite desperate vein, by the Hebraic Nietzscheans. To import either of these into
Jewish culture according to Ahad Haam, would be an adulteration po-

tentially fatal to Judaism. But Berdichevsky and the other Young Ones passionately proclaimed that they were not devoted to Judaism; they were devoted to Jews. The threats they feared were to the survival, the inherent worth of life, of individual Jews. And among these dangers, the dead hand of history, Jewish conventionalism in any form, including that favored by Ahad Haam, was in their eyes the most menacing and immediate.

Notwithstanding his harshness toward Ahad Haam, Berdichevsky had his own ambivalence regarding Jewish history and tradition: by no means did he wish to break cleanly with either. He was essentially a *maskil*, like Ahad Haam. He wished to liberate the present by a revolutionary break with the past—not because he rejected the past per se, but because this was the present need. For Berdichevsky remained continuously, profoundly, and productively involved with Jewish history, tradition, and religion. He undertook to restore a balance by regaining for his new Hebraic man those parts of his cultural heritage that were suppressed in the rabbis' canon of normative Judaism. He retrieved every hint of rebellion, every suggestion of heretical, countermoral, antirational, militant, antipietistic, self-assertive heroism contained in Hebrew literature and built upon them his own imaginative reconstructions. He led in his generation's restoration of dim figures of Jewish paganism that were suggested in the laconic phrases of the Bible and in early rabbinic literature. He heralded their new appreciation of Hasidism and other mystic or even pseudomessianic movements that had been held in low repute by the reigning intellectual traditions of their elders.

Where even Berdichevsky held back, another Hebraist of his generation who stood closest to the Second Aliyah committed himself fully. In the rejection of Jewish history by the proletarian editor, essayist, and novelist Yosef Haim Brenner, there were no defensive reservations, no search for a suppressed tradition of national glory with which to prop up one's battered identity. Instead there is the bold statement:

> . . . we have survived, we live. True, but what is our life worth? We have no heritage. Each generation gives nothing of its own to its successor. And whatever was transmitted—the rabbinical literature—were better never handed down to us.[3]

Such radicalism, while rooted in Berdichevsky's, had a consistency and ruthlessness that Brenner knew his friend could not share. Berdichevsky being a man of letters who sought to revolutionize a people's historic traditions, his sphere, in spite of everything, was the past, no matter how fiercely he insisted on immediacy and the primacy of the present.

Brenner's commitment to the living present was personal and actual, not literary, and his literary work was itself an immediate expression of his present agony of life. He suffered among the emigrant mass in London and ended his days among the workers in Zion. He did not choose to go to the people in a romantic haze of populist enthusiasm, like the *Narodniki* of an earlier generation. He *was* of the people; he was under no illusions as to their merits. Living in the London ghetto, he had no real hope for the proletariat; and living among the workers in Zion, he saw clearly why there was no reasonable basis for confidence in their future. But precisely because everything was hopeless, if one faced facts with rational honesty, the only honest recourse was to hold to life against rational calculation and in the face of hopelessness. In the state of rootlessness, one must nevertheless begin at the roots; one must, "nevertheless," build foundations. If he found himself, to a degree, in his life among the workers in Zion, it was not so because he took comfort from what they already had done there or because he had real faith in their future, but because they were beginning everything anew and working and building at rock bottom. He says in one of his autobiographical novels:

> This is what I have learned from my life's experience, and this is my
>   personal testament.
> Life is evil, but always mysterious . . . death is evil.
> The world is sorely complicated but colorful too, and occasionally
>   beautiful.
> Man is wretched, but sometimes splendid too.
> The Jewish people, rationally speaking, has no future.
> One must, nevertheless, work.
> As long as you breathe there are noble acts and ennobling moments.
> Long live labor, Jewish, human labor![4]

If there was one symbol that more than any other impressed itself on the consciousness of *haluzim* and gave their movement its self-image, it was Brenner's "Nevertheless!" The same theme, spoken out of an even sharper trauma of a later generation—one that suffered the disorder and bloodshed of the postwar days in Russia, the Ukraine, and Poland—was shaped into a new mythic symbol by the poet Yizhak Lamdan. In his poem cycle "Masada," which was built on the image of the desperate, suicidal last stand of the zealots against the Romans, Lamdan crystallized the fundamental mood of his generation of immigrants to Zion in verses like the following:

> Who are you that come, stepping heavy in silence?
>   —The remnant.
> Alone I remained on the day of great slaughter.
> Alone, of father and mother, sisters and brothers.
> Saved in an empty cask hid in a courtyard corner.
> Huddled, a child in the womb of an anxious mother.
>   I survived.
> Days upon days in fate's embrace I cried and begged
>   for mercy:
> Thy deed it is, O God, that I remain.
>   Then answer: Why?
> If to bear the shame of man and the world.
>   To blazon it forever—
> Release me! The world unshamed will flaunt this shame
>   As honor and spotless virtue!
> And if to find atonement I survive
>   Then answer, fate: Where?
> So importuning a silent voice replied:
>   "In Masada!"
> And I obeyed that voice and so I came.
> Silent my steps will raise me to the wall,
> Silent as all the steps filled with the dread
>   Of what will come.
> Tall, tall is the wall of Masada.
> Deep, deep is the pit at its feet.
> And if the silent voice deceived me,
> From the high wall to the deep pit
>   I will fling me.
> And let there be no sign remaining,
>   And let no remnant survive.[5]

This grim affirmation of the direct act and the living present was not only a current fashion among literati, where it might have had no more than transient influence; men and women who built and led the labor movement express a strikingly similar mood in their reminiscences of the Second Aliyah. Whereas the writers rebelled against history and an ossified tradition, the rebellion of men of action had a more contemporary focus: it produced an emotional strain against the rational analysis of the very ideologies to which they were attracted. The following excerpts transcribed from a talk by Berl Katznelson ascribe his *aliyah* to his contempt for the inauthenticity of deeds behind the words of all conventional current ideologies:

> Just as I was very skeptical on Zionist questions, so too, I was full of doubts in the matter of Hebrew, as to whether Hebrew had any function in the life of the people. . . . Just as there was good reason logically to oppose Palestine (To go to Palestine was to go to Abdul Hamid's country. We were fighting the monarchical regime here, and should we go to a land where Abdul Hamid ruled?) so, about Hebrew, logically one should say that the masses had no need of Hebrew. They could never learn it, to know it. But I did not want to close this account yet.
>
> I could tell you many things on this subject, how much renegadism there was. . . . I remember I lost all interest in the debate about Hebrew from the moment I saw how a group of men, themselves reared on Hebrew literature, how lightly they abandoned this cause. . . .
>
> . . . On that day my final decision was taken . . . both regarding Hebrew and regarding Erez Israel. I say again—it was not out of any Zionist conviction [that I came to Palestine], but out of pure shame, out of obstinate pride, out of unwillingness to be part of that generation that didn't even have the strength to expire honorably.[6]

In the case of Katznelson, the paradoxes of the above statement are understandable and consistent, for his whole career was marked by skepticism toward rational ideologies and by faith in the power of personal commitment. His socialist leanings were toward the revolutionary voluntarists—the utopians and anarchist syndicalists—especially those least encumbered with scientistic doctrines. Leaders of the Marxist Poalei Zion were not so likely to take his calmer attitude toward the current ideological positions of their diaspora party. Yet the outstanding Poalei Zion leader who joined the Second Aliyah, Yizhak Ben-Zvi, tells of the motives of his own migration in a vein not unlike that of Katznelson:

> In the name of the party I spoke [at a rally in October 1905, at the height of the revolution] to a public of ten thousand persons; in Russian, of course. I spoke as a Jew—about the Russian revolution, about the Jewish share in it, and about our aspiration to live as a free people in Zion. And as I spoke from the balcony of the theater my mind's eye was filled with

the living image of the holy city of Jerusalem ruined and desolate without her sons. . . . At that moment I asked myself: To whom am I making speeches? . . . Can we Jews truly share in this revolution and this victory? . . . At that time I came to the fixed decision that my place is in Erez Israel, that I must go there and devote my life to building it as soon as possible.[7]

For Katznelson, the personal commitment to build Zion took the place of ideology; for Ben-Zvi, it overcame ideology. In the case of another paramount leader and father image of the Second Aliyah, the venerable Aaron David Gordon, the direct act and personal commitment of living and working on the soil of Erez Israel became a fundamental postulate upon which an ambitious ideology was erected. Autoemancipation, conceived by some Zionists as the principle of political action and by others as the principle of cultural policy, became for him the rule by which man should lead his whole life in relation to the cosmos, and particularly in relation to his fellowmen.

Gordon's folk philosophy, drawing on simple vitalistic analogies, made life the supreme value, which was extended metaphysically to embrace the whole of nature in a single, biological chain of being. Health and strength—the amplification of life forces—were continuously derived from work on the soil and converted to a higher spiritual power by the natural units of human existence: the family, the nation, and the universal brotherhood of nations. The principle of this harmonious development was respect for life as an end in itself in all its manifestations.

The root of all evil, then, was the reduction of any manifestation of life to a mere means. Thus, the supreme virtue in man's relation to other entities—beginning with the soil and ending with one's neighbors—was conservation, respect for the ecological and social environment; or, as Buber would later put it, an I–Thou relation to the cosmos. The supreme vice, accordingly, was exploitation, parasitism: Buber's I–It relation. Only by creating an artificial environment, detached from nature, especially an urban one, and by creating an artificial self-interest, whether of simple individual egoism or of class interest, could such vice take root and thrive; for its inevitable consequence was debilitation and morbidity of the self. The Jews, through the workings of fate, not through choice, had been cast into such an environment and exposed to such vice. Only the powerful infusion of a will to live, transmitted from their ancient national origins, preserved them from total decline. What they needed vitally was to emancipate themselves from the exile, with its debilitating parasitism, and restore their symbiosis with nature and with mankind in the place where their roots were still attached—in the soil of Zion.

Autoemancipation was thus offered to youth by Gordon not as a doctrine of national salvation to which their lives must be subordinated but as a doctrine of personal salvation by which their lives must be elevated, for Gordon held self-sacrifice to be a cardinal sin, barely better than exploiting others or dependency on others. Echoing Ahad Haam's rejection of the Christian ethos of altruism, he declared self-sacrifice to be the obverse of parasitism, not its opposite. No man may make himself a means to the ends of others any more than he may exploit them for his ends; nor may he sacrifice his todays for his own or anyone else's tomorrows. Thus, Gordon argued against Zionist appeals to the impulse of self-sacrifice in recruiting young colonists, just as he rejected national subsidies to make the colonists' lot easier. The only authentic and, indeed, the only reliable motive for Zionist pioneering, he said, was the impulse of self-realization.

This attitude crystallized into the central principle of all *haluz* youth groups: the principle of *hagshamah azmit* (self-realization). The slogan, echoing Gordon's philosophy, was far from being unambiguous, as we shall see. But a major part of its effectiveness lay in the appeal of its vitalistic, Gordonian overtones to young Jews after World War I. This was a time when young men violently rebelled against subjecting the new generation and the present moment to either the past or the doctrinaire future. In particular, the German youth movements, rejecting the entire culture and society of their elders in order to start afresh in the lap of nature and the brotherhood of their peer groups, powerfully affected Zionist youth in formerly Austrian Poland. The poverty and desperation of postwar life in Eastern and Central Europe made the need to emigrate permanent and compelling. Against this background, the organization of *haluzim* not only offered a pragmatic escape but promised a new, elevated, meaningful life. The ideal of *hagshamah azmit* was imbued with a romanticism of sheer liberation, not only of release but of redemption from the hopeless impasse and the social and economic frustration of exile. These themes are powerfully accented in the following rhapsody concerning Klosova, a training camp for *haluzim* in Poland in the 1930s.

> Klosova! What associations are bound up with the name! Not a specific place, but a human ideal, an opportunity which appeared to every young man, to every simple son of Israel: to become a *worker*, to be different! It was an infectious dream which did not miss a single Jewish home, a possibility that I, you, he, everyone can attain and realize. The rumor that a simple man hewed stones and also sang and danced, and lived in a

commune, and that these were not exceptions, that everyone could live and be like them, had in it a magic power capable of transfiguring life. This was no myth of the Hero and the Leader, who commands us to follow in his tracks, to obey him, to do him homage. No! This idea was different: you and I can be different, we, all of us can make manifest that essential thing which is the depth of our being.[8]

The young workers of the Second Aliyah came from varied ideological backgrounds. A. D. Gordon's Tolstoyan gospel of self-realization, converting autoemancipation from a political doctrine to a principle of individual activism, undoubtedly expressed a mood common to all who identified with the self-image of pioneering labor Zionism. But the philosophy of voluntaristic idealism that it implied, and that Gordon explicitly formulated, was not one all could accept. It was especially congenial to those radicals who had been oriented primarily to activity in the WZO and to the Russian populist tradition. Those, on the other hand, who had been oriented primarily to the social democratic labor movement and to Marxist historical materialism were indoctrinated against such neo-Romantic utopianism; indeed, Gordon developed his doctrine largely in a continuing polemic against them.

The activism which the new immigrants considered to be their own special quality, distinguishing them from other Zionists, was at first a much grosser and simpler sentiment than in Gordon's elaboration; one may add at once that it was of more lasting effect in its cruder form. It was expressed, for example, in relation to the common witticism defining a Zionist as a Jew who collected money from another Jew in order to send a third Jew to Palestine; the labor Zionists proudly identified themselves as the "third Jew" in this aphorism and saw in this their radical break with conventional Zionism. In such a context, *hagshamah azmit* became defined as the commitment to perform personally in Zion whatever tasks were most necessary for the success of the movement, no matter how dangerous, difficult or menial.

If veteran Zionist leaders virtually conceded their political bankruptcy by turning to Uganda as a haven for Jewish refugees from the Kishinev pogroms, then young radicals had to demonstrate a heroic recalcitrance: those who organized self-defense groups in the face of pogroms must also go to live in Zion, which the others had practically forsaken. If, according to populist doctrine, the spoken language was the foundation of national culture and peasant labor was the just basis for national appropriation of a territory, then these constituted commitments to be carried out in person, and at once, under any conditions. Not negotiations for a charter to resettle, nor cultivation of the national spirit, not any merely preparatory measures whatever, but the essential act, the resettlement of workers speaking Hebrew, was the duty of Zionists; this duty the Zionist radicals adopted as their own. There was here a strong element of the very same self-sacrificial impulse that Gordon deplored.

In much of this, the young men and women of the Second Aliyah echoed views that were common ground among non-Herzlian Zionists at the time. Since the Rothschild policy switch in 1900, Zionist leaders had begun appealing for young volunteers to serve the faltering cause in its crisis. Proposals of this sort by men such as Ussishkin were highly pragmatic and narrow in scope, addressing the immediately pressing problems of the movement. Moreover, his challenge to the young was to set aside long-term career plans for a limited period of public service—not a challenge to commit themselves at the outset to a lifetime of pioneering.

Young Russian Jews of the late nineteenth and early twentieth centuries responded to such appeals not simply with pragmatic understanding of the Zionist movement's needs, but out of a personal need for release from immediately experienced pressures. Restricted access to schooling and oppressive economic and political conditions in Russia led a growing number to seek freedom and opportunity in other countries. Some began to train in occupations broadly relevant to the current projects for Jewish resettlement: not only medicine, now a profession aspired to by young women as well as men, but engineering, the applied sciences, and especially agronomy attracted socially sensitized young students. These were rather diffuse, unfocused inclinations in many cases.

The Kishinev pogroms, and the commitment to self-defense which energized a generation of young Jews, made the Palestine-oriented activists among them respond to the appeal for service with urgency and ardor, in a spirit of revolt against the Jewish situation in the diaspora. They called themselves the "new Bilu," renewing the mythic image of self-dedication to national service of their predecessors. But now they had to define themselves also in relation to the many new, elaborately developed, rival ideologies that contended against each other in the community. Their commitment to labor in Palestine could not be a simple, pragmatic response to the unquestioned needs of an existing organization. They began with specific, mainly socialist propensities beyond conventional Zionism, and they developed "objective" analyses of the Jewish crisis that posed a wider range of alternatives, both in Zionism and in socialism, than was suggested by the limited organizational problems that concerned Ussishkin.

Yosef Trumpeldor, who shared Ussishkin's attitudes perhaps more than others of his period, is a characteristic example. During the Russo-Japanese War, he served at Port Arthur, where he lost his left arm, was cited for heroism, and thereafter was raised to officer rank in the army reserves. He began to organize young Jews for Zionist service at first in a Japanese prison camp, and later continued this work as a student in Saint Petersburg and in southern Russia. He thought and worked along the same lines as Ussishkin: his recruits were to prepare themselves (by training on farms in Russia) for whatever labor or technical service was required by the Zionist project in Erez Israel. In other words, they were to submit themselves (under a military-style discipline) to the objective needs of practical Zionism and were to accept voluntarily whatever personal sacrifice this compliance might entail. But unlike Ussishkin, Trumpeldor conceived his activist program in the spirit of an overriding utopian socialism. His labor army was to combine military discipline with a Tolstoyan collectivist vision.

When the Poalei Zion turned to Marxism and adopted the Borochovist version of dialectical materialism, thereby attributing historical inevitability to the Jewish national restoration in Palestine as well as to the social revolution, they introduced a major ideological complication into the simple commitment to practical Zionism demanded by Ussishkin. After having used Borochov as his trusted aide in combating the territorialist and diaspora nationalist deviations, Ussishkin turned away from the social-democratic Zionists and gave his support to the Zeirei Zion, youth groups attached to the Russian Zionist federation. But this body of young enthusiasts, from whose ranks *haluzim* began to move to Palestine, had its own romantic, populist utopian socialist leanings, and it attached broad social and ethical implications to the act of *aliyah*, beyond the narrow pragmatic intentions of Ussishkin. They were especially open to the prophetic teachings and example of A. D. Gordon.

Yet neither the Poalei Zion nor the Zeirei Zion, nor even the strategic mind of Yosef Trumpeldor, set up procedures that effectively committed their followers to unconditional and immediate *aliyah*. Those who went from their ranks at once to labor in Palestine did so as deviant individuals, moved by their own compulsions and not under instruction nor even in accordance with the leaders' doctrines. Trumpeldor wanted his young recruits to go through a considerable course of prior training and to set up a collective of communal villages in Russia in order to ensure success when they should transfer their forces to Palestine. The first of his circle to migrate, the young romantic, Zvi Schatz, did so in 1910 out of the sheer urge for action, in spite of Trumpeldor's elder-brotherly advice. In 1911, Schatz returned to Russia for a visit, and at a conference in Romny he urged immediate *aliyah* and training for work in Palestine. He succeeded in persuading four comrades to join him. They began sending urgent letters to Trumpeldor, and in 1912 Trumpeldor followed, without his small army but intent on forming a string of communes united in a disciplined collective.

By that time, there was already a scattered community of *haluzim* in Palestine—some, like Katznelson, detached from any diaspora party or organization, but others drawn from the ranks of the Poalei Zion and Zeirei Zion. Neither of the latter organizations was committed to a strategy of *aliyah* in the same way as Trumpeldor. The Zeirei Zion developed an eclectic Zionist progressivism, in which diaspora nationalism was combined with Palestine-oriented practical Zionism of a romantic-populist kind. This was an atmosphere that fostered individual commitments to *aliyah* but neither required nor supported it in an organized fashion. The Poalei Zion party, which grew internationally by incorporating disparate elements—Austrian and American as well as Russian socialist Zionists, and disillusioned territorialists like Nahman Syrkin as well as diaspora nationalists like Chaim Zhitlowsky—had a Borochovist core that was committed to a well-defined, elaborate ideology. Their "prognostic" doctrine of the inevitable concentration of the Jews in Palestine did not propose the immediate immigration of labor pioneers: it was the displaced Jewish petty capitalist who would have to initiate the population transfer. This position was opposed by some who, though adhering to social-democratic Marxism, considered that the commitment to Palestine was a matter of principle, not of prognostic inevitability. Their commitment was personal, subjective, not objectively deduced—of the same kind that impelled Yizhak Ben-Zvi to his *aliyah* in spite of his loyalty to Borochov and Borochovism.

Those who came, each out of his or her individual needs, shared a common generational impulse—a common *mentalité*. They were divided, however, by prior attachments to rival parties and youth organizations of socialist-oriented diaspora Zionism.

II

The first wave of the Second Aliyah, from December 1903 through 1905, brought *haluzim* who aimed to become wage laborers in the New Yishuv, particularly in the *moshavot*, in order to save the settlements for the Zionist enterprise: to keep them from becoming Arab in population, French in culture, and Ugandist in political sentiment. These settlers

shared the general Zionist abhorrence of dependency, whether on subsidies or on administrators, but drove it to fanatical extremes: thus, they
rejected suggestions of financial assistance to become small proprietors
on the grounds that this would defeat their main purpose: to constitute
a Jewish farm workers' class.

Although these views aroused the sympathy and admiration of some
radical Zionists among the First Aliyah settlers, the new immigrants encountered what they perceived as an overwhelming response of rejection
and derision. At their way stations to Palestine, they met disillusioned
reemigrants, who gave depressing reports of Erez Israel. Then when they
arrived and sought employment, they found that the planters who came
to hire workers preferred to choose experienced, readily available Arab
farmhands, and the green Jewish youths were left standing idle. The
secular-nationalist and socialist leanings of the *haluzim* led traditionalist
planters in Petah Tikvah, the largest labor market among the *moshavot*,
to boycott them within a year of their first appearance. The unaccustomed heat, malaria attacks, primitive living conditions, and low-paying,
irregular, backbreaking toil defeated the vast majority of them; at a
rough estimate some 9,000 of about 11,000 who came seeking work
left the country after exposure to Palestinian conditions.

Those who held out were a band of beleaguered individuals, painfully
aware of their isolation. Some who had already bonded with each other
in the diaspora before they arrived, such as an early group from Romny
and the famous handful who had distinguished themselves as a self-
defense unit during the Gomel pogrom, held together for comfort and
support and served as an active core for major innovative ventures of
the Second Aliyah. Those who came alone, the great majority of the
haluzim, looked for similar ties of a common background, in the same
way as immigrants everywhere.

But there was another force of mutual attraction—their sense of a
common mission—that made the *haluzim* seek a broad base for union
and collaboration among all those who shared it. They were encouraged
by a few exemplary figures among the older settlers, who saw new hope
for the Yishuv in their coming. They formed small, local societies in Jaffa
and nearby settlements, where there were conducted lectures, discussions, and excursions into the countryside, and they tried to help newcomers find work.

After preliminary discussions in Petah Tikvah in July, they met in
Jaffa during the Sukkot festival in the fall of 1905 and formed a countrywide organization to revive spoken Hebrew and secular Hebrew culture and to reclaim and reform the First Aliyah villages by establishing

Jewish labor there. At the same time, the small band of *haluzim* split
into two camps in a dispute over the name chosen by the majority,
Hapoel Hazair (The Young Worker). Those among them who had belonged to Poalei Zion societies in the diaspora came with an already
developed sense of their collective identity; they felt it altogether appropriate that the new body too should call itself Poalei Zion (Zionist workers), since this name precisely fitted its declared purpose: to become
workers in Zion. The rejection of their name, which implied rejection of
their already established organizational loyalty, caused them to opt out
of Hapoel Hazair and to organize the Palestine party of Poalei Zion in
the following month.

Thus, the Second Aliyah had hardly begun before two organizations
identified with the new workers arose. The several, somewhat disparate
tendencies that motivated the Second Aliyah *haluzim* were combined in
characteristically different ways in Hapoel Hazair and the Poalei Zion.
The subjective drive to build a new life in revolt against the Jewish condition in exile, generally shared by the *haluzim*, was more clearly dominant in Hapoel Hazair. The compulsion to serve the objective requirements of a socialist Zionist solution for the problems of Jews, which was
felt by all, had more compelling specific effect among the ideologically
rigorous Poalei Zion. They were doctrinally committed to the social revolution and the class struggle, while the socialist leanings of Hapoel
Hazair were generally vague and sentimental. Nationalism was the conscious priority of Hapoel Hazair and their commitment to Hebrew was
overwhelming. The Poalei Zion liked to think of their nationalism as a
dialectical necessity of the class struggle and were torn between Yiddish,
the language of the diaspora Jewish labor movement, and Hebrew, the
language of national revival in Erez Israel and the medium that could
serve to unite the Sephardim, Yemenites, and Ashkenazim ingathered
there.

The two organizations were predisposed from the start to different
strategies and structural designs. The Poalei Zion began as an ideological
party, associated with a world movement; during the Sukkot festival of
1906, they propounded a Palestinian party platform closely following
the one adopted by the Poalei Zion in the Ukraine earlier that year.
Hapoel Hazair long debated, inconclusively, whether to consider itself
an ideological or a professional association; during the Second Aliyah it
never succeeded in defining a full-fledged ideological platform in spite of
fitful efforts to formulate one. Its principled, individualistic voluntarism
for years inhibited it from developing a tight organizational tie with a
worldwide movement of its own. The commitment to Zionist-Hebraist

pioneering, which was the doctrinal core of Hapoel Hazair, was viewed as an act of personal freedom and unregimented choice. Given such differences on fundamentals between the two organizations—one more attuned to the subjective appeal, the other to the objective demands of Zionist pioneering—it is understandable why disciplined collective units capable of deploying needed personnel to strategic tasks were generally organized among Poalei Zionists rather than by their rivals. The cooperatives and collectives, essential for the mutual support of the *haluzim*, that were initiated under the inspiration of Hapoel Hazair were more often marked by utopian romanticism.

A few years after the first arrival and initial organization of the Second Aliyah, these differences rooted in the diaspora background of the parties were overcast by new policies that responded to their common experience in Palestine. As new arrivals came in larger numbers, the veterans of Hapoel Hazair who tried to serve them abandoned some early purist attitudes. They continued to reject direct philanthropic assistance to individual immigrants and settlers, but sought such aid from Zionists for the services that they, as an organized body of workers, themselves provided: workers' kitchens, employment information, health care, and especially their literary journal and other cultural materials and activities. So too they now began to seek institutional ties to the diaspora Zeirei Zion. If that organization could not yet accept their single-minded commitment to *aliyah*, but continued to devote itself to diaspora *Gegenwartsarbeit*, it could at least direct those of its members who came to Palestine toward the facilities offered by Hapoel Hazair. In respect to both of these changing attitudes, Hapoel Hazair began to emulate the Poalei Zion, who from the start had close ties with its diaspora party and had no scruples about seeking its aid and material support. The difference between the two became a matter of the more forthright and effective reliance of the Poalei Zion on its diaspora supporters and also, as we shall see, on its greater ideological difficulties in regard to affiliation with the WZO—a problem that did not arise in the same way for Hapoel Hazair.

On the other hand, the Palestinian Poalei Zion found itself drawn into the line of policy most prominently championed by Hapoel Hazair. The preindustrial local economy offered no opportunity for class struggle at the level of development required by Marxist theory for the social revolution. The Poalei Zion began instead to concentrate on normalizing the Jewish economy by building a Jewish working class in Palestine, an aim that in any case had a pervasive appeal among all *haluzim* who came to Palestine. Moreover, like Hapoel Hazair, it laid particular stress on establishing Jews as farm labor. The other field that could absorb *haluzim*, one in which both parties were active, was the urban construction trades; but this task lacked the special prestige of labor on the land, which could bolster the Zionist right to claim the country as the Jewish national home.

A major policy change developed through an activity that was not initially accepted by either of the parties but was imposed upon them by the preferences of the young workers and by swiftly changing conditions in the country. Beginning in 1907, the plantation colonies entered a period of economic expansion that largely eliminated the problem of the first wave of Second Aliyah *haluzim* in finding work there. There was at the same time a temporary decline in the immigration of *haluzim*. The demand for farm workers exceeded what local Arabs were now willing to supply at the depressed wage scale that was offered, and there was a suggestion to import Egyptian labor for Petah Tikvah. It then appeared that even when work was available in the vineyards and orchards at the premium required by unskilled Jewish labor, the new immigrants were not willing to commit themselves permanently to such seasonal or casual labor. The single men and women who came to work on the land moved restlessly from one site to another. The only ones likely to stay in the *moshavot* were those who became skilled workers in the wineries or the orchards and were qualified for steady jobs at salaries sufficient to support a family.

The young workers were now attracted to the new settlement areas in the remote, northern regions of Erez Israel. The policy followed by ICA there produced settlers who, together with their families, actively farmed their own land, unlike the planters who merely supervised hired labor. When such men hired workers to help them, working together produced a kind of comradeship among them. Together with the romantic allure of opening up new and (given the continued prevalence of banditry and Bedouin raiders) dangerous areas of new settlement, this system allowed for the development of a social milieu that was more congenial to the young pioneers than were the set ways of the older villages.

At the same time, the WZO became more active in Palestine. The Jewish National Fund began to buy small blocks of land which had to be occupied and cultivated. They were not at first sufficient to support a significant program of resettlement, but they were put to symbolically important uses. An olive tree plantation fund to commemorate the name of Herzl gained popular support in the diaspora. With the arrival of Arthur Ruppin to head the WZO's program of practical work in Palestine, and with the encouragement of the WZO Palestine Commission headed by Otto Warburg in Berlin, a more elaborate strategy began to develop, based on land acquired by the Jewish National Fund or for private investors by the PLDC. Such tracts were now to be used—as in the ICA farm of Sejera in lower Galilee—to train Jewish workers in general farming. A particular interest of the women among the *haluzim*, to escape from their restriction to housework and train themselves for field work (especially in vegetable gardening and chicken farming), also found a sympathetic response in Ruppin; he regarded the failure of the plantation villages to provide suitable economic roles for women to be one of the main flaws of the First Aliyah's settlement strategy.

Implicit in such a program was the anticipation that the training farms would produce not simply hired workers who would occupy the land and secure it temporarily, but permanent, independent settlers. This prospect was increasingly attractive to some of the *haluzim*, though not in the same way as to the long-suffering, weary First Aliyah workers. What moved the young Second Aliyah workers was not the pressure of supporting a family but their rebellion against subordination to supervisors. The plans envisaged by the WZO called for eventual transfer of the training farms and other land acquisition to producers' cooperatives (or to individual owners or leaseholders) but only after a considerable period of training and demonstrated success. Frictions that arose with their farm directors caused some of the young people who worked under these terms to demand a speedy transition to cooperative self-management—at first, under sharecroppers' contracts, and eventually, at Um Juni (Degania) at the outlet of the Sea of Galilee, as an independent communal settlement with a long-term, indefinitely renewable leasehold of the Jewish national fund's land.

This turn of events was not initiated by the two rival workers' parties, who viewed them at first as deviations from principle. When Yosef Vitkin openly advocated independent settlement of the workers in 1907, the leading ideologue of Hapoel Hazair, Yosef Aronowicz, strongly condemned the idea as a betrayal of the central aim of his generation of *haluzim*: to create a Jewish agricultural working class. He saw it as a surrender to the very corruption they attributed to the First Aliyah workers who sought subsidies in order to escape from their hard lot and become landed settlers. When the WZO undertook to put into effect Franz Oppenheimer's plan for cooperative farm settlement, and some Poalei Zionist *haluzim* responded favorably to this proposal, Ber Borochov applied the whole weight of his prestige and Marxist dialectical skill to demonstrate the utopian futility of this idea.

Consequently, those who took up the new line of policy were members of Hapoel Hazair and the Poalei Zion who departed from the earlier party line. Another element of major significance were *haluzim*, who, coming later than the first waves, were unwilling to submit to the party division that had been drawn. They soon formed a "nonpartisan" grouping of their own, based on rejection of the issues and rivalries that divided the workers. They found a broader unity in the common regional tasks that arose first in the Galilee and later in Judea. These formed the basis for a number of special regional and functional organizations in which the party divisions were transcended and workers of both parties, as well as the nonpartisans, laid the groundwork for characteristic institutions that the Second Aliyah prepared for development by its successors.

A major role in these developments was played by small, cohesive groups within the larger framework of Hapoel Hazair and the Poalei Zion, formed by *haluzim* who came with special ties to each other from Russia or who developed them in Palestine. One such group was the Romny contingent; another was centered on the workers who came together in the ICA training farm at Sejera.

In 1903, the Anglo-Palestine Company, the Zionist bank, had begun accumulating land parcels for the Jewish National Fund, and by 1907 the WZO seriously undertook the task of establishing settlers on its holdings. Ruppin, who came to direct the work in Palestine early in 1908, found already organized nuclei of experienced workers, such as the Romny group, ready to take up this task. Workers in Sejera had begun to organize in a preliminary way the kind of functional and regional bodies that could respond to the changing needs of the Zionist project: "Hahoresh" (The Plowman), an attempt at a general organization of farm workers and peasants; a secret society, "Bar-Giora," which among its purposes aimed to provide Jewish watchmen and guards for Jewish settlements; and the "Collective," a compact of some of the Sejera workers to pool their earnings, join in full mutual responsibility for all their needs, and allocate their labor and skills according to a discipline subservient to class and national needs. The coincidence of these developments among the workers along with the new turn in WZO policy represented by Ruppin's appearance produced a complex relationship of growing cooperation arising out of successive conflicts.

The first "practical" project undertaken by the WZO Palestine Office was to prepare for planting the Herzl Forest by setting up an olive tree nursery at its Ben Shemen farm near Lydda (Lod), east of Jaffa. A storm of protest was raised when Moshe Berman, the agronomist in charge, hired Arab labor to do the work. Enraged workers dug up the saplings—and then replanted them—to demonstrate their determination that Zionist funds, at least, should be used to establish only Jewish labor. The Palestine Office ordered Berman to respect this demand. His complaint that he was unable to find Jewish workers was met by the Romny group, who volunteered for the job. They then developed a warm, cooperative relationship with Berman. A few months later, when he was entrusted with the PLDC farm that was to be set up at Daleiqa (Kinneret) in the Galilee, he invited the Romny group to join him as workers.

After the first year, the new project grew in scope, employing over 40 workers on different terms (annual, monthly, or day laborers) and wage scales. But as a result of Berman's extravagant personal lifestyle and patronizing attitude toward his first workers, relations between the two sides deteriorated into the more common bureaucratic relationship with a larger, more heterogeneous crew. Moreover, the rosy expectations of the original designers of the project, who had presented it to shareholders as being intended to produce dividends, could not be sustained when it was cut down to the scale of a farm school. The deficit incurred in the first year, and failure to finish the threshing of the harvest before the autumn rains of 1909, caused the administration once again to propose hiring Arab workers, leading to a strike by the Jewish workers. The Romny group left Kinneret, and the other workers demanded that Berman be dismissed and they themselves be entrusted with the farm management. A compromise eventually divided the area: Daleiqa, on the right bank of the Jordan at its outlet from the Sea of Galilee, continued as a managed farm school (with some of its workers employed as a collective body); on the left side, Um Juni (later Degania) was to be entrusted to a cooperative workers' group on a profit-sharing basis. Such a group was set up by Hahoresh from among the Galilean workers and, on completing its contract, it turned in a much heralded profit. But, with its members individually recruited, it was not a consolidated unit; the members dispersed after their successful year, and the Romny group was called in to take over. Having long worked together, they were a small, tightly knit community, drawing equal wages and working together. They settled permanently, at first as a hired work force with a right to share any profit (since they resisted becoming proprietors) and eventually as leaseholders, forming the first Palestinian communal village, a *kvuzah*.

The settlers of Degania found their most congenial broader association in the populist-nationalist milieu of Hapoel Hazair. At Sejera, the active leadership was predominantly drawn from those with a Poalei Zion background in the diaspora. Temperamental differences that divided the Poalei Zion in Russia—attitudes of "prognostic" Zionism versus Zionism "on principle"—developed in response to Palestinian conditions in a parallel but characteristically different division. The difference is strikingly illustrated in the distinguished careers of two brothers, Eliezer and Israel Shohat. Both came to Erez Israel in 1904 after having been active in early Poalei Zion groups, before Borochovist doctrines had been formulated and at a time when self-defense against pogroms was their major concern.

Eliezer, the elder brother, who came to Erez Israel at the age of 30 to work in the plantation villages, was one of the founding leaders of Hapoel Hazair. Like Vitkin, however, he pressed for permanent establishment of Jewish labor on the land and considered proprietary settlement as a desirable option. Like A. D. Gordon, he saw Jewish rural settlement in Erez Israel as, above all, a restoration of the Jewish national spirit, drawing once more from roots in its natural specific environment. He urged Judean workers to move to the new frontier in the Galilee. In Sejera, he was one of the founders of Hahoresh, which he projected as a general agricultural union of peasants and workers, not a narrowly conceived instrument of class interests. After Hahoresh lived out its time, he joined the second wave of Second Aliyah *haluzim* and the nonpartisan group they organized in reestablishing a Galilean agricultural workers' union. Thereafter, he was one of the founders of the first Israeli *moshav ovdim*, the small holders' cooperative village of Nahalal, and was an editor of literary and political publications for Hapoel Hazair.

Israel Shohat, barely 18 years old, came to Erez Israel with his elder brother. He found his closest companions among young *haluzim* who, like himself, were caught up in the spirit of militant self-defense that was evoked by the 1903 pogrom wave. Among the first *haluzim* to come were a famous group from Gomel and others who left southern Russia in part because their valiant defense against pogroms exposed them to official attention. They, like Israel Shohat, were especially sensitive to one glaring flaw in the First Aliyah settlements: their reliance on Arab or Circassian watchmen to protect them against theft and violence. They responded with ardor to the counsel of two veteran romantics and activists of the First Aliyah, Yehiel Michael Halperin and Israel Belkind, who urged them to train for this special task and provide the Yishuv with its own security force. They obtained weapons, which they wore with pride, demonstrating that Jews in Palestine intended to be respected for their strength.

The occasion to realize these dreams concretely occurred after the Eighth Zionist Congress in 1907, which both Shohat brothers attended:

Eliezer as a delegate for Hapoel Hazair; Israel, for the Poalei Zion. At the close of the Sukkot holiday, a restricted meeting in the Jaffa apartment of Yizhak Ben-Zvi set up a secret society, "Bar-Giora" (after the leader of the first-century rebellion against Rome), which was to serve as an elite corps of socialist-Zionist activists. Of the initial group, half went to Sejera with their leader, the 20-year-old Israel Shohat; there they soon managed to take over guard duty for the ICA farm in the village. Israel Shohat—but not his brother—also became part of the Sejera collective. Its leading spirit was Manya Wilbushevitz, another of the remarkable personalities of the Second Aliyah and later Shohat's wife. Manya Shohat was inducted into the Bar-Giora and became an equal partner of her husband in his career as a paramilitary leader.

Manya Shohat was one of the exceptional Second Aliyah leaders for whom collective social organization was not only a valued, pragmatic support for homeless workers but an ideal, a matter of ethical and ideological principle. Her dream of settling a collective group of trained and disciplined soldier-workers in the Hauran east of the Jordan, amid notoriously lawless tribesmen and villagers, had its appeal for young militants who liked to think of themselves as Jewish Cossacks and wished to adapt to the conventions and lifestyle that were honored by their Bedouin neighbors. But this was a remote dream, not immediately attainable. Meanwhile, the pressure of local security problems, which grew inordinately when the immediate effect of the Young Turk revolution in the Galilee eventually undermined public order, led other villagers in the area to turn to the Sejera collective for their guardsmen. The practice of the Bar-Giora leadership was to rely on Jewish workers in a village to support the full-time guards they supplied, and to demand that Jewish workers be hired wherever they entered into a contract. In April 1909, this task had assumed proportions that led the leadership to abandon the covert Bar-Giora structure and organize an open guardsmen's association, Hashomer, which extended its services to villages throughout the Yishuv that were willing to employ them.

Hashomer converted Ussishkin's broadly conceived program of national service and the romantic fancies of Belkind and Halperin into a detailed plan of organization and operation. Members of Bar-Giora and Hashomer were scrupulously selected, rigorously tested before acceptance, and trained for implicit loyalty to their comrades, swift obedience to command, and close adherence to well-defined operating principles. Since the aim was to compel respect for Jews while avoiding blood feuds with Arabs, Turcomen, Circassians, and Bedouin, strict self-discipline and intimate knowledge of Arab folkways were required. Hashomer members formed an elite corps, disposable throughout the country, and in the villages that they contracted to guard, they usually lived as a collective. All contracts were entered into by the central leadership, which assigned members to carry them out, received payments, provided equipment, insurance, and medical, legal, and other services, and, after deducting fees for such disbursements, paid wages to the guardsmen. Apart from members assignable at need, Hashomer would also hire Jewish workers in each place to fill its ranks, and such men might later be proposed for membership if they proved themselves.

With such aims and organization, Hashomer developed extensive relations, both cooperative and conflicting, with all rural sectors of the New Yishuv: the planters, the colonizing agencies, the other workers, and the workers' parties. They claimed to be expert not merely in policing techniques but in the methods of bargaining, negotiation, and general peacekeeping that were customary and effective among Arabs. Consequently their conditions for accepting a contract to guard a settlement included full control of the village's relations with its Arab neighbors. Their manual of operations called for backing up their professional patrols, made up of units of their membership and supplementary Jewish worker guards, by organizing and training all suitable manpower in a settlement to be available in emergencies. Thus, they usually stipulated in their contracts not only that they completely replace Arab guards, but that a substantial number of Jewish workers be hired for general work in the plantations. In this way, Hashomer hoped to use its professional reputation as a lever for reforming the whole structure of the First Aliyah settlements.

Demands like these were bound to bring Hashomer into conflict with the old-line planters. Those First Aliyah veterans considered reliance on Arab protection to be politically wise just as reliance on Arab farm labor was economically sound. Some did eventually engage the services of Hashomer after suffering losses or becoming involved in conflicts with their Arab guards. But the village councils in such cases insisted that their contracts leave unimpaired their authority to control their own relations with neighboring Arabs; they treated their Jewish watchmen as simply hired hands. Conflict on this and other issues caused Hashomer to withdraw from many of the southern settlements and concentrate its efforts again in the Galilee.

Not only the village elders but the young men of the *moshavah* were ultimately antagonized when the closed society of elite guards was introduced into some of the plantation villages. The children of the first rural settlers were subject to special strains in the crisis atmosphere of the colonies. They were the ones who in some *moshavot* were brought up to represent the Zionist ideal of a new Hebraic man, to despise the oppressed Jewish life of the diaspora which their pioneer fathers had cast behind them. Yet they were also the ones who, when sent abroad to study and seek a career, signalized the abandonment of their parents' hopes and ideals. Stalwarts who chose to remain in the settlements often did so in a spirit of irritable pride, defensive and rebellious alike, and were marked no less than the young worker-immigrants by an arrogant esprit de corps. In some cases, they allied themselves, at first, with the Second Aliyah workers in common rebellion against the authoritarian village councils; but the elitist character of both groups bore seeds of conflict between them from the start.

In Zikhron Yaakov, the clash became open and ideological when the settlers' sons set up their own paramilitary society, the Gideonites, in opposition to Hashomer. Against the avant-gardist pose and Eastern European culture of the Russians, they took pride in their own roots in Western European humane and scientific culture—a distinction most eminently exemplified by the paleobotanist Aaron Aaronsohn, the young discoverer of wild wheat. Insulted by the pretensions of Hashomer, the Gideonites, organized by Aaron's brother Alexander, entered the fray in a highly belligerent and polemical spirit.

Their social and cultural discordance was transposed into ideology. Against Hashomer's claim to a professional right to guard Jewish settlements, the Gideonites, who were born of the soil and were not newcomers from the despised diaspora, claimed their own birthright. Where Hashomer wished to control settlement relations with Arabs as a matter of expertise and demanded a Jewish rather than Arab workforce in the villages, the Gideonites, and Aaron Aaronsohn, formulated the opposing position in sharply defined terms. To employ local Arabs was not only an economic necessity, but a key to good neighborly relations. Even the village guards organized by the Gideonites were built on the model of the old *moshavah* practice: Arab watchmen were organized and commanded by Jewish chiefs of the Gideonite society.

Sharp differences also occurred between Hashomer and the two labor parties. The bond between Hashomer and Poalei Zion was preserved by Yizhak Ben-Zvi, the party's recognized ideological mentor and representative of the diaspora leadership, who served as a constant liaison and supporter from the beginnings of the watchmen's organization as a secret society. But Hashomer nonetheless continually drew fire from some Poalei Zion leaders. They were critical of its closed, elitist character and demanded that it submit to party guidance and directives. The watchmen's organization, proud of its Poalei Zion tradition of "proletarian" self-defense, was rather contemptuous of the intellectual pretensions of the Hebraist Hapoel Hazair. The latter, for its part, developed an opposing doctrine of self-defense, not centrally directed but based on local responsibility.

III

The degree to which farm labor and rural settlement came to dominate the attention of both Hapoel Hazair and the Poalei Zion was not originally intended by either. The proletarian leanings of the Marxist Poalei Zion theory made urban labor its proper primary concern. Hapoel Hazair leaned, of course, in the other direction, as mainly an agrarian-populist movement. But the program it outlined at the start called for serving the interests of all the new generation of young workers, both urban and rural. If a distinction was made, it was to confine normal trade union work to city workers, service farm labor was to be supplied by idealists. Moreover, both parties—Hapoel Hazair, to be sure, more forthrightly than the Poalei Zion—conceived themselves to be working in the broad national interest of Zionism, and not for narrow class concerns. This conception broadened the scope of their contacts, and of potential conflict as well as cooperation, with all other elements in the New Yishuv and the diaspora agencies that lent them support.

The Old Yishuv, which had continued a fairly close relationship of conflict with the First Aliyah, had little if any connection with the second, whose radical secularism was utterly repellent. Even so, the creeping modernization that invaded the enclosures of traditionalism brought these outer extremes of Palestine Jewry into occasional contact. The rapid growth of the Old Yishuv in Jerusalem severely strained the resources of the *halukah*, and the establishment, as well as the populace, had to seek other ways of sustaining the community. There was a large expansion of building, in which *halukah* funds as well as private capital were invested. There were traditionalist rabbis who encouraged young men to learn artisan crafts or settlement on the land. The Bezalel school turned out skilled craftsmen, especially among the Sephardi and Yemenite communities, and stonecutters and other construction workers were recruited from the Old as well as the New Yishuv. There was also a flow of migrants from Jerusalem to Jaffa or the colonies, where they came into the orbit of the New Yishuv.

At these margins of growth, Second Aliyah workers, as well as others in the New Yishuv, came into limited, and often problematic, contact with the traditionalist community. The Poalei Zion in Jerusalem organized a printers' union in 1908 which went out on strike for better wages and conditions. It met not only with a rabbinical ban, but with opposition from both the Jerusalem intelligentsia and the Jaffa leaders of the New Yishuv, and it ended after 11 days without success. There were somewhat more effective points of contact of the Second Aliyah activists with Sephardim and Yemenites. The Sephardi upper class, from the beginning, had cooperated with Ashkenazi modernists, both philanthropic and nationalist, and were also a major liaison between them and the Ottoman authorities. Both native-born Sephardim and Sephardi immigrants were found scattered among all the characteristic urban and rural work sites of the Second Aliyah. They were valued as an element that adapted to Ottoman and Palestinian practices and thus were more likely than the young Ashkenazi "idealists" to persist as laborers in the villages. The Yemenites, who began to arrive in larger numbers at the beginning of the Second Aliyah, were held in special regard for the same reason.

The extension of effective Ottoman control into Yemen at that time gave Zionists an opening to encourage a larger worker immigration from this source. In 1911, the WZO Palestine Office and Hapoel Hazair sent Shmuel Yavnieli to Yemen, posing as an emissary of the *halukah* and equipped with recommendations from the Jaffa rabbi, Abraham Hacohen Kook. The sharply increased number of immigrants that he stimulated were settled with official Zionist and Hapoel Hazair help in the plantation villages, where they became a permanent part of the workforce. But Hapoel Hazair was even less successful than the Jerusalem Sephardi establishment in integrating the Yemenites in their midst. The Yemenites who settled in Jerusalem in the 1880s after a series of quarrels broke away from the Sephardi communal structure in 1908, following the Young Turk revolution. The Yemenite farm workers that were sponsored by the WZO in Palestine and Hapoel Hazair formed a self-segregated community almost from the beginning, living in separate quarters near the villages where they worked. Their continuing relations with their Second Aliyah fellow workers were minimal.

The relations between the Second Aliyah *haluzim* and their predecessors of the New Yishuv were closer, but more contentious. They saw themselves from the start as directly opposed to the example of the First Aliyah farmers who relied on Rothschild subsidies—including the example of the struggling First Aliyah workers' organizations, who ended by seeking to become settled proprietors. They ultimately opted for settlement themselves, but under new forms of organization and relations with their Zionist sponsors that, in their view, were distinctly different in kind from the client-patron patterns of their predecessors. But their cooperation with Zionist agencies always had problems of its own. It matured only after many disputes, and it continued to develop in an atmosphere of recurrent tensions.

The Poalei Zion adopted the most equivocal attitude toward the WZO. Although the world union of these socialist Zionists participated in Zionist congresses as a separately affiliated federation, the several territorial Poalei Zion parties varied in their attitude. In 1909, the Russian party, from which most Palestinian party members originally came, derived from its neo-Marxist ideology the conclusion that they must withdraw from the WZO, since affiliation with that bourgeois organization was an act of class collaboration. The Austrian and American Poalei Zionists, on the other hand, maintained much closer relations with the major Zionist bodies, both international and local. The Palestinian party, under pressure of its local environment, moved gradually away from its Russian comrades toward the less inhibited nationalism of the Austrian and American parties. This shift, to be sure, was a source of divisions that opened up in their milieu in later years.

The nationalism of Hapoel Hazair was consistently more emphatic than that of the Poalei Zion; the same is true, for the most part, of the nonpartisan faction among the Second Aliyah workers. The relation of both these groups to others in the New Yishuv—especially among the intelligentsia and the bureaucrats concerned with resettlement—was often very close, and from time to time there erupted disputes sharpened by this very closeness. The major cause of Second Aliyah rebellions against their sponsors—next to their resentment of overbearing supervision—was the employment of Arab workers on projects launched by Zionist agencies and invested with special nationalist significance. The demonstrative uprooting and replanting of saplings in the Herzl Forest tree nursery was mentioned earlier. Similar vigorous protests were raised in 1908 when it was rumored that the Odessa Committee of the Hovevei Zion planned to bring Russian construction workers to erect a building in the Jewish suburb of Jaffa (later called Tel Aviv) for the Zionist-run Jaffa girls school. There were then unemployed Jewish stonecutters and carpenters in Jerusalem, and Hapoel Hazair demanded in vain that this public building at least be entrusted entirely to Jewish labor. A Jaffa contractor who took on the job failed to honor his commitment to employ a 50 percent quota of Jewish workers. Later, however, when the first story of the building, constructed by an exclusively Arab crew, collapsed, the representative of Hapoel Hazair who was appointed to serve on the inquiry committee succeeded in stipulating that the rebuilding be done entirely by Jewish labor. In the summer of 1908, the plan of Petah Tikvah planters to import workers from Egypt produced another uproar. Hapoel Hazair appealed to the WZO headquarters in Cologne, and the WZO annual conference of that year instructed "all Zionist institutions" to prevent the intended action—which, in the event, was not carried out by the Petah Tikvah planters.

If the Poalei Zion had reservations about the establishment based on class considerations, leaders of Hapoel Hazair were critical on nationalist grounds. Yosef Aronowicz repeatedly demanded that Zionist leaders be required to live up to what he considered primary Zionist obligations: if not to immigrate to Erez Israel, at least to adhere strictly to the principle of employing Jewish labor. Failure to do so should disqualify them for leadership. It followed that those who fulfilled basic Zionist obligations—in particular, the workers in Erez Israel—were most fit to determine and carry out its policies. The claim of those in Palestine to have a privileged voice in world Zionist councils began to emerge.

A. D. Gordon defined the underlying principle in clear terms in a letter composed in 1904, soon after he arrived in Erez Israel. Zionism suffered in comparison with other nationalisms, such as the Irish and Balkan movements, he wrote, because it was "detached from the land, from the soil which is the base and goal of the whole movement." Everything Zionist was imported: ideals, activists, immigrants, resources, lifestyles— in other words, life itself. This situation may have been inevitable in a people living in exile, but at a time when enough Jews had settled to permit "the budding of national life, we ourselves are now to blame for this abnormality." Autoemancipation, the fundamental principle of Zionism, is no more than a potted plant, he said, so long as it is not rooted in its natural soil:

> Seventy or eighty thousand people are not too small a number to be considered the beginning of the creation of a national life. And especially when our whole idea is to live a life of national labor in peace.
> . . . Accordingly, the problem [of the Second Aliyah] is, together with those settled Jews who are willing and able to work, in the *moshavot*, the cities, and particularly Jerusalem, to arouse an autonomous national movement, not dependent on anyone or anything from the outside.[9]

Gordon was at pains to add that he was not proposing to break the links with world Jewry, nor was he discussing organizational questions, such as those raised by Ussishkin's recent effort to create a united Yishuv. But nobody, he averred, could question that what the immigrant workers were doing was more important than any other Zionist activity, and its success would have an immense quickening effect on the movement everywhere.

The claims of the young workers to share in the governance of the local community were a more immediate issue than any pretensions they might have to leadership in the WZO. The issue arose when they first came to work in Petah Tikvah and other plantation settlements. They came with a sense of their peculiar mission: to reform the First Aliyah villages. They thus asserted a right to a voice in the internal affairs of the *moshavot*, totally disregarding the established practice which limited the village electorate to the landowning settlers. This stance was one of the reasons for the hostility they aroused in the village councils. So, too, Hashomer's demands to take over full control of the relations with Arab neighbors and their requirement that Jewish labor be hired to back up the guards was a provocation that aroused the hostility of established settlers.

On the other hand, the Second Aliyah *haluzim* developed close and cooperative relations with the Hebraist teachers and intellectuals. A close alliance developed, too, with a group of students in the Herzliya *gymnasium* who joined the ranks of the *haluzim*. Hapoel Hazair from the start undertook to commit its members to Hebrew, conducting its own meetings and correspondence in that language. The Palestinian Poalei Zion (though leaders like Ben-Zvi initially favored Yiddish as the Ashkenazi folk language) also came into the Hebraist camp under the pressure of local conditions and of partisans of Hebrew such as David Green (Ben-Gurion). Thus the Second Aliyah workers provided the Hebraist teachers in the *moshavot* with the invaluable backing of an organized, allied public. The periodicals published by the workers, particularly the journal *Hapoel hazair*, became a leading organ of literary expression by recognized and budding Hebrew writers, as well as a highly regarded forum for the reporting and discussion of current Jewish and Palestinian affairs.

These ties became of historic significance in the Yishuv's famous "language war" that broke out in 1913. The schools attended by children of the New Yishuv in the cities—apart from a few Zionist-oriented schools and the British Evelina de Rothschild school, on the one hand, and those of Christian missions, on the other—were divided between institutions supported by two philanthropic sponsors, the French Alliance and the German Hilfsverein. The latter, coming into the field late, was relatively more open than the former to the proposals of the Hebraist teachers. Nevertheless, there was a strong bias toward spreading German influence, and a general coolness toward Jewish nationalism, in the Hilfsverein's activity. It developed its network rapidly, adding to the Austrian-founded Laemel school, which it took over, a teachers' seminary in Jerusalem, and a German-style high school, a Realschule, in Haifa.

A legacy from the estate of the old Hovevei Zionist and tea magnate Kalonymus Wissotzky provided for the founding of an institute of technology—subsequently renamed Technion—in Haifa. The Kuratorium (board of trustees) of this projected school included old friends of Wissotzky and executors of his will such as Ahad Haam and Shmarya Levin, a member of the WZO Action Committee, together with a majority of Hilfsverein representatives. Since Levin gained the support of Jacob Schiff during an organizational tour of America, the views of this influential banker and philanthropist also became important.

The grumbling against the French and German philanthropists came to a head over the question of the curriculum of the projected technological institute. The Hebraist teachers, who were a significant element in the faculties of the Hilfsverein network, pressed for their own program of making Hebrew the language of instruction at all levels and in all subjects. Their intransigent radicalism went to extremes that were not shared by all the Zionist members of the Kuratorium, some of whom were not convinced that advanced scientific studies could yet be pursued in Hebrew. Nevertheless, when the majority of the Kuratorium forced a decision that made German the language of instruction in the Realgymnasium and the projected technology institute, Ahad Haam and the other Zionists resigned from the board in solidarity with their zealous Erez Israeli comrades. (Schiff in America took offense at the behavior of both sides—an attitude that brought added pressure on the Hilfsverein leaders.)

But it was in Palestine that decisive battles of the language war were waged. In Jaffa, the journal *Hapoel hazair* conducted its fierce campaign, and the activist Herzliya Gymnasium student group organized protests. In Jerusalem, the Hebraist faculty of the Hilfsverein teachers' seminary (generally more conservative than their Jaffa–Tel Aviv colleagues) resigned in protest. The rebellious teachers opened their own parallel schools, and drew a major part of the students away from the Hilfsverein institutions.

All this brought about a situation unforeseen, and not really welcomed, by the WZO. The rebels' success in setting up their rival institutions, which other Zionists perforce supported, bestowed upon the Zionist organization an unexpected, but costly and responsible blessing. It acquired all at once an extensive school system, across the full length of the New Yishuv, which expanded its active role in maintaining the structure and furthering the growth of the community in the critical years ahead.

● 8 ●

Growth of the Zionist Parties

World War I radically altered all current presuppositions of the Zionist enterprise. The British Balfour Declaration of November 2, 1917, and similar statements of other Allies held out the promise, at the war's end, of a new legal status explicitly favorable to the idea of a "national home for the Jewish people." The Mandate for Palestine, which recognized Zionist historic claims and granted the WZO the rights and powers that embodied essential elements of the charter that Herzl envisioned, made good this pledge.

On the other hand, the Yishuv, an already existing base for building the homeland, had suffered severely from siege and Turkish oppression. Cut off from overseas markets and sources of supply, the hapless community was saved from general starvation only by the emergency efforts of diaspora Jews. Political interventions by the diaspora spared the Yishuv from suffering the full ferocity of a suspicious and vengeful Turkish military governor, who considered Zionists, no less than Armenians and Arab nationalists, to be enemies of the Ottoman Empire. The Yishuv nonetheless lost a third or more of its prewar numbers, leaving something less than 57,000 Jews in the Holy Land toward the close of hostilities.

The wartime loss was not evenly distributed throughout the Yishuv, nor were the Yishuv's component groups equally able to make necessary adjustments in the face of crisis. The heaviest blow was suffered by those least able to organize to meet it: the Old Yishuv, comprising two-thirds of the prewar Jewish population. The Jews of Jerusalem and Safed were decimated by hunger and disease, and many emigrated in order to survive. The plantation colonies, hit by the loss of markets and by Turkish exactions, also lost ground, and Jaffa Jews were among those expelled. But, together with the rest of the New Yishuv, the coastal settlers responded actively to the crisis with emergency measures of cooperative organization.

Those in the most favorable position were the new grain-growing settlements and other colonists of the inland and northern regions. Their produce was a major source of food for the urban community during the war. The workers' new marketing cooperative, Hamashbir (The Provisioner), supplied the general public at reasonable, controlled prices. This was one of the factors that helped raise the Second Aliyah and its workers' organizations to new prominence in the Yishuv's developing communal structure.

Among the special targets of Turkish hostility were those most active in the Yishuv's newest leadership. Second Aliyah labor leaders, even though they had increasingly sought to identify with the Ottomans since the Young Turk revolution, were, as Russians, enemy aliens; and, as socialist militants too, they were particularly suspect. The new official Zionists, many of whom, like Arthur Ruppin, were German nationals and hence Turkish allies, were nevertheless held under suspicion as Jewish nationalists. These circles were carefully watched, from time to time arrested, and, in the end, many were exiled.

In the face of such hardships, both the official Zionist representation and the workers' leadership in Palestine gained great prestige through initiating and maintaining a growing Jewish communal structure set up in response to critical wartime needs. The Jaffa Zionist office and the new Zionist Anglo-Palestine Bank were the main channels for distributing the wartime largesse of diaspora Jewry; and with this backing they maintained by their credit and authority the balance and liquidity of a very shaky economy. They also were closely tied to the Western consulates and embassies who undertook the necessary political protection of the Yishuv. In addition, a makeshift communal structure, based on a Jaffa emergency committee and covering the settlements of the whole New Yishuv, was developed under the aegis of the colonizing agencies, led by the Zionists. In this structure, the laborers, who developed and unified their own organizations in vigorous response to the wartime crisis, played a special role. They were the section of the Yishuv who from the beginning were the most self-conscious politically. They were the one partisan element that successfully mobilized and acted as a dynamic force with clear immediate objectives and definite ideas regarding the new society they hoped to build in Zion.

Zionist ascendancy in the Yishuv was advanced still further by the postwar situation. In spite of resistance to the Balfour Declaration's policy, which was strongly evidenced by local British authorities especially during the military administration, the mandate gave official Zionists unprecedented authority in their community and prestige in the country at large. The war's end saw the return of many Jews who had fled or been exiled during the crisis. But the major influx was of new immigrants, and in the first years these were mainly young, radical workers, the natural heirs of the laborers of the Second Aliyah. These reinforcements primarily determined the form in which the highly individual labor Zionist attitudes that arose in the Second Aliyah were crystallized in institutions, creating historic facts that were decisive for the future of the new Jewish society and, ultimately, of the new Jewish state.

I

The approach of war revived the question of Ottoman citizenship as an urgent matter for the Yishuv. In spite of a campaign for Ottomanization following the 1908 Young Turk upheaval, very few Ashkenazim had become naturalized by 1914. The war renewed a tense, uncertain situation, half hope and half fear, like that which in 1908 produced appeals to the Yishuv to give up foreign protection and become Ottoman subjects.

In 1908 the Zionist movement as a whole welcomed the Turkish democratic revolution, seeing in it a chance to advance its own cause under the general and equal rights of a constitutional regime. For the Jews of the Yishuv, the expanded powers of municipal councils and the new opportunity of general elections invited, or rather challenged, them to participate in local politics—on condition of becoming Ottomans. However, the Zionist movement and the Yishuv, like others involved with the new regime, soon found their hopes largely disappointed and their fears too often realized. Zionists not only had to beware of the repressive attitude of the nationalist regime toward the minor nationalities whose hopes it had aroused; they also encountered active, politically aware opposition on the part of the new Arab nationalist spokesmen. The Zionists were placed on the defensive in their attempts to reach political agreement with both Turks and Arabs within the Ottoman system. The Yishuv lost ground steadily in its efforts to participate in local politics, and the community relapsed into quiescence in this field.

The global war looming in 1914 at once stirred up new hopes and projected sharper, graver fears. Whatever its outcome, the war was bound to shake the established structure and create a radically new political situation. During the war there was every reason to fear for the fate of national minorities under Turkish rule, especially those considered hostile or classed as enemy aliens. A new campaign for Ottomanization was launched in the Yishuv, in order to shield alien Jews against the danger of expulsion and to place the Jewish community in its best posture toward the Turks and the Central Powers during and after the war.

The most far-reaching conclusions were swiftly drawn by the Gideonites of Zikhron Yaakov. They responded at once to the Turkish call for general mobilization by enlisting in the army as Ottomans. But the Turks soon ended any attraction such patriotic gestures might have for Jews and other non-Muslims. Conditions of service were far from pleasant in the Turkish military under any circumstances, and only a few Ottoman Jews had entered the army and the military schools open to them on a plane of equality since the Young Turk revolution. Now, upon joining the world war, Turkey proclaimed a *jihad*, a holy war, hoping to arouse Muslims in solidarity throughout the empire and beyond. This meant that, once again, Muslims alone could bear arms; other Ottoman conscripts were relegated to labor battalions, where they were conspicuously ill-used and humiliated. Such treatment led Alexander Aaronsohn, for one, to revise his views radically and pin his hopes on a connection with the Allies rather than on a demonstration of the Yishuv's Ottoman patriotism. In time, his Gideonites were drawn into a pro-British espionage network, the so-called Nili group, led by his elder brother, Aaron.

Not only the native-born Gideonites but immigrant leaders of the Yishuv, and in particular Poalei Zion and Hashomer cadres, took a line of loyalty to the Ottoman Empire at the beginning of the war. While hopeful calculations concerning decisive political changes after the war played their part in this policy, it was still more important as a defensive measure against immediate dangers facing these groups. The new Turkish military rulers, especially the governors in Jaffa who ordered expulsions, conducted a general campaign against all the manifestations of Jewish nationalism, which had been continually cited by nationalist Arab anti-Zionist agitators since the beginning of the Young Turk regime. In particular, they demanded that the Yishuv disarm Hashomer and other civil guards; and when, under pressure of the Yishuv's leaders, some Jewish arms were turned in, they were used to equip a local Arab, Muslim militia.

Poalei Zion and Hashomer leaders, some of whom had become Ottoman in earlier years and joined the small group of Jews in Turkish schools in Constantinople, tried to gain Turkish consent for a parallel Jewish militia. At the same time they resisted the policy of voluntary disarmament urged by other Yishuv leaders and maintained their organizations. In the upshot their top leaders, such as Israel and Manya Shohat of Hashomer and Ben-Zvi and Ben-Gurion of the Poalei Zion, were exiled to distant Anatolia or expelled abroad. This event led the latter two to revise their views, as the Gideonites did, and eventually adopt a new orientation toward the Allied cause.

Some Zionist leaders took a pro-Allied stand from the outset. Living in England, Chaim Weizmann found it natural to build Zionist hopes on a pro-Allied orientation; and a relatively remote figure, Herbert Samuel, concluded on the day Turkey entered the war that British interests now ran parallel with those of Zionism. A similar conviction possessed Vladimir Jabotinsky, who was then covering the war as a correspondent in Bordeaux, and gave him an opening to renew his active career in Zionism in a new vein of militancy. He at once conceived the idea of a "Zionist Legion" to fight with the Allies and establish the Jewish right to present claims to Palestine at the peace conference after victory.

Such notions were rejected by most Zionist leaders as adventurist, likely to expose the Yishuv to reprisals by the Turks; and Jews generally, deeply hostile to tsarist Russia and inclined to take a pacifist stand on the war, considered them to be an opportunist betrayal of principle. But individuals such as Yosef Trumpeldor and, in a different way, Aaron Aaronsohn in the Yishuv, as well as Pinhas Rutenberg, Nahman Syrkin, Chaim Zhitlowsky, and Ber Borochov in the diaspora, embraced this approach at once. Ben-Gurion and Ben-Zvi, pursuing in exile their plans for a postwar wave of socialist Zionist immigrant volunteers, in the course of time also became ardent supporters of the Jewish Legion project.

The first military ventures of pro-Allied Zionists were relatively obscure, small-scale projects conducted by individuals on the fringe of the movement against strong opposition of the central leadership and the mass of Jews. The first public activity was the Zion Mule Corps, recruited by Trumpeldor in Alexandria among the refugees expelled from Palestine; it served with valor in the disastrous Gallipoli campaign of 1915. Apart from the honors accumulated by the Zionist soldiers, the project had little immediate political impact; and indeed, anticipating this result, even Jabotinsky had opposed from the start a project that relegated Jews to a labor battalion and was not directed immediately to Palestine.

In 1915, also, Aaron Aaronsohn and his associates laid their first plans for pro-British espionage in Palestine. Their initial contacts with British headquarters in Egypt during that year were without effect, and not until the leader himself escaped to London late in 1916 did significant activity develop. Meanwhile, rumors of the spy ring thoroughly alarmed and embittered the Yishuv, living as it did under the hard hand

and suspicious eye of the Turks in military government. Not until the Nili network gained British support and became a channel for distributing shipments of gold raised by Western Jews to aid the Yishuv was Aaronsohn's group accorded a certain cautious recognition by community leaders. But then the discovery and liquidation of Nili touched off such ferocious Turkish reprisals, and were accompanied by such violent episodes, by such terrible acts both of sacrificial heroism and of vindictive betrayal, that the Yishuv long afterward bore the scars of that internal conflict.

The issue of a Zionist pro-Allied military effort was meanwhile kept before the Jewish public and the British government by Jabotinsky's persistent agitation in London. With the Gallipoli campaign ended and the Zion Mule Corps disbanded, Trumpeldor came to London to help in the cause, as did a small contingent of veterans of the corps, who reenlisted as a company in the British army. Not until the summer of 1917 did they gain their point. In late August, with a new Palestine offensive being planned and with drafts of a pro-Zionist declaration about to be seriously considered, the British formally announced the formation of a Jewish regiment.

The new turn of events, resulting in a modest representation of Jewish military units in Allenby's Palestine invasion force, projected the idea of the Jewish Legion as a major issue around which party ideologists renewed Zionist discussion. The 38th Battalion of Royal Fusiliers, in whose organization Jabotinsky took the lead, was followed by the 39th, recruited in America, and the 40th, recruited in Palestine itself. In the latter two battalions, socialist Zionist leaders and socialist Zionist recruits, particularly members of Poalei Zion groups, were strongly represented. Trumpeldor, who was not permitted to join the 38th Fusiliers because he was a Russian officer, carried the legion idea to revolutionary Russia, where he planned a Jewish army of workingmen who would march across the European land mass to Palestine and build a socialist commonwealth there. This dream did not come true, but the spirit and conceptions of Trumpeldor's ideological vision had a sweeping, powerful influence upon the postwar immigrants, particularly those recruited in Russia by the new organization Hehaluz (The Pioneer), which was developed under his leadership.

Once it was taken up by socialists and adapted to the broad civilian objectives of these ideologists, the Jewish Legion concept was no longer an issue cutting across party lines and advocated by random individuals. It became one of those critical questions that, in the period after the Russian Revolution, had to be dealt with as party matters by socialist

Zionists, and it contributed significantly to the realignments and reorganizations of the Zionist left at that time. While a minority of activists in Hapoel Hazair joined the 40th Royal Fusiliers in Palestine, the leading spirits of that party remained opposed on grounds of pacifism and of their general aversion to power politics. The Palestinian Poalei Zion, on the other hand, was substantially united in support of the legion; joining it, its members cemented their bonds with "nonpartisan" Zionist workers who were their comrades in its ranks. The 1919 merger of the Poalei Zion and the nonpartisans in a new party, the Ahdut Haavodah (United Labor), was initiated in discussions in the barracks of the Jewish Legion. In subsequent years the impact of Trumpeldor's ideas and example among Eastern European immigrants continued to be a major force in the rapidly changing party structure of the Zionist left.

The whole Zionist movement underwent striking changes of party alignment and organization in the aftermath of the war. For the general Zionist groupings in the diaspora, such changes reflected a necessary readjustment to the altered relative strength of the several territorial Zionist organizations and the Jewish communities that supplied their constituencies. The issues involved were brought to focus primarily through the struggle for central leadership between outstanding figures who had been raised to powerful positions during the war. On the left, the regrouping was more ideological and was decisively affected by the critical quarrels in which all postwar socialist parties were caught up.

The World Zionist Organization, thoroughly disrupted by the war, approached its postwar reorganization in a slow and tentative manner. The old leaders in defeated Germany and war-torn Russia were unable to reassert themselves. The German central office willingly left the lead in world Zionist affairs to Weizmann and Louis D. Brandeis, whose base of power was in the victorious Allied countries. Raised to authority by local, external conditions, Weizmann had to acquire legitimacy within the world movement; and only after difficult internal disputes did he emerge as the acknowledged leader.

Immediately following the first British victories in Palestine, a new "Zionist" central institution for Palestine was created by the Allies. A few months after the Balfour Declaration was issued, permission was granted to send to Palestine a Zionist commission nominally endowed with broad powers: to act for all Jews, and particularly the Yishuv, in relation to the British and the Arabs; to coordinate relief, including repatriation, and restore the economy and emerging communal organization of the Yishuv; and to study possibilities of future development in all fields, including the specific proposal of a Hebrew University. Members of the commission were chosen initially in such a way as to represent, not the Yishuv nor the autonomous institutions of diaspora Jewry, but those Jewish circles upon whom certain Allied governments relied to defend their several national interests. The French were represented by an anti-Zionist, Sylvain Levi of the Alliance Israélite Universelle. The Italians chose a Jewish naval officer, Commodore Angelo Levi-Bianchini, who showed outstanding zeal not only in defending the Yishuv but in advancing Italian political and commercial interests in connection with the commission's work. The closest ties were maintained by the British, who appointed a political officer, Major William Ormsby-Gore, to serve as liaison with the commission. Apart from this appointment, they relied on the friendship of the Jewish people generally, sustained through the agency of their chosen instrument, Chaim Weizmann, who was the commission chairman. Americans were not represented in the first year, because of the United States' neutral position in the continuing war with Turkey. Their representatives assumed dominant positions in the commission for a time in 1919. These men, Zionists of long standing or of recent recruitment, were backed by a leader of international eminence, Louis D. Brandeis.

The direct influence of the Allied powers in commission affairs lasted only briefly. The French and Italian representatives speedily dropped out, as was natural at a time of growing hostility in those countries to the British position in Palestine. This meant not only detachment from those governments but also a loss of non-Zionist representation. In 1920 the commission was replaced by a Palestine section of the Executive of the World Zionist Organization, which derived its power structure from the internal politics of the diaspora Zionist movement. Within this arena the wartime shift of power to Britain and America was restricted and corrected as European Zionists reasserted themselves. Only by gaining their confidence did Weizmann make good his claim to leadership. Men such as Ussishkin and Ruppin returned to responsible posts in the WZO Palestine Executive, and apart from an old foe such as Aaron Aaronsohn, who disdained the old leaders and their methods, old friends of the New Yishuv such as Akiva Ettinger and Yizhak Wilkansky succeeded to the top professional posts. The American Brandeis group, who shared many of Aaronsohn's views, not only dropped out of the Executive but were driven into retirement as the greatly reduced American movement reshaped itself on traditional Zionist lines.

The Brandeis group's defeat decided the issue of the WZO's structure. It was not to become a depoliticized executive body, controlled by experts, each charged with a specific technical task such as public health or other preliminary investment prerequisite for private and cooperative development of Palestine on businesslike lines. Instead, the Executive, under instruction of Zionist Congress resolutions, would base its policies on broad ideological principles, responding to more or less effective popular pressure.

Such a structure and composition of the WZO necessarily fostered sharp opposition to the policy line that Weizmann was compelled to adopt. Relying on British goodwill, he had to refrain from political demands beyond what was explicit in the mandate, as officially interpreted in the Churchill White Paper of 1922. The progress of the Jewish national home toward its formally undefined goal of a Jewish state therefore depended on the developing "economic absorptive capacity" of Palestine, or of the growing Jewish sector within it, and that in turn was restricted by the inadequate funds that, after the first flush of enthusiasm, diaspora Jewry made available to the shrunken Zionist movement. The patient building of the homeland, "dunam by dunam," which Weizmann favored no less than Brandeis or Aaronsohn before him, was really the only policy that was open to the Zionist Executive under the circumstances.

Nor could Weizmann depend solely on the traditional structure and constituencies of the WZO in order to carry out such a policy. The nature and magnitude of the task required funds on a scale the Zionists could not hope to obtain without the cooperation of the whole Jewish community, particularly the wealthy non-Zionist philanthropists who were so influential in American and British Jewry. From his rise to the WZO presidency until ultimate success in 1929, Weizmann conducted a stubborn, continuous campaign for a form of organization, briefly achieved in the "enlarged Jewish agency," based on effective cooperation with non-Zionists. The latter, too, became a major issue debated by the WZO's European-centered parties.

In the crisis atmosphere of postwar Central and Eastern Europe, Weizmann's pragmatic and restrained leadership provoked sharp resistance. After the agonies of the war, young Zionists expected swift, radical liberation from the old, oppressive conditions of diaspora life. They hoped for recognition of the rights of the dispersed Jewish people to establish its sovereignty in Palestine without delay and to obtain national cultural autonomy in the succession states of the Russian and Austrian Empires. Weizmann's policy seemed to many to undercut these aims. Hence it met opposition not only in the minor parties but from new factions organized in the general Zionist ranks.

The proposal to reorganize the Jewish Agency in order to grant equal representation to non-Zionists was particularly repugnant to Polish Jews such as Yizhak Gruenbaum, who in their own country were struggling to give substance to the cultural and civil rights promised in the minorities treaty. Under their leadership, a Radical Zionist party was organized to fight for the creation of a World Jewish Congress, which would act for the worldwide Jewish nationality both in building Zion and in defending diaspora Jews in political issues of common concern. Such a congress would have to be based on democratically organized Jewish communities; its delegates could therefore be counted on to deal with Jewish interests in a spirit of national liberation. This party naturally regarded as a mortal threat to its entire conception Weizmann's negotiations with the wealthy, self-appointed oligarchs of Western Jewries to set up a bipartite directorate with those antinationalists for so central a nationalist activity as the upbuilding of the Jewish homeland.

Others opposed Weizmann's proposed reorganization of the Jewish Agency as part of his entire approach to Zionist policy, which they rejected basically and in detail. After the Balfour Declaration, old Eastern European Zionists and especially ardent young Zionists among prospective immigrants or in the Yishuv hoped for rapid, determined implementation of Zionist "aspirations" under the new dispensation. They expected the mandate regime to recognize the Hebrew language and the Jewish Sabbath and holidays as official. They demanded a dominant role, effective as well as symbolic, for world Jewry in the Palestine administration from the outset. They proposed that the Jewish battalions be retained as a main defense and internal security force. They pressed for the transfer of masses of Jews, especially young Jewish workers, to begin at once.

Demands for a dominant Jewish role in the Palestine government had to be publicly renounced by the Weizmann leadership from the very beginning in order to obtain British consent to a mandate draft that would meet even the minimal Zionist requirements. Other demands, such as the retention of the Jewish battalion as a garrison force, were slowly relinquished in the face of opposition from the British military administration. Demands for rapid, mass immigration were blocked not simply by the administrative and political requirements of a British colonial government constantly mindful of Arab resentment; the Zionist central leadership itself rejected such ideas as unrealistic, at least until the necessary planning and preparation had been done: swamps drained, malaria eradicated, roads built, an effective Zionist administration set up, social and economic conditions gradually created for absorbing mass immigration—and, as the prerequisite of all this, adequate funds placed at the disposal of the Jewish Agency. Such attitudes deferred the hoped-for final triumph of Jewish national liberation to a remote and uncertain future.

The general antagonism provoked by such policies were expressed in diverse forms. Workers who were inclined to regard their own class organizations as the primary instrument of the national liberation were confirmed in their distrust of the WZO and concentrated on their own local endeavors. A man such as Jabotinsky, however, considered political factors—the policy of the British and the status and authority they granted to Zionist agencies—to be of paramount importance. Only if the Jewish Legion were retained as a British force, if anti-Zionist British officials were replaced by men who were acceptable to the WZO and sympathetic to its aims, and if rapid Jewish resettlement were backed decisively by British policy, did he expect success for the Zionist cause.

In the first years of Weizmann's leadership, Jabotinsky tried to advance these views within the WZO Executive, joining what he called a Zionist "coalition." By January 1923, this attempt broke down and Jabotinsky, with typical radicalism, resigned from both the Executive and the Zionist Organization. As a free-lance critic of Weizmannism over the next two years, Jabotinsky aroused a lively response among other Zionists, particularly old colleagues on the Russian Zionist journal *Rasviet*, who shared his militant "activist" views. In April 1925 this group organized themselves as the "Zionist Revisionists" and decided to operate as a world union within the WZO, but with the reserved "right of independent propaganda in Jewish and non-Jewish circles."[1]

Unlike Gruenbaum's Radical party, which remained small and essentially confined to Eastern Europe, the Revisionists aroused a broad segment of the Jewish community and of Jewish youth, especially in Poland and in Palestine. They developed into a major opposition party, with a special attraction for all aggrieved groups who were disaffected from the Zionist establishment and open to the appeal of rightwing nationalist extremism. Under the influence of this constituency, the Revisionist ideology expanded from its initial base, the concern with Zionist external relations, to cover the Yishuv's internal divisions, and it responded increasingly to a sense of grievances among communal groups and economic interests outside the left-oriented Yishuv institutions.

The sharpest ideological divisions developed during and after the war in the ranks of the labor Zionists. They were compelled to adjust to radically new conditions in both the Yishuv and the diaspora. They were challenged particularly by the Russian revolution, which compelled all socialists to make unanticipated decisions. They were also challenged by new modes of thought and consciousness absorbed by Zionist youth in Europe under conditions of wartime and postwar trauma.

The end of war and the new Zionist opportunities it brought produced a powerful drive among labor Zionists in the Yishuv to renew ties with the diaspora and seek new recruits there. Second Aliyah veterans abroad, such as Trumpeldor and the Hapoel Hazair leader, Elija Munchik (Margalit), in Eastern Europe, and Ben-Zvi and Ben-Gurion in America, had already organized *haluzim*, who began to appear in Palestine. Delegations of leading labor Zionists now went from the Yishuv to meet the new groups, gain their adherence, and promote their activity in the diaspora. Old leaders of diaspora socialist Zionism, for their part, went to Palestine to reestablish the relations that had been disrupted by the war and the postwar internecine party conflicts. In either case, the emissaries encountered a radically altered situation.

The arrival of the Jewish Legion brought to a head what had been developing for several years before the war in the Zionist workers' community. The two labor parties that were organized by the first wave of the Second Aliyah had been yielding ground to the nonpartisan agricultural workers' organizations of Judea and Galilee. Hapoel Hazair's ideology of unconditional commitment to the "conquest of labor" and the Poalei Zion strategy of organizing the dialectic processes of class migration and class struggle had each been modified by the new doctrine of independent labor settlement in collective and cooperative villages, which was developed primarily in the agricultural unions. This new "constructivist" socialist Zionism not only responded generally to conditions in Palestine and the inclinations of young Jewish worker-volunteers, it reflected the specific impatience of a later generation of Second Aliyah immigrants with the dogmatic party chauvinism generated by their immediate predecessors. The same mood, heightened in intensity, prevailed among the postwar *haluzim*. The "nonpartisan" leaders who had fostered the new conceptions and general labor organizations in the prewar period pushed ahead decisively on the same lines, correctly anticipating the attitude of the postwar immigrants. Their first victory was the organization, following discussions in the Jewish Legion camps, of a new united labor Zionist body, the Ahdut Haavodah.

This was intended to be a complete, comprehensive union of Zionist workers, replacing the older parties and their competing services. In fact, however, it was a merger of only two of the three leading elements in the labor community, the Poalei Zion and the nonpartisans.

The former adopted wholesale the ideological approach of the latter. The socialist Zion was to be built, quite explicitly, by the personal commitment of pioneer youth, supported by the self-taxation of the Jewish people at large. From the outset, without awaiting a normal capitalist development, it would be based on producers' cooperatives and collectives. The working class would thus create a nuclear socialist society which, by its internal growth and absorption of immigrant masses, would ultimately integrate the whole redeemed nation of Jews in Zion. Adopting such views, the Palestinian Poalei Zion clearly marked itself as a distinct expression of the Yishuv within its own world union of socialist Zionists; for while a few diaspora leaders, such as Nahman Syrkin, shared this approach, it represented a crucial deviation from the line of other Poalei Zion parties and of the main diaspora leadership.

The nonpartisans, for their part, also underwent significant transformations in the course of merging with the Poalei Zion. They accepted an explicit identification with the Second International, which, after several failures, the Poalei Zion had succeeded in joining during the war. But precisely this identification, with class rather than with nation, was a cardinal point rejected by Hapoel Hazair in their refusal to merge with the new united organization.

If the nonpartisans accepted an explicit commitment to international socialism, their doing so was not simply a concession to terms for the merger proposed by the Poalei Zion. It also expressed the general mood of the revolutionary postwar era, which they fully shared. But it was not part of their intention, nor indeed was it a prevailing conception in international socialism at the time, to build a normal political party as their revolutionary instrument. They had in mind an activist society which, like the contemporary Russian or German soviets, would be not a mere faction within a prerevolutionary political regime, but the nucleus of a complete new polity—and in their case, even more clearly, a complete new society, culture, and economy as well—constructed without much reference to the old.

It was thus a failure of their undertaking when, because of the refusal of Hapoel Hazair to join their merger, the Yishuv's labor community, which was formerly divided between the Poalei Zion and Hapoel Hazair parties, now offered new immigrants a choice between the parties of Ahdut Haavodah and Hapoel Hazair. The drive for unity, reinforced by the obvious unwillingness of many newcomers to be restricted to such alternatives, led a year later, in December 1920, to a new expedient, a General Federation of Jewish Workers in Palestine (Histadrut Haovdim Haivrim be-Erez Israel). This body, which, together with the Jewish Agency and the Yishuv's general community organization, provided the major institutional framework for building the national home, arose by agreement between the two parties and a new nonpartisan third element, the mass of postwar worker immigrants. The latter groups, who often rejected the partisan identifications of their predecessors out of a sense of their own generation's distinct identity, were themselves divided and polarized by the turbulent ideological quarrels of postwar Europe.

The Russian revolution produced shock waves among socialist Zionists, as it did among all left-leaning contemporaries. The creation of the Third International, in rivalry to the discredited Second, forced a choice and a division among them. At an international Poalei Zion conference in Vienna in July 1920, the bulk of the Europeans demanded immediate and unconditional affiliation with the Third International, while the Palestinian Ahdut Haavodah and Western Hemisphere Poalei Zionists abstained in the vote on this issue, hoping for a new socialist International that would unite the third with other revolutionary socialist bodies. Not only was the conference then split in two; the whole Poalei Zion movement was weakened and divided, as further ideological splintering followed this initial cleavage.

The Left Poalei Zion, which dominated the European movement, found that its first step left it still a long way from its goal. The effort to combine Zionism with Bolshevism was not accepted by the Bolsheviks. The leftward drift ended for many with total adherence to communist anti-Zionism. The Left Poalei Zion ranks were decimated and were reduced to a dwindling, internally fragmented band of minor sectarians who stoutly maintained their embattled, shifting positions. Generally, they attacked Zionist Hebraism and defended Yiddish as the national tongue; they persisted in their Zionism while denouncing class collaboration with the Zionist organization; and they persevered in seeking admittance to the Third International without accepting the explicit anti-Zionism which was its prerequisite.

All this left a much-reduced company of European Poalei Zion who adhered to the federation based on Ahdut Haavodah and the American parties. However, their ranks were replenished by new associates from other sources. The intense political involvement of the period following the war, the Balfour Declaration, the revolutions and counterrevolutions, and the massacres of Jews by Ukrainians and Poles, regular troops and irregular pogromists, brought into the Zionist movement, and especially its youth organization, the Zeirei Zion, a flood of recruits, making them the largest organized group among Eastern European Jews in the early years. Like their contemporaries, these young people responded to the revolutionary socialism of the period and precipitated ideological divisions among the largely Hebraist youth committed to the WZO and its traditional goals and activities. The faction that emerged in the Russian-Polish area as a socialist Zionist part of Zeirei Zion then merged with the local Poalei Zion party which was still affiliated to the world union.

The dominant influence among Zeirei Zion groups in Europe after the war was the Palestinian party, Hapoel Hazair. This segment of the Second Aliyah had always drawn a significant part of its leaders and members from the Zeirei Zion. Veterans who returned from Palestine or were sent abroad for this purpose had kept Hapoel Hazair in close contact with its diaspora counterpart even before the war, and, after it, the Zeirei Zion owed its large share in the *haluz* movement of the Russian-Polish region to the efforts of such emissaries.

In Germany and Austria, a comparable young Zionist group, led by Chaim Arlosoroff with moral support from such luminaries as Martin Buber and, shortly before his death, Gustav Landauer, identified with the Palestinian party to the extent of using its name, Hapoel Hazair. The party journal was widely read by young Hebraists in Berlin and Vienna, and among German-reading Jews, the writings of A. D. Gordon were made known and exercised a strong influence, thanks to translations published in Buber's *Der Jude*—at the suggestion, as it happens, of the young Poalei Zion intellectual Zalman Rubashov (Shazar).

In 1920 Hapoel Hazair sent a delegation, including the venerable Gordon, to consolidate these relations with the diaspora. Up to that time, both Hapoel Hazair and the Zeirei Zion organizations had functioned more or less autonomously but, formally at least, within the several Zionist territorial organizations; and at the WZO Congresses they sometimes worked together by ad hoc arrangements as an ideological faction. Now, at Prague in March 1920, they created a world union of Hapoel Hazair and Zeirei Zion as a separate federation of the WZO.

Strong as was the moral influence of Hapoel Hazair upon its associates—much as they shared its Hebraism, its non-Marxist idealism, and its commitment to "self-realization," to personal fulfillment of the pioneer tasks of labor in Zion—like-minded Zionist youth were also subject to contrary, local influences. Like the rest of their generation, they were open to the revolutionary enthusiasm of their time, and they could not regard the name "socialism" as a shibboleth or consider affiliation to the socialist International taboo. The differences between Ahdut Haavodah and Hapoel Hazair in Palestine or between themselves and such a party as the American Poalei Zion, which was far from pure or rigid in its Marxist orientation, seemed to them to be exaggerated by the Palestinian party, and these grew less and less significant over the years. Hence they were a force that helped, in Palestine, to transcend party differences in forming the Histadrut in 1920, and nine years later, in 1929, their growing number in the Yishuv, as well as the convergence of ideas and interests between the two Palestinian parties, helped bring about the union of the Ahdut Haavodah and Hapoel Hazair in the Erez Israel Workers' Party, Mapai (Mifleget Poalei Erez Israel) and parallel mergers and unions in the diaspora countries.

II

In the postwar Yishuv, the new dominance of Zionist agencies such as the Palestine Executive of the WZO presented a special problem to the leaders of the Old Yishuv, especially the Ashkenazi traditionalists. Instead of repressing the modernists who dissented from or disregarded their own old-established authority, they now had to cope with modernists who were successfully exercising the authority of the Yishuv. The war, in the meantime, had greatly altered the terms in which they themselves could respond to this scandalous challenge. The community in the Holy Land and the Eastern European traditionalist Jewries were left broken and weakened, but now channels of influence and power were opened to traditionalists in the West. These developments encouraged new methods for resisting the modernist threat.

Within the traditionalist ranks, German and Hungarian Orthodox leaders rose to the fore, bringing with them their doctrine of Orthodox separatism. In such a policy there was always the implication that this group had a separate, direct relationship to gentile authorities, distinct from that of other Jews. This could easily lead to rivalry for political precedence—a competition in which German Orthodox leaders had considerable success in relation to their country's wartime occupation policy in Eastern Europe—or could lead to a claim that they were the exclusive legitimate representative of all Jews.

German-Hungarian modern Orthodoxy involved two attitudes quite foreign to Eastern Europe. It combined separation from the (liberal-dominated) Jewish religious community and acculturation to secular gentile standards of legitimacy. The unmodified tradition regarded the whole Jewish community, including its sinners as well as the pious, as an integral whole—one, to be sure, in which traditionalists were accustomed to exercising dominant authority. The notion of Orthodox separatism was inherently repellent to the Eastern Europeans, even though their involvement in the Zionist movement, through Mizrahi, had introduced them to a similar notion of parallel religious and secular organization in the limited field of culture and education. As for the relation of Jews to gentile authorities, Eastern European Ashkenazim preferred traditionally to keep these at a minimum.

With secular Zionists now asserting communal authority under sanction of the government, however, new, modern tactics were required, and the German-Hungarian Orthodox provided both leaders and the tradition of an active, separatist political approach. The Old Yishuv's Ashkenazim split under these opposed pressures. A right wing, mustered under the banner of Agudat Israel, which took up the battle with Zionism over the whole ideological front, eventually plunged into conflict on the central, constitutional issues. This change gradually developed out of clashes concerning the organization of the rabbinate and the whole communal structure of the Jews in Palestine, which was inspired by the new political situation and legal institutions introduced by the British. No matter how modestly formulated, the essential Zionist political ideal involved establishing a self-governing community of all Jews in Erez Israel. To build toward this end from the existing forms of communal autonomy was always feasible as an immediate Zionist objective, under Ottoman as well as British rule.

One method of approaching this task would be to unite the congregations, the *kehilot* and *kolelim*, which, as was already noted, had splintered the traditional community. With so large a proportion living in the holy cities as an act of devotion, the communal organization of much of the Old Yishuv was strongly related to ritual functions. This meant far greater weight for rabbinical than for lay authorities, and far less importance for officers in contact with gentile authorities, than was required in the diaspora. As a result, the inherent antihierarchical tendency of Jewish tradition was driven to manifestly unreasonable lengths. So, at any rate, it seemed to those who were responsible for contacts with the non-Jewish administration. Accordingly, in Ottoman times several abortive attempts were made to unite the main Jewish religious communities, often on the initiative of Sephardim, including the Haham Bashi of Constantinople. Zionists, especially those of Ahad Haam's circle who laid such stress on the communal consensus, naturally took the same attitude; from 1913 to 1915, successive attempts, initiated by Ussishkin's visit to Jerusalem, were made to unite the congregations in the holy city.

These efforts were taken up again when Weizmann arrived in 1918 as chairman of the Zionist Commission and, with considerably greater authority, by Sir Herbert Samuel, upon his assuming the office of high commissioner. Under the pressure of the Palestine administration and its new Jewish officials, a rabbinical assembly was convened in 1921 which elected a rabbinical council with lay participants. The new council assumed the official responsibilities that had been granted to the Jewish millet in Ottoman times: exclusive jurisdiction "in matters of marriage and divorce, alimony and confirmation of wills of members of their community other than foreigners"; jurisdiction in other matters of personal status, if all parties to an action consented to it; and jurisdiction in regard to "the constitution or internal administration" of charitable foundations established under Jewish law before rabbinical courts. It exercised its power as a court of appeal superior to local rabbinical courts, and the government undertook to enforce such rabbinical judgments with respect to "members of their community."[2] At the rabbinical assembly, too, the office of Haham Bashi, a Sephardi monopoly in Ottoman times, was superseded by two elected Palestine chief rabbis, one Sephardi and the other Ashkenazi.

These innovations were not adopted without opposition. Some Ashkenazi traditionalists in Jerusalem boycotted the rabbinical assembly, refusing to accept any hierarchical principle and to subordinate their own courts to the judgments of a rabbinical court of appeal. It should be noted, moreover, that unlike the Muslim courts, which retained from Ottoman times their jurisdiction over all Palestine Muslims, the official rabbinical authorities were granted jurisdiction only over "members of their community," adherence to which was voluntary. The ultra-Orthodox, in rejecting the rabbinical council's appellate jurisdiction, thus implicitly opted out of this community. This dispute soon became part of a larger quarrel over the creation of a general Jewish community organization in which rabbinical courts were only one major function. The implicit separatism of the traditionalist right wing became in this context an explicit separation.

In Ottoman times, Zionists made repeated attempts to unite the Yishuv in a countrywide secular organization. Ahad Haam's work toward this end during the crisis years of 1899–1900 led to a general conference of the new settlements and the dispatch of a Russian-Palestinian delegation to Baron Rothschild in 1901. In 1903, Ussishkin organized the enrollment of 2,000 Jews in the towns and villages and convened an elected assembly. When this body collapsed as a result of the Uganda conflict, the main Zionist and professional organizations of the New Yishuv established a self-appointed council. All these efforts, as well as subordinate activities (such as the network of Jewish arbitration courts) and partial organizations (such as the regional federations of villages and the agricultural unions) that developed in the Second Aliyah, had one common characteristic: they were essentially confined to the New

Yishuv, or to parts of it. The new postwar situation produced a radical change: Zionists now approached the task of countrywide community organization as self-evidently including the entire Jewish population of Erez Israel, old and new settlers alike.

Conferences were convened in November 1917, as soon as the British had successfully occupied areas of Jewish settlement, in order to organize the Yishuv and prepare for its postwar demands. The Jewish leadership intended to create a body of elected representatives of the entire Yishuv, in the whole area of Erez Israel, but the British did not renew their offensive and occupy the area of the northern settlements until a year later. Further delay was caused by the long process of peace negotiation, upon which the definition of the Jewish position depended. Hence, elections for the Yishuv's constituent assembly were not held until April 19, 1920 (except in Jerusalem, where communal riots caused further delay), on the eve of the San Remo agreement to allocate the Palestine Mandate to Britain. The elected assembly finally convened in October 1920, after the new, civilian high commissioner, Sir Herbert Samuel, had gotten well settled in the country.

During this period, immediate matters were dealt with, in the name of the whole Yishuv, by preliminary conferences, assemblies, and a provisional council. The issues that arose—such as the political structure of the community, its share in the British military effort, and security arrangements in Palestine—were treated as matters of more than local concern. Postwar demands advanced by the Yishuv's spokesmen included far-reaching authority claimed for the Jewish people as a whole, not only in the development of the national home but in the current administration of the country.

Such demands were dropped by the WZO leadership upon the insistence of the British and, as a result the competencies of various bodies concerned with the Jewish national home, had to be separated. Zionists were explicitly denied any share in the Palestine administration. The WZO, recognized as representing world Jewry, was authorized to cooperate with the administration primarily in regard to the national home's development. Under the circumstances, the proposed general organization of the Yishuv, in spite of a continuing major interest in broad political issues, had to find its specific functions in the remaining open field: the administration of the essentially local concerns of the Yishuv.

But this matter too was conceived by the mandate government far differently from the pattern envisaged by leaders of the New Yishuv. The latter thought in terms of a community organization that would be a nucleus of national autonomy even when the Yishuv represented a small minority. It would function on the same federal principle as the Austrian Social Democratic nationalities theory, which was adopted by Jewish nationalists in Eastern Europe, with the difference that in Palestine the Jewish community came to desire not merely "personal" but "territorial" autonomy. Their scheme envisaged a general organization to which all Jews belonged and were required to pay taxes, and one that undertook "municipal" responsibilities such as defense and economic welfare as well as narrowly defined cultural functions. The British, on the other hand, were predisposed to favor a form of voluntary religious association for Jews, with restricted ritual and charitable activities, as in England. British Jews such as Herbert Samuel understood, of course, that under the rubric of a voluntary religious community, Jewish tradition included a far wider range of functions than did a Protestant tradition, even in Episcopal England. Moreover, they took as their guide the status of an Ottoman millet enjoyed by Jews and other sects before British occupation, and that structure provided more extensive authority for the proposed communal organization than in England. Nevertheless, their conception was fundamentally different from the Yishuv's idea of a proto-national organization, since it built the community primarily on the base of its religious activities and, hence, of clerical authority.

In view of these differing conceptions, it took seven years before regulations for the Jewish community were adopted in a form acceptable to both the Yishuv and the government. In February 1926, the Palestine *Official Gazette* published an ordinance (the "Religious Communities Organisation Ordinance, 1926") permitting "each Religious Community recognised by the Government," in the exercise of its autonomy for internal affairs, to "make, vary or revoke" its own regulations, which, with the approval of the Colonial Office, would be recognized by the Palestine government.[3] At the end of 1927, such regulations were gazetted for the Jewish community.

While general in its terms, the "Religious Communities Organisation Ordinance, 1926" was applied by Jews alone and reflected to some extent their demands. The community organization, though based on voluntary membership, unlike the Palestine Muslim community, was nonetheless conceded a juridical personality and the right to levy enforceable direct "contributions" on its members. There was a considerable reduction of the clerical dominance characteristic of the millet, the model initially favored by the Palestine administration. The original proposals of the New Yishuv leadership had entirely neglected religious functions of the community, thus evoking indignant protest from the already established rabbinical council. In the gazetted regulations, the rabbinical council and local rabbinates were incorporated into the general community structure, and the articles relating to them were granted pride of place, preceding other items in the document. One result of this positioning was that questions were raised of general community authority in regard to the election and budgets of religious officers.

The emphasis of the regulations as a whole was on the secular authority of the community. This was most effectively symbolized by certain provisions stressing the "territorial" quality of Jewish autonomy. Far from being a voluntary federation of local Jewish communities, as the Palestine administration originally contemplated, the directly elected general assembly could "require or authorise a local Community to levy upon its members a rate or rates"; and where there was a regularly elected local council in a Jewish "township, village or quarter," the municipal officers would normally serve as the committee of the local Jewish community.[4]

Dissatisfaction with such newfangled arrangements had already been manifested by traditionalists during the organization of the rabbinical council. Even more rancor was aroused by the regulations for the new general community organization. Some who had accepted the reorganized rabbinical institutions now opted out. The major source of irritation for them, as for other groups whose interests were affected, was the proposed methods of election to the new governing bodies.

With their political background of Eastern European radicalism, the radical Zionist leaders could think of none but the most uncompromisingly democratic procedures as appropriate for electing the Yishuv's representative institutions. It was obvious to them that elections should be "general, direct, equal, secret and proportional."[5] Moreover, recent experience, not only in the Zionist organization and the community organizations of Central and Eastern Europe, but in some local communities of the Old Yishuv, proved that most of these principles had wide acceptance. "Equal" electoral rights, however, were a subject of dispute among traditionalists in every Jewish community, because they raised the issue of woman suffrage.

The exclusive prerogatives of men in the synagogue and their unquestioned dominance in community affairs were grounded in scriptural and rabbinic texts, as well as in traditional practice. But there was, as always, ample room for differences of interpretation, and there were traditional scholars who argued in 1920 that woman suffrage was not only permissible but commanded in the Torah. The Ashkenazi right wing in the Yishuv arose in passionate indignation against such ideas. It was mainly this issue that crystallized their opposition, to the point that they made common cause with Agudat Israel in an outright attack on the legitimacy of the newly forming community.

The proposal of women's suffrage had been raised as early as 1902, in Ussishkin's attempt to organize the community, and was then dropped in the name of unity. It was pressed after the war by newly founded women's organizations and by liberal and leftist Zionists. By successive stages, the emerging community approved, first, women's right to vote and, then, their right to be elected; on this basis the first elected assembly of Palestine Jewry, including women delegates, was eventually chosen by equal franchise in April and May 1920. But during two years of debate preceding this conclusion, the issue had opened ideological fissures that threatened to separate traditionalists from other Jews and to divide Orthodox Jews of various degrees of rigor.

Among the Orthodox Zionists of Mizrahi, opinion was divided on the questions of principle: some favored woman suffrage without reservation, a few were totally opposed, and an intermediate opinion thought tradition sanctioned women's voting but not holding office. Apart from principle, Mizrahi had to consider its role as representative and protagonist of traditional Jewry. It required a united front of all Orthodox Jews *within* the emerging general Jewish community. In Jerusalem, at any rate, the Agudat Israel, under the leadership of Hungarian Rabbi Isaac Sonnenfeld, had already adopted a position of principled separatism, and when the Jerusalem community united and elected a local committee, the Agudah position had attracted a part of the ultra-Orthodox Ashkenazim, who joined in their dissident congregation. Mizrahi, in taking a position on the issue of suffrage, had to consider the likelihood of similar developments in the emerging countrywide Jewish communal organization.

Orthodox attempts to reverse the decision in favor of woman suffrage began in 1919, as soon as it was made. The ultra-Orthodox Jerusalem Ashkenazi faction ran its own separate elections, excluding women, for the first elected assembly, and obtained validation of the results at a delegate–voter ratio double that in the general election. It then demanded that the assembly take up as its first order of business the repudiation of woman suffrage, and it suspended its participation when this demand was rejected.

Thereafter complicated negotiations took place over the participation of the Orthodox in subsequent assembly sessions, with Mizrahi seeking to gain concessions on both sides. Having succeeded at any rate in making woman suffrage problematic through negotiation, Mizrahi sought in vain to persuade the ultratraditionalists to continue the fight within the communal organization. By 1925, the community leadership bowed to the Orthodox demand that the abolition of woman suffrage be taken up by secret vote as the first business at the next session. The assembly, however, indignantly repudiated its chairman's agreement, and Mizrahi was sharply attacked as hypocritical in view of its previous support of women's voting rights and its participation in the WZO, where woman suffrage was fully accepted.

Mizrahi at this point withdrew from the assembly and set up a separatist community, with the participation of rightist Ashkenazi Orthodox groups and some Sephardi and Yemenite groups; however, upon the refusal of the Palestine Zionist Executive to grant recognition to the new body, it was abandoned. Nevertheless, the community leadership again had to yield to one of Mizrahi's demands, and approval was gained for a referendum on the woman suffrage issue, though not a referendum of men alone, as Mizrahi had proposed. This victory, however, was rejected by Orthodox ultratraditionalists, who refused to participate in any referendum. The elections for the second assembly were soon to be held, and Mizrahi had to make its decision. On November 1 it announced its unqualified participation in the community elections and stated that its aim in proposing a referendum had been solely to keep other Orthodox Jews in the community, as Mizrahi itself had always taken part in conferences with women delegates participating.

Such a positive position on a controversial question crystallized an ideological division among Orthodox Jews, whose lines had been firmly drawn on the other side by the Agudat Israel. When the draft regulations of the Jewish community were published in 1922, the Agudah had written to the High Commissioner refusing "to be subjected in any way . . . to the Jewish National Council." Its consistent separatism, already evidenced in the refusal to be part of the united Jerusalem community or the new rabbinical council, was put on a precise ideological basis: the draft regulations were unacceptable because they were "a solemn proclamation of the deposition of God and the Torah as sovereigns of the Jewish Nation."[6] Failing to persuade the high commissioner or the Colonial Office to reject the proposed regulations and replace them with a substitute draft recognizing the Torah, as interpreted in standard rabbinical codes, as the community fundamental law, Agudat Israel took other measures. Together with other Ashkenazi ultratraditionalists, it appealed to the League of Nations, claiming that the draft regulations of the Jewish community violated their freedom of conscience and demanding recognition as a separate community. This was denied them by the British, but the Orthodox right wing continued as an separatist entity outside the community. It maintained its direct opposition to that community's claims of legitimacy, in spite of occasional cooperation in specific matters of common concern. Mizrahi, within the general Jewish community, had to develop its policies under constant pressure and criticism from these Orthodox rivals on the outside.

The community organization envisaged by the left and liberal leadership, who commanded a majority, appeared to threaten not only the traditionalists but also vested interests of the long-settled Sephardim and the established planters and other property owners. These groups joined in a loose network of opposition forces and succeeded in obtaining a number of concessions and compromises that altered the original design for the community structure.

Both sets of groups enjoyed privileged positions in the local communities, the chief existing "power structures" which were to be integrated into the proposed countrywide community. In the major cities where the Old Yishuv dwelt, Sephardi rabbis were recognized by the Ottomans as the official representatives of Jewry, and in the new municipal councils produced by the Young Turk revolution, Sephardim, as Ottoman citizens, were in the best position to maintain a degree of Jewish participation. So, too, the self-governing institutions of the plantation villages were set up on the basis of a franchise limited to property owners or persons who paid taxes beyond a minimum amount. When the British Palestine administration recognized some other Jewish towns and village authorities as legally empowered "local councils," it accepted their qualified franchise; and occasionally when conflicts arose, it used its reserved powers to approve the elected officials, budgets, and other aspects of their local governments in favor of the more conservative elements of the Jewish community.

One of the first and relatively smoothest reorganizations of the postwar period was the already noted official recognition granted to Ashkenazim in the rabbinate and other institutions of the traditional community. The Sephardim, who had to yield their exclusive prerogatives, did not strongly resist the changes demanded by the new authorities, both Zionist and British. Indeed, they had cooperated in prewar attempts to unify the community, an action that also had required concessions from their side. But it was not long before they felt obliged to demand specific guarantees of their position.

Not only Sephardim but Yemenites and the Bokharan and Georgian *kehilot* voted en bloc and elected their own delegates to the Yishuv's first elected assembly in 1920. In the disputes of the early years, which were on general issues rather than on their specific communal grievances, the largest Oriental group, the Sephardim, sided with the conservative opposition to the labor-liberal majority. Some Sephardim and Yemenites, as was already noted, joined Mizrahi in its brief attempt in 1925 to set up a rival, rightwing assembly of the Yishuv. But in view of the basically communal sources of their opposition sentiments, such alignments with broad class-oriented factions could not fully absorb the Oriental blocs, nor were they long-lasting. Precisely while they formed part of a rightwing alliance, the Sephardi bloc in 1922 successfully insisted on representation, by its own designees, on the presidium of the National Council (Vaad Leumi) elected by the assembly to conduct the Yishuv's affairs between sessions. The Yemenites, for their part, whose history gave them close ties with the labor groups, ran a separate communal list of their own in the 1923 elections of the new general labor federation, the Histadrut. In the second elections of the Yishuv community organization, they conducted separate polls, claiming discrimination against them by the Tel Aviv electoral committee.

The question of safeguarding Sephardi and other communal positions became an immediate issue which had to be faced directly when the draft regulations of the Yishuv's community organization arose for discussion. From the beginning, Sephardim insisted on explicit provisions for their representation on all major lay and rabbinical organs of the community. Not only did the regulations that were approved in 1927 contain such guarantees, but in a three-year battle thereafter the Sephardim won the concession, for the forthcoming election, of a separate electoral curia for their community: they would be granted a number of delegates to the assembly proportional to the number of Sephardim enrolled in the community register, regardless of the number who actually voted; and separate polls would be conducted in which only Sephardi candidates could run, while Sephardi voters could exercise their franchise in that curia and no other. Because of this concession, a similar curia was set up for the Yemenites and the Ashkenazim, much against the will of the latter.

One of the collateral effects of the creation of the communal curia was to make more difficult the alignment of whole communal groups with class-oriented factions or blocs in the elected assembly. The Sephardi community, in particular, represented a substantial electorate, with the major parties contending for their votes by offering separate lists of Sephardi candidates in the curia polls. In 1931 five such lists shared the Sephardi vote; six General Zionists (right of center), five Revisionists (right wing), and four Labor delegates made up the fifteen assemblymen allocated to the community. Naturally, they voted with their Ashkenazi party comrades on most matters, though the predominantly conservative Sephardi delegates on critical occasions were part of the bloc of the right opposition, while the three delegates elected by the Yemenite curia usually voted with the labor-liberal majority.

Center party votes in the Yishuv's community organization were the least effective of all. The best organized "center" factions in early years represented professional interests, such as the artisans' guild, the teachers' union, and the private farmers' or the Judean settlements' federations. Their political positions varied on different issues. In addition, groups representing various shades of basic Zionist ideology, within the gamut referred to as General Zionist, sprang up briefly. Such groups were often opposed to each other rather than united on current issues.

The weak representation and political impotence that resulted were particularly resented by the more conservative General Zionists. Not only were they most frequently opposed to the majority decisions, but their weakness in the elected assembly contrasted sharply with their established power in Jewish local councils and municipalities. Representing long-established institutions, some of them had had a tradition of opposition to the labor factions that went back to earlier conflicts. The prewar clashes of interest between planters and labor, sharpened by younger men into such broader rivalries as between Hashomer and the Zikhron Yaakov Gideonites, took violent form in the wartime disputes between Hashomer and the Nili group, a pro-British espionage cell organized around Zikhron Yaakov leaders, who made a strong bid for the hegemony, if not control, of the entire Yishuv. The desperate adventurism of Nili precluded their gaining wide and lasting support as leaders of the Yishuv's propertied classes, but a fixed opposition to the labor factions was widely established among them. Eliezer Ben-Yehuda, through his newspaper *Doar Hayom* (The Daily Post), had emerged before the war as a spokesman of such sentiments, in opposition to the entente between Zionist officials such as Ruppin and the workers. The predominance of labor in the Yishuv's first elected assembly outraged Ben-Yehuda. He proposed in 1920 that the planters prevent the assembly by convening a meeting of the committees of local communities, who would form a federal union and elect a central governing group. This notion gained some support among the planters, but since other center groups such as the teachers and artisans and the municipal committees of Jaffa and Tel Aviv had been associated from the beginning with the plans for the new community organization, the project misfired.

A major issue was raised before the second session of the elected assembly, in 1922, when Ruppin proposed to levy community taxes on both income and property at progressive rates. The Farmers' Union and the Federation of Judean Settlements led an attack against this proposal, joined by Mizrahi and the Sephardim. Only when assured that alternative plans would be presented did they agree to participate. In the second elections of December 1925, the representation of propertied interests was even less satisfactory. The planters therefore demanded a predetermined representation of 3 out of 23 members of the Vaad Leumi—a considerable increase in ratio over their 9 members of the 221 delegates in the Second Assembly. Failing to gain this concession, they boycotted the elections to the Third Assembly, and subsequent negotiations led only to their admission as observers.

By the mid-1920s, the strength of the center was further fragmented by the emergence of the Revisionists, a party with an extreme position in Zionist external politics. In the Second Assembly elections of 1925 they gained 15 of 221 seats, and in the 1931 elections to the Third Assembly, 15 of 71 seats—in both cases, a number considerably larger than any other party with a strong appeal to middle-class voters. Yet, in their single-minded concentration on Zionist external affairs, they could not adequately represent the specific interests of planters and other center groups, while they hampered the concentration of center forces by drawing votes from these circles. Their relations with the community organization were almost as troubled as those of the planters' party. On several occasions they marched out of assembly meetings, and they withheld full participation with the Vaad Leumi because of conflicts over current political issues. However, their rebellion was climaxed not in the Yishuv's organization but in their secession from the WZO in 1935.

Following the 1931 elections, the Yishuv was unable to hold a new poll until 1944. In the elections of that year, the Oriental communities and the propertied classes again demanded a method of representation that was not based on the one-man one-vote principle, and they withheld participation when this was denied them. Thus, during a critical period of over 15 years, when its population base and other political circumstances were totally altered, the Yishuv's governing bodies were perforce constituted on the outdated election returns of 1931 or the dubiously representative poll of 1944.

On the one hand, this situation placed the propertied classes, like the traditionalists and the Oriental communities, in a rather humiliating state of weakness vis-à-vis the well-organized labor groups and their liberal allies in the organized Jewish community. On the other hand, they were able to rely on their strength in local community organizations—and on the Vaad Leumi's inherent weakness. Its claim to represent the Yishuv was constantly endangered by Agudah separatism, the abstention of the propertied classes, the chronically aggrieved posture of some of the so-called Oriental communal leaders, and Revisionist rebelliousness. Those who wished a share in the Vaad Leumi's power were often able to gain it by negotiation, following their boycott of Yishuv elections or withdrawal from the Assembly. Also, they were able on several occasions to weight the community's governing bodies in their favor by coopting eminent persons in times of emergency.

⋄ 9 ⋄

The Hegemony of Labor

How labor rose to dominance in the Yishuv (Palestine Jewish community), in the Zionist movement, and finally in Israel is a subject that has been thoroughly studied. The growth of the working population and the more effective political organization of labor compared with other parts of the Yishuv after World War I have been noted. But these were no more than relative advantages. The workers long remained a minority and, however well organized in comparison with others, they too were divided by numerous, bitterly factional differences.

Moreover, in the beginning the most effective force in the Yishuv was not its own communal organization, but the Palestine Executive of the World Zionist Organization (WZO); and in this body, until the 1930s, labor was an insignificant factor. The majority of the Executive was made up of General Zionists, on the strength of their preponderance in the WZO's diaspora organizations. The most important political and economic posts were in their hands. Labor was usually represented as a minor faction, on a par with Mizrahi, and for a short period following the Fifteenth Zionist Congress in 1927 it was completely excluded.

Although the workers at first gained little influence or prestige from their meager representation on the WZO Executive, they were always significantly involved in the most important and highly prized functional activities of that body. The whole conception of Zionist strategy under Weizmann depended on economic development: on resettling a large enough body of immigrants on sufficiently extended territories for an eventual claim to an independent national status. This goal was within the compass of organized Zionist effort in two primary respects: first, through the WZO's direct responsibility in regard to Jewish immigration and, second, through its program of land acquisition and occupation by permanent Jewish settlers. In both areas the labor Zionists turned out to be a critically important element.

I

In spite of Herzl's grand design of a charter to develop broad areas and a company to transfer mass populations, bag and baggage, it was not necessarily the Zionist intention to rely primarily on the immigrants whom they themselves recruited and transported or the lands the organization itself bought and held. They expected private initiative, both individual and corporate, to play a major role in the flow of immigrants and the settlement of land. Experience, on the whole, substantially supported this attitude.

In the first years of the mandate, as in earlier decades, the Jewish population and landholdings in Palestine seemed less likely to be increased by the WZO's direct activities than by independent forces. The British administration introduced immigration regulations which made Jewish labor the sole category for which the WZO bore direct responsibility. For other categories of immigrants (capitalists, professionals, students and ecclesiastics, dependents) the government granted visas individually on the basis of specific qualifications. Labor immigrants were admitted en bloc by quotas granted to the WZO Executive for distribution. The number admitted was based at first on Zionist guarantees of employment and later on estimates of the short-run "economic absorptive capacity" of the growing Jewish community.

The dominant view of official Zionists in the early years was that labor immigration should be delayed and restricted in the interest of a gradual, "organic" upbuilding of the national home. The mere fact that the Zionist Commission and later the WZO Palestine Executive underwrote prospective employment for the workers, and that after the first year their funds were seriously short, was enough to induce a cautious approach. But the policy was also based on more general considerations. It was felt by many that before bringing in workers en masse, a large-scale, publicly funded project to drain swamps and build public health facilities was necessary. An even more widely accepted prerequisite was substantial private investment, both by investors abroad and, in particular, by Jewish "capitalist" immigrants.

Thus, while trying to restrain the impatient drive for immediate mass immigration which was proposed on political grounds by Max Nordau and angrily demanded by East European *haluzim* who were already on the move, official Zionists pressed for concessions to develop state lands, Dead Sea salts, hydroelectric power plants, and other possible capital investments. This order of priorities was approved even by men such as

Ussishkin, who came into conflict with the Western leadership over his determination to buy up for the Jewish National Fund (JNF) large tracts of private land that became available.

After the rush of *haluzim* in the first years, other immigrants, outside the labor quota, began to arrive in significant numbers. Jewish traders and artisans in Poland, already under the pressure of a nationalist boycott before the war, found their prospects in the postwar era increasingly hopeless, and the severe depression that followed the monetary reforms of the rightwing, anti-Jewish Grabsky regime in 1924 caused a large increase in Jewish emigration from that country. The new American Immigration Acts of 1921 and 1924 sharply reduced admission to the accustomed haven of earlier years. The U.S. share of world Jewish immigration dropped from 72 percent (237,000) in the four-year period 1920–23 to 30 percent (123,000) during the eight years of Palestine's Fourth Aliyah, 1924–31. Palestine's Jewish immigration in the same years rose from 10 percent (33,000) to 21 percent (82,000) largely because of the sharp increase in the Polish Jewish influx. Registered immigrants from Poland went from 2,175 in 1923 to 17,640 in 1925, and in 1926 they were 55 percent (7,647) of all registered Jewish immigrants to Palestine. Over the whole period of the Fourth Aliyah, Polish Jews were 49 percent (39,000) of the total, compared with 31 percent (9,158) of the total over the five years 1919–23.

While referred to as "middle class," the immigrants of the Fourth Aliyah included a very substantial proportion admitted as "laborers." This was particularly true of the nearly 40,000 who came from Poland, no more than 10,000 of whom qualified for admission as "capitalists" by proving (sometimes quite nominal) possession of the £500 required. Nevertheless, the capital and the commercial outlook brought in by a good part of the Fourth Aliyah had a major impact on the New Yishuv.

Palestine again saw a real estate boom like that of 1890, but under circumstances more favorable to the productive absorption of investment. The growth of Tel Aviv and Jerusalem and the new Jewish quarter in Haifa provided opportunities for investment in urban land and buildings on a much larger scale than was available earlier. Conditions for absorbing rural investment were also improved. After the collapse of the 1890 boom, more than a decade passed before methods were developed for obtaining adequate returns from some farmlands acquired at that time. By 1927, there was enough experience with various crops to demonstrate the natural advantage enjoyed by the *shamuti* orange, which was native to Palestine, and Jewish settlers had experimented successfully with new methods of cultivation and marketing to enhance the advantage. Rural lands that had been privately acquired in the speculative market of 1925–1926 expanded the base for the major development of citriculture that occurred after 1927.

The WZO had no general policy of seeking to regulate or control the welcome inflow of private funds. Zionists for decades had sketched out ambitious projects for Palestine's industrial development. Now that such plans had become feasible, following the installation of a civil administration, the WZO Executive in London and Jerusalem supported the companies organized by Pinhas Rutenberg and Moshe Novemejsky in their bids for the electrification and Dead Sea salts concessions in Palestine. With regard to land acquisition, however, Zionists felt that regulation as well as support of the private market was desirable, and they were always eager to increase the area held permanently as a Jewish national possession.

To be sure, official Zionism had no exclusive commitment to the principle of the national ownership of land. When Ruppin, like Vladimir Tiomkin before him, tried to organize Jewish land purchase in Palestine, he did so not only because he feared the effects of uncontrolled speculation but because he hoped to harness the power of private demand for the advancement of Zionist goals. He set up the Palestine Land Development Company (PLDC) in 1908 as a central service agency to help private as well as public investors meet the financial, legal, and technical requirements of rural and urban land acquisition. At the same time, it was Ruppin under whose administration Zionist policy most fully realized the inherent advantages of national land, bought and permanently held by the JNF.

The whole doctrine of Zionist farm settlement, beginning with the First Aliyah, was developed in opposition to the methods of Baron Edmond de Rothschild's administration, the latter based on private land acquisition. Not only labor Zionists, but official Zionists considered it a primary aim to build villages that would not be dominated by Arab labor. Ruppin, together with the Second Aliyah workers, demonstrated that this goal might be accomplished by use of JNF land and Zionist labor settlers—that is, by combining natural resources under Zionist control with human resources committed to Zionist discipline. There was, further, the scarifying experience of the real estate boom and bust of the 1890s. This drove home the lesson that a speculative private market drove up prices and created a constant danger of the resale of Jewish-owned land, ending all possibility of using it for the settlement or employment of Jews. The publicly owned, inalienable lands of the JNF were thus a strategically critical asset.

The real estate boom of 1925–26 ended in an even greater bust than that of the 1890s. Immigration in the following years dropped, and emigration rose to the point of a net decline in Jewish population in 1927–28. Renewed development and immigration in later years provoked Arab hostility, with armed violence breaking out, and this raised political issues of critical significance. The British administration began to consider reports recommending, on political as well as economic grounds, severe restrictions on Jewish land acquisition and Jewish labor immigration. The prospect grew increasingly imminent that the British might decide to terminate their obligation to facilitate gradual growth of the Jewish national home; the Zionist project faced the approach of a time when the degree of national independence it would obtain would depend on the lands it held and the population it had already settled. In the face of this danger, activities directly controlled by the WZO itself, the land it bought for permanent possession and the labor immigration it had successfully absorbed, grew increasingly important.

The idea of a Jewish National Fund was as old as the Zionist movement, but it was not until the Fifth Zionist Congress (Basle, 1901) that the fund was finally established. The policy then adopted was not to begin purchasing land in Palestine and Syria until a capital of £200,000 had been accumulated. This policy was demanded by business considerations, as well as the unwillingness of political Zionists to begin practical work in Palestine before receiving their charter. Nevertheless, at the next congress (Basle, 1903) the restriction was removed and land acquisition by the JNF in Palestine began, with an initial annual budget of £600. In 1908, when Arthur Ruppin came to head the WZO in Jaffa, the total landholdings of the JNF were only about 4,000 acres, scattered in four different regions of Palestine. But with these small areas, still for the most part unoccupied, and with the meager capital and annual receipts of the Zionist funds, the practical Zionists initiated a program intended to remedy immediately some major defects of previous Jewish settlement policy, and to deal with others as fiscal resources and other necessary conditions made doing so possible.

On areas as small as these, it was, of course, quite impossible to approach the Zionist task of resettling Palestine on a scale adequate for a claim to Jewish sovereignty. But it was possible, nonetheless, to attempt a task symbolically essential for the larger goal: to demonstrate that a farmer-worker class, not dependent on Arab labor, could be recruited from the Jews of the ghetto and successfully settled on the soil of Palestine. Together with the Second Aliyah labor settlers, the Palestine office under Ruppin took up this challenge. They used methods that both partners adopted in conscious reaction against the defects, as Zionists saw them, of the Rothschild-sponsored colonization.

At the very beginning of his work, developing views current among earlier critics including the labor settlers themselves, Ruppin proposed to make "mixed farming" rather than fruit plantations or grain growing the basis of Zionist villages. He foresaw that certain crucial advantages could be secured by their combining plantations with cereal crops and adding other farm branches seldom found in Jewish settlements, such as a dairy, poultry run, and vegetable gardening. Such a mixed farm would provide work throughout the year for the settlers themselves, as well as for hired labor. If workers had regular work in small holdings of their own, they could settle in and around the old plantation villages. Doing this would make unnecessary the casual or seasonal employment of local Arabs, who themselves did such work as a supplement to their other sources of subsistence and could thus live on wages inadequate to support Jewish workers. It would also solve the cardinal problem of "drawing women into agricultural work." The new crops, moreover, would enrich the diet and raise the cash income of the workers.

Ruppin conceived a use for the existing small JNF holdings that would fit in with this plan: they were to serve as a school for Jewish farm workers. Here, again, he was developing current ideas, but with a distinctive stress on one element: he strongly defended the principle that the settlers must choose their own forms of social organization and conduct their communal affairs autonomously. This did not mean that he thought administrators could be dispensed with on his projected farm schools. Cultivation was to be directed in such new settlements by expert administrators, with the immigrant apprentices serving as hired labor. However, the workers-in-training should be dealt with as organized co-operatives, free of the administrator's authority in all or most of their communal functions, such as their medical care, their communal kitchen, and, above all, their cultural activities.

After training, the workers were to be settled on JNF leasehold land, if available, or acquire their own land from the ICA or through the new Zionist land agency, the PLDC. Here, too, having encouraged the co-operative organization and communal initiative of the settlers during their training, Ruppin was consistent. He did not favor exclusively individual settlement on private homesteads; he also contemplated permanent settlement in cooperative groups. The cooperative principle, made popular among Zionists by the writings of Franz Oppenheimer and others, gained Ruppin's support on the basis of his own direct experience as well. He witnessed during the Second Aliyah how the Zionist settlers' social idealism formed them into dedicated bands of nationalist enthusiasts, and he appreciated the practical value of their esprit de corps.

The labor settlers were in accord with Ruppin's ideas on all these points. But what he suggested in a moderate and far from exclusive spirit, they often demanded should be applied much more radically, as a matter of principle. Thus Ruppin planned to make pragmatic use of existing JNF landholdings. The workers bound themselves by oath not to acquire land privately but to settle only on nationally owned land; and they undertook not only to refrain from hiring Arab labor, as required by the JNF lease, but to hire no labor at all, committing themselves as socialists to the principle of "self-labor."

The special situation of workers' settlements on JNF land enabled the labor Zionists to carry out one of Ruppin's proposals that had little success with private Jewish farmers. Mixed farming was not widely adopted in the private Jewish settlements; it became a labor Zionist specialty. The light soils of the coastal plain returned too attractive a profit from citriculture to be put to other uses, and most new private investment, Arab as well as Jewish, was attracted to this branch. Arab labor, which monopolized the work in Arab citrus orchards, also continued strongly dominant in the Jewish plantation villages. The grain-growing settlements that were established with Rothschild funds by the ICA in the remoter inland areas remained virtually stagnant. Few new settlers joined them and the veterans carried on the same, relatively extensive cereal farming with which they had begun, employing Arab labor and methods not greatly different from those of the *fellaheen* (Arab agricultural laborers).

However, the conditions on which JNF land was leased virtually dictated intensive methods of cultivation based on mixed farming, and the aims of the labor settlers themselves objectively demanded such methods. As was noted, the JNF leasehold contract explicitly forbade hiring Arab labor. The use of Jewish hired labor was not banned but it was discouraged by a policy of apportioning land in small units calculated to support a single farm family through the labor of all its members. Not only were the labor settlers—who renounced landownership—largely dependent on leaseholds for their farm settlements, their principle of "self-labor" also made it necessary to seek farm programs capable of employing all their adult members throughout the year. Mixed farming on JNF land was eventually recognized as the form in which these labor Zionist principles could most readily be realized.

Ruppin's greatest virtue in the eyes of the labor Zionists was his understanding of and support for the worker-settlers' rights to determine the form and to conduct the affairs of their socialist farms autonomously. This, too, was a principle that they developed with radical consistency far beyond the original contemplation of even as progressive a Zionist civil servant as Ruppin. The Zionist Organization's school-farms, like similar ICA-sponsored settlements, saw disputes between administrators and the Second Aliyah worker-settlers no less intense than earlier "rebellions" in the Rothschild villages. But now the outcome was not, as before, the complete defeat and cowing or expulsion of the rebels. The farm workers won the right to contract directly with the WZO as a cooperative group and to take over the entire management of their farm, without an administrator. Beginning with an experimental annual contract, this system took hold in a broader, more permanent form which became predominant in all settlements on JNF lands.

When the war's end made practical Zionist work again possible, men such as Ussishkin and Ruppin were prepared to take up land settlement once more on already established lines. In spite of objections from Western Zionists, large stretches of available lands were bought from Arab landlords with whatever funds could be diverted immediately. The new lands were quickly occupied by newly organized collective and cooperative workers' groups. But at that time, the WZO no more based its hopes on lands that the JNF could acquire in the open market than it expected labor immigration certificates to be as crucial an issue as they later became.

Zionists initially planned to extend the Jewish national home by settling Jews on Palestinian state lands. However, in spite of Britain's commitment under Article 6 of the mandate to "encourage, in cooperation with the Jewish agency . . . close settlement by Jews on the land, including State lands and waste lands not required for public purposes," no significant areas were made available from these sources for Zionist settlement. The Palestine government proceeded very cautiously in settling title to state lands. No more than 660 out of over 20,000 square kilometers (including 11,000 in the arid Negev) that might be public lands had been finally demarcated by 1945, and most of this was used, if at all, "for public purposes": roads, railways, and riverbeds, antiquities, forests, army sites, and the like. The government also gave priority to the needs of local Arab cultivators, including future generations, so that some public lands that were sought for Jewish settlement came into the hands of the WZO only after Arabs to whom the government transferred title later sold them to the JNF.[1]

Lands that were privately acquired by Jews might also serve Zionist policy, even though they were not directly controlled by the organization. JNF acquisitions, which did not begin until after two decades of private purchase by Rothschild and immigrant groups, continued to be a minor factor in the first years of the mandate; and even after a decade of accelerated activity, JNF holdings amounted to less than 120,000 acres in September 1939 compared with more than 220,000 acres privately owned by Jewish companies and individuals. Moreover, much of the privately owned Jewish farmland was concentrated in Palestine's orange-growing belt, where the population density was highest. The total population, the Jewish population, and even—in spite of the heavy employment of Arab labor—the number of Jewish farm workers supported by an acre of such plantation land were substantially greater than the comparable numbers supported by mixed farming in the heavy soil areas where JNF land was concentrated. It might seem, therefore, that the best way to achieve close settlement of Jews on the land would be to foster just such private land purchases.

But Zionist experience contained a store of horrible examples of the dangers of the private land market. The speculative market of 1890, repeated in 1925–1926, and in 1932–35 extending beyond urban and suburban plots to distant agricultural sections, proved that private land acquisition was a totally unreliable and inordinately costly tool of Zionist policy. Exorbitant prices set in the boom years interfered with long-negotiated plans for JNF purchases, and in the subsequent collapse of the market Jewish private investment in land sharply declined, or on some occasions registered a net loss of holdings. In the late 1930s, when new difficulties in marketing Palestine's large citrus crop were added to inflated real estate prices, the JNF was left virtually alone to add to the area of Jewish-owned land.

Collateral effects of the speculative private land market were equally disturbing. A good part of the recent settlers reemigrated in 1927, and large-scale unemployment reduced chances for renewing the Yishuv's growth through accelerated immigration. The relatively rapid economic recovery that followed was based in good part on exports of oranges grown on private lands; but Zionist aims were not as well served by the continuing dominance of Arab labor there. Only in a few mixed farms on JNF land could Jewish workers be said to be settled permanently. Such lands were also sought as a base of support for Jewish labor groups that were at least temporarily settled near the plantation villages or partially employed there in a continuing struggle to entrench and, if possible, enlarge the Jewish state in this vital area.

In the second decade of the Palestine Mandate, political issues abruptly heightened the strategic significance of JNF land and of labor immigration. Arab outbreaks against the Jews in 1920 and 1921 had been followed by restrictions on Jewish immigration, which, while much resented by the Zionists, were avowedly temporary. The far greater violence of the 1929 attacks was followed by British inquiries and government statements contemplating new restrictions of a permanent nature. In particular, the Hope Simpson Report and the accompanying (Passfield) White Paper published on October 20, 1930, were based on the conclusion that Arab cultivators already had insufficient land to support them, and thus none was available for new Jewish settlement under existing conditions. Moreover, Jewish immigration began to be viewed in the light of the doctrine, gaining strength in British quarters, that the "rights and position" of the Arabs would be prejudiced if Jews were allowed to increase beyond a third of the population.

Although it was able to prevent direct applications of this doctrine until the 1939 White Paper, the Jewish Agency operated throughout the 1930s under the pressure of such ideas, gradually prevailing in the British administration. After the major Arab uprising in 1936, the termination of Zionist development became an imminent possibility; new suggestions for a territorial partition of Palestine further underscored the significance of existing Jewish landholdings. With the Yishuv not yet constituting even a third of Palestine's population and occupying a minuscule fraction of its area in scattered holdings, its urgent need to extend its bounds to cover the essential minimum for a viable Jewish polity grew steadily clearer. In the face of these prospects, which were inherent in the Zionist situation, the combined role of the JNF and the labor settlers had a strategic significance generally understood from the start and increasingly valued as the mandate wore on.

Buying lands in remote areas of Palestine, often by acquiring, piecemeal, scattered strips or blocks amid hostile Arab villages and Bedouin encampments, was always a considerable risk. In the 1930s, new laws for the protection of tenants, drawn up to appease Arab political opposition to Jewish land purchase, made it even more vital to occupy land as soon as title was transferred. Otherwise, squatters would certainly appear and claim tenancy, with the purpose either of extorting compensation or of blocking Jewish expansion. Only organized labor groups could readily mobilize trained groups capable of occupying and defending the new lands. Their ability to fulfill this function, already proven during the Second Aliyah, gave them a close tie with major departments of the WZO Executive, and above all with the JNF. On the other hand, by specializing in recruiting and training immigrants abroad for the task of frontier settlement, the labor Zionists came to depend increasingly on the availability of new nationally owned lands and Zionist funds.

The mutual involvement began even before immigration, in the process of the training of young *haluzim* abroad. Labor Zionist groups were engaged in this before the WZO was prepared for their immigration and in spite of official Zionist attempts to delay the process. As the British responded to Arab pressure by restricting immigration, at first temporarily but soon with more permanent implications, the labor immigration quota became a prime political issue for the WZO Executive as well as the labor Zionists. The issue was heightened when Hitler's rise produced a new flood of Jewish refugees. At that time of crisis, not only did the traditional countries of refuge close their doors but the very land mandated by the League of Nations to be the Jewish national home was administered in a spirit that was increasingly hostile to Jewish immigration. The *haluzim* who were trained for occupying JNF land now also put their skill and organization into the transport and reception of immigrants who had not been granted entry legally by the British. As they continued to work in a disciplined relationship with the Jewish Agency, in this field as in others, they became a major instrument, as well as a major influence, in the Agency's growing resistance to the policy of the 1939 British White Paper.

From the start, the WZO followed principles for allocating its quotas of labor immigration certificates that were rather roughly related to its generally understood aims. An appropriate age (between 18 and 35), knowledge of Hebrew, and preliminary agricultural or craft training were the qualifications set for labor immigrants. On these broad foundations, the labor Zionist groups who trained *haluzim* established their own, far more specific requirements. They trained prospective immigrants, sometimes organized in tight groups long before their departure, so that they would fit precisely into the same framework—the particular type of collective settlement or political and social orientation in the Yishuv—from which their instructors had been detached for temporary duty in the diaspora.

In the course of years the number of *haluzim* so organized in the diaspora outran the capacity of the WZO to absorb them rapidly in Palestine. A backlog accumulated of organized groups who had to wait long years for new JNF land or WZO funds to become available for settlement. Those who had already immigrated struggled to maintain themselves in the meantime as hired plantation workers in competition with Arab labor. If their settlement was too long delayed, the organized groups might collapse under the strain and members might drift to the towns, perhaps even revert to petty trade and other middle-class occupations. Thus, the availability of JNF land and WZO funds, from the labor point of view, not only became the essential condition of healthy growth of the Jewish national home but was the sine qua non for the health and growth of their own various organizations. Even more crucial was the availability of labor certificates for the *haluzim*, individuals or groups, who were waiting in increasingly trying conditions in diaspora training centers for their turn to be admitted to Palestine. If this goal were endlessly deferred, groups would disperse and the scattered and disillusioned *haluzim* might defect to anti-Zionist movements.

After the first decade, when labor immigration certificates were left more or less unchallenged by other Zionist parties to *haluz* groups, the tightening of British restrictions caused a competitive demand for these visas, as well as others. Requirements for a "capitalist" visa were raised from £500 to £1000 in 1933, a sum high enough to bar many poor Polish Jewish craftsmen who were clamoring for admission. The WZO Palestine offices in diaspora countries had to allot some of the labor certificates for such claimants, and the proportions allotted were continually protested as insufficient by "middle-class" protagonists. For their part, the *haluz* movements also complained of unfair treatment.

In the late 1930s the Palestine government placed quotas on all categories of Jewish immigration. Even before this final measure, the government set aside part of the labor immigration schedule for its own use: deductions on account of travelers remaining illegally, allotments for relatives of Palestinian residents, and so on.

Under these circumstances, the *haluz* groups relied on their political influence in the WZO to secure at least priority in the share-out of labor immigration certificates. Zionist Congress resolutions set aside 50 to 55 percent of the labor schedule for young people with 18 months of agricultural or other vocational training and for members of recognized artisans' organizations. In view of the special circumstances allowing Hitler's rise to power, resulting in a swift increase in organized *haluz* groups in Germany, the ratio was increased to 65 percent. Among themselves the *haluz* groups argued bitterly for greater allocations in the subdivision of these certificates. Claims were based on ratios of their enrollment in diaspora training centers, their group membership, and (as with other parties outside the labor Zionist fold) on their factional strength in the latest Zionist Congress.

The portion of the labor schedule actually taken up by *haluz* groups in any year varied with the pressure of other applicants. It declined when political or economic oppression in the diaspora swelled the stream of Jewish emigrants and increased demands on the labor schedule, and it rose when potential immigrants from other sources were discouraged by political or economic setbacks in Palestine. Thus after the 1929 pogroms in Hebron, Jerusalem, and Safed, 85 percent of the labor immigrants in 1930 were members of Hehaluz (The Pioneer). Following the rise of Hitler, they comprised only 43 percent in 1933 and 40 percent in 1935. The Arab revolt that broke out in 1936, as well as mass Hehaluz recruitment in Germany, caused the ratio to rise once more to 49 percent of "labor" immigrants in 1936, 57 percent in 1937, and 60 percent in 1938.

In those years also the position of the labor Zionists in the WZO Executive was continually strengthened. Moreover, by long usage, the conventions of the close relationship between labor Zionist groups and the departments of immigration and settlement in the WZO Executive were entrenched and developed in an elaborate institutional form. The principle of this relationship was recognition of the autonomy of the labor settlers in conducting all their economic, social, and cultural affairs.

This principle was well enough established even in the 1920s, before labor Zionists won major positions in the WZO Executive, so that outside experts, accustomed to methods employed in parallel cases elsewhere, described the Zionist system as a veritable dictatorship of the settlers over the colonizing agency. Exaggerated as such a description may be, it had more than a grain of truth.

But if there was a "dictatorship of the settlers," it was not exercised directly by them as a single, compact group, united in their common interest. The autonomy of the worker-settlers was exercised mainly by the numerous partial organizations, groups, and factions who were in competition within the workers' camp itself. The inner political organization and divisions of labor Zionism were thus a major influence in determining how the strength and influence of labor affected the general development of the Yishuv.

II

Any detached observer must be struck by the strange mixture of idealistic romanticism and pragmatic, if not opportunistic, realism pervading the history of Zionism in its every aspect. The continual polemics surrounding the movement, in which hostile critics stress one side and sympathizers stress the other side of the picture, have made the complex situation familiar in regard to Israel's political history. It is no less evident in the history of Israel's domestic institutions.

Interest in cooperative methods was widespread in the Zionist movement, as has already been noted. Herzl was attracted by current versions of technocratic utopianism (for example, by the idea of an "industrial army") and Nordau was sympathetic to socialism. Franz Oppenheimer's social theories, based on agrarian land reform and credit, consumers', and agricultural (but not industrial) producers' cooperatives, were given practical application by way of experiment when the WZO in 1911 began to build the colony of Merhavya according to his plans. American Zionists such as Brandeis were inclined to similar ideas, responding to Henry George's "single tax" theories, and their Pittsburgh program in 1918 called for national ownership of land and encouragement of co-operative enterprise in Palestine. Nevertheless, actual Zionist policy in the early years of the Palestine mandate, was generally conducted in a cautious spirit far removed from radical enthusiasm.

The special background of the labor Zionists included an even richer variety of decidedly radical, collectivist social ideas; but skeptical realism, as well as the diversity of approaches, precluded a general commitment to any particular vision. Nahman Syrkin as early as 1898 proposed to build Zion from the outset on cooperative lines, as a socialist Jewish state, but Borochov's cool Marxist analysis strongly deprecated any such utopian idea and counseled labor Zionists to rely on capitalist development to build them a normal "strategic base" for the class struggle in Palestine. The Jewish petty bourgeois, unable to find security for their capital or for themselves elsewhere, would be driven to Zion, whose Levantine, small-scale, essentially commercial economy would offer them opportunities, available precisely because they were too marginal to attract other investors. Jewish proletarians and déclassé artisans, as well as unemployed intellectuals, were driven to settle in Palestine for similar reasons, but their establishment in Zion depended on prior investment by Jewish small capitalists. In line with these views, Borochov strongly criticized the proposal to adopt Oppenheimer's cooperative colonization project, which was debated at the world conference of Poalei Zion in advance of the Ninth Zionist Congress in 1909. In the same Poalei Zion meeting, however, the Oppenheimer plan was strongly defended by Shlomo Kaplansky, on behalf of the Poalei Zion of Galicia, where cooperatives and other "constructive" radical theories had long enjoyed support.

"Constructivist" versions of labor Zionism, which advocated immediate labor initiative toward settling on land in cooperatives and collectives, the cells of an embryonic socialist society, gained increasing acceptance among Second Aliyah workers. But theories held by prewar advocates of this method were widely diverse; while their efforts converged, they were not directed by a common, fully elaborated doctrine. There was a rather eclectic use of inherently opposed ideas, which, in later periods, formed the base of rival ideologies. Thus, while Hashomer was allied with the Marxist Poalei Zion, collectivist activism was preached by a few enthusiasts in their ranks, people with anarcho-syndicalist, social revolutionary rather than social democratic leanings, such as Michael Helpern and Manya Wilbushevitz (Shohat).

Another example of this eclecticism was the program adopted by a commune of potential *haluzim* in the Ukrainian town of Romny in 1911. This document, drawn up by Yosef Trumpeldor, proclaimed its aims to be both national liberation, by achieving Jewish independence in Erez Israel, and social liberation, by building communist settlements there. It combined ideas upon which later *haluzim* elaborated rival ideologies: to build settlements on the economic base of industry as well as of agriculture and animal husbandry so that communes could absorb the mass of Jews—an approach later associated with Yosef Trumpeldor's own name and influence by his immediate disciples—and at the same time to foster personal freedom and preserve family and religion as private domains. The liberal tone of the latter objectives was associated in later years with Eliezer Jaffe and the *moshav ovdim*, in opposition to the collectivist followers of Yosef Trumpeldor. The poet Zvi Schatz, who in 1911 was the leading spirit of the Romny group, also emerged in later years as an ideological foe of quasimilitary collectivism. Personal freedom was the core value of Schatz's anarchistic vision of the commune, and he regarded the collective as sublimated family, based on the brotherhood of comrades.

Although Schatz found no difficulty in accepting Trumpeldor's eclectic program in 1911, the polemical necessities of later years forced him to distinguish more sharply between its various elements. He declared in decisive terms that the rule of a communal brotherhood must be one of "living in depth, not in breadth." He insisted that "the spirit rejects large cooperatives ... instead, small communes of 8 to 10 close, congenial persons will spring up on the land."[2] This statement represented a polemical position in the postwar period, when Trumpeldor's sweeping conceptions were taken up by disciples committed to the large commune as an industrial army. But the 1911 document that Trumpeldor composed implies just such social relations as Schatz envisioned when it provides that "communal labor groups should be made up of 15 persons"; yet, at the same time, it stipulates that "the project must be set up from the beginning on a wide scale."[3]

Clearly, then, the postwar immigrants found no well-established framework within which to work out their socialist Zionist idealism. The Second Aliyah veterans had not gone beyond a stage they themselves regarded as experimental. They were hardly ready to crystalize their own various ways of life in final form, let alone offer them as a completed environment into which newcomers could be inducted en masse. The Second Aliyah offered no more than a general ideal and several specific models of exemplary labor Zionist performance. Newcomers could identify with and, in a general way, pattern themselves upon the legendary Hashomer or the new Galileean communes. But if the veterans wished new recruits, they urgently needed to define their own organizing ideals more concretely and in a way that was responsive to the new values the immigrants represented.

With the British conquest of Palestine, Second Aliyah veterans, and some young leaders of the Third Aliyah, formulated specific plans, drawing on accumulated labor Zionist experience and anticipating the needs and character of the newcomers. Sharply opposed alternatives were thus offered to the immigrant workers, leading to new ideological controversies and new political groupings and social formations.

Communes in the Second Aliyah had been rather loose, ill-defined arrangements used pragmatically by workers in various connections: as a common home base for day laborers in the plantations; as collective contractors; and as the social form of some, though not always all, workers in certain farm settlements. It was possible for both the mobile Hashomer and settled villages such as Degania and Kinneret to have members of a commune living and working together with comrades who were not members of the commune. The commune was a form of living chosen by elite groups among the workers because it best expressed their social idealism and because it enabled them to be more effective. It was not necessarily construed by its members at the time as an immediately available instrument for absorbing and organizing the mass of worker-immigrants.

Those in the Second Aliyah whose foremost concern was mass settlement of farmer-workers were likely to think of private or cooperative villages rather than communes as the appropriate instrument. In Hovevei Zion circles, proposals to settle workers on small plots around the plantation villages, enabling them to supplement wages with the income and produce of their own farmers, attracted attention; Beer Yaakov was founded in 1907 near Rishon Lezion, and Ein Ganim in 1908 near Petah Tikvah, on this plan. But the worker-farmers in these and similar settlements became planters themselves, and even employers of Arab labor, defeating the original purpose.

The Merhavya cooperative farm-school, established in 1911 on lines drawn up by Franz Oppenheimer, attracted some labor Zionists in an attempt to initiate extensive settlement of workers while overcoming the shortcomings of those earlier schemes. The plan was based on a single large farm, to be worked initially under the direction of trained farm managers and with modern mechanized methods. Each of the workers, whose wages would be graded according to skill and industry, was also allotted a small family plot near his dwelling as a supplement to income. Sales and purchases outside the settlement would be cooperatively effected, as would the provision of services to members in the village. This scheme, supported by the Austrian Poalei Zion, was rejected by those Second Aliyah workers who founded Degania in the same year as a fully communal farm group. The workers who came to Merhavya soon revolted against the administrators who were imposed upon them; in the end, Merhavya was reorganized as a commune, and a smallholder's cooperative settlement was also set up on its land.

The Second Aliyah reacted against this and similar administered villages, such as the ICA farms, by creating self-administered farmers' communes like those of Degania and Kinneret. However, these experiments, which gave the workers their full autonomy and satisfied the social idealism of some, were not generally considered suitable for absorbing mass immigration. This was one of the arguments used by Eliezer Jaffe, one of the leaders of the Kinneret commune, who drew up an alternative plan during the troubled war years to found *moshavei ovdim* (sing., *moshav ovdim*: a cooperative farmers' settlement) as the most appropriate labor Zionist method for establishing a peasant-workers' class.

Jaffe regarded the workers' communes as useful provisional arrangements, but he argued that they were inherently antithetical to basic human needs and values. The communal structure was necessarily antagonistic to personal freedom and privacy and it was out of harmony with the fundamental human institution of the family. The peculiar kind of commitment required to live such a life permanently could not be shared by many. Whatever advantages labor Zionists sought through the communes could, in the long run and on a much broader scale, be secured equally well by the *moshav ovdim*, which was based not on exotic but on universal human motivations. The *moshav*, as Jaffe planned it, would be built on JNF land held on long-term lease, and it would establish workers as self-employed farmers who neither employed others nor were themselves part-time hired laborers, and who managed their individual farmsteads and cooperative services autonomously, without depending on administrators.

One difficulty that could prevent newcomers from joining *moshavei ovdim*, critics argued, was the degree and range of skills needed to make a success of a smallholders' mixed farm. The commune, with a large labor force assignable as needed, could divide its membership (in rotation, if desirable) among the several farm branches, appoint trained specialists to head each branch, and thus fit unskilled newcomers into a going economy while it gradually trained them. The *moshav*, where each member had to operate individually all branches of a mixed farm, could not undertake this task. In point of fact, the *moshav ovdim* in later years was built by closed groups of veteran farm workers, each of whom had learned the necessary skills during years of labor in communes or collective labor groups; it did not generally attract inexperienced newcomers. But Jaffe did not believe the objection was insuperable. Suitable methods could be devised to make the *moshav* as effective as the kibbutz in the labor Zionist task of absorbing the unskilled and using the special skills of its members.

The *moshav's* broadly human appeal and capacity to absorb masses rather than the select few that were fit for communes were not, however, the sole considerations for Jaffe in advancing his project. He was interested primarily in other objectives, and for these, he and those who felt as he did would be willing even to defer the rapid settlement of immigrant masses. His labor Zionism was of the idealistic anarchist variety preached by A. D. Gordon and favored by the agrarian-populist Hapoel Hazair, of which party Jaffe was a leader. He considered crucial not how quickly the largest possible number of Jews could settle on the land in Palestine but how profoundly the Jewish farmer would be rooted in his soil. Only the *moshav ovdim* promised to create the deeply personal—because private—possession of the family homestead, the total investment of the workers' powers in a natural place, and the direct bond between culture and nature without which the new Hebrew nation could not arise. Only the *moshav ovdim* could end once and for all the ingrained mercantile habits and alienated psychology of diaspora Jews and build family and nation on the secure base of a self-supplied, near-autarchic economy.

The task was one that Jaffe expected to see accomplished only through the dedicated efforts of generations of idealistic pioneers. He did not go as far as Ahad Haam or A. D. Gordon, who denied emphatically that the Jewish national home must serve as a primary haven for Jewish emigrants and be built in response to their needs. But he did insist on personal idealism as the single motive essential to Zionist success, and he clearly expected the goal to be reached by long, slow years of toil by the Zionist elite, the worker-settlers.

Any approach based on materialistic motivations or on political shortcuts, he rejected as bluntly as did Gordon. He opposed the project of a Jewish Legion, as did many in Hapoel Hazair, and refused to rely on political promises such as the Balfour Declaration, for he held that no people could be *given* their land: they had to possess it by their labor. It goes without saying that he opposed the merger of labor Zionists in Ahdut Haavodah party, united as it was with the Marxist World Union of Poalei Zion and with the Second International.

The activist idealism of a Jaffe had a great appeal to men like Buber and the postwar generation of young Zionists, especially when backed by the noble figure of A. D. Gordon at the Prague conference of Hapoel Hazair and the Zeirei Zion in 1920. But other aspects of this approach did not attract them equally. Young East European Jews were caught up in the contagious enthusiasm of the Russian Revolution. They too might hold traditional party organization in contempt, but they could not understand a conception that rejected power politics and political mass organization as main tools for a swift conquest of Zionist aims. Central European Zionist youth, for their part, were deeply committed to the collective eroticism of their own youth movements and "youth culture." Whatever they would build in Zion, it would have to stand on the brotherhood of their *Büende*, on the intimate "nests" of comradeship within their movement; and they could hardly respond to proposals to build anew on the base of the family and the private individual and reproduce social forms embodying the very tyranny of the parent that they rejected.

This was a generation to whom the commune, and not the *moshav ovdim*, could serve as an ideal, if presented in a way that responded to their drive for revolutionary mass action. Such an approach was offered at Kinneret, where Shlomo Levkovitz (Lavi) formulated the concept of the large, variegated, open commune: the kibbutz. In the nearby Jordan valley commune of Degania, where the rival concept of the *kvuzah*—the small, select, homogeneous, purely agricultural commune—was developed, the pressure of new members was met by their dividing the communal lands among two (initially three) groups rather than expanding the social unit beyond its capacity to promote brotherly intimacy and retain its agricultural purity. In Kinneret the problem was met in another way: the commune there opened itself to new members without rigid tests of compatibility or tight limits on numbers, and consequently accepted the responsibility for economic diversification on a scale that could absorb a constantly increasing membership.

Sweeping and daring as the conception was, it still bore seeds of future conflict with still wider-ranging ambitions that prevailed among some of the new immigrants. Levkovitz was a man of the Second Aliyah and his idea of the large commune was one of the ways in which his generation sought a stable, local attachment after long years of transient labor and mobile service. Even in Hashomer, with its traditions of romantic nomadism, the swing to fixed communal settlements—on the exposed frontiers, to be sure—gained strength shortly before and during the war. They, too, founded permanent settlements in Galilee, notably Kfar Giladi in the far north. But the new generation, imbued with Trumpeldor's vision of a workers' army, was inclined to extend its collectivism beyond any fixed locality and sought an activist role over the entire land and the whole social structure.

Such a conception was strongly favored by postwar conditions in Palestine. Even if there had been a well-established design for absorbing the mass of newcomers in old or newly built villages, the WZO had neither the land nor the facilities for doing so. The first major postwar land purchases, which permitted an initial spurt of rural settlement in 1921, were not followed up with sufficient investment to provide for an adequate, steady rate of colonization. Instead, the labor Zionists first found employment in road construction, begun by the military government and continued by the civil mandate administration as well as by ICA and the WZO. In later years they took up construction trades in the towns. The peculiar requirements of these construction jobs, given the loosely radical leanings and collectivist enthusiasm of the workers, produced characteristic new forms of workers' organization.

III

Those who provided the first jobs for the immigrant workers in the Third Aliyah were the labor bureaus of the workers' parties. As primary or subcontractors, they were able to secure work on road construction from the government or from Jewish agencies, and they considered it their chief purpose to provide such employment as the first stage in the absorption of immigrants into the labor community. But the Second Aliyah veterans had proved unable to overcome their partisan differences even under the prompting of the new, nonpartisan elements in the Jewish battalions. The strife between Hapoel Hazair and the Poalei Zion was succeeded by an equally bitter rivalry between Hapoel Hazair and Ahdut Haavodah. Many new immigrants, who had to seek employment through the offices of the two parties, strongly objected to being involved in their conflicts, which they considered irrelevant to their generation.

Even though their employment was obtained by party-affiliated bureaus, and notwithstanding their sympathy and identification with Second Aliyah ideals, the newcomers were not compelled to adjust to the existing conditions. They were not a mere scattering of individuals added to the Yishuv, as the Second Aliyah had been. The immigrant influx in the years 1920–1922 represented an annual increase of 11 to 13 percent relative to the war-stricken Yishuv of those years. Workers continued to be a significant part of the influx during the peak years of the Fourth Aliyah, when immigrants were 15 percent in 1924 and 28 percent in 1925 relative to the settled Yishuv. Not until the Hitler era and the mass immigration immediately following the independence of Israel were similar proportions again attained. The Third Aliyah was also composed of more young, single, male workers than was any other wave of immigrants, and they outnumbered from the start the small band of veteran labor Zionist settlers.

It should be noted further that, unlike the Second Aliyah, these newcomers did not come as dissociated individuals, largely without the backing and direction of their diaspora movements. The new workers' aliyah was in good part a migration of groups that were bound together by diaspora associations which continued beyond the time of their arrival. The broadest common association was their affiliation to Hehaluz, the diaspora organization of pioneers-in-training; most of them had spent considerable crisis-laden periods under its discipline before their emigration, and some had taken part in the epic movement across war-torn borders to reach Palestine, with or without legal authorization, which Hehaluz had inspired and conducted. Hehaluz consequently emerged as a distinct, articulate, and effective force which remained active in the Yishuv after its avowed object of training *haluzim* and bringing them to Zion had been accomplished.

The primary reason for the persistence of this migrant organization after its objective was achieved was the newcomers' dissatisfaction with the mutually opposed options offered to them by the Second Aliyah parties, and their impatience with the veterans' inability to achieve a full and firm union of all labor Zionist forces. These feelings were shared by Second Aliyah "nonpartisans" such as Berl Katznelson, who had regarded the prewar agricultural unions, rather than the labor parties, as the primary labor Zionist instrumentality. Joined with new immigrants in a nonpartisan bloc, they had formed the largest faction at the national convention of agricultural workers and at the general labor convention, including urban workers, held in Petah Tikvah in early spring 1919, where Ahdut Haavodah was formed. This partial merger could not satisfy the nonpartisan leaders in Ahdut Haavodah any more than it did the newly arrived Hehaluz leadership. New plans then being discussed in WZO circles—especially plans for a Workers' Bank to finance cooperatives and labor-contracting bureaus—made a full labor Zionist union urgent, in their view, in order to obtain independent labor control of such projects and to influence Zionist policy in general, including on education and colonization. Hehaluz thus joined with Ahdut Haavodah in pressing for the conference which at the year's end created the general labor federation, the Histadrut (*Histadrut klalit shel haovdim haivrim be-Erez Israel*). Upon the creation of this comprehensive union of Zionist workers, Hehaluz disbanded as a separate body in Palestine and confined itself to the role of a training organization in the diaspora.

Although, in principle, the Histadrut had a broad mandate to assume all constructive labor Zionist tasks, it nevertheless fell short of the full unity and the total program envisaged by Ahdut Haavodah and Hehaluz leaders. The general labor federation was produced after a party compromise which eliminated "socialist" from the proposed title of the new organization and nominally excluded "politics" from its functions. The effect was to concede a legitimate sphere for the party organizations in conducting labor Zionist politics; and the survival of two major parties, in some ways, gave them a primary role in determining the general organization's policies. But the rival parties remained under pressures that drove them to converge on a common position, with both of them committed to the Histadrut as the primary instrument of labor Zionist policy.

As was noted earlier, Hapoel Hazair's natural allies in the diaspora, the greatly expanded Zeirei Zion cohorts, were strongly affected by the socialist current of the time; and when they came to Erez Israel, many joined Ahdut Haavodah. That party, in turn, was reinforced by the merger with the nonpartisans in attitudes that even before the war had divided the Palestinians from the diaspora Poalei Zionists: their Hebraism, often tinged with anti-Yiddishim; their increasingly definite cooperativist-collectivist version of socialism, which traditional Marxists could only condemn as utopian; and their growing disregard for proletarian-Marxist scruples about "class collaboration" with functional agencies of the "bourgeois" WZO. On all these points the dominant trend of diaspora Poalei Zionists in the early 1920s was directly opposed. But as the majority Poalei Zion factions in Eastern Europe were steadily dissolved and absorbed by their communist milieu, the remaining diaspora parties were mainly those who shared most of the attitudes of Ahdut Haavodah. Between that position and the position of Hapoel Hazair sympathizers who, at the same time, professed themselves socialists, the difference grew quite insignificant. In 1929 the two parties in Israel joined to form the Erez Israel Workers Party, Mapai, and similar mergers then took place in the diaspora. Thus, the union of labor, begun on a broad scale by compromise between its two major parties, was now crowned by their merger.

In building Mapai, as in their fight to unite all labor in Ahdut Haavodah and the Histadrut, men such as Berl Katznelson were inspired by vague notions of a form of political labor organization that transcended the conventional political party. Such leanings are, of course, common and natural in a socialist political body that aims to alter radically the system within which it operates; even German social democracy, for that generation, the classic model of a parliamentary socialist opposition, had devoted at least as much attention to its own inner structure of disciplined comradeship as it did to its external power struggle. The labor Zionists were largely products of a Russian radical milieu which, in 1905 and 1917, repudiated the German model, renounced the parliamentary approach, and, through the general strike and the workers' and peasants' soviets, united a rebellious mass at once into a disciplined striking force and a potential nucleus for a radical new polity and social organism. The same predispositions, if not conceptions, were strongly manifested by Second and Third Aliyah leaders. When Katznelson fought to unite the Zionist workers, he was interested primarily in controlling the undisciplined expansive force of the labor community and directing it more efficiently toward the goal of his constructive strategy: building the working class into the socialist nation. The Mapai merger might improve labor's parliamentary position in the Zionist movement but, more important, could also help achieve the dream of the Histadrut as a total working community, one that responded unequivocally to central policy through the finely attuned initiatives of all its autonomous, organically collaborating elements.

But by 1929 there had already grown up opposition groupings which proved strongly resistant to Mapai's centralist ambitions. They arose primarily in the sector that was the core and model of Mapai's own strategy: the agricultural labor community. In most cases, moreover, the dissidents shared the vision of integral labor organization, one not based on conventional political or trade union functions but aimed at forming a full community and exercising all social functions. They defined themselves, however, by increasingly partisan ideologies and strategies, dissenting from the consensus that was sought by the Mapai. The paradoxical outcome was that not only did they defeat Katznelson's vision of universal labor community harnessed in tandem to a common goal; in the course of doing so, they themselves relapsed into increasingly conventional political parties and helped Mapai reduce itself to the same status.

While Hehaluz, the most comprehensive organization of the new immigrants, disbanded as a separate force in Erez Israel and confined itself to recruitment and training in the diaspora, the newcomers developed other highly autonomous and mutually competitive associations that represented their attitudes and interests in the Yishuv. From the beginning, veteran settlers of the Second Aliyah who joined the road and construction gangs attached themselves to the new organizations and helped mold their ideologies.

As was noted earlier, a group of Trumpeldor's Russian disciples in Hehaluz, the so-called "Crimchakes" (Crimeans), including a core of Red Army veterans, organized the Gdud Haavodah, a Legion of [Defense and] Labor in the name of Yosef Trumpeldor—the bracketed expression was kept secret—at the construction camp on the Zemakh-Tiberias road in August 1920, shortly after their immigration. The Marxist-syndicalist temper of these Crimean immigrants strongly attracted Poalei Zion veterans of the most militant activist type. Hashomer leaders such as Israel and Manya Shohat, returning from exile, and Shlomo Levkovitz, the advocate of the large, open, variegated kibbutz, turned to the Gdud Haavodah as the most suitable means for realizing their bold new ideas.

Shohat and her friends, recognizing the affinity of Hashomer and the Trumpeldorian legion in style and conceptions, tried to carry out through the Gdud Haavodah specific plans for the postwar Yishuv's defense which the established leaders and the labor Zionist consensus had rejected. The question of defense became acute in the early years of British administration, when, as has been noted, attempts to maintain the Jewish Royal Fusilier battalions as an internal security force of the mandate government failed. During the April 1920 Arab attacks on Jews in Jerusalem, Jabotinsky had openly deployed units of a new paramilitary body of the Yishuv, the Irgun Haganah (Defense Organization), thus asserting a legal status and claiming government recognition for their activity. The upshot was his own arrest and conviction, together with other Haganah men. For Jabotinsky, even after Jewish protests yielded an amnesty that ended his long-term prison sentence (but also freed Arab activists), this experience powerfully reinforced his conviction in the doctrines he had evolved: that the only way to gain the Zionist objective was to exert political pressure on Britain for a definite, explicit, commitment to a Jewish state and recognition of a Jewish military corps under British command to enforce that policy; and he held that the Haganah must be organized and utilized in accordance with that aim. This view was not shared by most other Zionists, however, and leading Haganah activists continued the organization as a semisecret, voluntary paramilitary force.

While there was a consensus that the Haganah must perforce function as a nonofficial body, the Yishuv, and labor Zionists in particular, differed sharply on the strategy and organization of the corps. Shohat and other Hashomer stalwarts, who reluctantly disbanded their own organization in 1919 under pressure of Ahdut Haavodah, wished to continue its tradition in the proposed new militia defense formation. They demanded that command of the Haganah be delegated to an elite corps drawn from their ranks. They insisted on unhampered discretion in the central command, not simply for the sake of swift and decisive reaction to attack in emergency situations. Their private strategy was based on the vision of the Haganah as the arm of a workers' revolution against British imperialism, and this aim, they felt, required a conspiratorial type of organization quite incompatible with control by existing public bodies.

These views were rejected by the labor Zionist consensus and by Ahdut Haavodah as well. The latter led in the organization of Haganah as a general defense corps of the Yishuv, under control of public bodies in spite of its necessarily clandestine, semilegal character: first Ahdut Haavodah and then the Histadrut Executive exercised a more or less formal control of the Haganah. Hapoel Hazair, the other major party in the Histadrut, strongly opposed not only revolutionary aims but any strategic objectives for the Haganah at all, beyond self-defense closely tied to specific labor functions. They failed to have this condition made explicit in the Histadrut resolution that assumed responsibility for the Haganah, but in fact the defense organization developed in early years along the lines of residential and settlement self-defense of chiefly static and reactive character.

In the face of the rejection of its own plans, Shohat's group reconstituted itself within the new Legion of Labor as a secret military collective preparing for a revolutionary role. Its activities, particularly in diverting funds and arms purchases to its own use, provoked bitter undercover conflicts in the labor movement. In the Gdud Haavodah it contributed to a military syndicalist tone and an adversarial stance toward the majority in the Histadrut. It established its base in a frontier kibbutz, Kfar Giladi, in the Galilean area where Trumpeldor had met his death.

The aim of another veteran, Shlomo Levkovitz (Lavi), who joined the Gdud Haavodah in order to build the large commune, had a broader, more critical impact. The Legion of Labor was a natural choice for such a project, for it tended toward a broad-gauge collectivism both by inclination and out of the logic of its situation.

The immigrants employed in road gangs in 1919–20 organized themselves, on the basis of hometown or youth movement ties, or simply because they met on the job, into small collectives of a dozen to fifteen comrades, moving their camp with the advancing roadhead. They got their jobs under contracts undertaken by the two labor parties, and later by the Histadrut's labor and public works bureau. Cooperation in a small group provided essential services and also the advantages of pooled work and income. It served as a form of mutual insurance for the cooperating members, who, as newcomers to the country and novices at manual labor, greatly needed such collective support.

The small work group who founded the Legion of Labor thought from the start in much broader terms than this. Their leaders undertook to build a broad, open organization comprising many—potentially all—such mobile collectives into a single countrywide industrial army, which would achieve a Zionist communism. Numerous collective road gangs at one or another construction divided daily wages equally among their members for the duration of the job; individual accounts were settled at the end. The Gdud Haavodah organized a growing number of affiliated collectives on an extension of the same principle, receiving payments centrally on all its contracts and distributing the proceeds equally after deducting costs of administration, services, and investment; and very soon, the Gdud formally abandoned the whole principle of individual accounts for the workers.

Such a collective of collectives was, in principle, open for unlimited expansion of its membership and its functions and thus seemed eminently suited to carry out a plan like Levkovitz's. It had already, at the very beginning, committed some of its members to the frontier Hashomer-organized rural commune of Kfar Giladi. It was soon won over to the project of building, as part of its structure, a large, open, variegated commune, permanently settled on JNF land.

For this purpose Levkovitz needed also to win the consent of the

WZO to grant his untried group a land-lease. In order to achieve this end, he and the Labor Legion needed the support of some established political faction. The choice of Levkovitz's own party, Ahdut Haavodah, was obvious, since Hapoel Hazair strongly favored either the small, tight commune like Degania, or the new proposal of a *moshav ovdim*, for which Eliezer Jaffe was organizing a group of experienced, time-tested veterans of the Second Aliyah. With Ahdut Haavodah and Histadrut support, the project of a large commune was permitted to have its trial. When the new JNF lands that were acquired in Emek Jezreel were allocated for settlement, Jaffe's *moshav ovdim* was granted the leasehold of a swampy block of land in the western Emek, where Nahalal was founded in August 1921; and eleven days later, the commune of Ein Harod was founded on Levkovitz's plan near the springs of the Nuris tract, in the eastern Emek. A few months later the Gdud Haavodah set up another encampment immediately to the east of Ein Harod on the Nuris lands; they named it Tel Yosef (Joseph's mound) after Trumpeldor.

Within two years, sharp differences divided those leaders who considered the large communal settlement as central from those who considered it incidental to the purposes of Gdud Haavodah. The critical dispute arose over disposition of the income of the rural commune.

Levkovitz, Yizhak Tabenkin, and others wished to separate Ein Harod's finances from the general Gdud treasury. They intended to use both the WZO funds granted them and Ein Harod's own surplus, if any, primarily to consolidate and expand the economy of the settlement. They considered the working groups of the Gdud who were employed in the general Yishuv economy to be temporary expedients, important chiefly in training prospective settlers for independent, fixed communes. The equalization and pooling of income in such labor groups through the central Gdud treasury was a valid principle; but it could not be legitimately accomplished by the diverting of WZO funds that were specifically granted for investment in the settlements, nor should settlement surpluses be used to subsidize the nonsettled Gdud contingents. The primary, most strategic use of all such funds generated by the settled communes was to consolidate the communes themselves, for they, rather than the nonsettled *havurot* (collective work groups) employed on the roads or in the towns and plantation villages, were the basic units that would grow into a full-scale Zionist socialist society. Moreover, diverting WZO funds would cause them to be cut off, whereas if Ein Harod, by reinvesting its income, could prove that collective settlement was an efficient and economical method of colonization, the communes would become the preferred instrument of Zionist policy and increasing WZO investment funds would be directed to their channel.

Menah Elkind scoffed at such conceptions as being naive and utopian. He argued that the way to ensure a flow of Zionist funds was not to demonstrate efficiency and economy in fixed settlements, but to speed the approaching takeover of the movement by socialists as part of the general social revolution. To suppose that the collectives could grow organically from within by the attraction of their example, and thus come to dominate the Yishuv, was no more than utopianism in the obsolete style of Robert Owen. Moreover, the conception was based on naive autarchical fancies of a self-sustained and self-supplied collective economy, independent of the basically capitalistic environment. In fact, however, the Gdud Haavodah, precisely because it operated through the entire range of the Yishuv's economy, could be an effective instrument for converting the whole Jewish community into a socialist commune; and the mass market which it already offered the settled commune was a better economic base for growth than were fanciful ideas of economic self-sufficiency based on combining agriculture with industry in the rural unit. Thus, there was no reason to treat Ein Harod differently from any other collective unit of the Gdud.

The dispute raged fiercely through the winter of 1921–22 in the joined commune of Ein Harod–Tel Yosef. With the Gdud leadership deadlocked, the Histadrut was brought into the picture and appointed a commission to resolve the issue. But the commission findings, that WZO funds granted to Ein Harod must not be diverted to general Gdud purposes, were no less bitterly opposed by Menahem Elkind and the dominant Gdud leadership. The result was a split in which the union of Ein Harod and Tel Yosef was severed; Ein Harod left the Gdud Avodah in 1923.

Having repudiated the authority of the Histadrut consensus, the Gdud Haavodah drifted into a position of deepening sectarianism and, ultimately, disorganization. Leaders such as Elkind, who enjoyed wide discretion to act in the Gdud's name, in view of their indirect, informal election and highly centralized authority, followed their personal bent for political activism. From a collective faction within Ahdut Haavodah, they became an independent partisan force in the Histadrut and formed a radical bloc, together with other collectives that stood apart from the established parties. But Elkind came more and more to question the validity of producers' cooperation as a way to socialism; he stressed instead that the Gdud should strive primarily for a consumer's communism. Such a view could not be shared by the remaining settled communes in the Gdud—Kfar Giladi, Tel Yosef, and Ramat Rahel, the urban commune in the outskirts of Jerusalem, or by other radical settled communes. Drifting further to the left, Elkind and some of his comrades then abandoned Zionism altogether, and, following a further split in Gdud Haavodah in December 1926, departed for the Soviet Union, where most came to tragic ends. Others joined the Yiddishist Left Poalei Zion splinters in various cities. The settled Gdud Haavodah communes eventually joined the federation of collectives that grew up around Ein Harod.

In the period before the split of 1923, when the prospect of rural settlement on a broad scale opened up for Gdud Haavodah, it was a center of attraction around which other workers' collectives might well have gathered in a single, comprehensive organization. Affiliation with the Gdud was actively considered at that time by the other two groupings of collectives that arose in the Second Aliyah, the Hashomer Hazair group and Havurat Haemek, both of them led and largely made up of Polish rather than Russian immigrants.

The differences in European background produced many other barriers to implicit understanding between Hashomer Hazair and the Gdud leaders. The young Polish immigrants came out of a scout movement that reflected the romanticism of the German Wandervogel, a mood antithetical to the revolutionary materialism of the neo-Marxist Russians. Their movement had built close ties to Hapoel Hazair, and their first groups came to Zion under that party's aegis. Their collectivist ideal was basically that of the small, intimate commune preached by Zvi Schatz and exemplified by Degania, the polar opposite of the industrial army to which Ahdut Haavodah circles leaned and the Gdud Haavodah represented.

Nevertheless, other factors, which soon caused Hashomer Hazair to take its distance from its official Second Aliyah mentors, brought them close to the Gdud. The Second Aliyah models of the Zionist scouts included not only Hapoel Hazair but Hashomer, whose adventurous, broad-gauge activism had a strong appeal; in addition, Hashomer Hazair was subject to the same swing to leftism that affected other youth of the time. Moreover, the young scouts not only suffered the usual difficulties of immigrants in adjusting to the hard climate and difficult conditions, the wasting disease and unfamiliar severe demands of labor in Palestine, but they experienced a feeling of strangeness among their comrades who did not share the background of their own movement. From the first, Hashomer Hazair immigrants tended to cling together and took comfort from continuing the rites and customs, the group confessionals and collective intellectualizing, of their scouting days. Later groups brought word of a decision of the movement in the diaspora to maintain Hashomer Hazair as a separate body in Zion. When the Emek Jezreel land purchases offered the chance of settlement, a construction collective of Hashomer Hazair was one of those who contested the Gdud Haavodah's claim to develop the whole eastern tract; and they were granted a leasehold to the east of Tel Yosef, where they founded their own commune of Beit Alfa in 1923.

The closeness to the Gdud was not merely territorial, and there was a discussion in Beit Alfa of affiliation. The split in the Gdud, which eliminated this possibility and confirmed the separateness of the Hashomer Hazair communes, did not end the growing affinity. The developing leftism in Hashomer Hazair led it to ally itself with the Gdud radicals as an opposition bloc in the Histadrut. But Hashomer Hazair leftism developed under different conditions and in different ways from those of the Gdud, and led to different consequences.

The leftist drift of the Gdud was focused in the political development of its leaders under conditions of increasing disorganization of the movement. The participation of rank and file was primarily an implicit continuous testing of individual members' confidence in their individual leaders. In Hashomer Hazair, the whole collective worked out its painful advance toward the left through town meeting procedures, in which each new policy was thoroughly discussed by the group. The leaders went as far and as fast as was needed to maintain collective solidarity within their own camp. Their strategy was determined largely by this consideration and not, as with Gdud leaders, by their changing tactical position in the arena of Histadrut politics. The primary focus of Hashomer Hazair, members and leaders alike, was thus on the growth and consolidation of their settled communes, and their tactics in Histadrut politics *reflected* the changes in this field instead of *determining* them. Consequently, leftism did not take Hashomer Hazair out of the Zionist camp; it consolidated it as a labor Zionist faction.

Another grouping among the collective road gangs of the early 1920s, the Havurat Haemek, was made up largely of Polish Jewish immigrants, but with different background and perspectives than those of Hashomer Hazair. With neither Russian revolutionary nor the Central European youth movement background, these immigrants most closely paralleled the central Ahdut Haavodah and Histadrut leadership in their aims and assumptions. They formed their *havurah* on May Day 1921 at the Nazareth-Afuleh road camp, as a means for overcoming the deficits and disorganization that afflicted both central administration and the various employees' collectives of that construction job. By taking on and administering its own contract, and with careful attention to the social and cultural side of its group life, Havurat Haemek ended its first job with a small profit and high morale. A part of the group then continued on the same lines, extending their activity into every available avenue and using their experienced personnel as the core of new groups, open to all immigrants and with the intent of absorbing them smoothly in work and into a labor society.

Havurat Haemek thus swiftly developed into a large, countrywide collective, with its veteran cadres constantly detached to work with newcomers wherever construction contracts were available. Such nomadism caused increasing strain the longer it continued, and many *havurah* members sought permanent settlement, both for themselves and as a base for the organization. In 1923, discussions were underway with the Gdud Haavodah and Beit Alfa for union toward this end, but the split in the Gdud closed this door to Havurat Haemek. After the split, Ein Harod made an offer to the *havurah*, which was accepted by a large part of the membership. As a result, not only did the *havurah* achieve permanent settlement in Ein Harod, but Kibbutz Ein Harod developed as a widespread collective whose base and bulk were in the Nuris block settlement but which had affiliated settled collectives and temporary working crews all over the country.

Whatever their differences, all the communes had common interests which justified a union of their forces. Attempts to organize such a union began early and were constantly renewed, although continually frustrated by the growth of partisan groupings. In 1920, the existing communes first convened in council to discuss their problems: the financial stringency, loss of membership, seasonal variations in labor, and their own growing differences. Subsequent similar meetings led to a conference late in 1925 which attempted to set up the Hever Hakvuzot, a league of communes, as a permanent organization comprising all the small, locally concentrated *kvuzot* and the large, extended *kibbutzim* in a single organization. But this effort took place at the height of the disputes generated by the Gdud Haavodah crisis. At a second conference, held in Haifa in February 1926, the majority bloc of Gdud Haavodah and Hashomer Hazair collectives controlled the organization and tried to impose their views. The attempt to convert the Hever Hakvuzot into a solid organization then collapsed, leaving its component segments to seek their own consolidation separately and reducing Hever Hakvuzot to its former functions of occasional consultation.

Two years later, when a second attempt at general union seemed ripe, the major groupings were the nationwide associated collectives of Kibbutz Ein Harod and the collectives of Hashomer Hazair. The main force for general unity came from the former body, backed by Ahdut Haavodah and its Histadrut leadership. Those upon whom this imposed the greatest strain were the Hashomer Hazair collectives, who were then establishing themselves as a leftist opposition force. In April they protected their own internal unity and confirmed their ideological separatism by setting up a national collective of Hashomer Hazair, Hakibbutz Haarzi-Hashomer Hazair, which consolidated most of its units and members. Some, however, left to join the more general grouping—Hakibbutz Hameuhad, a united collective, which was created in August around the Kibbutz Ein Harod nucleus. A grouping of small communes led by the Second Aliyah veterans of Degania remained unaffiliated to either of the countrywide kibbutz federations, and maintained a loose contact among themselves through the largely inactive Hever Hakvuzot.

By the 1930s the Zionist labor settlements had been largely organized into the three major federations. Hakibbutz Hameuhad, which continued the tradition of the Gdud Haavodah, was a large, open collective of settled communes and provisional working groups. While it professed no fixed political allegiance, it was identified chiefly with Mapai, the union of Ahdut Haavodah and Hapoel Hazair. The individual *kibbutzim* of the federation accepted a considerable degree of central direction from their federation secretariat and councils, especially in detailing personnel for movement service or work groups for special tasks vital to the Histadrut or the WZO; each sought generally to achieve maximum growth by combining agriculture, industry, and crafts along with outside work at hire, and by accepting for trial membership without rigid selection immigrant workers sent by Hehaluz through federation channels.

Hakibbutz Haarzi and Hever Hakvuzot followed a more selective principle in regard to membership. They restricted the growth of their individual units at first to the maximum determined by their standards of social coherence and compatibility and also by the carrying power of their land area, which was developed as a purely agricultural enterprise. But, especially in view of the dynamic drive of Hashomer Hazair, the limited economic perspective was abandoned while the principles of social selectivity were strongly maintained. In Hakibbutz Haarzi both tendencies—to accelerate growth and to preserve tight social consolidation—were heightened because the Kibbutz served from the start as the center and frontline of a worldwide youth movement with increasing political definition. As in Hakibbutz Hameuhad, but unlike in the loosely federative Hever Hakvuzot, its individual units accepted considerable central direction, and it detailed personnel freely for tasks considered vital by its own movement. In the Histadrut it figured increasingly as a distinct opposition group. Hever Hakvuzot, like Hakibbutz Hameuhad, was not formally aligned with any party but in fact identified with Mapai, after Hapoel Hazair submerged itself in that union.

As was noted, the communal federations, more than any other grouping in Palestine or in the Histadrut, were able to detach their members for service in Hehaluz, training prospective immigrants. While this was service to the general Histadrut, which directed Hehaluz on behalf of the WZO, each federation developed a more particular attachment of its own. Hakibbutz Haarzi was the product of Hashomer Hazair and continued to function in close and exclusive connection with that youth movement. Not until 1934 did Hever Hakvuzot develop such a bond with a diaspora youth movement—Gordonia (after A. D. Gordon), which it fostered and which provided it with new recruits, preformed and selected to fit its own requirements. Hakibbutz Hameuhad, true to its principle of nonselective openness, had no exclusive connection with any youth movement, though several such movements, organized under the aegis of the general Histadrut or the parties united in Mapai in Palestine and the diaspora, trained their members to join its ranks. It identified itself generally with Hehaluz and drew from its members at large, in accordance with the broad general identification with the Histadrut and the whole labor class which it professed.

Because of these connections and functions, the three major kibbutz federations exercised significant power within the Histadrut and the Yishuv generally. The differences between them, based primarily on distinct approaches to their special, parochial tasks, had important repercussions upon the whole institutional structure of the Yishuv and upon its policies.

IV

The relative strength of the labor parties in Yishuv politics was based solidly on their own growing numbers and unity and bolstered by the disunity of their rightwing opponents. During the 1930s, the same factors also brought labor to a dominant position in WZO politics.

At its founding conference in 1920, the Histadrut represented less than 5,000 workers, or no more than 7 percent of the Yishuv. By the mid-1930s (end of 1936), there were some 90,000 workers and workers' wives in the Histadrut, representing well over 20 percent of the whole Yishuv and, of course, a considerably larger proportion of the adult, voting population. The total number of workers in the Yishuv was counted at nearly 17,000 in late 1922 and rose to 85,000, at the end of 1935, and the proportion organized in the Histadrut rose from half to two-thirds.

The two leading labor parties who divided their votes in Histadrut elections in the 1920s (some 40 to 50 percent going to Ahdut Haavodah and about 20 to 30 to Hapoel Hazair), combined as Mapai in 1929, and commanded over four-fifths of the total Histadrut electorate in the December 26, 1932, election. Also, in the Zionist movement the united labor Zionist party made a strong recovery from the decline of its component parties at the Fourteenth and Fifteenth Zionist Congresses in 1925 and 1927. Aided by the double weight accorded to Yishuv votes in the WZO and by the growth of its associated diaspora parties, Mapai in 1927 and 1931 controlled enough votes to return its members to important positions, including the Political Department of the Jewish Agency. In 1933, when the other parties split in bitter disagreement over Weizmann's policies, Labor's 44 percent of the congress delegates gave it decisive power in the reorganizion of the Zionist Executive. Ben-Gurion came in as chairman, Moshe Shertok (later Sharett) as head of the Political Department, and Eliezer Kaplan as head of the treasury of the Jewish Agency.

The labor settlements, especially the kibbutz movement, also grew both absolutely and relatively during this period, but hardly in proportions that could explain their continuing influence and prestige. Starting with 12 communes and 4 *moshavim* in 1921, the Histadrut network of labor settlements rose to 43 communes and 35 *moshavim* in 1935. The members of these settlements rose from 404 in communes and 160 in *moshavim* in 1921 to 6,205 in communes and 4,048 in *moshavim* in 1935. In the fall of 1936, Histadrut communes counted 12,614 members, divided among the federations as follows: the Hakibbutz Hameuhad, 6,590; Hakibbutz Haarzi, 3,308; Hever Hakvuzot, 1,765; others, 951. But the kibbutz population remained relatively insignificant in numbers in spite of this growth. The nearly 17,000 strong kibbutz population of late 1936 represented less than 5 percent of the Yishuv, and the nearly 13,000 adult kibbutz members were perhaps 10 to 15 percent of the Histadrut members, including wives.

The number who permanently became members of *kibbutzim* is not, however, a true measure of those in the Histadrut who identified significantly with the principles and leadership of the kibbutz federations. As was mentioned, kibbutz activists, detached for this purpose by their federations, provided practically the whole top leadership of Hehaluz. This organization prepared not only the greater part of immigrant Histadrut workers but a major fraction of all Jewish workers in Palestine before their settlement. A census of Jewish workers conducted in March 1937 by the Histadrut, with the cooperation of two religious labor unions and the Union of Yemenites, found that 42.7 percent of that total were former Hehaluz members. (The remainder included workers born in Palestine and immigrants from Asian and African countries, where Hehaluz activities were not intensive, as well as immigrant workers trained by non-Histadrut parties and organizations more or less in line with the kibbutz-oriented Hehaluz principles.) The kibbutz influence was thus extended, by exposure to kibbutz leadership at a most impressionable age and under particularly favorable circumstances, well beyond the organized settlements into a broad periphery of the Histadrut's general membership.

Former members of Hehaluz differed from other immigrants and native-born workers, and they approached the model of the *kibbutzim*, in the work they first took up and in their ultimate settlement. Those most likely to undertake the pioneer tasks that were most highly valued by *kibbutzim* were young men and women trained in the youth movements affiliated with Hehaluz and those trained in Hehaluz city and farm work centers in the diaspora. The 1937 census indicates that former members, who were 42.7 percent of all workers counted, constituted more than half the Jewish workers in agriculture, women's employment, and the building trades—in general, in heavy work—and in all new, undeveloped places. Trades with a low proportion of former Hehaluz members, such as the tobacco industry, the printing trade, and medicine and other professions, were either highly skilled urban occupations, often manned by so-called Oriental Jews, or skilled crafts and professions characteristic of the European diaspora.

What was true of Hehaluz immigrants in general was even more marked in the case of those who had been in Hehaluz training centers abroad. Constituting 63.4 percent of all the former Hehaluz members enumerated, these men and women were 85.4 percent of former members among the artisans in the communal settlements, 79.9 percent among the transport workers, 78.8 percent among the building workers, 72.3 percent among the service workers (including a large proportion of working women), 69.8 percent among the unskilled workers, 69.3 percent among the farm workers, and 68.5 percent among those employed in quarries and building materials plants. The distribution among various forms of settlement in Palestine of those who had been in training centers, other Hehaluz members, and nonmembers is shown in Table

TABLE 9.1 *Distribution of Workers Among Settlement Types, 1937*

	Former Hehaluz members from training centers	Other former Hehaluz	Other workers	Total no.	%
In communal settlements	17.8%	10.4%	3.1%	8,544	8.2%
In *moshavim*	5.2%	5.8%	5.2%	5,515	5.3%
In *moshavot*	32.2%	26.8%	22.4%	26,780	25.7%
In cities	44.8%	56.9%	69.4%	63,288	60.8%
Total number	28,145	16,271	59,706	104,127	
Total percentage	27.0	15.6	57.3		

9.1. As the table clearly indicates, former Hehaluz members were far more likely than other workers to be found in rural settlements (with the exception of *moshavim*) and particularly in the *kibbutzim*, and this was true in even greater degree of those who had been in Hehaluz training centers.[4]

If these figures were drawn not from a cross-section at a given moment but from personal history studies over the whole period from immigration to final settlement, the degree and extent of involvement of worker immigrants with *kibbutzim* would be even more evident. All *kibbutzim* experienced a high turnover in their membership, and Hakibbutz Hameuhad in particular served as a first home for many workers who ultimately settled elsewhere. Those who left were not always disillusioned with the ideals and leadership of their *kibbutzim* but often retained a strong identification, and others often sought in other ways to realize the general purpose of Zionist labor pioneering that the *kibbutzim* represented to a notable degree, as everyone acknowledged. But equally characteristic, and perhaps even more conducive to a continuing bond with the *kibbutzim*, were those who belonged to provisional working collectives and were unable to achieve permanent settlement.

Entire collectives of this sort, and any number of workers and leaders, found their energies diverted from their original goal and directed by circumstances to the work of the Histadrut in the cities. Such men, particularly in the 1920s, reluctantly submitted to the fate of urban settlement. Not only did Hapoel Hazair resist the organization of the Histadrut as a union of both rural and urban workers, but so typically urban a union as the construction workers belonged to the Histadrut's agricultural center. Major sources of the settled communes, the Gdud Haavodah, Havurat Haemek, and Hashomer Hazair all had important urban collectives in the early 1920s. The most notable early leaders of the Histadrut, Berl Katznelson, David Ben-Gurion, Eliezer Jaffe, and many others came out of a background of leadership in the early agricultural unions.

Such men, in building the Histadrut increasingly upon an urban base, sought to form it on principles closely similar to those being followed in the construction of the rural collectives. Especially those kibbutz federations with broad, national scope and dynamic identification with the Zionist labor class as a whole served as their model.

The Histadrut structure was strongly affected by efforts to apply to the whole working population of the Yishuv an approach characteristic of such bodies as Gdud Haavodah. Its formative principle, ideally, was to organize the whole working class, under conditions of total mutual responsibility and under strong central direction, to a common strategy for the achievement of Zionism. On the other hand, this very task required the Histadrut to incorporate urban as well as rural workers; among the former, who grew increasingly predominant in the ranks, trade unions that were dedicated to the special interests of particular trade and professional groups were the most natural form of expression. The peculiar characteristics of the Histadrut arose out of its success in imposing upon an urban, trade unionist clientele syndicalist principles and forms of organization as nearly similar as possible to those of the farm and construction gang national collectives. It was as though the IWW and not the AFL had emerged as the dominant form of labor organization in American cities in the late nineteenth century.

In the end, Gdud Haavodah attempted to impose a rule of equal pay for all work without differentials for skill, a system that had developed in its own ranks. Such a rule was not imposed upon the recalcitrant trade union base, but sufficient cash allowances were provided on grounds of social welfare—for example, augmentations according to the number of workers' dependents—to yield a wage system hardly matched for its egalitarianism in any modern country, whether socialist or capitalist.

Living as they did in cities, the workers tried to retrieve as much as they could of the atmosphere of communal living they had known in the construction camps and settled communes. With the help of the Histadrut central bodies, workers' quarters were built in the cities. These were originally to have been governed autonomously by the residents in a similar manner to the council and committee government of *moshavim* and *kibbutzim*. In the end, they turned into labor-sponsored housing developments, without member selection by collective approval, and their councils turned into little more than tenants' committees such as are common in cooperative housing.

The greatest impact of collectivism was upon the system of Histadrut governance and organization. Every effort was made to subordinate the pressures of special interests, of trade union "economism." Instead of being a federation of trade unions, the Histadrut was built from the beginning as one big union, and trade unions in particular were subordinated to the central control. The governing organs of the Histadrut were not constituted of delegates from component organizations, but a convention was elected by the whole membership on a one-man (or woman), one-vote basis, and the convention elected an executive council which in turn chose a secretariat and secretary-general to manage the whole organization. Dues were paid by all members of the Histadrut individually to the central treasury, which then determined and paid out the budgets approved for the subordinate bodies, such as trade unions. Officers of these subordinate bodies, too, were chosen subject to approval of the central body.

The whole system was so constructed as to rob the trade unions in particular of their autonomy, since they were suspect as special-interest agencies that might fail to give due precedence to the general class strategy. Wage negotiations and strike calls of trade unions were subject to approval of the whole Histadrut membership, both nationally and locally; the Histadrut had set up local versions of its central bodies in labor councils, based on the whole Histadrut membership of a town or village, thereby more or less effectively controlling the local unions of particular crafts.

In addition, of course, the Histadrut's distinctiveness lies in the astonishing array of independent labor institutions that it established. The Workers' Bank with which it began was used not only to supplement loans granted to rural settlements but also to finance sales and purchasing cooperatives, joining together town and country urban producers' cooperatives of all sorts, and above all financing contracting and manufacturing firms that were set up as direct subsidiaries of the central Histadrut body itself. In addition, the central body took over and expanded a system of social services for its members: Kupat Holim (the Workers' Sick Fund), which developed a network of hospitals and clinics; a complete system of primary and secondary schools; a theater and athletic association; newspaper and publishing house; and a variety of insurance schemes and special services to particular crafts.

The main principles underlying these ramified operations were the total mutual responsibility of the whole working class to each of its members and of each member to the class, and the coordinated direction of all their efforts to the common goal: to build the socialist Jewish nation-state out of the sound nucleus created by the independent collective efforts of the workers. In order to attain this goal, the Histadrut sought to combine strong central direction with complete individual commitment of Histadrut members, to the goals and policies of their chosen leaders, cooperating spontaneously in subordinate bodies such as trade unions and rural communes.

It is obvious that any such scheme of democratic centralism may fall short either in democratic participation or in central authority. In its urban sections, which were the overwhelmingly dominant part of the Histadrut, the leaders insisted more on central authority in that they were less certain of spontaneous individual commitment. The rural settlers represented the model of such commitment in the eyes of Histadrut leaders and members alike, and they were also the part of the Histadrut that enjoyed the greatest autonomy vis-à-vis the central Histadrut authorities.

The whole scheme of constructivist-revolutionary or utopian syndicalism, as envisaged by such a man as Berl Katznelson, depended on the greatest possible unification of labor settlers as a class. Party division within the labor movement was a direct contradiction of the ideal and a mortal blow in principle to its potential realization. The unification of 1929 which produced Mapai was a giant step toward Katznelson's goal within the framework of the Histadrut at large. It fell short precisely in relation to the kibbutz movement. Not only did Hashomer Hazair remain apart and, increasingly sharpen its opposition, although refusing to call itself a party; attempts to unite the Hakibbutz Hameuhad and Hever Hakvuzot, both substantially identified with Mapai if not formally so defined, were continually defeated as a consequence.

To men like Berl Katznelson, it was a bitter omen that the Histadrut, and the whole Zionist movement in its wake, might not go in the way of his vision. In later years, precisely when the Histadrut camp attained hegemony in the whole Zionist movement, his foreboding was indeed borne out. But the Jewish national home and later the Jewish state were marked profoundly by as much of that way as they had traveled.

• 10 •

The National Home

Global events had an overwhelming impact upon the growth of the Jewish national home under the mandate. The political turmoil of Europe in the 1920s, the world economic and political crises of the 1930s, and the cataclysms of the 1940s all left a deep imprint upon the Yishuv's development. Yet the effect was more often inversely related to general world trends than it was a direct reflection of them.

Global history invaded even such a backwater as Palestine by many channels during the interwar period. By far the most important influence, especially for the Yishuv, was the flood of Jewish immigration. The migrations of the mandate period, like the *aliyot* of Ottoman times, were produced in reaction to contemporary events in the diaspora; and the emigrants were impelled in large part by the same revulsion against the conditions of exile as had motivated the first *haluzim*. In these circumstances, the Yishuv was able to absorb a relatively huge influx of outer forces through the continuous development of its autonomous principles and institutions.

The political instability characteristic of Central and Eastern Europe, from the Danube to the Rhine, was particularly marked during the interwar years, 1919 to 1939. The postwar regimes of Russia, Germany, and Hungary were formed in revolution and counterrevolution. The boundaries between those countries and Rumania, Poland, Lithuania, Czechoslovakia, and Austria were fought over in 1919–22 in a succession of invasions, counterinvasions, and local uprisings which left bitter territorial disputes in their wake.

Leftist and liberal-progressive groups continually declined in influence under the prevailing conditions in the area between France and Russia. In the agrarian zone which covered a large part of it, peasant parties, constantly growing in strength, turned increasingly chauvinistic and conservative. Everywhere, explicitly antisemitic, fascist-style organizations emerged; not only did they harass Jews on the streets and railways, in the universities, and even in their own stores and shops, but in the 1930s they gained power over government in Austria, Hungary, Poland, and Rumania, either directly or through antisemitism engaged in by other, ruling parties. Hitler's rise to the German chancellorship in 1933 climaxed a trend that was equally apparent elsewhere. It added an advanced industrial state to the block of backward agrarian societies where Jewish existence was being made intolerable by political oppression.

After 1929, the economic hardships that marked the initial postwar period were followed by the devastating, long, worldwide depression of the 1930s. The mass of Jews in Central and Eastern Europe, already desperately poor before the war, were still further ground down, as inflation, deflationary monetary reforms, and then the collapse of trade amid mass unemployment struck successive blows. Those few successful speculators, especially on the western fringes of Central European Jewry, who were clever enough, and in the right position, to profit by the rapid changes of the market only fed fuel to the soaring fires of anti-Jewish agitation. Antisemitic boycotts and government policies of nationalistic discrimination bore heavily against the Jews, as ethnic majorities tried to ease their own burdens by weighing down those of others.

The history of the Yishuv stood in an odd, inverse relation to that of Jews in Europe during that time. The period of political revolution and economic turmoil that followed World War I produced an immediate upsurge in the resettlement of the Yishuv. The first economic crisis in Palestine, in 1926–1927, on the other hand, came at a time when Europe had reached an initial recovery from its political and economic troubles. For the remainder of the 1920s, the Yishuv remained relatively stagnant while Europe remained relatively stable. The economic and political calamities of the Western world in the 1930s again set off a major expansion of the Yishuv's strength, which continued until World War II, in spite of such local disturbances as the Italian invasion of Ethiopia in 1935 and the Palestinian Arab revolt of 1936–39. Thus, crisis in Europe produced political and economic growth in Palestine. The link between them was the flow of Jewish emigration from the diaspora.

For half a century, population pressure in densely populated Jewish regions of prewar Europe had found an outlet in emigration. Flowing at an annual rate estimated to be 1.7 percent of the total Jewish community, double that of any other ethnic group, emigration had nonetheless failed to draw off the full natural increase by a considerable margin, but it did allow the young and energetic to escape from crushing frustration to new hope. The same release was sought by hard-pressed Jews in the interwar period; but limited by mounting restrictions, first in the

United States and thereafter in the accustomed secondary destinations of Canada, Argentina, and South Africa, the venturesome emigrants had to seek new havens widely dispersed in every quarter of the globe. An outstanding role in this world movement of Russian and Rumanian, Polish and Lithuanian, and, later, German, Austrian, Czechoslovak, and Hungarian Jews was that played by the Jewish national home in Palestine.

The share of overseas Jewish immigration to the United States fell from 70 percent in 1920–23 to 27 percent over the period 1924–25. Secondary havens in the prewar years, such as Argentina, Canada, and South Africa, rose sharply in their share of overseas Jewish migration during 1924–31, when American quota restrictions were imposed, though only in the case of South Africa did this shift represent a rise in the absolute rate of immigration. But restrictions were soon tightened further in those countries as well, reducing their shares, both absolute and relative, far below the initial magnitudes. During the critical Hitler years and the wartime Holocaust of the Jews, only the United States noticeably increased its contribution to what had become, in the direct, most literal sense, an emergency rescue operation. And this too was a belated, grudging contribution.

Under the circumstances, the role of the Jewish national home in Jewish life changed significantly from its prewar function. While Zionism and Jewish migration had been tied together in theory by Herzl and the socialist Zionists, so that Zionism was to solve the emigration problem and the need to emigrate would convert Zionist dreams into a political reality, the actual relation between them had been very tenuous in the initial period. The emigration movement had, indeed, become a major historic force, but its dynamic thrust was directed toward the new Western hemisphere Jewries. Palestine lay well outside the trodden paths of Jewish emigration; no regular steamship lines flourished on the profits of this traffic and no commercial agents drummed up this trade. The Yishuv did nonetheless increase, but its members were selectively recruited from among those who responded to traditional religious and new nationalistic motivations and not simply to the generally oppressive situation in the diaspora. The Yishuv did not share significantly in solving the emigration problem at that time, nor did it grow to the size of a major Jewish community, even of the second rank.

After World War I, Palestine became a major destination and, in the early Hitler years, the foremost destination of Jewish emigrants; the Yishuv steadily rose to the proportions of a major Jewish community. Solid Zionist traditions and a strong Hehaluz organization remained important factors in the disproportionate share of Polish and Russian (so long as emigration was permitted) influx to Zion. Upon Hitler's rise to power, Zionists responded to the challenge with a rapid, massive expansion of their organized activities in Germany, too. But the movement to Palestine during the interwar years was also based firmly on the general, unorganized stream of Jews ejected by oppressive local conditions. From 10 percent of overseas Jewish immigration in 1920–23, Palestine's share rose to 21 percent in 1924–31 and 53 percent between 1932–38, the early years of Nazi rule. From a community reduced to 56,000 in 1918, roughly the size of Italian Jewry, the Yishuv grew to nearly half a million by 1939, greater than the French, British, Argentine, Czechoslovak, Hungarian, or, by that time, declining German Jewry. Comprising nearly a third of the total Palestine population in 1939, and widely distributed socially and occupationally, the Yishuv was incomparably more significant an element than any Jewish minority anywhere relative to the social-economic structure of its country.

It was also a community whose composition was strongly affected by its rapid growth, in which immigration had a phenomenally large share. In peak periods, the rate of immigration relative to the size of the whole Yishuv ranged from 13 to 9 percent in 1920–23, went from 15 to 28 and back to 9 percent in 1924, 1925, and 1926, and stood at 18 to 20 percent in 1933–35. The share of immigration in the net growth of the Yishuv was 82 percent in 1919–23, 69 percent in 1924–31, and 82 percent again in 1932–38.

With such massive immigration, in which young age groups and unmarried males were disproportionately represented, the Yishuv as a whole was strongly weighted in the young, economically productive, childbearing population strata. Also because immigration came primarily from Europe and the Americas rather than Africa and Asia in the interwar period, the preponderant Ashkenazi section of the Yishuv rose to a position of dominance; and among Ashkenazim the New Yishuv elements greatly outgrew the Old.

But, of course, the New Yishuv itself was far from uniform. The proportion of newcomers drawn respectively to the cities, plantation villages, and labor settlements or representing various specific diaspora backgrounds, generations, and political leanings was not necessarily the same as in the already settled Yishuv. The differences challenged the absorptive capacity of the Yishuv's already established institutions and produced pressures for innovation and change.

The institutions created by European Jews in Palestine had from the beginning developed in relative isolation from the local environment.

Protection by European consuls had enabled the Ashkenazim of the Old Yishuv to live detached from the Ottoman regime. The settlers of the New Yishuv developed their colonies by avoidance of the Turkish government, and their relations with older communities in Palestine, not only Arabs but Old Yishuv Jews, ranged from remote neighborliness to guarded hostility. Even the various types of Zionist settlers pursued their several paths in diverging directions, so that the New Yishuv too grew up as a set of compartments, that were considerably insulated from one another.

By the 1930s, the trend had turned to much greater interaction between sections of the Old and New Yishuv. The overarching institutions sponsored by the mandate regime and by the Jewish Agency, the sheer growth of the Yishuv, and the common problems of contact with Arabs forced greater integration of the distinct communities, an integration inspired by partisan ideologies. The Yishuv, still wrestling with the problem of coordinating its contending established elements, now also had to fit into its emerging pattern the flood of immigrants, or had to revise the pattern to fit its divergent needs.

I

The most obvious immediate goal of Zionist policy in building the New Yishuv was to supply a rural, agricultural base for the Jewish national home. The Old Yishuv was, of course, totally urban, residing in the four holy cities of Jerusalem, Safed, Hebron, and Tiberias. The minor beginnings of farm and village settlement before 1914 were steadily advanced during the period of the Palestine Mandate; and by the end of 1939, when World War II broke out, approximately a fourth of the Jewish community lived in rural settlements and roughly 19 percent were occupied in agricultural pursuits.

Cities, nevertheless, rather than villages and farms, were the main centers of settlement of the New Yishuv as well as the Old. From 1922 to 1942 the Jewish population of Palestine rose from roughly 84,000 to 484,000; and three-fifths (238,000) of this increase was absorbed in Jerusalem, Haifa, and the twin cities of Jaffa and Tel Aviv. Of these, only Jerusalem had been a traditional center of the Old Yishuv, and its character, too, was steadily transformed by New Yishuv immigrants and institutions. Thus, in absolute terms, these towns, which together with the urbanized villages and farms in their immediate region represented perhaps four-fifths of the total Jewish population, constituted the bulk of the New Yishuv built up during the mandate.

If holy Hebron, Safed, Tiberias, and old Jerusalem grew up under the seal of tradition, Tel Aviv, Haifa, and the new Jerusalem arose under the aegis of Zionism. Yet there was a difference between the Zionist spirit prevailing and Zionist institutions arising in the towns and the spirit and institutions intimately connected with the New Yishuv's more remote rural sectors and, above all, the labor settlements. The WZO contributed a far smaller share of investment and exercised a far less direct influence in the towns and nearby plantation villages than it did in the more purely agricultural frontier settlements.

Jewish investment in Palestine from the British conquest to World War II amounted to about $500 million. Of this amount, roughly one-fifth was either contributed or lent to the WZO and other public agencies and was thus subject to their policy. The remainder, constituting the vast bulk of investment that built up the New Yishuv, was brought in by an estimated 39,000 heads of immigrant families who were able to transfer their capital assets from the diaspora. Thus by far the most significant influence in shaping the Jewish national home as a whole by way of investment was private interest, which responded to market conditions, rather than the WZO's nationally and socially oriented investment policy. Moreover, private investment was directed almost entirely to the new towns and nearby plantation areas, while the WZO was able to spare only a relatively small part of its funds for investment there.

There was, of course, a continuing effort to influence development in the towns and plantation villages in line with Jewish national aims. Timokin's ill-starred attempt to organize Jewish private land purchase demonstrated not only the dangers but also the importance of some control over the private real estate market. Affiliates of the WZO, like the PLDC under Ruppin and the JNF under Ussishkin, and also an agency such as the Palestine Economic Corporation (PEC), organized by the Brandeis group in the public interest, invested in urban land with a view toward influencing or even controlling the market, in the national interest. In the plantation villages, public investment also played an important role, as did major investments of the Rothschild and Zionist agencies in initial land purchase and amelioration, by supporting agricultural research and extension services, which were a major factor in the success of Jewish agriculture. Attempts to stimulate industrial development were more represented by sales promotion and political support for Jewish concessionaires and investors than by direct WZO investment of this sort.

Zionist visionaries had originally conceived of their approach to urban-industrial, no less than to rural-agricultural, development as a planned, systematic, research of the country's potential, followed by the constructive application of scientific technology. This plan implied a major role for WZO agencies, if not WZO funds, in initiating projects and guiding their growth in line with national interests. A fair approximation of this vision was achieved in Zionist rural settlement, especially in the labor sector. Urban growth followed a different pattern, however. Apart from a few major projects specially encouraged by the WZO, such as the electrification and Dead Sea Salts concessions, urban and industrial growth was neither initiated nor directed by Zionist policy. The generating force was the spontaneous immigration not organized by the WZO, and the guiding principle of growth was the inflated real estate market and the construction industry produced by the immigrants themselves. Under these conditions, Zionist policy took a different turn. Plans were now directed toward the control and regulation, rather than initiation and direction, of urban-industrial growth.

Visionary bureaucrats in the JNF and PEC plotted a course based on acquiring public land reserves and drafting tax reforms to keep the overflowing current of private real estate investment within safe and productive channels. While the JNF, which had fostered the initial development of Tel Aviv, acquired a significant share in land and construction in Jerusalem, and the PEC did the same in Haifa Bay, their influence on the growth of these towns, and particularly of the industrial and plantation economy of the Yishuv, remained minor. They could not pretend to be guiding these major components of the Yishuv's economy, which represented the bulk of both employment and foreign trade, according to their conception of public interest.

The major Zionist contribution to the growth of the cities and villages where most of the Yishuv settled was in the field of education, health, welfare, and other services. If Zionist policy was unable to control, let alone sponsor, the main part of the Yishuv's economic base, it had a dominant influence in the services that largely determined how the greater part of the Yishuv lived.

Beginning with the Old Yishuv, educational institutions had always been a major part of the communal structure and a primary channel for diaspora involvement. The traditional *halukah*, such as Rothschild and von Lämel, and agencies such as the Alliance Israélite Universelle, were active before the first Zionists appeared, and the varied types of schools these circles supported continued to expand during the mandate—but now in a growing measure of involvement with the major Zionist effort.

Along with rural colonization, the main focus of Zionist activity was a widening network of Hebraist schools. While conceived as a primary instrument for the revival of the Hebrew language and the renewal of a continually evolving, secularized Hebrew culture, the Zionist schools at first did little more than add a new element to the range of Jewish education in Palestine. After the language dispute with the Hilfsverein der Deutschen Juden, the Teachers' Association aided by Zionists took over central responsibility not only for the Technion but for Hebraist schools throughout the country. This responsibility was confirmed and overwhelmingly increased under the Mandate, when the Jewish Agency and the Vaad Leumi administered a system that educated the bulk of the Yishuv's schoolchildren. About 80,000 children, two-thirds of them in Zionist-organized schools, attended the Jewish schools in the late 1930s, nearly half the number of schoolchildren in all Palestine. The Vaad Leumi school budget at that time ran to half a million Palestine pounds (£P517,940 in 1941–1942). The Palestine government's school budget then amounted to little more than half that sum, including its £P56,000 grant to the Jewish schools.

The Jewish schools were decisively important in achieving one cardinal Zionist aim which triumphed in the cities no less than in the rural settlements. Everything else about the Zionist project might be justly considered an "experiment" as late as the 1940s, but the revival of the Hebrew language and culture was an established and well-recognized fact as early as the 1920s. The Yishuv's first protagonists of living Hebrew, Eliezer Ben-Yehuda and his associates, were a small band of enthusiasts. The Second Aliyah gave the cause a settled, mass base both in the ardent ranks of labor immigrants and among the Hebrew-educated second generation in some of the towns and plantation villages. But with the Third Aliyah, Hebrew established itself as the dominant common tongue of the Yishuv at large; it united town and country, Ashkenazi and Sephardi, and, despite the ideological opposition of some ultratraditionalists and some leftwing Yiddishists, it united the political partisans of a much divided Yishuv. The native Hebrew speech of the "Sabras" (cactus plants), as the Palestine-born Jewish youth were called, was their mark of recognition setting them off from all earlier generations and immigrant sectors of the Yishuv.

Zionists also administered a predominant part of other public services to the Yishuv, particularly health care. As in the case of education, the quasigovernmental responsibilities carried out by the Jewish nationalist movement reflected in part the limits the Mandate government defined for its own activity. While the British did useful work in sanitation, including malaria control, and provided hospitals and medical care for the Palestine population at a higher level than formerly prevailed, they restricted themselves to roughly the per capita expenditures required to make marginal improvements in the situation of the majority Arab population. Zionists from the beginning aimed at far higher standards, and in order to approach their own goals, they developed an independent countrywide network of health services covering the bulk of the Yishuv.

About one-third of the land purchased by Jews by the late 1930s required swamp drainage. In preparing these lands for settlement, Jews contributed a major share to the elimination of malaria as a health problem for the entire Palestine population. Other endemic diseases of the country were also attacked vigorously by Zionists from the beginning of the British occupation of Palestine.

Louis D. Brandeis, much impressed with the human costs of disease in the construction of the Panama Canal by Goethals, insisted on major sanitation and health measures as a preliminary to Zionist resettlement in the postwar period. In this spirit, American Zionists, especially the American women's Zionist organization Hadassah, took up health care as a special responsibility. It was, of course, a major activity of the Vaad Leumi and other Yishuv institutions, especially of the labor federation, the Histadrut. By 1939, the combined effort of these Jewish organizations was supported by an expenditure more than double that of the Palestine government. It resulted in the virtual eliminaton of eye diseases such as trachoma, a sharp reduction in endemic digestive disorders, and increased life expectancy and reduced infant mortality to Western European standards among Jews. Palestine Arabs, whose health standards were generally higher than those of neighboring Arab countries, also showed a marked improvement in these respects in the areas of Jewish settlement where the effects of Jewish sanitation and health care were manifested.

The unusual development of public services performed by the Yishuv with major support from diaspora Jewry resulted, of course, from the special circumstances of the Palestine Mandate. The British administration until the 1930s was willing to be held responsible for permitting but not for actively fostering the development of a Jewish national home; this political reservation, together with general parsimony and a policy of maintaining rather than radically improving Arab positions, produced the meager budgets for education and health care. Jews had to organize voluntarily if they were to obtain the kind of services that were required by their own standards and were necessary to advance toward the goal of a Jewish commonwealth.

The public services of the Yishuv were, of course, organized and supported by non-Zionists as well as Zionists. Also, the continuous tradition of Jewish communal service, no less than the special political circumstances of the Palestine Mandate, shaped the emerging institutional structure. In their long history, Jews learned to provide education, health care, and numerous other charities to all in the community who needed them, through voluntary yet communally obligatory methods. Religious duty as well as the obligation of membership in an autonomous ethnic community were motives for performing these functions. In the modernist movements of recent times, whether inspired by emancipation liberalism or by Jewish nationalism, more dynamic motives were added. The traditional, autonomous communal services by which Jewry was maintained in exile were now transformed into instruments of social work or politics suitable for radically reforming the Jewish condition. In Palestine the whole gamut of traditional and modern Jewish approaches to the communal services were applied, and a variegated structure arose.

The service institutions of the Old Yishuv continued to exist and further develop in the new circumstances of the Mandate. *Kolelim* and *kehilot* built new synagogues and maintained traditional schools for their children and for pietists who devoted their lives entirely to study, prayer, and scholarship. The old *halukah* administration did not regain its former power over the community on the basis of its control of personal grants, upon which so large a part of the Ashkenazim had lived; however, in the new forms of political partisanship, such as through Agudat Israel, its successors maintained a continuing authority over their adherents. Western philanthropic agencies such as the American Joint Distribution Committee, as well as their own traditional supporters, helped develop the Old Yishuv's educational system and other charities— orphanages, old-age homes, clinics, and housing developments. They maintained their separatism in the face of the Vaad Leumi's (Elected Assembly) claim to embrace the entire Palestine Jewish community, and while they sometimes cooperated with the Zionist unbelievers in other fields, they kept their schools rigorously isolated against any contagion of modernism, including revived, but secularized, spoken Hebrew.

Western philanthropic agencies, which added independent variants to the range of educational and other services in the Yishuv, proved less separatist. The Alliance Israélite Universelle, without a battle over Hebraism such as had embroiled the Hilfsverein in 1913, transferred schools to local communities under Vaad Leumi supervision. The Alliance, various women's Zionist organizations, and other Western Jewish benefactors who supported education adapted their activities to the standards of Zionist Hebraism while stressing their own special interests, such as French or other Western culture, child care nurseries and kindergartens, and vocational education. So, too, hospitals and clinics that were established by Hadassah in the cities were transferred to the municipalities in the 1930s.

Thus the Zionists of the New Yishuv gradually absorbed and unified diverse, independently sponsored services in the course of developing a general Jewish community. At the same time, Zionist parties based on divergent social ideologies gained new scope for expression. Partisan political ideas and interests were pursued not only through the governing councils of the community but in the whole construction and functions of its service institutions.

The earliest source of such division was Mizrahi. As was noted earlier, the major condition demanded by the religious Zionists for their working within the WZO was support for autonomous Orthodox cultural institutions—at least until the whole movement could be won over to full acceptance of Orthodoxy. In 1914, when Zionists took on major responsibilities for education in the wake of the language dispute with the Hilfsverein, the Mizrahi school, Tahkemoni, was also brought into the network of Zionist-supported schools. Mizrahi education expanded along with other Zionist schools under the Mandate; continuing on the lines established before the war, religious Zionist schools formed a largely autonomous section under the general supervision of the Vaad Leumi's department of education. Moreover, all the extensive activities of the new chief rabbinate became closely associated with the religious Zionist party. Agudat Israel and other ultratraditionalists boycotted this section of the secularist-dominated Jewish community organization.

The Mizrahi precedent regarding education was followed after World War I by the labor Zionist movement. They, too, created autonomous institutions within the Zionist-supported school system supervised by the Vaad Leumi's education department. Like Mizrahi, the Zionist workers accepted curricular standards set by the general Zionist educational program for general studies and Hebrew culture but added special requirements of their own: Mizrahi schools devoted a fourth of their hours to the traditional rabbinic texts, in addition to intensive study of the Bible; labor schools devoted the same proportion to scientific and vocational training for labor and the inculcation of attitudes appropriate to workers, according to the version of socialism favored in one or another workers' settlement. Commitment to the special purposes of Mizrahi and labor schools was further strengthened by party control over the administration and teaching staff of the respective schools. Supervision by the nominally superior central body was mainly indirect and limited to general subjects in the curriculum.

The labor Zionists were motivated in part by the same considerations that made Mizrahi insist on autonomy. Their ideological position, going to issues of basic social philosophy, required freedom to determine their own subjects and methods of study and to maintain a staff committed to their point of view; subordination to the general system had to be limited to matters of general Zionist consensus. There was in addition a special motivation which activated the labor drive toward autonomy. In all aspects of their broad-gauge activity, the Zionist workers believed themselves to be building a new, organic society. What primarily concerned Mizrahi was the need to protect their children from demoralization by a secular, general education. The socialist workers had a similar apprehension about bourgeois values in the general schools, but this was secondary. They were motivated mainly by their commitment to start afresh, autonomously, in every sphere of human activity—including education.

II

Like the Zionist Yishuv at large, the labor community grew predominantly in the towns and nearby plantation villages rather than in the outlying rural settlements that most clearly expressed labor Zionist ideology. They too had to adjust to a market and community dominated by the play of private interests rather than by national policy. Like other Zionists, unable to build a complete urban society based on their own "revolutionary constructivist" principles, they constructed service agencies for their part of the society in order to exercise influence and deploy power over the whole.

Three major formative pressures shaped the communal structure of the Yishuv and also the organization of labor institutions: Jewish tradition, the patterns of Western society, and the dynamic ideologies of Zionism and socialism. The strain between modern Western and traditional Jewish (or Ottoman) conceptions of ethnoreligious organization, and the resistance of the Yishuv to British, Western patterns in this field, have already been noted. The workers too followed a traditional Jewish model and resisted modern Western precedents in building their mutual aid institutions. Instead of serving special private interests and relying on limited, private associations, they built a voluntary network of schools, clinics, trade unions and similar services into a common structure of collective responsibility and autonomy. More successfully than the Yishuv, they constructed an integrated organization instead of a series of loosely connected, variously assembled membership associations.

They were also more effective than the New Yishuv at large in expressing Zionist dynamism against the pressures of opposing Western patterns of organization. The New Yishuv had made its schools a major instrument of the Hebraist cultural revival, but in other respects its school and other institutions served limited functions which implied a stable, self-perpetuating social structure. According to both traditional and Western ideas, the labor Zionist schools, clinics, and trade unions should also have been peripheral agencies, alleviating social pressures and conserving a static structure. Instead they were infused with principles of social reconstruction and activated in a campaign to build a new Jewish society, to be modeled as far as possible on the *kibbutzim*. Under this ruling conception, the various service institutions were informed with a common spirit and articulated into a common, centrally guided organization.

The theory and practice of "revolutionary constructivism," not undeservedly hailed as a unique, original socialism, arose, stage by stage, out of a rapid succession of ideological conflicts in the Histadrut. The definition of policy provoked opposition at all stages, and as the line of debate shifted, a changing alignment of partisans, supporting or opposed to the consensus, developed among the workers. New groupings also coalesced in the Yishuv around issues presented by the changing course of consensus opinion in the labor community. Histadrut policy was thus as important in Zionist political history as Zionist policy was in the history of the Yishuv.

The basic dispute between Hapoel Hazair and Ahdut Haavodah and its compromise solution at the Histadrut's founding convention have already been noted. The united labor organization did not call itself "socialist" as Ahdut Haavodah had proposed, but neither did its title contain the description "nonpartisan" as Hapoel Hazair had desired. As a result, it was a moot question how far the new body could act politically as representing the Jewish working class in Palestine and abroad: for example, the affiliation of the Histadrut with the Trade Union International was left to be decided by the council elected at the convention.

So, too, the question whether the Histadrut should conduct "cultural" activities was less than clearly settled. The Histadrut was empowered to act for all the workers in all "resettlement, economic, and also cultural matters." The phrase "and also" (instead of simply "and") was meant to suggest a distinction between an unlimited sphere for the Histadrut's economic activity and a more restricted scope for its cultural activity; left moot was, for example, the question whether such a strongly political expression of culture as a labor newspaper was authorized. The further specification that, in addition to providing Hebrew language training, "general, agricultural, and vocational" education, technical libraries and classes, and "labor literature," the Histadrut was also to provide "a vocational press and bulletin of the General Federation" glossed over rather than decided this issue, since out of a "bulletin" a full-fledged daily newspaper could (and ultimately did) grow.

Similar issues arose in regard to the Histadrut's function of organizing potential worker-settlers abroad as well as its responsibility for paramilitary self-defense in Palestine. Compromise formulas sanctioned both these functions under vaguely implied restrictions. The unstable compromises upon which the Histadrut was founded were inherently weighted against Hapoel Hazair federalism and in favor of Ahdut Haavodah organicism, because of the dominant influence of Zionist agrarianism in both groups. Hapoel Hazair was strongly committed to the models developed by Second Aliyah agricultural workers. It initially opposed uniting urban and rural workers in a single body for fear that urban trade unionism would impose itself on the farmer-workers, but when it accepted this radical innovation and found with some gratification that rural models were imposing themselves on urban workers instead, its capacity to resist related developments was undermined.

The third major force in the merger, Hehaluz, which had held the balance in the convention, underscored the point with emphasis. Its own preference for a total organization of the farmer-worker class reflected both the European postwar enthusiasm for peasant-proletarian revolutionary syndicalism and its identification with Second Aliyah principles. It appealed to the precedents of the Yishuv's prewar agricultural unions, which had functioned above and apart from party lines, and demanded that the competitive labor exchanges and health services the parties had organized be reunited in the general Histadrut. When it disbanded its separate organization after this demand was accepted, and merged in the general body, it indicated clearly that the organicist ideas these young radicals favored were in the ascendant.

Hapoel Hazair's resistance to the prevailing trends in the Histadrut was further undermined by pressure from the left. Within the ranks of its own natural recruits, the diaspora Zeirei Zion groups, the socialist current ran strong and identification with the working class was desired. The balance within the party swung to acceptance of the socialist tag, and those still vehemently opposed tended to split off and join, or found, rightwing nationalist parties, as we shall see. Thus the distance between Hapoel Hazair and Ahdut Haavodah was decisively narrowed.

Leftist pressures of a different kind came from the leftwing Poalei Zion groups who remained outside Ahdut Haavodah. While in other cardinal points they were diametrically opposed to Hapoel Hazair, they shared the same objections to the centralization and extensive scope of the Histadrut, and they remained opposed long after Hapoel Hazair learned to approve the trend.

These leftists demanded two separate federations for urban and rural workers, a world wide revolutionary organization of Jewish proletarians, and a political organization in Palestine comprised of Jews and Arabs that would operate outside the new labor organization in a manner vaguely reminiscent of the relation of the soviets to the government in revolutionary Russia. Concretely, the leftists proposed close organizational ties to world communism and to the diaspora Jewish proletariat (which some held were represented by the left-leaning World Union of Poalei Zion), and active, even if separate, organization of Arab workers as a major Histadrut function—whence it followed that the organization should not name itself a General Federation of *Hebrew* Workers.

The premises from which these positions derived were directly opposed to those of Hapoel Hazair. The aim was to organize an economic and political weapon of the primary revolutionary class, the urban proletariat, and to deploy it in the context of the world revolution, not of the local situation of a national home in the first stages of construction. If, in backward Palestine, the embryonic proletariat needed other oppressed classes as its allies, the revolutionary coalition should be based on the Arab masses, not merely on the small Jewish working class. A Hebrew Histadrut comprising rural worker-settlers and basing itself not only on trade unions but on cooperatives, especially producers' cooperatives, smacked of heretical utopian socialist, populist theory and implied in practice nationalist collaboration with petty bourgeois Zionism. The Marxist instincts which sensed these implications in the Histadrut's structure were, of course, accurate. But those who continued to oppose the Histadrut's course on these grounds soon found themselves on the far fringe or altogether outside the organization. Their demand that the labor federation reorganize as a conventional trade organization was shared mainly with rightwing, bourgeois anti-Histadrut elements. Within the federation, the concept of merging urban with rural workers, combining trade union and cooperative functions, and uniting producers', consumers', and service organizations within a common, centrally directed body became a consensus item of unquestioned constitutional status.

The leftists stemming from the Poalei Zion split off in splinter groups reflecting the division in the diaspora movement. Neither the Yiddishism of some nor the increasingly anti-Zionist communism of others was attractive to large sections of the labor Yishuv. The communist faction was further reduced by police surveillance and the emigration of its members to the USSR. The Yiddishist party Left Poalei Zion remained a collection of fringe groups with little or no power to affect the Histadrut consensus other than to harden it by their opposition.

In Left Poalei Zion's politically impotent position, it was a reasonable calculation for it to favor a loose, federal construction of the Histadrut with every possible provision for magnifying the impact of minority parties. For Hapoel Hazair, on the other hand, the fact that unlimited support of federalism enhanced the disruptive potential of these Marxists tended to undermine their own support of this principle. The challenge of defending the Histadrut's constitutional structure, which faithfully expressed many of their own agrarian values, helped ease their acceptance of a centralized organization reflecting the Ahdut Haavodah conception.

The highly individual formal structure of the Histadrut was crystallized in a rapid succession of specific decisions occasioned by diverse problems. The rudimentary central structure of the federation established by the First Convention in December 1920 was developed further by unusual methods of labor organization in the next two years and was consolidated in the constitution adopted at the Second Convention in February 1923.

The Histadrut Convention was directly elected by the entire membership in a manner that facilitated full expression of all ideological variants. Delegates were chosen in strict proportion to votes cast for the several parties who submitted candidate lists. Such a system of proportional representation, based on single ballots for party lists, tends to encourage centralism by denying the right to split tickets; but with such small numbers involved, the individual candidates proposed by the party leaders were normally known and accepted by the bulk of party members. In the politics of the convention proceedings themselves, this electoral system encourages minorities and hampers the effective formation of a ruling majority.

Essentially the same principle was applied for electing the Histadrut Council that was to act as the legislative authority between conventions. While chosen indirectly by vote of the convention rather than directly by the membership, the council members represented the several party delegations in accordance with the ratios derived from the general election. The first council thus included representatives from the Hehaluz party list even though this faction disbanded at the close of the convention. A departure from direct proportionality to the general election results was made in order to give special representation to the Yemenite workers. Another constituency, women workers, organized themselves politically during the convention and demanded similar representation, which was granted. In both cases, these deviations in fact reinforced the basic tendency of the proportional representation system: to encourage the greatest expression of variant ideologies and interests within the labor community and, hence, to hamper rather than encourage effective centralization. Both the electoral system and its consequences conformed to the tradition of Eastern European radicals, whose political position required maximum freedom for the dissenting minority together with tight inner factional discipline.

However, day-to-day control of Histadrut activities was exercised neither by the convention nor by the council. A Central Executive of seven members was named by the Histadrut council to direct the organization and administer its affairs. This body, the true leadership of the Histadrut, was elected by the Council on the centralist principle of majority rule, the first Executive being a coalition of Ahdut Haavodah and Hapoel Hazair and excluding minority delegations such as the Left Poalei Zion. In 1921 the third Histadrut Council reorganized the Executive, further strengthening its centralist character. Retaining the two-party majority coalition, the new eleven-person Executive had a larger proportion of responsible department heads and fewer ideological specialists than before. David Ben-Gurion, returning from a party assignment in London, joined the Executive as secretary-general of the Histadrut, powerfully reinforcing the weight of functional, pragmatic rather than ideological influences on Histadrut policy. So, too, in electing Ada Fishman Maimon, head of its Working Women's Council, to be a member of the Executive, the Histadrut gave weight to a constituency based on concrete common interests rather than abstract ideological principles. In its subsequent development, especially after the merger of the Ahdut Haavodah–Hapoel Hazair coalition into a single party, Mapai, the Executive, based on majority rule and functional representation, steadily increased the Histadrut's centralization. The frequent, regular meetings of the council and the infrequent general election of new delegates for irregularly scheduled conventions served chiefly to keep the labor federation in touch with its various ideological constituents under conditions of proportionate representation.

The Histadrut's main organizing effort had to be directed to the cities and plantation villages, to which most workers were attracted after road construction and government employment of Jews dropped off in 1920–21. Models of craft and industrial unionism, as practiced in advanced Western economies, were discussed as alternative approaches but in the end a distinctive new method was evolved. The leftist factions, seeking the tactical position most advantageous to a marginal political minority, strongly favored a system based on fully autonomous craft unions, with a weak federative local labor council composed of craft union representatives. Some union leaders fought for direct control of membership dues of their own craft unit. The Histadrut, however, built a local organization that was based initially on craft union representation, to be sure, but one whose constituent unions were decisively subordinated to central control. Dues were collected by the local Histadrut branch from all its members directly, and particular union budgets were approved by the local labor councils' decision.

At the end of December 1920, the first Histadrut Council meeting decided that every locality with Histadrut members elect a single workers' committee. These committees replaced the earlier distinct committees of the parties and became representative agencies of the local Histadrut branch for internal and external affairs. Furthermore, the workers' committees were chosen at a general assembly of the local Histadrut members by an election proportionate to the several crafts. The centralization thereby provided was heightened afterwards as Histadrut branches gradually shifted from a workers' council representing the constituent local trade unions to one directly elected by the local membership. Since these elections were conducted on the same plan as the general, national elections—that is, on the basis of single ballots, party lists, and proportional legislation—central control of such matters as the choice of union leaders, budgets, and decisions on strikes and work contracts was exercised by a joint council representing local party strength rather than the local trade union leadership. In the course of time, moreover, the Histadrut central bodies took over the function of dues collection centrally, and the budgets, organizing staff, and major collective bargaining decisions of local unions, proximately controlled by the local workers' council, were under ultimate control of the national central bodies. In this way, the stable majority that controlled the Histadrut Executive exercised indirect but effective control also of its local labor organizations.

These organizational patterns that the Histadrut developed for its city and town membership represent a fair equivalent of certain principles that characterized the rural labor settlements and contracting communes. The democratic centralism of the Histadrut, conceived in the spirit of contemporary Eastern European radicalism, implied a disciplined membership of mobilized volunteers. It was a social structure of the same order, if not exactly the same kind, as the line of rural communes from Hashomer to Degania and the Legion of Labor. A consensus ideologically responsive to the free commitment of the members, together with individual commitment responsive to central policy, were achieved not through frequent general meetings, as in settled communes, but by formal elections, delegated representative organs, and parliamentary procedures. The centralist approach assumed the principles of total responsibility of the organization for its members and total obligation of the members to the organization, such as prevailed in the kibbutz. Applied to a largely urban-based, countrywide organization, with an increasingly formal structure and growing distance between leaders and members, Histadrut collectivism could hardly reproduce its simple rural models, but the force of the rural ideal left powerful traces on the strikingly unconventional shape of the Histadrut's urban institutions.

The largest section of the organized city workers was in construction trades. Apart from those laborers in the Old Yishuv whom the Histadrut was able to organize, largely from the so-called Oriental communities, the building workers were new immigrants, initially unskilled. A good many belonged to communal groups aspiring to rural settlement, and, as was noted earlier, the Histadrut construction workers at first defined themselves as an agricultural union.

It was soon obvious that building and construction, as well as other urban trades, would be a permanent, occupation for a major part of Histadrut workers. This fact of life was recognized in a characteristic formula later used to solve many similar ideological dilemmas. The Histadrut as a body, it was decided, must establish itself as a permanent contractor in the building and construction trades; for individual workers, preferably organized in collective groups, such employment was to be temporary. The new workers would thus learn crafts, acquire work habits, gain experience in management and organization, consolidate their finances, and build up their group solidarity and habits of cooperative living while waiting for land to be made available to them for settlement. Town living and employment, in other words, was to serve as an extension of the cadre training (*hakhsharah*) begun in Hehaluz camps in the diaspora.

Relying on this principle, the Histadrut entered upon its remarkable career in collective entrepreneurship, including from the very beginning collective finance. Arthur Ruppin, characteristically, supported and encouraged this development. During the discussions and maneuvers in the labor camp that led to the creation of the Histadrut, Ruppin, who had returned to Palestine as an officer of the Zionist Commission, proposed a Zionist-backed bank to finance the labor contracting groups then entering the construction industry. Berl Katznelson and other labor leaders, deeply interested in Ruppin's plan, insisted on an organization of the bank that would give labor secure control of its operations; this was one of the factors, Katznelson argued, that made labor unity an immediate, urgent necessity. The Histadrut Convention in December 1920 voted to establish the Workers' Bank. On December 1, 1921, after negotiations with the WZO and a successful campaign among its members and diaspora supporters for funds to buy the "founders' [voting] shares," the Histadrut was able to open its own financial institution, essentially under labor control. Ruppin, representing the WZO Executive (whose loan of £40,000 provided the bulk of the bank's capital), gave careful guidance as overseer in the beginning; but after a time the management reverted entirely to the Histadrut.

The Workers' Bank, which ultimately extended its operations to a wide range of corporate labor enterprises in agricultural settlements, producers' and consumers' cooperatives, and urban industry was only one example of central Histadrut entrepreneurship. Another, far more closely involved with the workers' daily lives, was Solel Boneh. The workers employed in the cities and villages by this labor contractor (the merger of two similar agencies operated by the main parties before the Histadrut) were in part organized in smaller contracting collectives, divisions of the Legion of Labor and other countrywide combines of rural and urban, settled and urban workers. Their individual commitment and discipline, together with the comprehensive responsibility for their maintenance and welfare, were mainly concentrated in the particular collectives to which they belonged, with central agencies such as Solel Boneh and the Histadrut itself more remotely related. But another part of Solel Boneh, growing to dominant proportions, were individual, detached breadwinners with no other attachments to the young labor establishment than the Histadrut itself, of which they were members, and such Histadrut corporations as Solel Boneh, which employed them. For these, the central labor agencies tried to institute the same mutual relationships of commitment and responsibility that prevailed in the membership collectives.

Thus, efforts were made, repeatedly but with dwindling success, to involve the workers in direct responsibility for Histadrut enterprises that gave them employment. Sporadic efforts were made (especially in later years) to introduce at least the participation of workers in the management boards of some Histadrut enterprises, but in many cases these met with lack of interest among the workers and growing resistance among Histadrut managers. The self-managing labor enterprises that were successfully organized with Histadrut support in the cities were mainly producers' cooperatives, especially transport cooperatives, not under direct Histadrut management. Such autonomous cooperatives, especially the bus companies, soon produced new problems for the socialist-minded federation by becoming employers (i.e., "exploiters") of other workers on a considerable scale.

The collectivist principle of total mutual responsibility worked itself out effectively in regard to workers' wages and income, and above all the provision of employment. The mass of workers employed by Solel Boneh individually, not as collective groups, were chosen by the Histadrut labor exchange and governed by the local labor council, in accordance with its own criteria. The principle followed was to assign jobs in such a way that all workers in a locality would be provided, as nearly as possible equally, with enough days of work to maintain themselves. Opponents of the Histadrut, on the left and right alike, denounced this control of the labor market by the Histadrut local labor council as a method of political pressure; but for most of those served by the system it provided a guarantee of equality and mutuality, under conditions of deprivation and strain, as nearly as possible like that of the collectives.

The labor federation consistently, though not always successfully, opposed the dole as a method of unemployment relief. They regarded such charity as reducing the worker to the level of a pre-Zionist *halukah* dependent, and they insisted that work projects be initiated instead, in spite of the greater expense. This task, moreover, was one they took upon themselves directly; carrying it out was one of the main functions and demanded the creation of such agencies as Solel Boneh and the Workers' Bank.

One of the by-products of Histadrut enterprise in construction was a series of "workers' quarters" built in the cities. The agricultural-collective model was held in mind here, too. Everything possible was done to foster a spirit of mutual responsibility, and a corporate sense, in Histadrut housing developments such as the Shekhunat Borochov suburb of Tel Aviv and Kiryat Hayim in Haifa Bay. Built on National Fund land by Solel Boneh, served by Histadrut cooperatives, clinics, and schools, and intensively organized by the labor parties, youth movements, and the Histadrut's own councils of Working Women and Working Youth (Hanoar Haoved), these sections of the urban Yishuv were corporately distinct and self-determined to no less extent than, in their own way, were the *kolelim* and *kehilot* and distinctive housing quarters of the Old Yishuv and its later equivalents.

The Histadrut bureaucracy, while growing into a major segment of the Yishuv's economy, also grew up to a considerable degree in the image of the agricultural collective. A good many of the leading officials were members of *kibbutzim* detached for long or short periods of general service, and still more had been members of *kibbutzim, moshavim,* or *havurot* in their youth. For this large segment, the service professions, the Histadrut, under the pressure as well as influence of its agricultural leadership, adopted an unusual wage scale. The wages that had prevailed in the competing markets (in private, government, and even Jewish Agency employment), which rewarded skill and training and responded to the demand-and-supply curves, were not effective in the internal Histadrut economy. Other considerations, such as the number of a worker's dependents and other special needs, were often able to outweigh skill and rank. The result was a far-reaching egalitarianism within the Histadrut economy. Histadrut bargaining power, as well as its growing numerical weight and political preponderance, along with other factors, helped to extend a high degree of egalitarianism to the Yishuv at large.

Some of the principles of centralized Histadrut organization were from the outset inapplicable to the rural labor settlements. For example, there was no need for the apparatus of trade union organization for members of a kibbutz or *moshav,* since these Histadrut comrades were self-employed. The local Histadrut branch was the settlement itself, and the general meeting and officers of the settlement preempted any possible function of a workers' council, the main instrument of Histadrut governance in the towns and plantation villages. However, the provisions for centralizing the Histadrut's economic institutions adopted at the Second Convention in February 1923 did cover the rural as well as the urban sector.

A major and highly characteristic feature of the extraordinary constitutional structure created at the convention was the corporate Hevrat Ovdim (Workers' Society). The "revolutionary constructivism" upon which the Histadrut consensus was founded implied a dual form of organization: on the one hand, the Histadrut, as revolutionary, "represented the workers"—that is, conducted its trade union and (in spite of the restrictions adopted at the First Convention) its joint political affairs; on the other hand, as "constructivist," it fostered and controlled its cooperative, collective, and corporate economic enterprise. Hevrat Ovdim was established as the central organ for the latter functions, just as the voting membership and officers of the branches, councils, and conventions of the Histadrut governed the former.

Hevrat Ovdim was set up as a legally recognized corporate entity, able to buy and sell, lend and borrow, sue and be sued, and in general enter into contractual relations as a legal personality. All members of the Histadrut, and only its members, were members of Hevrat Ovdim; Histadrut conventions, councils, and officers served as Hevrat Ovdim conventions, councils, and officers. The functions of the society were defined as "organizing, developing, and intensifying the economic activity and enterprise of the collectivity of workers in all branches of settlement and labor in country and town on a basis of mutual aid and responsibility." The nature of such economic activity was further specified in the full title of Hevrat Ovdim, "The Cooperative Society of Hebrew Workers for Settlement, Manufacture, Contracting and Supply."

The powers granted Hevrat Ovdim by the convention were defined as follows:

> Hevrat Ovdim is the proprietor of all financial and cooperative institutions of the General Federation. It establishes institutions, enterprises, funds and owns the founders' shares of the Workers' Bank, *Hamashbir*, and other subsidiaries of the Society. It is authorized to impose fees, determine wages in its institutions and enterprises (insofar as a wage system is in effect in them), and fix price schedules for products. Hevrat Ovdim sees to the mutual adjustment of the activities of the several institutions, supervises their management, approves their programs, reviews their fulfillment, and directs their activity to the requirements of the collectivity of workers.[1]

Representatives of Hevrat Ovdim were to serve on the management board of each Histadrut subsidiary. Such subsidiaries, subject to the by-laws and decisions of Hevrat Ovdim, would operate autonomously.

Following the adoption of these provisions, the Histadrut established Solel Boneh as its central subsidiary for urban enterprise and Nir (Furrow) as its central subsidiary for rural enterprise. (Subsidiaries were added for additional functions such as marketing, housing, cooperation and others as the need arose). Through Nir, which was a shareholding cooperative of all members of the Agricultural Union, the Histadrut was to act as a guarantor for its agricultural settlements and institutions and to be a party to their contracts with Zionist and other colonizing agencies.

Ruppin had long favored such a "Settlement Association" organized by the labor Zionists as a useful instrument for rational planning and control; for while mortgage banks and colonizing agencies should properly consider the security of only such loans as they granted, a group of settlers jointly sharing the risk as guarantors of loans to settlers could check suitability and performance of individuals as well. Berl Katznelson, the main protagonist of Nir, extended this notion into a general concern for, and indeed ultimate supervision of, the national and socialist commitment of the settlers who obtained settlement loans. In order to safeguard such aims of the labor collective, the Histadrut leaders, as in other subsidiaries they created, reserved a majority of the founders' shares for Hevrat Ovdim, giving its representative on the board of Nir a reserved veto power that might be used to prevent actions contrary to the constitutional principles of the parent body. In this matter, as Katznelson pointed out, the Histadrut followed a practice Herzl had adopted to secure WZO control of its subsidiary, the Colonial Trust; but the democratic centralist spirit of contemporary Eastern Europe was also strongly apparent.

But Nir was not accepted by rural labor Zionists as smoothly as was Solel Boneh by the urban workers; nor did the WZO Executive grant it the extraordinary rights proposed by the Histadrut. Nir encountered fierce opposition from Eliezer Jaffe and other leaders of Hapoel Hazair, who viewed it as an attempt to regiment the free farm worker, to impose on him an urban proletarian domination, and to turn voluntary cooperation into forced collectivization. This critique was fought off at the 1925 convention of the Agricultural Union only by long and detailed arguments, and also some amendments, stressing that Nir was to be an instrument not of the mainly urban Histadrut at large, but of its highly independent Agricultural Union. Moreover, the WZO Executive refused to accept Nir's signature as a party to loan contracts with the settlers; the whole matter of such contracts was suspended.

Nir remained a more or less symbolic body until the 1930s, when rural settlement, now based on formally contracted loans to the settlers, was revived. It then functioned as a fiscal agent through its own joint stock corporate subsidiary, which underwrote considerable loans to labor settlements. In other words, instead of an all-comprehensive organization, like the Legion of Labor on a larger scale, it became a limited-function organization, comparable in this respect to Solel Boneh. But it was not, like Solel Boneh, an employer in direct relations with individual workers; as a fiscal agent it dealt mainly with settlements, and very often with the settlements through the mediating agency of their settlement federations. The latter became a major power not merely in the agricultural sector, but in the politics of the Histadrut and, hence, of the Yishuv at large.

III

In the spring of 1922 a first attempt was made to unite and organize the communal settlements. In 1921, some 15,000 acres in two large blocks in the eastern and western sections of Emek Jezreel had been purchased as an emergency action by the WZO Executive. With even rasher determination, labor settlers, competing for the right to realize rival schemes of cooperative and collective settlement, had planted *moshavim* and large and small communes (*kibbutzim* and *kvuzot*) in the uncleared, malarial swamps. These additions to the prewar settlements and those founded during the war increased the number of collectives to the point where joint central services might be sustained, and the growing internal divergences of the collective movement made central coordination seem essential. A commission of *kvuzot* was convoked in 1922 to meet the evident need, but because of untoward circumstances, it was unable for years to do more than provide minor services of communication and technical advice.

The primary obstacle was the intensity of the quarrels in which the collectives were at once involved, especially the major dispute within and about the Gdud Haavodah. As was already noted, Shlomo Levkovitz's doctrine of the large, open, variegated commune had been adopted by the Legion of Labor, and Levkovitz and other Second Aliyah veterans, especially former Hashomer members, had joined the legion in order to carry it out. This group laid claim to the entire eastern section of the Nuris block of the 1921 Emek Jezreel land purchase and, after a sharp political struggle, was recognized as the permanent settler of part of it. There the Gdud Haavodah built two adjacent camps: a lower one, Ein Harod, at the spring amid the swamps, to be developed in field crops; a higher one, Tel Yosef (Yosef's Mound, in memory of Yosef Trumpeldor), where plantations were to be installed. The Gdud itself moved its central headquarters, workshops, and general services for its far-flung labor divisions to Ein Harod.

By that time a cutback in government construction and the inability of the WZO to invest large funds either in farm settlement or in urban projects had produced unemployment and a crisis atmosphere lasting through 1923. The Gdud leaders, inclined to consider mutual support and equal sharing among all its members as its primary obligation, applied to its general budget, which was overloaded with losses incurred in construction contracts and urban projects—funds Levkovitz had obtained from the WZO, with Histadrut assistance, for investment in the Ein Harod settlement. When he refused to be responsible toward the WZO and the Histadrut for the diverted funds, the Gdud leadership undertook to expel him.

This dispute was then taken up by the Executive of the Histadrut Agricultural Union, and Levkovitz was sustained by them in his view that loans for investment in Ein Harod were to be applied only for that purpose. This decision, in effect, recognized the right of the settled commune to fiscal autonomy within the wider collective, to which it belonged, Gdud Haavodah; on the other hand, it was a decision imposed by the central Histadrut authorities upon Gdud Haavodah as one of its own, thus subordinated, constituents. The resentment of the Gdud leaders was correspondingly double-edged: they grew more hostile to the Histadrut central consensus as a reactionary force, and they regarded Levkovitz and Ein Harod as renegade elements in their avant-garde movement. The quarrel broke up the Gdud; a minority were settled in Ein Harod and the majority reorganized around headquarters in the neighboring commune of Tel Yosef.

The commune of Ein Harod had no sooner split off from Gdud Haavodah than it turned into a combine closely resembling its parent organization. It was joined immediately by a large contingent from the countrywide collective contracting group, Havurat Haemek, and later by other communes. Kibbutz Ein Harod, as the new organization was called, respected the fiscal autonomy of its major and associated settled communes, unlike the Gdud Haavodah; but it resembled the Gdud in its commitment to large, variegated, intensively developed rural-industrial units and its commitment to seek contracts and send out labor divisions in every economic field—a commitment, to be sure, that it carried out in an unflagging militant-Zionist spirit.

After the split, Gdud Haavodah retained a number of settled communes in addition to Tel Yosef, especially those with strong Second Aliyah connections to Hashomer, such as Tel Hai and Kfar Giladi in northernmost Galilee and the urban kibbutz Ramat Rahel at the southern edge of Jerusalem. However, the Gdud leadership went through a course of oppositional radicalization that brought it into close union with the developing city communist factions and, like them, to an ultimate conclusion that Jewish settlement in Palestine was by its nature a counterrevolutionary activity. This soon led to conflicts with Hashomer veterans and others in the Gdud. While some of them cultivated a version of paramilitary communism of their own, they remained committed Zionists with strong ties to the several communal settlements they had founded; their resistance to Gdud plans to merge Tel Hai and Kfar Giladi, in which they had Histadrut backing, led in 1926 to another split in the Gdud. By 1928, many of the remaining Gdud leaders had reached a firm anti-Zionist position and adopted the logical conclusion of emigrating to the Soviet Union, where, in the Stalin years, they shared the tragic fate of many old Bolsheviks. As Gdud Haavodah declined, many of its Zionist units, as they split off or were left behind, joined Kibbutz Ein Harod, which was steadily growing.

In the disturbed and sharply polarized atmosphere of the times, however, other collective groups aspiring to communal settlement avoided organizational commitment to a larger collective organization or, like the collectives and settlement groups of Hashomer Hazair, grouped around their own centers of attraction. Meanwhile, the communal settlement movement had received a new impetus when the WZO Executive, under Histadrut pressure, overcame its reluctance to initiate new settlements and, in 1925, allocated to new labor settlements blocks of land acquired along the Kishon stream at the northern rim of Emek Jezreel and in the coastal plantation zone. The additional *moshavim*, *kibbutzim*, and *kvuzot* that sprang up, with new ones being planned, revived interest among leaders of the communal settlements in another attempt at central coordination, and the nearly dormant Commission of Kvuzot convoked a council, which produced a league of *kibbutzim* and *kvuzot* (Hever Hakvuzot Vehakibbutzim) to achieve this. The heated differences of 1925–26 left no possibility of success, and the league amounted to little more than the commission of *kvuzot* and *kibbutzim* before it. In 1927, when the communes did finally coalesce in larger union, two federations rather than one, were formed. The first, Hakibbutz Haarzi (National Commune) of Hashomer Hazair, arose in April and comprised most of the close-knit groups arising out of that youth movement. They had by now developed their own doctrine of commune settlement; they sought a larger, more varied economic base than the *kvuzah* but insisted on homogeneity, even intimate affinity, of the members of the commune, unlike in the open kibbutz. In line with this purpose, they further innovated the doctrine of ideological collectivism: the whole movement, and of course each of its communes, was to develop a consensus on all major, successively arising, issues of a political ideology which, once agreed upon, would thenceforth be binding on all members of the movement.

The kibbutz federation built by Hashomer Hazair for its own movement precluded a wider federation, which Kibbutz Ein Harod tried to build around itself as the nucleus, in 1927. As a result, the "united collective" federation (Hakibbutz Hameuhad) which developed out of Kibbutz Ein Harod in August 1927 represented only a partisan grouping based on the principles of the large, open variegated commune and not, as was planned, a centralized organization of the collective union as a whole, as an arm of the centralized Histadrut. The original aim, to form a union of all the collectives conforming to the unity of the Histadrut itself in scope and concept, remained characteristic of Hakibbutz Hameuhad. It was manifested particularly in the sources of recruitment that Hakibbutz Hameuhad cultivated. In principle it opened its ranks to all members of Hehaluz in the diaspora and to the Working Youth organization that was directly created by the Histadrut in the Yishuv, rather than restricting itself, like Hakibbutz Haarzi of Hashomer Hazair, to youth groups organized and trained under its own immediate control, in strict conformity with a developing political line. At the same time, the Hakibbutz Hameuhad actively organized youth movements committed to its own style of collective organization and kept close touch with other youth movements aligned with Ahdut Haavodah, and later Mapai, the dominant party in the Histadrut.

With the emergence of two kibbutz federations, each based on a large national collective, the earlier coordinating body, Hever Hakvuzot Vehakibbutzim, lost its raison d'être. There nevertheless remained a group of communes, largely small communes (*kvuzot*) like Degania, their model, that maintained the same kind of communication. In the 1930s a youth group named Gordonia (in dedication to the ideas and image of A. D. Gordon), which had grown up in the diaspora, joined the *kvuzot* in a new league, the Hever Hakvuzot, which was founded in 1932.

Each of these collective federations, like their predecessors in labor Zionism—Hapoel Hazair, Ahdut Haavodah and, for that matter, the Gdud Haavodah and the Histadrut itself—arose protesting that it was not a party but an organic movement. Yet each in its own way developed a strong political party identification.

Both of the main labor parties were strongly committed to rural settlement in a variety of forms: small holders' cooperatives and small communes were approved by Hapoel Hazair and Ahdut Haavodah alike, and groups from both parties were responsible for founding new *moshavim* and new *kvuzot* in the 1920s. A difference between them arose over the concept of the large collective, the kibbutz. Hapoel Hazair often shared the skepticism and distrust of general Zionists toward this form of social experimentation. Ahdut Haavodah gave it approval, among other forms of labor settlement, and strongly defended the kibbutz from the start in the Zionist movement. When the merger of the two parties into Mapai occurred in 1929, Hever Hakvuzot and Hakibbutz Hameu-had did not merge, and their separation helped perpetuate the strain of old divisions in the new united labor Zionist party.

A major factor preventing the general union of the collectives was the separatism of Hashomer Hazair in its own Hakibbutz Haarzi. The primary base of the communes' separatism, the commitment to congeniality based on a common youth movement experience of their members, was reinforced and gradually transformed by a secondary development: beginning with the doctrine of ideological collectivism, they swiftly developed a doctrinaire Marxist-style program, and they made acceptance of this their minimum condition for joining other collectives in any projected union. By insisting on this demand, Hashomer Hazair effectively prevented not only a general union of the three labor Zionist collective federations, but also a partial union of the two Mapai-oriented federations; for Hakibbutz Hameuhad steadfastly refused to go into a union that would not include Hakibbutz Haarzi as well as Hever Hakvuzot.

The doctrine that Hashomer Hazair developed moved steadily leftward. The erstwhile Zionist scouts, raised on the ideas of Baden-Powell and Buber, Gustav Wyneken and Freud, became orthodox Marxists, combining this with their Zionism as did the Left Poalei Zion. Marxism was also the prevailing doctrine taught by the schoolmasters and youth leaders of Hakibbutz Hameuhad, though the federation made no demands of ideological conformity upon its members. In addition, however, Hashomer Hazair adopted positions on Arab policy that were opposed to those of the Histadrut leadership as well as the WZO majority. Hakibbutz Hameuhad, on the other hand, kept strongly to a line of Zionist militancy inherited from such forebears as Hashomer and Trumpeldor.

Such differences between the collective federations had far-reaching effects in the entire Histadrut, Yishuv, and WZO political structure. The merger of the two older labor parties in Mapai did not end the rivalry between veteran partisans who now were united in one framework; and the separate organization of Hever Hakvuzot and Hakibbutz Hameuhad served to focus these rivalries on a larger range of issues, especially some involving the separate youth movements of each federation. Hashomer Hazair, for its part, extended its political influence far beyond its own borders, finding political allies in the city among Left Poalei Zion groups and other opponents of the establishment. By the 1930s, Hashomer Hazair organized its former members and others sympathetic to its political program as a Socialist League, conducting its activities in essentially the manner of a political party.

At the Second Convention of the Histadrut in 1923, Ahdut Haavodah won a clear majority of the seats. The previous restraints on Histadrut authority, which had been rather lightly regarded in any case, were now formally discarded. The implied restriction in the constitutional provision that the Histadrut should "also" conduct cultural activities for the workers was removed by dropping the word "also"; accordingly, it was decided to establish the federation's daily newspaper, *Davar*. The markedly political cast of the Histadrut was reinforced by approval of entry into the International Federation of Trade Unions and by resolutions on current issues facing the Yishuv that implicitly ratified political activity already being carried out by Histadrut central and local organs in the Vaad Leumi and in municipal elections.

The central Histadrut executive organ might now have been constituted by Ahdut Haavodah alone, on the strength of its commanding majority, but, seeking to achieve a more comprehensive political union, the leadership maintained the earlier coalition. This meant that Hapoel Hazair continued to share major responsibility for determining and executing policy, but under new conditions that produced policies decisively affected by, and closely conforming to, basic Ahdut Haavodah conceptions. Younger Hapoel Hazair recruits to the leadership such as the brilliant Chaim Arlosoroff, reflecting the mood of their diaspora movement, favored this ideological rapprochement. And for its part, by exerting a powerful influence on the diaspora Poalei Zion toward conformity with the Erez Israel model, Ahdut Haavodah fostered convergence toward local party mergers, complementing the creation of Mapai in 1929. During this process, and afterwards as well, the majority party operated through the persuasive form of a coalition executive but governed with decisive effect through its massive predominance. Coalition bargaining with Hapoel Hazair, under conditions of increasing acceptance of Ahdut Haavodah positions, did not impede, and in many ways served to smooth, the acceptance of majority views.

The coalition approach was extended beyond the two major parties but was not able to absorb minor groups on the left and the right into the developing merger. On the left, the national collectives of the Gdud Haavodah (until its collapse) and Hashomer Hazair persisted in opposition. Together with splinter Left Poalei Zion groups in the towns, they developed an internal critique of Histadrut policy that sought to combine Zionism with Marxist proletarian internationalism. In particular, they increasingly diverged from the Histadrut's Arab policy.

Thus Ben-Gurion, for example, gradually abandoned the hope of organizing Jews and Arabs in joint unions (as had been more or less successfully done only in the union of government railway, telephone, and telegraph workers) and came to feel that a federation of Hebrew workers must confine itself to encouraging parallel Arab unions, separately organized but linked to the Histadrut. So, too, Ahdut Haavodah, after some soul searching among its former Poalei Zion adherents, adopted the strong line of Hapoel Hazair on the right of "organized" (i.e., Jewish) labor to strike and picket against casual Arab–employment in Jewish plantations. In opposition, Hashomer Hazair joined Left Poalei Zion groups in fighting for joint Arab–Jewish unions, which would, of course, make Arabs, as "organized" workers, entitled to a share of employment in Jewish vineyards and orchards. They also independently developed a doctrine of binationalism, joining periodically with liberal Zionists outside the Histadrut in opposition to the vaguely outlined consensus of the Zionist movement on the political future of Palestine.

Opposition also developed on the right, especially among men formerly identified with Hapoel Hazair. The resistance to the growing ties to socialism, no matter how nationally minded or reformist in temper, was not overcome among all those in that party. Some reacted against the trend in the Histadrut by joining other forces in new antisocialist groupings in the Yishuv and the Zionist movement. These men were a significant element in the emergence, for example, of the anti-Weizmann and anti-Histadrut Zionist Revisionist party.

The primary impulse in this development was a sharp opposition to the political line accepted by the WZO consensus. Instead of displaying patient cooperation with the mandate government under obscure formulas, restrictively interpreted, Jabotinsky and his adherents demanded an active political struggle to redefine the mandate formulas and secure a positive and dynamic commitment of the British to the speedy establishment of a Jewish majority and a Jewish commonwealth in Palestine, including Transjordan.

In the labor movement of the early 1920s, there was general agreement with the attitudes expressed in such later Revisionist demands. More than any other Zionists, the labor leadership insisted on immediate, large-scale immigration and continuous rural settlement, regardless of obstacles. Only among a section of Hapoel Hazair, where pacifist voices had been raised against both the Jewish battalions and the proallied Zionist diplomacy of the wartime period, were some temperamentally inclined to the cautious gradualism Weizmann resorted to in the immediate postwar aftermath. Others in that party, and most of Ahdut

Haavodah, strongly pressed for more active political pressure against the developing British policy of the time.

A wedge of difference between Jabotinsky and the labor leaders was introduced by the issue of self-defense. The local experience of the labor groups, no less than their fundamental bias toward autonomy, left them little or no confidence in a neo-Herzlian tactic that staked everything on the chance of altering British policy. In going ahead with the organization of the Haganah organization as a nonauthorized, voluntary, and semisecret paramilitary defense force, they parted ways with Jabotinsky. The initial breach was widened by differences among the Haganah activists themselves.

Haganah was accepted first by Ahdut Haavodah and then also by the Histadrut as a labor responsibility; but the self-defense formations of the Yishuv always included other elements as well, especially in the towns and plantation villages. As was noted earlier, Ahdut Haavodah and Histadrut representatives concerned with the Haganah clashed with some Hashomer stalwarts over the desire of the latter to retain a separate, quasiprofessional staff control that was not subject to the "civilian" authority of the labor parties or federation. A similar quarrel arose in the towns between the central Histadrut leadership of the Haganah and some of the local captains, such as Abraham Tehomi in Jerusalem. The Hashomer opposition, which was drawn to the left, produced fantasies of military communism; some urban dissidents from the Haganah consensus were drawn to the right, to the new political and paramilitary formations grouping themselves around Jabotinsky. Other rightwing paramilitary traditions, prevailing in the same circles that had given birth to the Gideonites and Aaronsohn family's Nili group in First Aliyah settlements, were fostered by the association of settlers' sons, the Bnai Binyamin.

The rapprochements and prospects of a merger between Hapoel Hazair and Ahdut Haavodah split off some of the adamant antisocialist nationalists of the former party on issues of social and communal concern. At first such men were active as a rightwing opposition in the Histadrut itself, where they fought to restrict the federation to those trade union functions common in Europe. They were also strongly opposed to the class consciousness and class struggle motifs that were prevalent in the Histadrut under Ahdut Haavodah domination; they argued that the interests of Zionism demanded constructive collaboration between classes, given the rudimentary existing economy. They favored, as did bourgeois elements outside the Histadrut, a system of compulsory arbitration of labor disputes, and labor exchanges conducted by employer as well as union representatives—both of these to be under public control by the WZO Executive or the Vaad Leumi, rather than class-controlled by the Histadrut.

With views like these, the rightwing workers, who increasingly aligned themselves with Jabotinsky and eventually set up a national workers' federation outside the Histadrut, introduced the sharp edge of conflict over social issues into the relatively limited initial disagreement between Labor and the Revisionists. Moreover, initial divergence on Zionist policy grew wider as the Histadrut leaders aligned themselves increasingly with Weizmann's party in the WZO. The clash heightened to the point of street battles and Revisionist strike-breaking. The red flag of the Histadrut was opposed to the brown shirts of Italian-style Revisionist youth formations in a confrontation heightened by the obvious contemporary European parallels. The bitterness reached a climax of irreconcilability when labor leaders held Revisionists responsible for the murder of Arlosoroff in 1933. An attempt to bridge the gap through an agreement negotiated between Ben-Gurion and Jabotinsky, including arrangements to preclude trade union wars, was defeated by a Histadrut referendum in March 1935. A month earlier, a Revisionist conclave had rejected the prospect, implied in the agreement, of renouncing independent political activity outside the WZO.

By combining opposition to the Histadrut on domestic labor–capitalist issues with their primary militant opposition to Weizmann's moderate Zionist foreign policy, the Revisionists moved into the role of a far-right opposition—this in spite of Jabotinsky's own nineteenth-century Herzl-style liberalism and the old ties between leading Yishuv Revisionists and the labor movement. Other opponents of the Histadrut were concerned with standard bourgeois interests of property and profit and were committed to a relatively simple, conservative type of liberal ideology. Still others were interested primarily in the cause of religious Orthodoxy. The heightened political importance and activity of the Histadrut in many cases aroused the latent opposition of such center groups and sharpened its ideological edge, but other factors, which neutralized and deflected their opposition, impeded their development into tight, united, active parties capable of offering a serious challenge to labor Zionism.

Among the religious and general Zionists alike, the role the labor Zionists played in assuming the hard, constructive, pioneering tasks of Zionist populism undermined opposition. Indeed, there arose in these circles settler groups and youth movements that emulated the labor Zionist example. General Zionists and religious Zionists, not to mention

Revisionists, organized cooperative and communal settlements and groups of urban workers that adhered to these ideologies.

Some of these remained within the Histadrut framework as an opposition. Both rural and urban religious workers, organized outside the Histadrut, but not, as the Revisionists ultimately did, in order to constitute a competitive union. Their separation was based on the cultural functions of the Histadrut and the ideological complexion of its rural and urban settlements, and was designed to make possible their cultivation of an Orthodox style of life, rejuvenated by commitment to the standard revolutionary Zionist tasks. In other matters, such as collective bargaining and health care, they collaborated with the Histadrut central bodies and shared Histadrut services.

This group then served as a left opposition in the religious Zionist camp; a similar grouping of religious workers and labor settlers developed also in the anti-Zionist Agudat Israel. Their growing relative strength in the Orthodox camp had significant political consequences: it complicated the problems of forming a united Orthodox political force— already handicapped by the conflict between Mizrahi and Agudat Israel—and by precluding the automatic alignment of the whole clerical front with the rightwing bourgeois parties, as was commonly the case elsewhere, it helped institute an Orthodox strategy based on balance-of-power politics and neutrality, or balance, on nonreligious issues.

To the extent that the "Oriental" Jews—those derived from Muslim countries—were a significant element in the Yishuv's politics, the picture was about the same. They were unable to form a solid, united bloc, not only because of the differences in tradition, local backgrounds, and loyalties among them, but also because the Histadrut exercised a certain appeal for some while it strongly antagonized others. The Yemenites in particular were a group cultivated by the labor Zionists; the Sephardi communities, however, especially those who were relatively long settled and prosperous Ottoman citizens, tended to align on social and communal issues with the bourgeois anti-labor factions.

Split as the opposition was among disparate elements, the labor Zionist Histadrut bloc encountered continual strong opposition in the politics of both the Yishuv and the WZO. In the Vaad Leumi, as was previously noted, the power of the labor electorate was frustrated by boycotts and noncooperation of rightist groups directed against the Yishuv's voluntary communal institutions. In the municipalities and large plantation villages, the government backed up mayors and councils elected by a restricted franchise against the democratic clamor of the labor factions. In the WZO, the dominance of labor in the Yishuv—

augmented in force when the per capita representation of the Yishuv was raised to double that of diaspora Zionists—was effectively counteracted by the strength of other Zionist parties in the diaspora. Nevertheless, by the 1930s, labor Zionists achieved a dominant plurality in the WZO as well as in the elected institutions of the Yishuv.

The political activity of the dominant labor Zionist Histadrut coalition in the 1920s was marked by strong differences in spite of the gradual convergence of the two parties, Hapoel Hazair and Ahdut Haavodah. The divergence between the two approaches emerges clearly in the relative concentration of each, as separate spheres of activity, on the Yishuv or the WZO.

What was common to both labor parties—and equally characteristic, for that matter, of all Zionist factions that shared in the work of Palestine—was the concentration on a particular function or approach, which each, according to its ideology, singled out as centrally important to the success of the entire Zionist enterprise. Religious Zionists devoted themselves to the regeneration of traditional Judaism through the creation of a self-sustaining Orthodox settlement of pious Jews in Palestine. Cultural Zionists hoped for a revival of the national ethos through Hebrew language and literature, based on a solid Jewish society in Palestine, and constituting a value system that would restore Jewish creativity and active solidarity throughout the diaspora. Labor Zionists hoped, in two different versions, for a revolutionary restoration of the Jewish people as an active historic entity: Hapoel Hazair, through the construction of a Hebraic, populist, cooperative farmer-worker society, which would heal the corruption of the Jewish urban ghetto by striking new roots in the ancestral soil; the Poalei Zion, and especially Ahdut Haavodah and the dominant Histadrut leadership, through the concerted, centrally directed, voluntary commitment of all workers in Palestine to the creation of a new Jewish nation out of the constructive achievements of the new Jewish working class. All of them, Mizrahi, Hebraists, populists, and socialists alike, were convinced that the function they alone were carrying out was the key element of the solution of the Jewish problem for all Jews, and all expected that the social forms and institutions they were creating would ultimately encompass the entire, redeemed Jewish people in Palestine.

What emerged from these diversely single-minded, ardent efforts was a highly pluralistic society. The partisans were united in their common ultimate perspective only because and insofar as it was not clearly focused. Only by concentrating their absolute ideological claims on limited, immediate tasks that could be pursued side by side, were the jostling parties saved from frontal clashes. This was true of Hapoel Hazair and Ahdut Haavodah, as well as of more widely divided parties, even during the period of their steady rapprochement.

It was inherent in their ideological positions that the Poalei Zion as well as the Ahdut Haavodah leaders through the Histadrut, should direct their efforts toward the whole Yishuv and be inhibited in relation to the WZO, while Hapoel Hazair tended to isolate itself in the Yishuv and to work easily with the WZO. The proletarian-minded, Marxist-oriented labor Zionists were inclined to think in terms of masses and were strongly attuned to the territorial politico-economic frame of social action. Their ideological propensity for working through the proletarian, indigenous mass, and not through small, segregated bands of idealists, carried over into the Histadrut and underlay the strong involvement of its Ahdut Haavodah leaders in urban union organization and the political arenas of the municipalities and the Vaad Leumi. All this interested much less the Hapoel Hazair agrarians, who, in the context of the Yishuv, devoted themselves primarily to the agricultural sector, or at most to Hebraic education and culture in the towns.

As for the WZO, the Poalei Zion had been wary of this bourgeois organization on grounds of class consciousness, and Ahdut Haavodah leaders of the Histadrut retained a suspicion of bourgeois, diaspora Zionism, reinforced by their strong sense of the superior Zionist quality of settlers in Zion over Zionist supporters of the Yishuv in the diaspora. They cooperated mainly with the Settlement Department of the WZO, the Jewish National Fund, and similar Zionist agencies that were directly involved in practical work in Palestine, but they viewed with distrust other Zionist departments, especially the Political Department, during the early 1920s.

Hapoel Hazair, on the other hand, was a direct, though radical offshoot of the traditional populist Zionism of the Hovevei Zion period. Its resistance to doctrinaire socialism came together with an affinity for the broad nationalism of the WZO. In its own peculiar fashion, Hashomer Hazair had a similar relation to the WZO, in spite of its increasingly radical doctrinairism in regard to the local economic politics of Palestine: their two-stage doctrine (a reworking of conceptions of Nahman Syrkin) required them to be class conscious socialists after entering Palestine but simply nationalists in the diaspora prior to resettling. This philosophy enabled them to be leftist opponents of Histadrut policy in Palestine and, simultaneously, prime favorites of moderate or progressive general Zionists in the diaspora.

These differences in relation to the WZO were reinforced by complementary differential attitudes of general Zionists to the two major labor Zionist factions. The chief example of radical social experimentation which bourgeois critics thought to be impractical and downright dangerous to Zionism was the large, open kibbutz. It was Ahdut Haavodah, the main contender in Histadrut class struggle unionism, that also took up the defense of this form of settlement in the inner-Zionist debate. Hapoel Hazair shared the skepticism of bourgeois Zionists toward this form of centralized collectivism, though it strongly supported other types of cooperation, such as consumers' and service cooperatives, smallholders' settlements, and small, romantic-idealistic communes; and Hapoel Hazair was also less than enamored of urban trade unionism, let alone the class struggle. It accordingly enjoyed the special regard of the bourgeois Zionists who, in large part, had strong agrarian-populist inclinations of their own.

The impact of these differences on the relationship of the two major factions of the Zionist workers to the WZO is clear. The seat of Labor in the Palestine Executive of the WZO was usually held by a member of Hapoel Hazair, whereas in the Vaad Leumi men of Ahdut Haavodah were most prominent. At the 1923 Zionist Congress Ahdut Haavodah and Poalei Zion delegates boycotted the elections to the Executive altogether. On the other hand, the dominant Histadrut leaders maintained close working relations with the Zionist civil service active in Palestine, especially men, such as Ruppin who allocated development funds. Many experts of the type of Akiva Ettinger, Yizhak Elazari Volcani, and Shlomo Kaplansky, active in the settlement department, were themselves socialist Zionists, some of them belonging to Ahdut Haavodah. These relations were highly useful in launching such institutions as the Workers' Bank and helped induce bold WZO ventures such as the 1921–1922 and 1925 land acquisitions and new settlement projects.

By 1926–1927, when the boom of the Fourth Aliyah burst, the chronic criticism of overextended, high-risk, dubiously economic Zionist settlement activity, and especially of radical, experimental social forms like the kibbutz or *kvuzah*, swelled to new heights. In the Zionist Congress of that year, a hostile Executive was elected without any labor representation at all. Moreover, in the same year, negotiations for an expanded Jewish Agency with prospective non-Zionist representation swiftly matured. A commission of experts came to survey the Palestine economy and ecology, and its subsequent published report contained a slashing attack on the communes and on other aspects of the labor Zionist special relation to the WZO Settlement, Immigration, and other departments. The need to resist such attacks was a strong element which induced the two large labor Zionist factions to close ranks and work for a party merger.

In the aftermath of the crisis, labor Zionist planners grasped the critical importance for their work of close collaboration with the WZO. They began to draw up schemes for national loans to be guaranteed by the assets already built by the Zionist resettlement agencies; and in order to achieve this, they set themselves seriously to the task of writing contracts for the consolidation and repayment, together with current interest, of investments already made or to be made in the labor settlements. They proposed that communal groups working in plantation villages loan their savings to the JNF in order to participate in the purchase of new lands for their own settlement, the sums advanced to be accounted for in their subsequent rent and other charges.

At the next Congress, in 1929, Labor recovered strongly from its defeat in the Zionist movement. A now united Mapai, backed by diaspora labor Zionist delegates, was able to claim more than the minor portfolios previously held in the Executive, on a par with Mizrahi. Chaim Arlosoroff came in as head of the Political Department in Jerusalem, a post previously reserved for a diaspora figure personally close to Weizmann.

Upon the heels of the Congress, and the creation of an expanded Jewish Agency which it ratified, came the bloody Arab attacks upon towns and villages of the Yishuv—and then the second shock of the sharp turn against its Zionist commitments by the British Labor government: the Passfield White Paper of October 1930, which represented a clear attempt to arrest the further development of the Jewish national home. The effect of this succession of blows was multiple and decisive.

In the Yishuv, while consolidating the main labor Zionist forces, the effect was to radicalize their opponents. On the left, the Jewish communists were led, or driven, to a line, dictated by the Comintern, of welcoming as revolutionary and progressive such acts as the Hebron massacre of defenseless yeshiva students who were not even by any stretch of the imagination Zionists. On the right, dissatisfaction with the unpreparedness and inadequate activity of the Haganah in the crisis was one of the factors that contributed to the estrangement of a number of paramilitary formations (especially in towns), to their growing detachment from Histadrut central control, and to their drift toward the Revisionist affiliation strongly represented among their officers.

In the WZO, on the other hand, the trauma of the 1929 events rapidly consolidated the bonds of collaboration and unity between the Histadrut and WZO leadership. Labor entered energetically into the two central functions of the WZO, its Political Department and Treasury. The Emergency Fund collected by the newly enlarged Jewish Agency was utilized for a "Thousand Family Plan" of expanding the network of labor villages through new land purchases, amelioration, and settlement. The workers and workers' institutions now participated in these efforts with their own savings and by their established and prospective assets, committed under loan contracts, which the Jewish Agency Treasury was able to use as a credit base for large loans.

The decade of the 1930s brought Hitler and the catastrophic tragedies of European Jewry, which placed Palestine under a pressure of Jewish immigration beyond anything imagined before. The Yishuv and the WZO faced tasks—political, social, fiscal, and technical—incomparably greater than anything in their earlier experience, and unprecedented anywhere.

The Zionist movement entered upon these immense tasks with a consolidated labor Zionist force that was firmly established in the leadership of the Yishuv and the WZO. The Histadrut membership rose from roughly 4,000 at the end of 1920 to nearly 23,000 at the end of 1927, and it raised the proportion of organized laborers in that period from 50 to 70 percent of the whole. By the Fourth Convention in 1933, the 34,000 Histadrut members were nearly 75 percent of all the Jewish workers and more than a third of the whole Yishuv. The labor Zionist movement was now led by a mass party representing over 80 percent of voters and controlling powerful positions in all Yishuv and WZO institutions. All this strength and experience, together with a ready skill for innovation, were needed to cope with the trials of practical work that now had to be undertaken. The political trials that accompanied these efforts were an even greater strain, under which the established structure of the national home cracked, buckled, and shifted, but held firm and found new strength.

The Transition from Yishuv to State

The new State of Israel, born to independence on May 14, 1948, arose upon the foundation of a society that was itself young and incomplete. In the first years of its existence, Israel absorbed a mass of immigrations equal in number to its original population but sharply different in many significant social, economic, and cultural traits. What does it mean, then, if under these circumstances one speaks of the social structure of the new Jewish state?

Obviously, an analysis of the structure of a society implies a description of its stable elements. But only the future can really tell us how far and in what respects Israel today exhibits the elements of stability characteristic of older, better-established societies. Thus, a description of Israel's social structure is necessarily a venture in prediction. The best approach may be to analyze Israel's most significant unsolved social problems—that is, those, whose solution is likely to have the most significant historic effect.

In this respect Israel is similar to other states that have emerged in our time. History and social structure are inseparably joined in such states, as they are in all revolutionary—or, as we now call them, rapidly developing—situations. The contemporary social problems of the new "developing" nations are clearly rooted in their history, while the shape of their historic future is being decided by the very policies through which they attempt to solve these contemporary problems. Thus the extreme poverty and wretched conditions of India's "untouchables" are closely connected with the religious tradition of Hinduism; and on the other hand, whether India will become a united, stable, and powerful modern nation greatly depends on its raising the level of literacy, the degree of social acceptance, and the economic productivity of the pariahs and other depressed groups.

These relationships are usually well understood by those responsible for determining the policies of new or rejuvenated nations. Even half a century ago the Young Turks under Kemal Pasha Ataturk held the veiling of women and other Muslim traditions responsible for the cultural stagnation and social debility of the Ottoman regime. Consequently, they made "Westernization" a paramount aim of nationalist policy. Thus, measures intended to abolish social ills were also intended to accomplish historic—or more precisely, political—aims.

The same observations apply to Israel. The Jewish state is one of those modern societies that seeks to make itself more easily understood by proclaiming its fundamental purposes (not only political, but social, economic, and cultural) as elaborately articulated principles. Israel is both a state and a social structure conceived before its birth as a means of solving a specific social problem—the modern Jewish Problem—in all its ramifications; moreover, since its establishment, Israel has continued to regard the solution of the Jewish Problem as a fundamental purpose. Consequently, the institutions and values of Israel, both the state and the society, have been and continue to be structured by their functions in solving this problem. This, at least, is an ideological demand that Israel recognizes. History alone will decide how far reality will conform to the ideal.

Thus the Zionist movement before the rise of Israel proclaimed, in addition to the goal of political sovereignty, the following nationalist objectives: to develop Hebrew as a spoken language and as the foundation of a Jewish national consensus; to transfer to Palestine all Jews who could not or did not wish to live in diaspora countries; to establish a Jewish community in Palestine free from the particular social, economic, and cultural problems that beset the Jewish status as a minority people scattered throughout the world; and to carry out the transformations in the Jewish social and economic distribution, to create the appropriate social institutions, and to foster the cultural changes that were the necessary means for attaining the above ends.

The State of Israel has committed itself no less clearly and comprehensively than did the Zionist movement before it to elaborately articulated ideological principles. Upon the creation of the state in 1948, the ideal of national independence was institutionalized in the ultimate form, that of political sovereignty. By that date, too, the Jewish community in Palestine had already developed institutions that realized the related nationalist aims. Hebrew was a spoken language, widely enough disseminated to become the national tongue of the new state, and social and economic institutions had been developed, an occupational distribution achieved, and cultural values established in conformity with the ideal of a self-sustaining, balanced community capable of controlling its own destiny in the same way as other free peoples do. But following 1948, in extending its welcome to all Jews who could not or would not remain in their old homes, Israel received a mass immigration that, for the most part, did not possess the national attributes already developed by the settled population. In consequence, Israel's tasks henceforth included the following: to enable the newcomers to master the language and share in the other elements of social consensus existing in the settled community; to enable them to participate in the social institutions and cultural life of the settled community; and to transform the social and occupational distribution of the new immigrants so that they would conform to the settled population and become self-supporting, at the same time helping the state become economically self-sustaining.

From this survey, it is evident, that in certain respects Israel is sharply different from the other new states to which we have compared it. The problem intended to be solved by acquiring sovereignty in Israel and establishing a free Jewish society there was not the problem of an autochthonous community whose pattern of living was rooted in centuries of adjustment to its own locale. It was instead the problem of a people suffering exile. Its first stage was the return of the people to a homeland to which were intimately attached only their dreams but not the minute details of their diverse ways of life. In the very act of migration, the returning Zionists, like emigrants everywhere, implicitly committed themselves to renounce habits that might not be suited to the new country; also their adjustment to modern requirements in the new country, was relatively free from the handicaps of a rigid local tradition. Thus the establishment of new patterns of living, rationally suited for adjustment to the social, cultural, and economic as well as political requirements of a modern nation in Palestine, was made far easier than for the native Asian and African communities that have acquired independence in our time. A rather more suitable comparison would be new nations of the Western Hemisphere, colonized by immigrants from Europe.

Another major difference from the new Asian and African states (and here, too, the situation may properly be compared with other modern societies built up by colonization) is closely related to the first. Israeli society as it stood in 1948 represented (at least, in conception, and to a considerable degree in fact) a successful solution of the social problems with which the Zionist movement is concerned. While the mass influx of new immigrants after 1948 undoubtedly produced severe new social problems, one might contend that Israel had already succeeded in developing the social institutions, or at any rate the values and principles, which in appropriate application could solve the new problems. If this were a fully satisfactory description of Israel's present situation, Israel would then resemble the United States during the mass immigration of 1880 to 1920 more than it does a country like India or Egypt today. Its major task would be *merely* social—how to absorb a "formless" mass of newcomers into an already established social milieu—rather than historic—how to devise new institutions or convert traditional social forms into a suitable environment for "modern" living.

The differences from other "developing" countries in this respect must indeed be recognized from the outset, but it is equally essential to recognize how different in magnitude and kind was Israel's task from the integration of immigrants in rapidly developing nineteenth-century America. If there is a proper comparison, it would more nearly be to the impact of immigration in colonial America or, later, just behind the moving Western frontier, because the relative scale of immigration to Israel was so great that the "established" institutions had to adjust to the immigrants no less than the immigrants to the institutions. In addition, the change from a community living under a mandate government to an independent Jewish state, with all the other political, social, economic, and cultural upheavals that attended it, undoubtedly loosened the underpinnings of the old institutions. It could be said, therefore, that Israel's social institutions and values were and are more in flux than they are fixed.

In sum, the study of Israel's pressing domestic problems today can and should be more than a study of *merely* social issues. The questions that demand solution, if we may put the issue in technical terms, probably arise from something more than a merely frictional maladjustment, and the answers to them may represent something more than the restored equilibrium of a stable, "boundary-maintaining" social structure. The solutions of Israel's social problems are likely to have historic significance. They may determine the shape in which still undefined Israeli social institutions and values eventually become fixed and stable.

Any social structure that is at all involved in historic processes is, to that extent, a structure of hypotheses and of provisional values that are continually challenged by alternatives. In a situation as fluid as that of Israel, such alternatives assert themselves with special force. In no rapidly developing country that absorbs large numbers of immigrants do the newcomers have to adjust to a monolithic code of values; instead, they find a range of nuanced alternatives that are recognized as legitimate by the social consensus of the settled community. In no rapidly developing country are the newcomers integrated into a direct social relationship with all or even a representative sample of the settled population; instead, they enter into complex relationships of reciprocal acceptance and rejection with selected elements among the old settlers according to the particular social functions they take up or are assigned. Where the relative weight of the immigrant population is so large as it is in Israel, the support the newcomers lend to alternative values, which may lie latent among the older settlers, could well force the revision of the patterns of society throughout the whole range of its functions—political, economic, cultural, and purely social.

So large an immigration relative to the settled population could also force recognition of quite new alternatives to Israel's institutions, now represented even as latent, deviant trends among the older settlers. Moreover, the right of Jewish immigrants to determine the patterns of Israel's future existence has a strong ideological grounding in Zionist principles. Israel exists, according to its own proclamation, in order to solve the problem of the homelessness and lack of independence of the Jewish people—that is, to provide a rational solution for the problem of Jews in exile and to allow the Jews of the dispersion, in returning to the homeland, to become masters of their own national destiny. This surely means that the new immigrants are not less entitled to advocate their own patterns of living as appropriate for Israeli society than were their predecessors who established the social institutions with which Israel began in 1948.

I

In all the new states that have emerged in our day, the conversion from dependency to sovereignty has produced new, complex social problems and raised issues of historic significance. Israel's independence was won in rebellion and war, and the conditions under which Israel had to plan its future after the hostilities subsided were radically different from all that had existed under the Mandate and from anything that could be anticipated beforehand. From the very beginning, the Jewish state was confronted not only by the ordinary readjustments to independence, taxing enough in all cases, but by unusual difficulties.

In Israel, as in many other instances, the colonial administration did not hand over to the new state functioning institutions and trained officials fully able to cope with the responsibilities of sovereignty. On this count alone, the transfer of authority to Israel could not be smooth. It came as an abrupt challenge that had to be met at the first shock by improvised expedients, with many attendant difficulties. Over the long pull, the readjustment to a new governmental structure placed a severe strain on many institutions of the Yishuv, which had been built up in the absence of a Jewish state, and here, too, difficulties similar to those of other new states arose.

In some ways, however, Israel was much better equipped for sovereignty by the legacy of the Mandate period than were other ex-colonial areas. Even though the Mandate administration was unable to create a legislative or advisory council that would enable the population to gain experience in government at the highest level, a fair number of Jews were employed in the higher ranks of various government departments. Additional personnel with general administrative experience could be drawn from the many welfare and development agencies with which the Yishuv was so well supplied. The Jewish Agency, the Histadrut, and the minor party organizations conducted social, economic, cultural, and political activities in many ways parallel to those of a state. There were, nevertheless, many important functions not paralleled or adequately represented in the experience of the Jewish public institutions. The Mandate government, bitterly hostile to the United Nations' resolution to partition Palestine and particularly antagonistic to the plan for a Jewish state, did nothing to help, and a great deal to hinder, Jewish preparations for statehood during the brief transition from Mandate to independence in 1947–48. The United Nations Palestine Commission worked to the best of its ability under difficult conditions to help the Jews meet this problem, and the Jews applied themselves vigorously to the task. Because of these efforts as well as the well-established infrastructure of a modern state that the Yishuv bequeathed to Israel, the new Jewish polity was able to avoid the crippling confusion, conflict, and general political instability that has often beset early years of independence in other states. Even so, Israel at its birth had to struggle with severe and urgent problems of reorganization in order to, convert its existing institutions and improvise supplementary agencies capable of preserving its independence. The extraordinary extent of the activities carried on by the Yishuv's partisan organizations separately, as well as by most of them jointly through the Jewish Agency and the Vaad Leumi, was a curse as well as a blessing in the first years. The new state was born with relatively well-developed organs of self-maintenance, education, and self-defense. The difficulty was that it had not one but many well-staffed agencies for absorbing immigrants, not one but many full-scale school systems, and, worst of all, not one but many military organizations, each seeking to establish and defend the Jewish state according to its own strategic and tactical plans.

Israel was very early able to overcome its inherited, plural form of military organization. The clear and present danger of defeat was enough to make the Israeli government take drastic measures and the Israeli population support them. The state, however, represented, a new force intent upon unification not only in military matters but over a wide range of inherited institutional structures, and in these unifications it did not have the same support. There were strong interests, and strong functional demands as well, for the continuation of the pluralistic institutional structure that Israel derived from the New Yishuv. This applies even to Israel's political institutions.

The values and habits essential to the efficient functioning of a state were not lacking in Israel to such a dangerous extent as in many another new state. Although large numbers of the new immigrants came from countries where industrial civilization and democratic government were not familiar, the Yishuv had long been accustomed to modern ways of administration and was prepared by experience to induct newcomers into its advanced institutions.

Nevertheless, there were certain respects in which the sudden assumption of new governmental functions, and the sudden expansion of central bureaucracies, sharply altered the conventional attitudes of the Yishuv. The Yishuv had valued expansion, growth, dynamism, and initiative as much as any modern code of rational values could wish, and it had generally favored the idea of planning. But from the beginning of the Second Aliyah, it had also strongly stressed the autonomy of small groups and the right to experiment with a variety of approaches to social, economic, and cultural problems. It had grown into a pluralistic society even more diverse, perhaps, than was desired by the protagonists of group autonomy themselves—for each partisan group thought, after all, that the others ought to accept the principles it upheld. But not only did the rise of the state machinery, with its broad-range drive toward unity, endanger the vested interest of established partisan organizations, also the value it placed on central authority, discipline, and obedience ran counter to the established values of grass-roots autonomy, spontaneity, and initiative that were conventional in the Yishuv. Thus the sudden rise of the state machinery forecast possible conflicts not only over matters of social organization but over values. Not only were the vested interests of the Yishuv challenged, but its ideals were questioned and its sensibilities shocked.

The assumption of sovereignty, then, meant the rise of social problems and historic issues for Israel, as for other new states of our time, though not of the same kind or severity. The circumstances in which Israel gained its independence and had to defend it in the early years raised almost unique difficulties. Not to recognize the legitimate existence of new states is an innovation not infrequent in our times, but few new states are so completely encircled as Israel by neighbors that deny its right to exist. Undeclared, cold, and other varieties of unconventional war are also not without precedent in our times, but few states are so harried with blockades, boycotts, and border clashes as Israel has been since its birth. As a result, Israel has been an armed camp, and its entire population, a citizen army.

The social and cultural consequences of a virtually total conscription policy have been far-reaching and significant. The army has been the meeting place of all Israelis, segregated so sharply in their civilian capacities. The common danger and the common service have inspired a high esprit de corps throughout the nation, one particularly responsive to outer threats. For the immigrants, the army has served, by conscious plan, as a primary school of Israeli naturalization.

No less significant have been the economic and political effects of Israel's exceptional security situation. Only by a high productive capacity can Israel sustain relatively huge military capabilities. Cut off from its immediate hinterland, Israel has been forced to seek economic ties abroad. It has had to compete in the markets of the advanced industrial countries of the West; and it has had to seek economic as well as political relations with distant, new territories emerging into independence in Asia and Africa. Unable to rely on resistance to Arab blacklisting by foreign transport lines, Israel has been driven to organize its own merchant marine and airline, to develop new ports and expand its airline terminal facilities.

Even an Israel left at peace by its neighbors would face extraordinary social and economic problems. The new country was half arid, and the great mass of entering immigrants was unprecedented. The insecurity of Israel immeasurably complicated the situation. As political refugees, most immigrants entered in a state of utter deprivation and many in poor health. So, too, the supply of capital and the location of industry and agricultural settlements, the methods of absorption and the aims of acculturation of immigrants were all different in the encircled Israel that arose out of the Arab–Israeli conflict than would otherwise be the case.

Like other new countries, independent Israel faced social and economic readjustments that developed from its having severed the ties that bound it to another people during its colonial period. But the new Israel not only broke its bonds with Britain, the far-off colonial power; after the war of independence, it also found itself separated from a major part of the local population of prewar Palestine, the Arabs. Both changes involved drastic revisions in the social and economic relationships contemplated for the new state.

It was, of course, the fundamental purpose of Zionism to make the Jews autonomous not only in their political but in their social and economic institutions. Nevertheless, success in achieving sovereignty brought with it unexpected problems arising from the sudden erection of a state apparatus. So, too, when Zionism achieved an intrinsic aim by freeing Israel from the subordination of its judiciary to British legal practices and authorities, it encountered the unexplored difficulties of living according to a Jewish law.

British control of Palestine's economic policy had been a major obstacle to Zionism, most serious after the adoption of the 1939 White Paper. The advantages of Britain's departure were clear. Israel now had a free hand to explore the mineral resources of Palestine and plan the intensive development of land and water without restriction. Another economic grievance had been the tariff policy of the Mandatory, which, Zionists charged, was unduly rigid in granting equal access to the Palestine market for all League of Nations members while being unduly responsive to the commercial interests of neighboring countries, and inconsistent with the rapid development of a modern industrial economy in Palestine. With independence, Israel obtained the freedom to adopt such foreign trade policies as would best serve its ends.

The economic consultants of the Zionist Organization, in criticizing British economic policy in Palestine, had proposed alternatives that assumed the continuance of the Mandate—that is, the persistence of an economic connection with Great Britain. They proposed, for example, the inclusion of Palestine within Britain's imperial preference scheme. But the immediate effect of Israel's independence, even before the formal proclamation, was the severance of all economic ties with Britain. Palestine was removed from the sterling bloc. The new Jewish state was not obliged to devise policies that could support a more or less stable currency upon the sole basis of its own economy instead of sharing, as previously, in a balance comprising total economic activities of the sterling bloc.

Whether or not the severance of economic ties with Britain had critical economic significance, it gave new prominence to a task that Zionism had not clearly considered earlier, and it required an emphasis on somewhat different economic criteria. In the many plans that Zionists had made for the economic development of Palestine, the stress had been strongly technological: how to derive maximum yields from the land and to achieve the most efficient employment of all available men and women and capital. The criterion of a profitable balance at a given level of productivity was given less prominence, being regarded as an economic goal that could be deferred until the prior aim of raising the level of productivity to a maximum had been achieved. The question the Zionists asked was how they could best use *any* piece of land in Palestine and in what way they could best provide employment for any immigrant who might come, not which lands should be exploited first and at what point land became submarginal or how many immigrants should be allowed to enter at a given time. The latter, of course, were the criteria that a hostile Mandatory government pressed upon them. After Israel was created and cast upon its own resources to achieve a balance of its accounts, the objective situation required Israel itself to make solvency, not merely efficiency, a major economic aim.

Much more far-reaching were the effects of separation from the Palestinian Arabs. In their economic planning during the Mandate period, Zionists had elaborated proposals for large-scale land acquisition throughout Palestine. This included gradually but radically reducing the overwhelming preponderance of Arab landownership and extending to the maximum the area cultivated by the advanced methods of the Jews. It also included specific plans for raising Arab agriculture, to the highest level on the reduced areas available. The idea was to begin with the resources and techniques available to the Palestinian *fellaheen* (peasant farmers) and, by a graded progression, supply them with new facilities and accustom them to new methods, arriving by a different route at the same destination as Jewish agriculture.

The fighting of 1947–48 brought in its train the mass flight and some expulsions of Arabs out of the area of Israel. All at once, instead of by gradual stages, virtually the whole land area became available for development by Jews. The problem became one not of slowly purchasing occupied areas but of rapidly settling vacant areas, which would otherwise run to weed and which, unoccupied, might be overrun by the unopposed incursion of border raiders and enemy forces. Plans for agricultural retraining now had to be designed in terms of new Jewish immigrants with virtually no farming tradition, not in terms of the much less pliant Arab *fellaheen* with their set ways and ancient precedents.

The absence of the Arabs also altered the terms in which the problems facing Jewish agriculture itself had to be understood. In spite of the Zionist aim to build a balanced economy in which Jews would themselves produce all their own necessities, at least to the same extent as other nations in their own land, Jewish farming under the Mandate had an uneven development. Many characteristic farm products, natural to the Palestinian soil, were provided to the Jewish economy either entirely or in large part by the Palestinian Arab farmers. Unable to compete with local Arabs in growing native grains and certain fruits and vegetables, Jewish farms, like those of the Arabs, produced citrus for export and dairy products for the Yishuv. We have referred to the many factors that threw the new State of Israel on its own resources: the Arab boycott and blockade, and the severance of economic ties with Britain. The disappearance of so many Arab farmers from Israel and the cessation of trade with Arab suppliers across the border had a similar effect. Jewish farmers now had to plan to supply many basic commodities previously available from Arab sources. In view of the new importance of national solvency, Israel now also had to plan to use the whole area at its free disposal in the light of the requirements of Israel's foreign trade balance.

The sudden absence of the Arabs from Israel's countryside and from the cities where they had been neighbors of the Jews obviously had direct social and cultural effects. Among these, one in particular had a significant impact on the Israeli code of values. Living next door to a hostile neighbor nurtured the militancy inherent in the Zionist ethos as surely when the Arabs lived in close conjunction with Jews throughout a common land under the Mandate as when they were separated by political boundaries after independence. In the earlier period, the fact that Jews and Arabs would some day have to reach a modus vivendi was brought home to the Zionists in every field of their daily activity: at work, in the marketplace, at home, and on the roads. After independence, the need for an understanding with Arabs became remote and was relegated mainly to the field of external politics, in which the Israeli individual-on-the-street was personally involved only when mobilized for military service.

Another value of the Zionist ethos was affected, too, in a more tenuous form. The principle that Jews, in order to liberate themselves from economic dependency (or "parasitism"), must become workers had a specific relevance and impact when Arab farmers and workers were available in numbers sufficient to supply the Yishuv. Jewish labor and Jewish self-supply, the slogans of the socialist Zionist parties, found considerable opposition from the middle-class party. They were, nonetheless, ideals generally recognized by the consensus of the Yishuv, and the constant clash of these ideals with Palestinian realities made Jewish labor a particularly live issue in the community. Those who dedicated themselves to the realization of this part of the Zionist ideal enjoyed an undisputed elite position. With the flight of most of the Arab population, the whole question was sharply depreciated in significance. Now the Jewish community had to supply itself to the fullest extent possible, quite apart from any ideals involved. Now many of the new immigrants had to become workers and farmers; and it was a bureaucracy, not an idealistic youth movement, that proved best suited to the task.

II

In achieving independence, the new State of Israel achieved or incurred sharp changes in the conditions under which it would thenceforth have to pursue its national purpose. In some respects, the transition was smoother for Israel than for other new states of our era. Before becoming independent, the community had already created a social infrastructure quite capable of supporting a modern polity. There would undoubtedly be strains to overcome, in the long as well as the short run, but the fundamental political stability of Israel was beyond question.

In other respects, Israel's situation was unusually difficult. The land was small and poor. The Israeli policy of open doors for all displaced or unsettled Jews presented unprecedented problems of economic absorption and social adjustment. These difficulties had been foreseen and were more or less inherent in the essential purpose of Zionism. Other problems had not been expected and were due to extraneous circumstances. The sudden collapse of the Mandate, the sharp conflict with and persisting hostility of the Arab states, and particularly the vacuum created by the absence of the Palestinian Arabs abruptly and totally altered the conditions under which Israeli policy would thenceforth have to be formulated.

The changes were no less significant for Israel's domestic problems than for its foreign policy. To some of the new demands of the times, Israel was able to adjust its institutional structure rapidly and effectively. To others, the adjustment is still to be made. The problems involved are not only the major social questions that concern the people of Israel today but the historic issues that will shape the institutions of Israel in the future.

Notes

1. THE SOCIAL SOURCES OF ZIONISM

1. Christian Wilhelm von Dohm, "Concerning the Amelioration of the Civil Status of the Jews," in Paul R. Mendes-Flohr and Jehuda Reinharz, eds., *The Jew in the Modern World: A Documentary History*, 2d ed. (New York: Oxford University Press, 1995), pp. 28–36.
2. Leon Pinsker, "Auto-Emancipation: An Appeal to His People by a Russian Jew," in Arthur Hertzberg, ed., *The Zionist Idea: A Historical Analysis and Reader*, reprint (New York: Atheneum, 1981), pp. 181–98.
3. David Gordon, "Yishuv Erez Israel," *Hamagid* 26, no. 13 (1882), 107; cited in Israel Klausner, *Behitorer am: haaliyah harishonah mi-Russyah* (Jerusalem: Hasifriyah Hazionit, 1962), p. 181.
4. Moshe Leib Lilienblum, "*Al Israel veal arzo*," *Hashahar* 10, no. 8 (1882), 403.
5. See Theodor Herzl, "A Solution of the Jewish Question," in Paul R. Mendes-Flohr and Jehuda Reinharz, eds., *The Jew in the Modern World: A Documentary History*, 2d ed. (New York: Oxford University Press, 1995), pp. 533–38.

3. THE YISHUV, OLD AND NEW

1. Quoted in Nahum Sokolow, *History of Zionism, 1600–1918* (New York: Ktav, 1969), pp. 267–69.
2. Quoted in Simon M. Dubnow, *History of the Jews in Russia and Poland*, vol. 2 (Philadelphia: Jewish Publication Society of America, 1918), p. 306.

4. SETTLERS AND PATRONS

1. Quoted in Yaakov Ariel, "A Neglected Chapter in the History of Christian Zionism in America: William E. Blackstone and the Petition of 1916," *Studies in Contemporary in Jewry*, 7 (1991), appendix 1, "The Petition of 1891," p. 80.
2. Ahad Haam, "The Jewish State and the Jewish Problem" in Arthur Hertz-

berg, ed., *The Zionist Idea: A Historical Analysis and Reader*, reprint (New York: Atheneum, 1981), pp. 262–69.

3. Ahad Haam, "*Emet mi-Erez Israel*," in *Kol kitvei Ahad Haam* (Jerusalem: Hozaah Ivrit, 1947), p. 25.

4. "The Basle Program," in Paul R. Mendes-Flohr and Jehuda Reinharz, eds., *The Jew in the Modern World: A Documentary History*, 2d ed. (New York: Oxford University Press, 1995), pp. 540–41.

5. THE CONFLICT OF TRADITION AND IDEA

1. Quoted in Samuel Chernowitz, *Bnei Moshe utekufatam* (Warsaw: Zfirah, 1914), pp. 31–32.

2. Ahad Haam, *Al parashat drakhim*, vol. 4 (Berlin: Jüdischer Verlag, 1930), p. 208.

3. Rachel Elboim-Dror, *Hahinukh haivri be-Erez Israel*, vol. 1 (Jerusalem: Yad Yizhak Ben-Zvi, 1986), p. 142.

4. Ahad Haam, *Al parashat drakhim*, vol. 4, p. 227.

5. Theodor Herzl, *The Complete Diaries of Theodor Herzl*, vol. 2, ed. Raphael Patai, trans. Harry Zohn (New York and London: Herzl Press and Thomas Yoseloff, 1960), pp. 578–79.

6. Herzl, *Complete Diaries*, vol. 2, p. 654.

7. *Zionisten-Congress in Basel (29. 30. und 31. August 1897) officielles Protokoll* (Vienna: Erez Israel, 1898), p. 114.

8. *Stenographisches Protokoll der Verhandlungen des II. Zionisten-Congresses gehalten zu Basel vom 28. bis 31. August 1898* (Vienna: Erez Israel, 1898), p. 222.

9. *Stenographisches Protokoll der Verhandlungen des II. Zionisten-Congresses gehalten zu Basel vom 28. bis 31. August 1898*, p. 78.

10. Y. L. Hacohen Fishman, "*Toldot hamizrahi vehitpathuto*," in *Sefer hamizrahi* (Jerusalem: Mosad Harav Kook, 1946), p. 169.

11. *Stenographisches Protokoll des X. Zionisten-Congresses in Basel vom 9. bis inklusive 15. August 1911* (Berlin: Jüdischer Verlag, 1911), pp. 336–37.

6. ZIONISM AND THE LEFT

1. *The Complete Diaries of Theodor Herzl*, vol. 4, ed. Raphael Patai, trans. Harry Zohn (New York: Herzl Press, 1960), p. 1626.

2. *Aaron Liebermans briv*, ed. Kalman Marmor (New York: YIVO, 1951), p. 16.

3. Quoted in Abraham Ascher, *Pavel Axelrod and the Development of Menshevism* (Cambridge: Harvard University Press, 1972), pp. 19–21.

4. "*Der vendpunkt in der geshikhte fun der yidisher arbeter bavegung, 1895*" in *YIVO historishe shriftn* 3 (1939), 650–51.

5. Henry J. Tobias, *The Jewish Bund in Russia from Its Origins to 1905* (Stanford, Calif.: Stanford University Press, 1972), p. 212.

6. "*Der vendpunkt in der geshikhte fun der yidisher arbeter bavegung,* 1895," p. 650.
7. A reference to Ahad Haam's essay "*Avdut betokh herut,*" which was written in 1891 as a reply to Russian Jewish opponents of Hovevei Zion; see *Kol kitvei Ahad Haam* (Jerusalem: Hozaah Ivrit, 1947), pp. 64–69.
8. I. S. Hertz, "*Der Bund un di andere rikhtungen,*" in *Di geshikhte fun Bund,* vol. 1 (New York: Farlag Unser Tsait, 1960), p. 351.
9. Chaim Zhitlowsky, "*A yid tsu yidn,*" *Gezamelte shriftn* 6 (1917), 49–51.
10. Simon Dubnow, *Nationalism and History: Essays on Old and New Judaism* (Philadelphia: Jewish Publication Society, 1958), p. 164.
11. Phillip Menczel, "Jüdische National and Realpolitik," *Die Welt* 5, no. 4 (January 25, 1901), pp. 3–4.
12. Martin Buber, "Gegenwartsarbeit," *Die Welt* 5, no. 6 (February 8, 1901), p. 4.

7. THE YOUNG WORKERS

1. Haim Nahman Bialik, "*Al hashhitah,*" in *Kol shirei H. N. Bialik* (Tel Aviv: Dvir, 1966), pp. 252–53.
2. "*Mahshavot ziknah ubaharut,*" in *Kitvei Mikha Yosef Berdichevsky* (Tel Aviv: Dvir, 1960), p. 22.
3. Yosef Haim Brenner, *Haarakhat azmenu* (Jerusalem: Hozaat Hasharon, 1914), p. 111.
4. "*Mikan umikan,*" in *Kol shirei Y. Haim Brenner,* vol. 1 (Tel Aviv: Hakibbutz Hameuhad, 1960), p. 369.
5. Yizhak Lamdan, "*Sarid,*" in *Masadah* (Tel Aviv: Dvir, 1966–67), pp. 29–30.
6. "*Darki laarez,*" in *Kitvei Berl Katznelson,* vol. 5 (Palestine: Hozaat Mifleget Poalei Erez Israel, 1947), pp. 386–88.
7. Yizhak Ben-Zvi, *Zikhronot ureshumot,* ed. Rahel Yanait Ben-Zvi and Yehuda Erez (Jerusalem: Yad Yizhak Ben-Zvi, 1967), pp. 61–62.
8. Yizhak Tabenkin, "*Hinukh ledmut haadam vehapoel,*" *Dvarim,* vol. 1 (Tel Aviv, Hozaat Hakibbutz Hameuhad, 1967), pp. 453–59.
9. A. D. Gordon, *Haumah vehaavodah* (Jerusalem: Hasifriyah Hazionit, 1952), pp. 77–85.

8. GROWTH OF THE ZIONIST PARTIES

1. See Vladimir Jabotinsky, "What the Zionist Revisionists Want," in Paul R. Mendes-Flohr and Jehuda Reinharz, eds., *The Jew in the Modern World: A Documentary History,* 2d ed. (New York: Oxford University Press, 1995), pp. 594–97.
2. Arieh Morgenstern, *Harabanut harashit le-Erez Israel: yisudah veirgunah* (Jerusalem: Shorashim, 1974), pp. 33–35.
3. Menahem Friedman, *Hevrah vedat: haortodoxyah halozionit be-Erez Israel, 1918–36* (Jerusalem: Yad Yizhak Ben-Zvi, 1977), p. 185.

4. Paul L. Hanna, *British Policy in Palestine* (Washington, D.C.: American Council on Public Affairs, 1942), p. 89.
5. Friedman, *Hevrah vedat*, pp. 146–47.
6. Morgenstern, *Harabanut harashit le-Erez Israel*, p. 133.

9. THE HEGEMONY OF LABOR

1. See Foreign Office, *The Constitutions of All Countries* (London: His Majesty's Stationery Office, 1938), vol. 1, pp. 539–45.
2. Zvi Schatz, *Al gvul hadmamah-ktavim* (Tel Aviv: Am Oved 1990), p. 97.
3. Quoted in Shulamit Laskov, *Trumpeldor: sipur hayav* (Haifa: Shikmona, 1972), pp. 55–58.
4. *Pinkas hahistadrut haklalit shel haovdim be-Erez Israel*, 8 (January 1938), esp. table 8, "*Hashayakhut le-Hehaluz ulehakhsharah behuz laarez*," p. 55.

10. THE NATIONAL HOME

1. See "*Hevrat Ovdim*" in *Pinkas histadrut haovdim be-Erez Israel* (Jerusalem: Histadrut haovdim haivrim be-Erez Israel, 1923), pp. 6–7.

A Note on Bibliography

The growing body of literature on Zionism and the State of Israel is voluminous. This scholarly corpus exceeds the scope of any single study. Nonetheless, a few words are in order concerning major works in the field that are accessible to an English-reading audience. For comprehensive lists of recent articles on Zionism and the State of Israel see the yearly bibliographies compiled in the *Journal of Israeli History* (formerly *Studies in Zionism*).

A few texts serve as touchstones in the field of Zionist history. Ben Halpern's *The Idea of the Jewish State*, 2nd rev. ed. (Cambridge: Harvard University Press, 1969), is still the best treatment of the evolution of the concept of Jewish sovereignty. Gideon Shimoni's *The Zionist Ideology* (Hanover: University Press of New England, 1995) is an analysis of Zionism's diverse ideological manifestations. Walter Laqueur's *A History of Zionism*, 2nd rev. ed. (New York: Schocken Books, 1989), remains the best single volume on the political history of Zionism. Shlomo Avineri's *The Making of Modern Zionism: The Intellectual Origins of the Jewish State* (New York: Basic Books, 1981) and *The Zionist Idea: A Historical Reader and Analysis*, ed. Arthur Hertzberg, reprint (New York: Atheneum, 1984), are useful resources. Finally, *Essential Papers on Zionism*, ed. Jehuda Reinharz and Anita Shapira (New York: New York University Press, 1996), is an anthology of seminal essays by leading scholars in the field.

Several important monographs examine the rise of Jewish nationalism and the movement's ideological origins. Among the most significant of such studies are Shmuel Almog, *Zionism and History: The Rise of a New Jewish Consciousness* (New York: St. Martin's Press, 1987); Jacob Katz, *Jewish Emancipation and Self-Emancipation* (Philadelphia: Jewish Publication Society, 1986); George L. Mosse, *Confronting the Nation: Jewish and Western Nationalism* (Hanover, N.H.: University Press of New England, 1993); David Vital, *The Origins of Zionism*, vol. 1 (Oxford: Clarendon Press, 1975); David Vital, *Zionism: The Formative*

Years, vol. 2 (Oxford: Clarendon Press, 1982); David Vital, *Zionism: The Crucial Phase,* vol. 3 (Oxford: Clarendon Press, 1987).

The literature dealing with nationalism and state building is too vast to summarize here. A good place to start would be *International Political Science Abstracts* published in Paris by the International Political Science Association. Three excellent general surveys of nationalism, each of which include thoughtful discussions of Zionism, are Ernest Gellner, *Nations and Nationalism* (Oxford: Basil Blackwell, 1983); Elie Kedourie, *Nationalism* (London: Hutchinson University Library, 1971); and Anthony D. Smith, *Theories of Nationalism* (New York: Holmes and Meier, 1983).

Useful studies of Jewish state building are *Pioneers and Homemakers: Jewish Women in Pre-State Israel,* ed. Deborah S. Bernstein (Albany: State University of New York Press, 1992); Mitchell Cohen, *Zion and State: Nation, Class and the Shaping of Modern Israel* (London: Basil Blackwell, 1987); S. N. Eisenstadt, *The Transformation of Israeli Society* (London: Weidenfeld and Nicolson, 1985); Dan Horowitz and Moshe Lissak, *Origins of the Israeli Polity: Palestine Under the Mandate* (Chicago: University of Chicago Press, 1978); Henry Near, *The Kibbutz Movement: Origins and Growth, 1909–1939* (Oxford: Oxford University Press, 1992); Derek J. Penslar, *Zionism and Technocracy: The Engineering of Jewish Settlement in Palestine, 1870–1918* (Bloomington: Indiana University Press, 1991); Yaacov Shavit, *Jabotinsky and the Revisionist Movement, 1929–1948* (London: Frank Cass, 1988).

The following works trace the triangular relationship between Jews, Arabs, and the British in mandatory Palestine: Yosef Gorny, *Zionism and the Arabs, 1882–1948: A Study of Ideology* (Oxford: Clarendon Press, 1987); Neville J. Mandel, *The Arabs and Zionism Before World War I* (Berkeley: University of California Press, 1976); Benny Morris, *The Birth of the Palestinian Refugee Problem, 1947–1949* (Cambridge: Cambridge University Press, 1987); Kenneth W. Stein, *The Land Question in Palestine, 1917–1939* (Chapel Hill: University of North Carolina Press, 1984); Mark Tessler, *A History of the Israeli–Palestinian Conflict* (Bloomington: Indiana University Press, 1994); Bernard Wasserstein, *The British in Palestine: The Mandatory Government and the Arab–Jewish Conflict, 1917–1929* (London: Royal Historical Society, 1978); Ronald W. Zweig, *Britain and Palestine During the Second World War* (Suffolk: Boydell Press for the Royal Historical Society, 1985).

Sergio I. Minerbi's *The Vatican and Zionism: Conflict in the Holy Land, 1895–1925* (New York: Oxford University Press, 1990) is a path-breaking study of the Vatican in relation to both the Great Powers and the Zionist movement in Palestine.

Anita Shapira's *Land and Power: The Zionist Resort to Force, 1881–1948* (New York: Oxford University Press, 1992) is a comprehensive and insightful examination of Jewish militarism and self-defense in Palestine. For histories of the Israeli army, see Zeev Schiff, *History of the Israeli Army: 1874 to the Present* (New York: Macmillan, 1986); Edward Luttwak and Dan Horowitz, *The Israeli Army* (New York: Harper and Row, 1984).

There are many useful monographs concerning the impact of Jewish nationalism and Zionism on Jews in the diaspora. Among the best are Stuart A. Cohen, *English Zionists and British Jews: The Communal Politics of Anglo-Jewry, 1895–1920* (Princeton, N.J.: Princeton University Press, 1982); Jonathan Frankel, *Prophecy and Politics: Socialism, Nationalism and the Russian Jews, 1862–1917* (Cambridge: Cambridge University Press, 1981); Ben Halpern, *A Clash of Heroes: Brandeis, Weizmann and American Zionism* (New York: Oxford University Press, 1987); Samuel Halperin, *The Political World of American Zionism*, reprint (Silver Spring, Md.: Information Dynamics, 1985); Ezra Mendelsohn, *Zionism in Poland: The Formative Years, 1915–1926* (New Haven: Yale University Press, 1990); Jehuda Reinharz, *Fatherland or Promised Land: The Dilemma of the German Jew, 1893–1914* (Ann Arbor: University of Michigan Press, 1975); Gideon Shimoni, *Jews and Zionism: The South African Experience, 1910–1967* (Cape Town: Oxford University Press, 1980); Melvin I. Urofsky, *American Zionism from Herzl to the Holocaust*, reprint (Lincoln: University of Nebraska Press, 1996); Mark A. Raider, *The Emergence of American Zionism* (New York: New York University Press, 1998). Of related interest is Ezra Mendelsohn's *On Modern Jewish Politics* (New York: Oxford University Press, 1993), which compares Poland and the United States, the two dominant Jewish communities during the interwar period.

Several useful biographical studies of major Zionist figures are *Dissenter in Zion: From the Writings of Judah Magnes*, ed. Arthur A. Goren (Cambridge; Harvard University Press, 1982); Ernst Pawel, *The Labyrinth of Exile: A Life of Theodor Herzl* (New York: Farrar, Straus and Giroux, 1989); Jehuda Reinharz, *Chaim Weizmann: The Making of a Zionist Leader*, vol. 1 (New York: Oxford University Press, 1985); Jehuda Reinharz, *Chaim Weizmann: The Making of a Statesman*, vol. 2 (New York: Oxford University Press, 1993); Anita Shapira, *Berl: The Biography of a Socialist Zionist* (Cambridge: Cambridge University

Press, 1984); Gabriel Sheffer, *Moshe Sharett: Biography of a Political Moderate* (Oxford: Clarendon Press, 1996); Shabtai Teveth, *Ben-Gurion: The Burning Ground, 1886–1948* (Boston: Houghton Mifflin, 1987); Steven J. Zipperstein, *Elusive Prophet: Ahad Haam and the Origins of Zionism* (Berkeley: University of California Press, 1993).

Religious and cultural questions are dealt with by, among others, *Zionism and Religion*, ed. Shmuel Almog, Jehuda Reinharz, and Anita Shapira (Hanover, N.H.: University Press of New England, 1998); Robert Alter, *Modern Hebrew Literature* (New York: Behrman House, 1975); *The Great Transition: The Recovery of the Lost Centers of Modern Hebrew Literature*, ed. Glenda Abramson and Tudor Parfitt (Totowa, N.J.: Bowman and Allanheld, 1985); Ehud Luz, *Parallels Meet: Religion and Nationalism in the Early Zionist Movement, 1882–1904* (Philadelphia: Jewish Publication Society, 1988); Aviezer Ravitzky, *Messianism, Zionism and Jewish Religious Radicalism* (Chicago: University of Chicago Press, 1996); Eliezer Schweid, *The Land of Israel: National Home or Land of Destiny* (Cranbury, N.J.: Associated University Presses and New York: Herzl Press, 1985).

Index